hamlyn
QuickCook

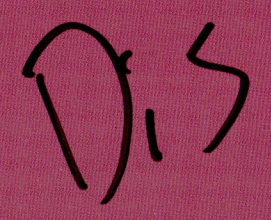

hamlyn
QuickCook
Healthy Feasts

Recipes by Joy Skipper

Every dish, three ways—you choose!
30 minutes | 20 minutes | 10 minutes

An Hachette UK Company
www.hachette.co.uk

First published in Great Britain in 2013 by Hamlyn,
a division of Octopus Publishing Group Ltd
Endeavour House, 189 Shaftesbury Avenue
London WC2H 8JY
www.octopusbooks.co.uk
www.octopusbooksusa.com

Distributed in the US by Hachette Book Group USA
237 Park Avenue, New York NY 10017 USA
Distributed in Canada by Canadian Manda Group
165 Dufferin Street, Toronto, Ontario, Canada M6K 3H6

Copyright © Octopus Publishing Group Ltd 2013

All rights reserved. No part of this work may be reproduced or utilized in any form or by any means, electronic or mechanical, including photocopying, recording, or by any information storage and retrieval system, without the prior written permission of the publisher.

ISBN 978 0 600 62668 8

Printed and bound in China

10 9 8 7 6 5 4 3 2 1

Standard level spoon and cup measurements are used in all recipes.

Ovens should be preheated to the specified temperature. If using a convection oven, follow the manufacturer's instructions for adjusting the time and temperature. Broilers should also be preheated.

This book includes dishes made with nuts and nut derivatives. It is advisable for those with known allergic reactions to nuts and nut derivatives and those who may be potentially vulnerable to these allergies, such as pregnant and nursing mothers, people with weakened immune systems, the elderly, babies, and children, to avoid dishes made with nuts and nut oils.

It is also prudent to check the labels of prepared ingredients for the possible inclusion of nut derivatives.

The United States Department of Agriculture (USDA) advises that eggs should not be consumed raw. This book contains some dishes made with raw or lightly cooked eggs. It is prudent for more vulnerable people, such as pregnant and nursing mothers, people with weakened immune systems, the elderly, babies, and young children, to avoid uncooked or lightly cooked dishes made with eggs.

Contents

Introduction 6

Snacks and Light Meals 20
Recipes listed by cooking time 22

Meat and Poultry 86
Recipes listed by cooking time 88

Fish and Seafood 132
Recipes listed by cooking time 134

Vegetarian Dishes 180
Recipes listed by cooking time 182

Cakes and Desserts 232
Recipes listed by cooking time 234

Index 280
Acknowledgments 288

Introduction

30 20 10—Quick, Quicker, Quickest

This book offers a new and flexible approach to planning meals for busy cooks, letting you choose the recipe option that best fits the time you have available. Inside you will find 360 dishes that will inspire and motivate you to get cooking every day of the year. All the recipes take a maximum of 30 minutes to cook. Some take as little as 20 minutes and, amazingly, many take only 10 minutes. With a little preparation, you can easily try one new recipe from this book each night and slowly you will be able to build a wide and exciting portfolio of recipes to suit your needs.

How Does it Work?

Every recipe in the QuickCook series can be cooked one of three ways—a 30-minute version, a 20-minute version, or a superquick-and-easy 10-minute version. At the beginning of each chapter, you'll find recipes listed by time. Choose a dish based on how much time you have and turn to that page.

You'll find the main recipe in the middle of the page accompanied by a beautiful photograph, as well as two time-variation recipes below.

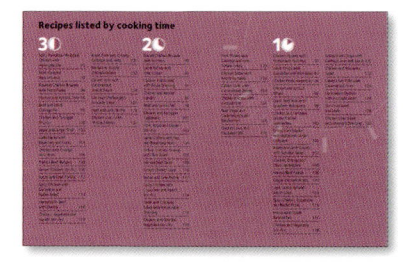

If you enjoy your chosen dish, why not go back and cook the other time-variation options at a later date? So if you liked the 30-minute Horseradish Beef with Quinoa, but only have 10 minutes to spare this time around, you'll find a way to cook it using quick ingredients or clever shortcuts.

If you love the ingredients and flavors of the 10-minute Salmon and Grapefruit Salad, why not try something more substantial, such as the 20-minute Breaded Salmon with Grapefruit, or be inspired to make a more elaborate version, such as the Salmon with Grapefruit Dressing and Roasted Vegetables? Alternatively, browse through all 360 delicious recipes, find something that catches your eye—then cook the version that fits your time frame.

Or, for easy inspiration, turn to the gallery on pages 12–19 to get an instant overview by themes, such as Mood Boosters or Superfoods.

QuickCook online

To make life even easier, you can use the special code on each recipe page to e-mail yourself a recipe card for printing, or e-mail a text-only shopping list to your phone. Go to www.hamlynquickcook.com and enter the recipe code at the bottom of each page.

HEA-SNAC-NIF

INTRODUCTION 7

QuickCook Healthy Feasts

For the past few years, people have started to realize that the foods we eat can have a real effect on our health and how we function on a daily basis. Despite this, the number of people developing diabetes and cardiovascular disease is on the increase. Obesity is also a growing problem, particularly in the Western world.

The information about what we should and shouldn't eat seems to change on a regular basis, which can be confusing. However, eating a balanced, healthy diet is not difficult, and should be something you enjoy. The recipes provided in this book will help you to eat a variety of great nutritious foods, with minimum effort required to prepare and cook them.

A Healthy Diet

So what is the best way to make sure your diet is healthy and nutrient rich? The easiest way is to cook meals from scratch—it is not as difficult or time-consuming as you may think, and you can start by trying some of the recipes in this book.

Planning your weekly menu can also help you to eat a healthy, balanced diet. Meals for the week should include good-quality protein (fish, eggs, poultry, lentils and beans, and meat) and filling, but nutritious carbohydrates. Choose recipes that are made with unrefined foods (such as sweet potatoes, whole-wheat pasta, brown rice, and quinoa), essential fats (oily fish, such as salmon, sardines, and mackerel), nuts (such as walnuts), and seeds (such as pumpkin, sesame, and sunflower), and eat a variety of fresh fruit and vegetables to make sure your intake of vitamins and minerals is sufficient. Fruit and vegetables also provide daily fiber—very important for detoxifying unwanted toxins from the body. Drink plenty of water to help the fiber pass through the body.

Dairy products, such as cheese and yogurt, are important sources of calcium and vitamins, but some, in the case of butter and cream, have a high fat content, so they should be eaten in smaller amounts. Some people find they are intolerant to dairy products, but these days there are plenty of alternatives, such as soy, almond, and rice milks, and dairy-free yogurts and cheeses.

The Mediterranean Diet

A research paper published in 2008 showed that following a strict Mediterranean diet reduces the risk of dying from cancer and cardiovascular disease, and the risk of developing Parkinson's and Alzheimer's disease. The diet is based on fresh produce and cooking great ingredients from scratch. It includes a high intake of olive oil, legumes, unrefined cereals, fruits and vegetables, a moderate intake of dairy products (mostly as yogurt and cheese), and a low consumption of meat.

The Role of Fat

We have never been more obsessed with dieting, eating low-fat foods, and even trying to cut fat out of our diets completely. This is not a healthy way to eat. It is best to eat food in its most natural state—milk does not come out of a cow as low in fat! The fat you consume does not make you overweight (unless you are eating the wrong kind in huge amounts, of course); what does is eating too much sugar and not burning it off, causing it to turn to fat in the body. Research has shown that low-fat diets can lead to cravings, binge eating, risk of fat-soluble vitamin deficiency, depression, problems with blood-sugar regulation, and skin problems.

Fat is one of the things that makes food tasty, and there is plenty of scientific evidence to show that we need it in our diets, but the important factor is the type of fat. Fats can be divided into two main types: saturated and unsaturated. Saturated fat is solid at room temperature and usually comes from animal sources. This fat is associated with an increased risk of heart disease. Unsaturated fats include the omega fats that are essential in the diet. We need healthy fat in our diet:

- For energy
- For body and organ insulation
- To keep toxins out of circulation
- For steroid hormone production
- To provide and circulate fat-soluble vitamins (vitamins A, D, E, and K)
- For cell membrane structure, keeping cells supple
- To help fight against inflammation

Healthy fats are found in oily fish, avocados, nuts, and seeds.

Choosing Healthy Ingredients

Buy fresh, local produce that is in season—not only for its nutritional value (it will probably have been picked more recently if it has not had to travel), but also for the flavor. Eating foods out of season usually means the product has been grown in and traveled from another country, and, therefore, has started to lose some of its nutrients and flavor.

Spend time at your local fish dealer's and butcher's stores, letting them know that you care about where your produce comes from, that it is sustainable, and that you are willing to experiment with new foods. Take their advice about seasonal produce and hopefully you will learn how to cook new cuts of meats or fish that you previously would not have bought.

Try cooking with ingredients that have added health benefits (you will find recipes that use these in the book).

Coconut Oil: This is used widely in Indian cookery and is known to be antimicrobial, antifungal, and antibacterial as well as an antioxidant, mainly due to the presence of lauric acid. It can be used as a substitute for butter or olive oil because it is not broken down into trans fats when heated.

Agave Syrup: Natural agave has been harvested in Mexico for hundreds of years. Ranking fairly low on the glycemic index, a small amount provides more sweetness than sugar, so a little goes a long way. It is great stirred into cooked fruit or yogurt, but can also be used in cooking.

Avocados: These green-skinned, creamy fruits provide nearly 20 essential nutrients, including potassium, Vitamin E, fiber, the B vitamins, and folic acid, as well as unsaturated fats.

Oily Fish: Including mackerel, salmon, trout, and sardines, this type of fish is rich in Omega 3 essential fats, which are required by the body for almost every function, from producing hormones to reducing inflammation. Omega 3 is also vital for a healthy, effective brain.

Canola Oil: Unlike other vegetable oils, cold-pressed canola oil contains Omega 3, 6, and 9 essential fats. While Omega 6 can be found in many food sources, it is harder to include Omega 3 in our diet, so the high ratio of Omega 3 to Omega 6 in canola oil helps to redress this issue.

Nuts and Seeds: A healthy component of any diet, these are rich in minerals and essential fats.

If you buy prepared foods, be sure to read the ingredient labels so you know what the food contains—aim for the least amount of preservatives and chemicals as possible. Learn what the different E numbers are (some of them are not harmful) and how they may affect you.

Food Preparation and Cooking

The way food is cooked affects how nutritious your diet is. Careful food preparation and cooking can help to retain certain nutrients. Follow the following guidelines for best results:

- Avoid peeling and chopping fruit and vegetables until the last minute before cooking, because exposed surfaces oxidize and lose vitamin C; you can see this when apples turn brown.
- Don't leave vegetables sitting in water, because this causes them to leach vitamins.
- Cook for the minimum amount of time in the gentlest way possible—steaming is best.
- If you want to cook a stir-fry, you could add a little liquid, such as water, stock, or soy sauce, then cover and steam-fry instead, for a slightly healthy option.

How and When to Eat

Eating when you are in a relaxed state helps the body to absorb nutrients from the food, so eating "on the go" or while you are doing something else is not good for your health. Take the time to relax and focus on what you are cooking and eating. Chewing food thoroughly helps it to be broken down in the body more efficiently and allows for the nutrients to be absorbed more readily.

To help maintain energy levels throughout the day and prevent the body going into stress through hunger, aim to eat regularly, possibly every few hours, to keep your blood sugar in balance. Three meals a day and a couple of snacks is ideal. Breakfast should never be missed, and the old saying: "Breakfast like a king, lunch like a prince, and dinner like a pauper" is a good one—aim to eat your main meal in the middle of the day.

Mood Boosters

Healthy, mood-enhancing feasts that are guaranteed to lift your spirits.

Nutty Granola 28

Smoked Mackerel and Horseradish Pâté 32

Warm Smoked Duck and Asparagus Salad 54

Spicy Chicken with Cucumber and Radish Salad 114

Curried Chicken with Avocado Salad 126

Chicken Liver Salad with Mustard Dressing 130

Broiled Lemon and Mustard Sardines 154

Salmon and Grapefruit Salad 160

Shrimp and Goat Cheese Salad 176

Lemon and Raisin Scones 236

Cocoa, Orange, and Pecan Oat Bars 242

Oaty Raspberry Dessert 278

Superfoods

Packed with nutrients, vitamins, and antioxidents, these dishes taste super, too!

Broccoli and Black-Eyed Pea Soup 38

Smoked Haddock and Kale Soup 40

Avocado, Red Pepper, and Olive Salad 50

Smoked Mackerel Superfood Salad 56

Beet and Goat Cheese Salad 58

Calf Liver with Caramelized Onions 124

Shrimp and Spinach Curry 152

Broiled Salmon with Avocado Salsa 172

Asparagus and Pea Quinoa Risotto 202

Cheese and Spinach Quesadillas 214

Oat, Banana, and Ginger Muffins 248

Whole-Wheat Blueberry Pancakes with Lemon Yogurt 270

Weekend Treats

Want something special for the weekend? Look no farther!

Breakfast Smoothies 26

Guacamole 34

Mini Smoked Trout Quiches 60

Rosemary Oatcakes 62

Grilled Zucchini Bruschetta 72

Chicken Dippers with Homemade Hummus 90

Roasted Pork Loin with Creamy Cabbage and Leeks 120

Smoked Haddock with a Cider and Cheese Sauce 164

Mushroom, Tomato, and Herb Pancakes 208

Pea and Mint Pancakes 210

Sesame Cookies 252

Whole-Wheat Raspberry Coconut Muffins 262

Good for Getting 5-A-Day

Kick-start your nutritious, balanced diet with these healthy feasts.

Hummus with Carrot and Celery Sticks 36

Salmon and Chickpea Salad 52

Pork, Apple, and Ginger Stir-Fry 102

Chicken and Vegetable Stir-Fry 118

Cod Loin with Roasted Tomato Ratatouille 148

Smoked Mackerel and Spring Vegetable Tabbouleh 168

Butternut, Broccoli, and Mushroom au Gratin 188

Simple Baked Leeks and Sweet Potatoes 222

Cheesy Spinach-Stuffed Mushrooms 226

Crunchy Pesto Broccoli with Poached Eggs 230

Berry and Mint Compote 254

Caramelized Fall Fruits 274

GALLERY 15

Spicy Meals

These tasty, nutrient-rich dishes will leave you feeling hot, hot, hot!

Tuna Open Sandwiches 74

Spicy Barbecue Beans on Toast 76

Harissa Beef Fajitas 108

Ginger Chicken Soup 110

Salmon and Rice Bhajis 140

Keralan Fish Curry 162

Red Pepper and Coconut Curry 186

Moroccan Vegetable Stew 190

Lima Bean and Mushroom Tagine 198

Falafels with Spicy Sauce 228

Sweet Semolina with Cardamom Poached Apricots 244

Gingered Sesame Fruit Kebabs 268

Taste of the Med

Impart some healthy, Mediterranean magic into your food!

Gazpacho 44

Mediterranean Beans 68

Pancetta and Cannellini Bean Bruschetta 80

Chicken and Tarragon Risotto 100

Bacon and Leek Tortilla 112

Moules Marinières 136

Salmon Ceviche 144

Baked Sole with Fennel Pesto 150

Fava Bean and Feta Tagliatelle 192

Greek Pita Pockets 204

Roasted Honey Peaches 250

Strawberry and Almond Desserts 258

GALLERY 17

Light Summer Dishes

These fresh summer dishes will put a spring in your step!

Melon, Mint, and Strawberry Smoothies 24

Warm Lentil, Tomato, and Muenster Cheese Salad 46

Peach, Feta, and Watercress Salad 48

Chorizo and Olive Tapenade Toasts 70

Shrimp and Zucchini Spring Rolls 84

Lamb Cutlets with Pea and Rosemary Mashed Potatoes 104

Chicken with Orange and Olives 106

Nectarine-Glazed Chicken Kebabs 122

Jumbo Shrimp Caesar Salad 166

Roasted Bell Peppers 196

Berry and Meringue Desserts 240

Tropical Fruit Salsa 260

Light Winter Dishes

Hearty yet healthy food to warm you up on a cold winter's day.

Roasted Butternut, Sage, and Cashew Nut Soup 42

Chicken and Apricot Stew 96

Beef and Lentil Chili 98

Fish Casserole 174

Chunky Cod, Red Snapper, and Shrimp Stew 178

Cauliflower Cheese Gratin 194

Lentil, Mustard, and Chickpea Soup 216

Mushroom and Tofu Stew 224

Oat-Topped Pear and Ginger Dessert 238

Blackberry Brûlées 246

Spicy Fruit Bread Puddings 256

Winter Fruits with Orange Ricotta 264

GALLERY 19

QuickCook
Snacks and Light Meals

Recipes listed by cooking time

30

Melon, Mint, and Strawberry Soup	24
Breakfast Muffins	26
Nutty Granola	28
Sardine Bean Burgers	30
Warm Mackerel, Horseradish, and Potato Salad	32
Smoked Salmon and Avocado Terrines	34
Carrot and Muenster Cheese Salad with Hummus Dressing	36
Broccoli and Black-Eyed Pea Curry	38
Smoked Haddock and Kale Soup	40
Roasted Butternut, Sage, and Cashew Nut Soup	42
Red Pepper Tarts	44
Lentil and Tomato Flatbreads	46
Roasted Feta-Topped Peach and Watercress Salad	48
Peperonata with Avocado and Olives	50
Salmon en Papillote with Warm Chickpea Salad	52
Smoked Duck and Asparagus Tarts	54
Smoked Mackerel Superfood Salad	56
Roasted Beet and Goat Cheese Salad	58
Smoked Trout Phyllo Quiche	60
Rosemary Oatcakes	62
Cheese Soda Bread	64
Cheese, Cumin, and Apple Scones	66
Mixed Bean Goulash	68
Chorizo, Onion, and Olive Tart	70
Zucchini Lasagna	72
Spicy Tuna Pasta Casserole	74
Spicy Bean Quesadillas	76
Salmon and Sesame Skewers	78
Pancetta-Wrapped Asparagus with Cannellini Bean Salad	80
Chickpea and Bean Sprout Curry	82
Shrimp, Chicken, and Vegetable Spring Rolls	84

20

Minty Melon and Strawberry Salad	24
Breakfast Muesli	26
Nutty Muesli Muffins	28
Bean and Sardine Salad	30
Smoked Mackerel and Mashed Potatoes with Horseradish	32
Shrimp and Avocado Salad	34
Hummus with Carrot and Celery Sticks	36
Broccoli and Black-Eyed Pea Soup	38
Smoked Haddock Fish Cakes with Kale	40
Butternut and Sage Mashed Potatoes	42
Gazpacho	44
Lentil and Tomato Soup	46
Peach, Feta, and Watercress Bruschetta	48
Muenster Cheese with Avocado, Red Pepper, and Olive Salsa	50
Broiled Salmon with Chickpea Curry	52
Pan-Fried Duck Breasts with Grilled Asparagus	54

10

Smoked Mackerel Superfood Soup	56
Beet Soup with Goat Cheese	58
Mini Smoked Trout Quiches	60
Rosemary Scones	62
Whole-Wheat Cheese Straws	64
Cheese, Cumin, and Apple Salad	66
Bean and Garlic Stew	68
Chorizo and Olive Potatoes	70
Grilled Zucchini Bruschetta	72
Tuna Salad Niçoise	74
Spicy Barbecue Beans on Toast	76
Broiled Salmon with Sesame Salad	78
Pancetta and Cannellini Bean Spaghetti	80
Chickpea and Bean Sprout Patties	82
Vietnamese Shrimp Spring Rolls	84

Melon, Mint, and Strawberry Smoothies	24
Breakfast Smoothies	26
Homemade Nutty Muesli	28
Smashed Bean and Sardine Dip	30
Smoked Mackerel and Horseradish Pâté	32
Guacamole	34
Hummus and Carrot Wraps	36
Broccoli and Black-Eyed Pea Salad	38
Spicy Smoked Haddock and Kale Pasta	40
Butternut, Sage, and Cashew Nut Dip	42
Mediterranean Pepper Salad	44
Warm Lentil, Tomato, and Muenster Cheese Salad	46
Peach, Feta, and Watercress Salad	48
Avocado, Red Pepper, and Olive Salad	50
Salmon and Chickpea Salad	52
Warm Smoked Duck and Asparagus Salad	54

Smoked Mackerel Superfood Toasts	56
Beet and Goat Cheese Salad	58
Smoked Trout Baked Eggs	60
Mixed Salad with Rosemary Dressing	62
Cheese and Pickle Toasts	64
Cheese, Cumin, and Apple Toasts	66
Mediterranean Beans	68
Chorizo and Olive Tapenade Toasts	70
Quick Zucchini Pasta	72
Tuna Open Sandwiches	74
Boston Baked Beans	76
Pan-Fried Sesame-Crusted Salmon	78
Pancetta and Cannellini Bean Bruschetta	80
Chickpea and Alfalfa Sprout Salad	82
Shrimp and Zucchini Spring Rolls	84

1 Melon, Mint, and Strawberry Smoothies

Serves 4

1 small watermelon, peeled, seeded, and chopped
14–16 strawberries, hulled
12 mint leaves
small handful of ice

- Place all the ingredients in a blender and blend until smooth.
- Pour into 4 glasses and serve immediately.

2 Minty Melon and Strawberry Salad

Put ¼ cup granulated sugar, 1 cup water, and a 2-inch piece of fresh ginger root in a small saucepan and bring to a boil. Simmer for 5 minutes, then let cool slightly before removing the ginger. Divide ¼ peeled, seeded, and cubed watermelon, 16 hulled and halved strawberries, and 12 mint leaves among 4 bowls. Pour the ginger syrup over the fruit and mint and serve sprinkled with 2 tablespoons toasted slivered almonds.

3 Melon, Mint, and Strawberry Soup

Place 1 small peeled, seeded, and chopped cantaloupe in a blender and blend until smooth. Pour into a small bowl, cover, and chill for 20 minutes. Using a clean blender, repeat with 1 small peeled, seeded, and chopped honeydew melon and then 1 cup hulled and chopped strawberries. When ready to serve, pour a ladle of each fruit puree into a bowl and make a pattern by dragging a knife through each one. Serve sprinkled with 2 tablespoons hulled and chopped strawberries and 2 teaspoons chopped mint.

24 SNACKS AND LIGHT MEALS   HEA-SNAC-QEV

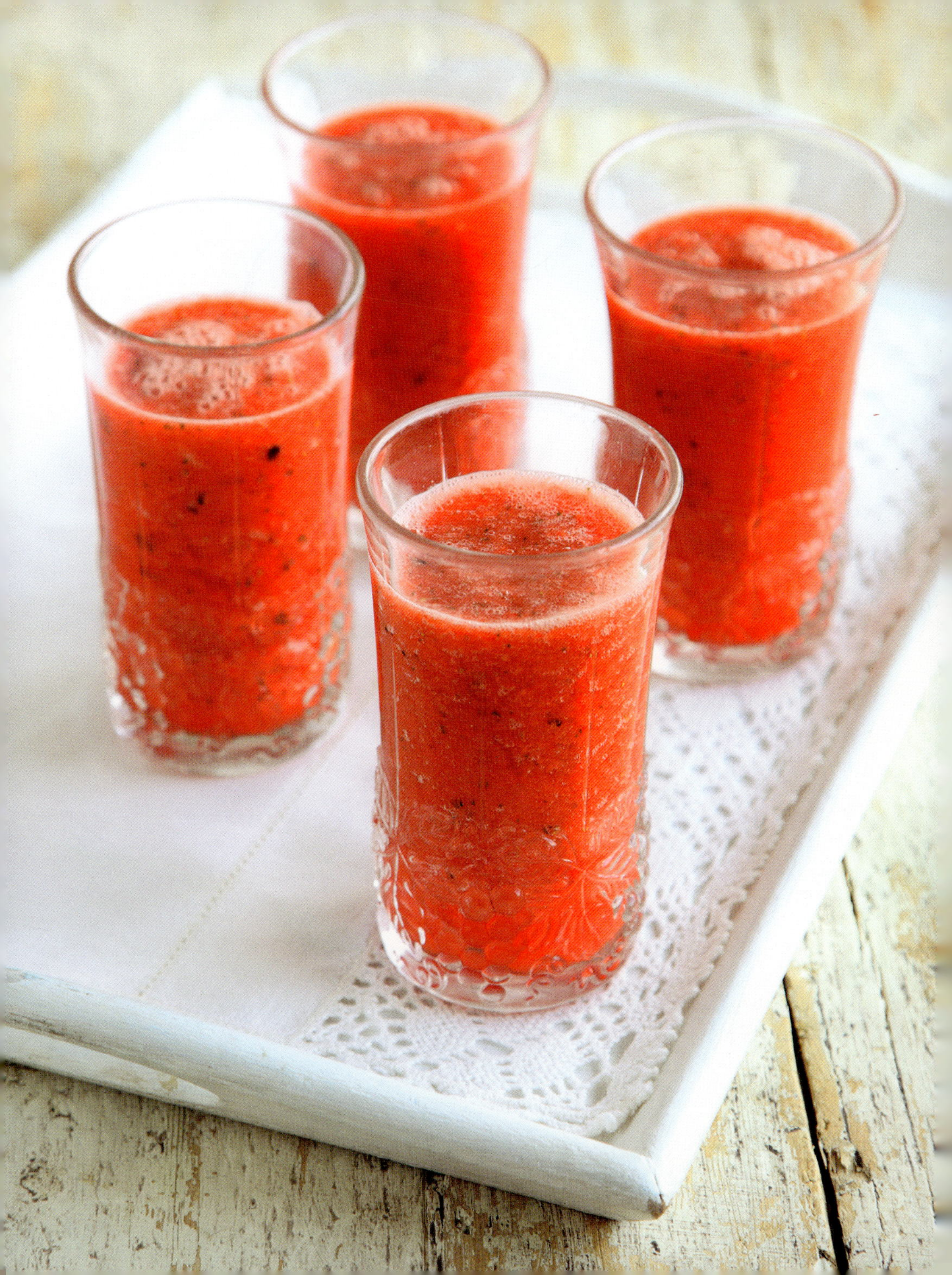

1 Breakfast Smoothies

Serves 2–3

1 tablespoon pomegranate juice
1 small banana, chopped
1¼ cups soy milk
1 tablespoon almonds
1 tablespoon rolled oats
½ teaspoon honey
½ tablespoon ground flaxseed
2 tablespoons plain yogurt

- Place all the ingredients in a blender and blend until smooth and creamy.
- Pour into 2 glasses and serve immediately.

2 Breakfast Muesli

Mix together 2 tablespoons rolled oats, 2 teaspoons ground flaxseed, 1 tablespoon slivered almonds, 1 tablespoon goji berries, and 2 peeled, cored, and grated apples in a large bowl. Pour in 2½ cups soy milk and let stand for 15 minutes. To serve, spoon into 2 bowls and top each one with 2 tablespoons plain yogurt, 1 small chopped banana, and 1 teaspoon honey.

3 Breakfast Muffins

Mix together 1 cup whole-wheat flour, sifted, ¾ cup all-purpose flour, sifted, 2 teaspoons baking powder, ¼ cup rolled oats, ½ cup firmly packed dark brown sugar, ⅓ cup golden raisins, and ½ cup slivered almonds in a large bowl. Beat together ½ cup melted coconut oil, 2 lightly beaten eggs, and 2 tablespoons soy milk in a small bowl, then pour into the dry ingredients, add 4 mashed bananas, and mix together until just combined—do not overmix. Divide the mixture among 8 paper muffin liners arranged in a muffin pan and bake in a preheated oven, at 375°F, for 20 minutes, or until golden. Transfer to a wire rack to cool.

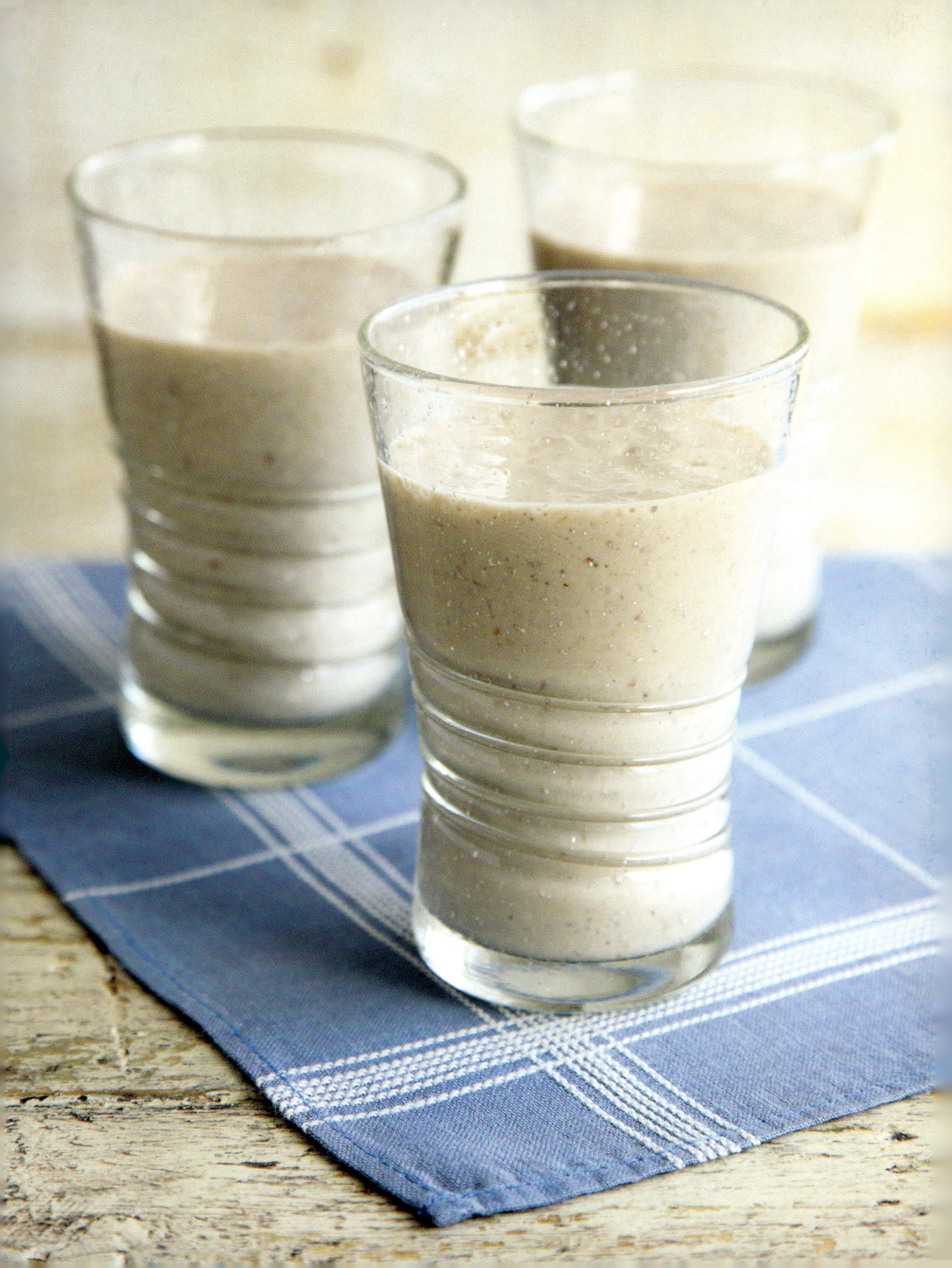

30 Nutty Granola

Serves 8–10

½ cup honey
1½ cups rolled oats
¼ cup slivered almonds
3 tablespoons sunflower seeds
3 tablespoons golden raisins
3 tablespoons dried cranberries
1 tablespoon chopped hazelnuts
1 teaspoon sesame seeds

To serve

plain yogurt
fresh fruit

- Melt the honey in a large saucepan over low heat for 1–2 minutes. Add the remaining ingredients and mix together thoroughly.

- Spread the mixture out on a baking sheet and bake in a preheated oven, at 350°F, for 10–12 minutes, until starting to turn golden. Stir the granola, turning it over a little, then return to the oven for another 4–5 minutes.

- Pour onto a cool pan or into a large bowl and let cool. Store in an airtight container.

- Serve with plain yogurt and fresh fruit.

1 Homemade Nutty Muesli

Mix together 2 cups rolled oats, ¼ cup slivered almonds, ⅓ cup golden raisins, ⅓ cup chopped dried apricots, 2 tablespoons shredded dried coconut, ¼ cup chopped walnuts, 1 tablespoon chopped hazelnuts, and 2 teaspoons sesame seeds in a large bowl. Store in an airtight container. Serve with milk and fresh fruit.

2 Nutty Muesli Muffins

Mix together ⅓ cup all-purpose flour, ⅔ cup whole-wheat flour, 2¼ teaspoons baking powder, ½ cup store-bought nutty muesli, and ⅓ cup firmly packed dark brown sugar in a large bowl. Beat together ½ cup sunflower oil, ⅔ cup soy milk, and 1 egg in a small bowl, then pour into the dry ingredients and mix together until just combined—do not overmix. Spoon into 10 paper muffin liners arranged in a muffin pan and bake in a preheated oven, at 400°F, for 15 minutes, until well risen and golden.

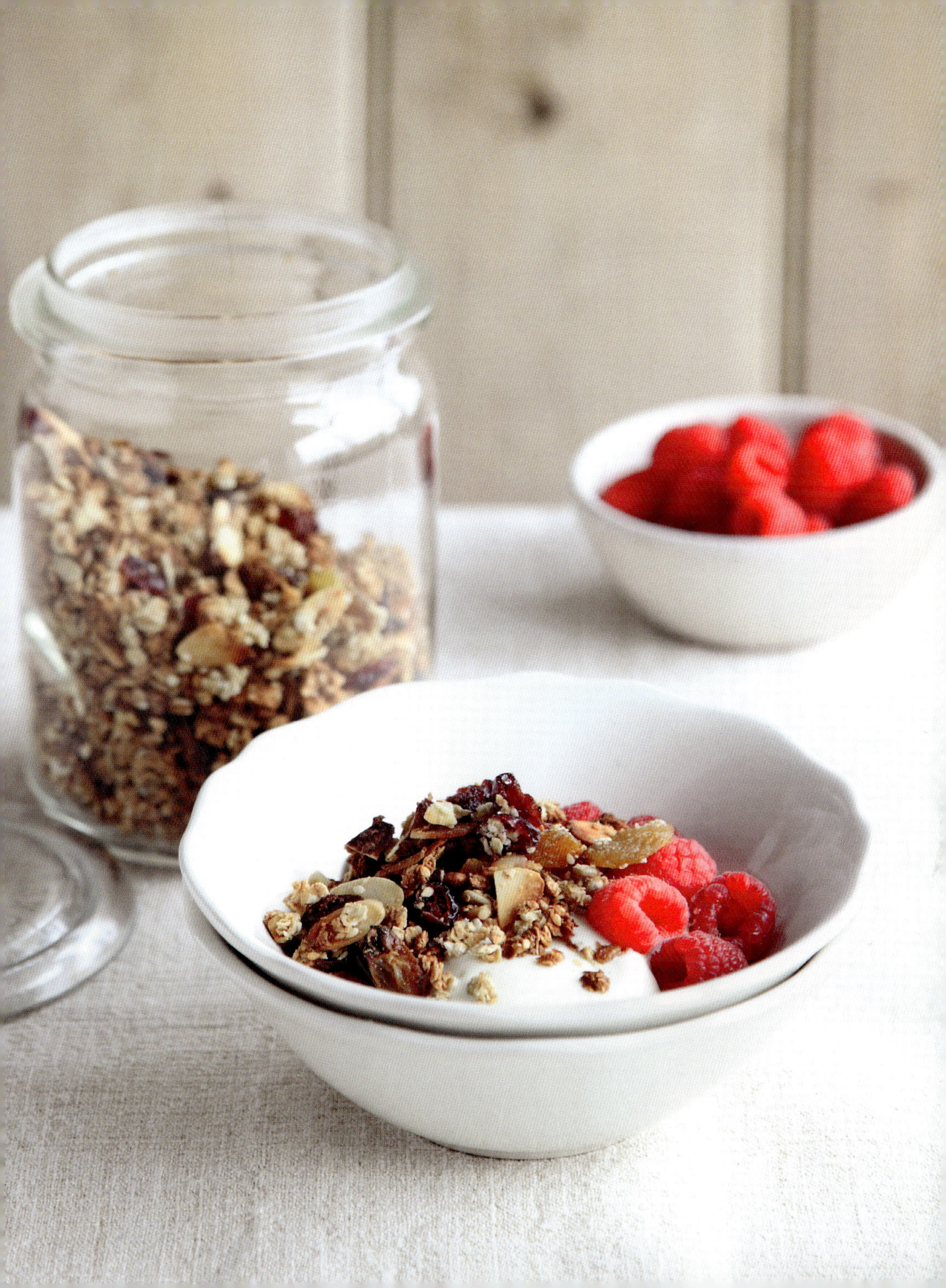

10 Smashed Bean and Sardine Dip

Serves 4

1 (15 oz) can cannellini beans, rinsed and drained
1 (15 oz) can chickpeas, rinsed and drained
2 garlic cloves, crushed
juice of 1 lime
1 teaspoon ground cumin
1 (3¾ oz) can sardines, drained
½ cup thick plain yogurt
1 tablespoon chopped cilantro
1 tablespoon olive oil
salt and black pepper
vegetable crudités, to serve

- Place the beans and chickpeas, reserving 1 tablespoon of each, in a food processor. Add the garlic, lime juice, cumin, sardines, and yogurt and process until smooth.
- Stir in the reserved beans and chickpeas with the cilantro and season to taste. Transfer to a bowl and pour the oil over the dip.
- Serve the dip with vegetable crudités.

20 Bean and Sardine Salad

Steam 2 cups trimmed green beans until just tender. Drain and refresh under cold water, then drain again. Rinse and drain 1 (15 oz) can cannellini beans and 1 (15 oz) can kidney beans, then place in a bowl with the green beans, 2 (3¾ oz) cans sardines, drained and halved, 2 sliced celery sticks, 1 diced red onion, 1 diced apple, and 2 tablespoons chopped parsley. Whisk together 1 tablespoon cider vinegar, 3 tablespoons olive oil, 1 teaspoon granulated sugar, and ½ teaspoon Dijon mustard, then toss into the salad. Serve sprinkled with ½ cup toasted walnuts.

30 Sardine Bean Burgers

Lightly crush 2 (15 oz) cans kidney beans, rinsed and drained, with 1 (3¾ oz) can sardines, drained, in a large bowl. Mix in 1 cup dried whole-wheat bread crumbs, 2 teaspoons chili powder, 2 crushed garlic cloves, 1 tablespoon chopped cilantro, 1 egg, and 1 cup chopped tomatoes and season. Divide the mixture into 4 and, using wet hands, shape into patties. Cover and chill for 10 minutes. Meanwhile, to make a salsa, mix together 2 cored, seeded, and diced red bell peppers, 2 peeled, pitted, and diced avocados, 3 diced tomatoes, 1 tablespoon olive oil, the juice of ½ lime, 4 sliced scallions, and 1 tablespoon chopped cilantro in a bowl. Cook the patties under a preheated medium broiler for 5–6 minutes on each side, until golden. Toast 4 halved burger buns and spoon the salsa over the bottoms. Top each one with a burger and a spoonful of sour cream, if desired. Replace the lids and serve.

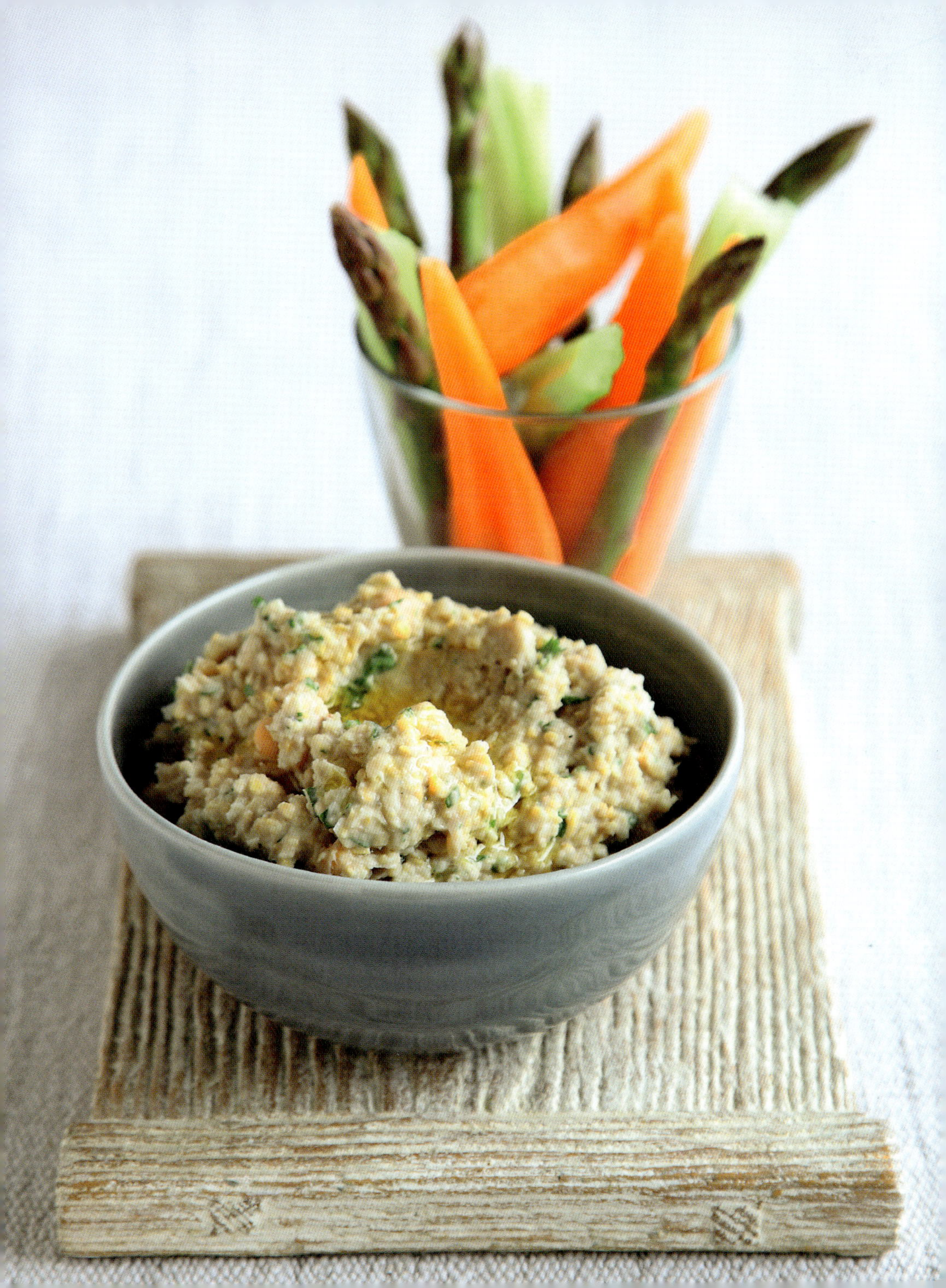

1 Smoked Mackerel and Horseradish Pâté

Serves 4
1½ lb smoked mackerel fillets
2 tablespoons plain yogurt
2 teaspoons creamed horseradish
juice of ½ lemon
black pepper
oatcakes, toast, or vegetable crudités, to serve

- Skin and flake the mackerel into a bowl. Add the remaining ingredients and mix well.
- Serve with oatcakes, toast, or with vegetable crudités.

2 Smoked Mackerel and Mashed Potatoes with Horseradish

Cook 6 peeled, chopped russet potatoes in a saucepan of boiling water for 12–15 minutes, until tender. Meanwhile, cook 4 (4 oz) smoked mackerel fillets, under a preheated medium broiler for 2–3 minutes on each side, until heated through. Place a large handful of basil leaves, 2 tablespoons toasted pine nuts, 1 garlic clove, 1 tablespoon grated Parmesan cheese, and ¼ cup olive oil in a food processor or blender and process to form a pesto sauce. Drain the potatoes, then mash with 2 tablespoons butter, 1 tablespoon plain yogurt, and 1 tablespoon creamed horseradish. Serve with the mackerel, drizzled with the pesto.

3 Warm Mackerel, Horseradish, and Potato Salad

Cook 8 oz new potatoes in a saucepan of boiling water for 15–20 minutes or until tender. Drain, then coarsely chop and place in a large bowl with 2 peeled, cored, and sliced apples, 1 tablespoon creamed horseradish, and 2 tablespoons sour cream. Season to taste. Toss together 3 cups salad greens, 3 tablespoons olive oil, 1 tablespoon lemon juice, 1 teaspoon Dijon mustard, and 1 teaspoon honey in a bowl. Broil 4 fresh mackerel fillets under a preheated hot broiler for 2–3 minutes on each side. Divide the salad greens among 4 plates, then top with the potato salad and mackerel. Serve with lemon wedges.

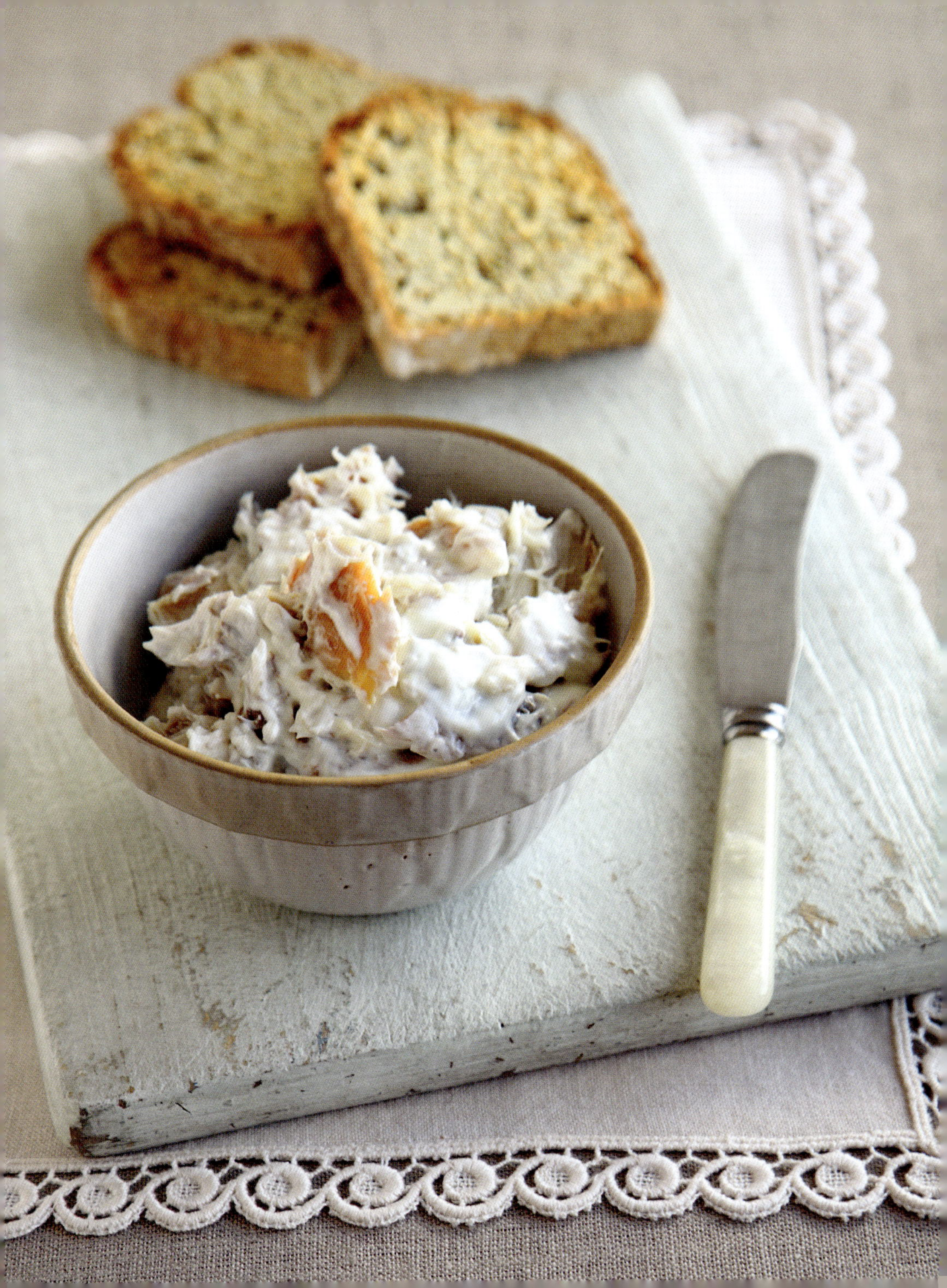

10 Guacamole

Serves 4

2 ripe avocados, peeled, pitted, and chopped
juice of 1 lime
6 cherry tomatoes, diced
1 tablespoon chopped cilantro
1–2 garlic cloves, crushed
oatcakes or vegetable crudités, to serve

- Put the avocados and lime juice in a bowl and mash together to prevent discoloration, then stir in the remaining ingredients.

- Serve immediately with oatcakes or vegetable crudités.

20 Shrimp and Avocado Salad

Prepare 8 oz vermicelli rice noodles according to package directions until just tender. Drain, refresh under cold running water, and drain again, then place in a bowl with 8 oz cooked, peeled jumbo shrimp, 2 peeled, pitted, and sliced avocados, ½ thinly sliced cucumber, and 4 sliced scallions. Next whisk together ½ cup coconut milk, the juice of 1 lime, and a 1-inch piece of fresh ginger root, peeled and grated, in a bowl. Pour the dressing over the salad and gently toss together to serve.

30 Smoked Salmon and Avocado Terrines

Line 4 ramekins with plastic wrap. Divide 8 oz thinly sliced smoked salmon among the ramekins, lining each dish and letting plenty of the salmon overhang. Mix together 2 oz soft goat cheese, 2 tablespoons snipped chives, 2 peeled, pitted, and chopped avocados, and the juice of 1 lemon in a bowl and season to taste. Spoon the mixture into the dishes, then press down and fold the salmon over to cover. Cover and chill for 10–12 minutes. Turn out onto plates and serve with a green salad.

SNACKS AND LIGHT MEALS

HEA-SNAC-ZUY

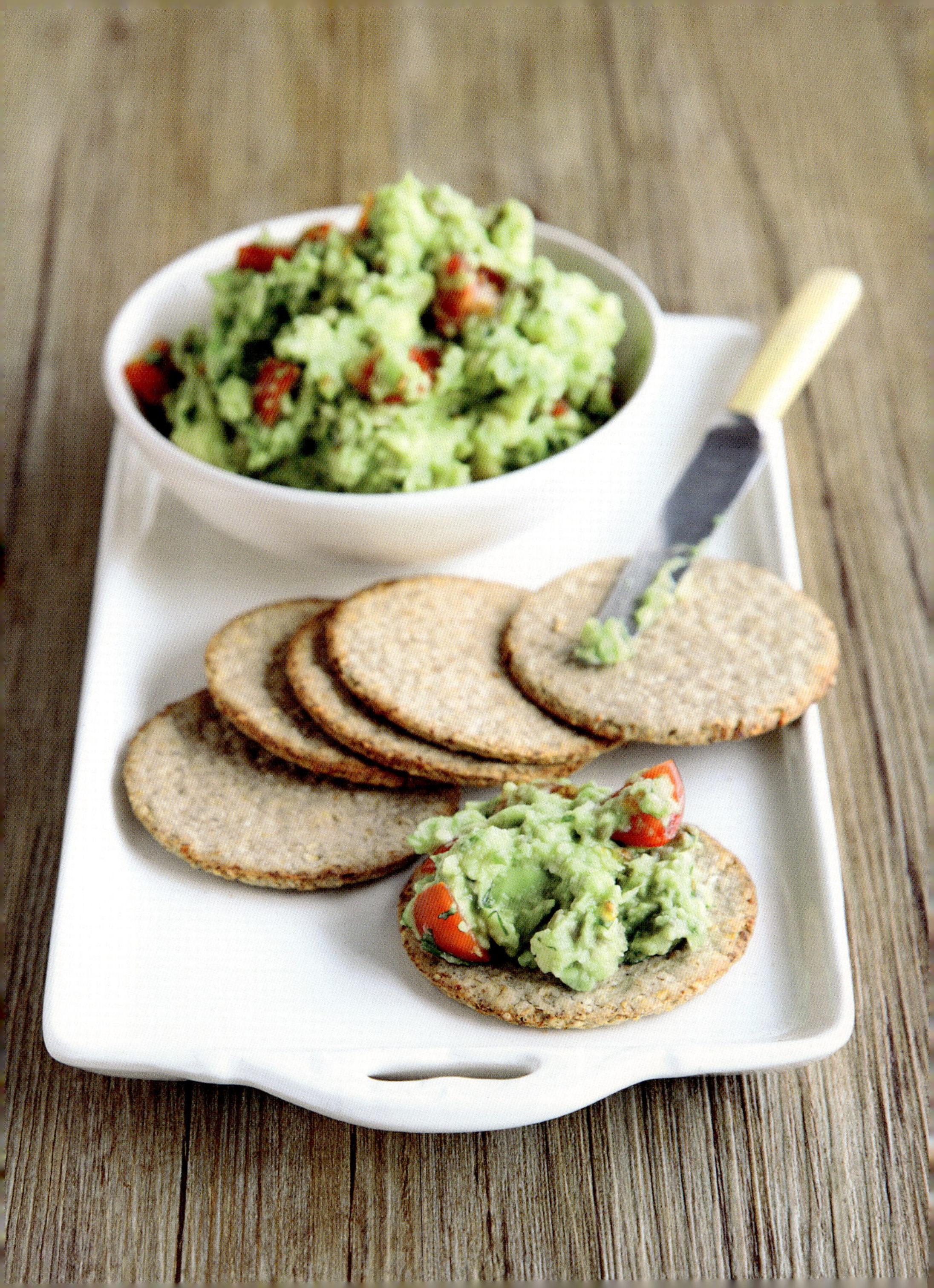

Hummus with Carrot and Celery Sticks

20

Serves 4

⅓ cup extra virgin olive oil, plus extra for brushing
2 garlic cloves, crushed
⅓ cup walnuts
1 (15 oz) can chickpeas, rinsed and drained
1½ tablespoons tahini paste
juice of ½ lemon
½ tablespoon chopped cilantro
salt and black pepper

To serve

2 whole-wheat pita breads
2 tablespoons sesame seeds
2 large carrots, peeled and cut into batons
4 celery sticks, cut into batons

- Heat 4 tablespoons of the oil in a skillet, add the garlic, and cook for 2–3 minutes. Remove from the heat and let cool slightly.

- Heat a nonstick skillet over medium-low heat and dry-fry the walnuts for 3–4 minutes, stirring frequently, until slightly golden and releasing an aroma.

- Place the chickpeas, tahini, lemon juice, garlic oil, and toasted walnuts in a food processor and process until smooth, adding a little water to loosen the mixture, if necessary. Stir in the cilantro and season to taste. Spoon into a bowl.

- Toast the pita breads under a preheated medium broiler for 4 minutes, then turn over, brush with the remaining oil, and sprinkle with the sesame seeds. Toast until golden, then cut into strips.

- Serve the hummus with the pita strips and the carrot and celery sticks.

---

10 Hummus and Carrot Wraps

Spread ¾ cup store-bought hummus over 4 seeded tortilla wraps. Peel and shred 4 carrots and sprinkle them over the hummus. Top each one with a handful of arugula leaves, a small handful of cilantro leaves, and a sprinkling of lemon juice and olive oil. Roll up the wraps and serve.

30 Carrot and Muenster Cheese Salad with Hummus Dressing

Mix together 3 peeled and chopped carrots and 1 tablespoon olive oil in a roasting pan. Place in a preheated oven, at 400°F, for 20–25 minutes, adding 2 tablespoons walnut halves 5 minutes before the end of the cooking time. Meanwhile, sprinkle 8 oz cubed Muenster cheese with ½ teaspoon dried oregano, then dry-fry in a nonstick skillet for 2–3 minutes on each side, until golden. Mix together 2 tablespoons store-bought hummus and ⅓ cup plain yogurt in a small bowl. Toss together the cheese, roasted carrots and walnuts, 4 chopped tomatoes, and 1 sliced red onion in a bowl. Place 2 cups baby salad greens on 4 plates, top with the carrot salad, and serve drizzled with the hummus dressing.

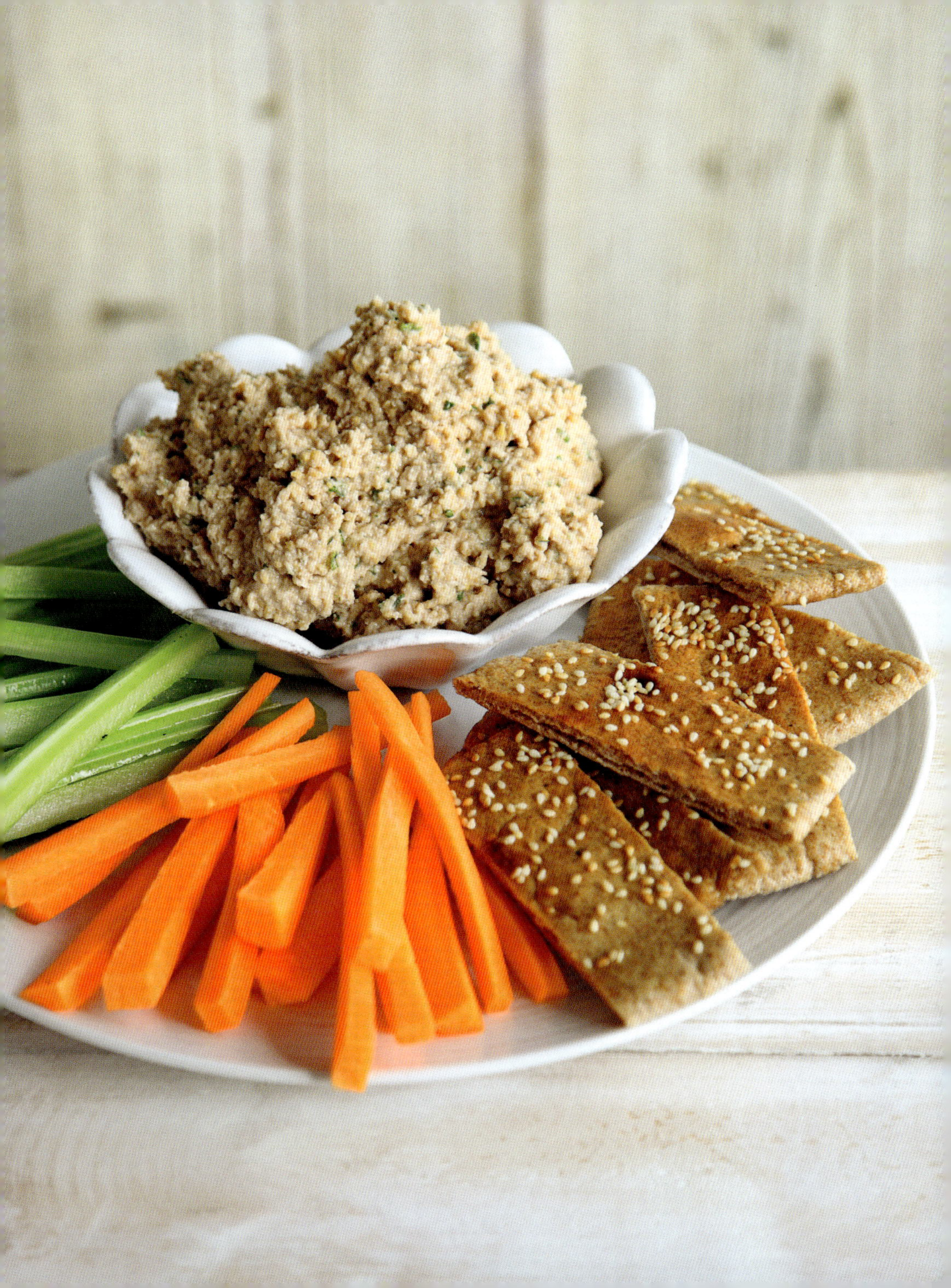

Broccoli and Black-Eyed Pea Soup

Serves 4
2 tablespoons olive oil
2 large carrots, peeled and diced
8 scallions, sliced
5 cups hot vegetable stock
3 cups chopped baby broccoli
1 (15 oz) can black-eyed peas, rinsed and drained

For the croutons
1 slice of crusty whole-wheat bread
3 oz goat cheese

- Heat 1 tablespoon of the oil in a large saucepan, add the carrots and scallions, and sauté for 2–3 minutes. Pour in the stock and add the broccoli. Bring to a boil, then reduce the heat and simmer for 10 minutes, until the broccoli is tender.

- Add the black-eyed peas and cook for another 4–6 minutes, until the beans are heated through.

- Meanwhile, make the croutons. Toast the bread under a preheated hot broiler for 2–3 minutes on each side, then top with the goat cheese and broil until the cheese is bubbling. Cut into squares.

- Ladle the soup into bowls, then top with the croutons and sprinkle with the remaining oil.

Broccoli and Black-Eyed Pea Salad

Cook 3 cups broccoli florets in a saucepan of boiling water for 4–5 minutes, then drain, refresh under cold running water, and drain again. Whisk together 3 tablespoons olive oil, 1 tablespoon balsamic vinegar, 1 teaspoon honey, and 1 teaspoon Dijon mustard in a large bowl. Gently mix in the broccoli, 1 (15 oz) can black-eyed peas, rinsed and drained, 1 sliced red onion, 1 (7 oz) jar roasted red peppers, drained and cut into strips, and 1 bunch watercress or 2 cups arugula. Serve with crusty whole-wheat bread.

Broccoli and Black-Eyed Pea Curry

Heat 2 tablespoons olive oil in a saucepan, add 1 large chopped onion, and cook for 3–4 minutes, until softened. Add 2 crushed garlic cloves, 1 tablespoon curry powder, 1 teaspoon ground cumin, and 1 teaspoon turmeric and cook for another 1–2 minutes. Stir in ¼ cup lentils, 1 (15 oz) can black-eyed peas, rinsed and drained, ⅓ cup raisins, and 3 cups broccoli florets. Pour in 1 (14½ oz) can diced tomatoes and 1¼ cups hot vegetable stock and bring to a simmer. Cook for 20–22 minutes, stirring occasionally. Serve with steamed long-grain rice.

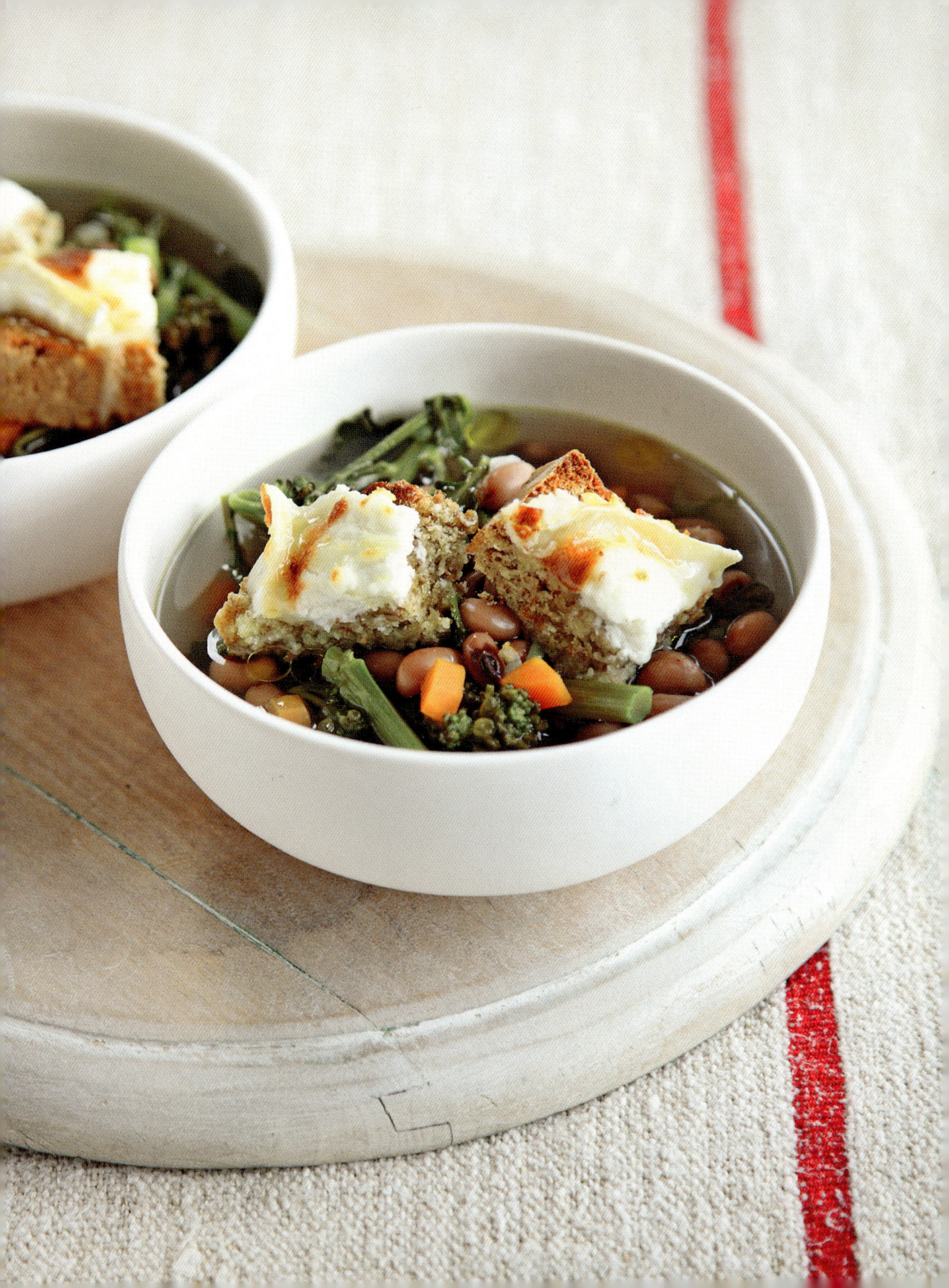

30 Smoked Haddock and Kale Soup

Serves 4

1 tablespoon olive oil
2 shallots, diced
3 garlic cloves, crushed
1 large potato, peeled and diced
1½ cups soy milk
2 cups water
4½ cups shredded kale
10 oz smoked haddock, skinned and chopped
salt and black pepper

- Heat the oil in a saucepan, add the shallots and garlic, and cook for 3–4 minutes, until softened. Add the potato, milk, and measured water and season to taste. Bring to a boil, then reduce the heat and simmer for 5–6 minutes.

- Stir in the kale and cook for another 10–12 minutes, until the vegetables are tender. Stir in the haddock and simmer for 2 minutes or until cooked through.

- Ladle the soup into bowls and serve immediately.

10 Spicy Smoked Haddock and Kale Pasta

Heat ¼ cup olive oil in a skillet, add 2 seeded and sliced red chiles, 3 sliced garlic cloves, and 6 finely chopped anchovy fillets, and cook for 1 minute. Stir in 6 cups shredded kale and gently cook for 7–8 minutes, until tender, adding a little water, if necessary. Add 4 oz skinned and chopped smoked haddock 4 minutes before the end of the cooking time. Meanwhile, cook 1 lb store-bought fresh penne in a saucepan of boiling water according to the package directions. Drain and toss with the kale, the juice of ½ lemon, and 3 tablespoons grated Parmesan cheese. Serve sprinkled with 2 tablespoons Parmesan shavings.

20 Smoked Haddock Fish Cakes with Kale

Cook 12 oz smoked haddock under a preheated hot broiler for 4 minutes on each side, then skin and flake into a large bowl. Mix in 1 (24 oz) container store-bought fresh mashed potatoes, 1 tablespoon chopped, rinsed, and drained capers, the grated rind of 1 lemon, 2 tablespoons chopped parsley, and 1 beaten egg. Mix well, then shape into 8 fish cakes and dust with a little flour. Heat 2 tablespoons olive oil in a skillet and cook the fish cakes for 3–4 minutes on each side, until golden. Meanwhile, heat 2 tablespoons olive oil in a separate pan, add 4 cups chopped kale, and cook for 3–4 minutes, until wilted. Serve with the fish cakes.

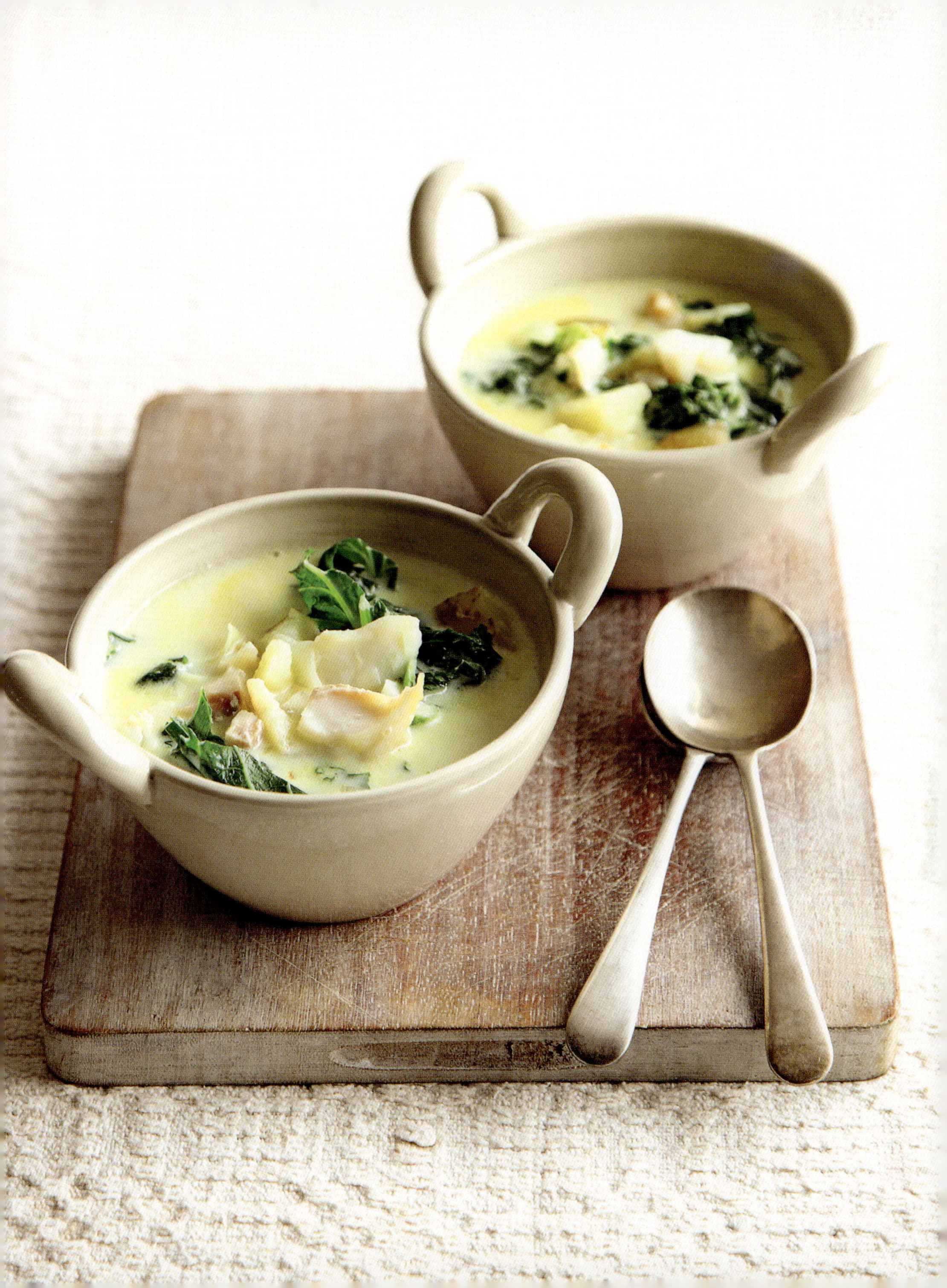

30 Roasted Butternut, Sage, and Cashew Nut Soup

Serves 4

1 (2 lb) butternut squash, peeled, seeded, and chopped into ½ inch chunks
2 tablespoons olive oil
1 tablespoon chopped sage
2 tablespoons pumpkin seeds
1 onion, chopped
1 garlic clove, chopped
½ tablespoon mild curry powder
2 tablespoons cashew nuts
2½ cups hot vegetable stock
½ cup plain yogurt
salt and black pepper

- Place the butternut squash in a roasting pan and toss with 1 tablespoon of the oil and the sage. Place in a preheated oven, at 425°F, for 18–20 minutes, until tender and golden.

- Meanwhile, heat a nonstick skillet over medium-low heat and dry-fry the pumpkin seeds for 2–3 minutes, stirring frequently, until golden brown and toasted. Set aside.

- Heat the remaining oil in a saucepan, add the onion and garlic, and cook for 4–5 minutes, until softened. Stir in the curry powder and cook for another minute, stirring.

- Add the roasted squash, cashew nuts, and stock and bring to a boil, then reduce the heat and simmer for 3–4 minutes. Stir in the yogurt. Using a handheld blender, blend the soup until smooth. Season to taste.

- Ladle the soup into bowls and serve sprinkled with the toasted pumpkin seeds.

---

1 Butternut, Sage, and Cashew Nut Dip

Cook 2 cups peeled, seeded, and finely diced butternut squash in boiling water for 6–7 minutes, until tender. Drain and cool for 1 minute. Meanwhile, dry-fry ¾ cup cashew nuts until golden. Place in a food processor with 1 tablespoon tahini and 2 garlic cloves and blend until smooth. Add the squash, the juice of ½–1 lime, ½ tablespoon chopped sage, and a pinch of chili powder. Season, then blend with 1–2 tablespoons olive oil to the desired consistency.

2 Butternut and Sage Mashed Potatoes

Cook 5⅓ cups peeled, seeded, and chopped butternut squash and 3 peeled and chopped russet potatoes in a saucepan of boiling water for 12–15 minutes, until tender. Meanwhile, cook ½ shredded savoy cabbage in a separate saucepan of boiling water for 4–5 minutes, then drain and keep warm. Bring a saucepan of water to a gentle simmer and stir with a large spoon to create a swirl. Break 2 eggs into the water and cook for 3 minutes. Remove with a slotted spoon and keep warm. Repeat with another 2 eggs. Drain the squash and potatoes, then mash in the pan with 1 tablespoon plain yogurt, 1 tablespoon chopped sage, and 2 tablespoons butter. Season well and stir in the cabbage. Serve topped with the poached eggs.

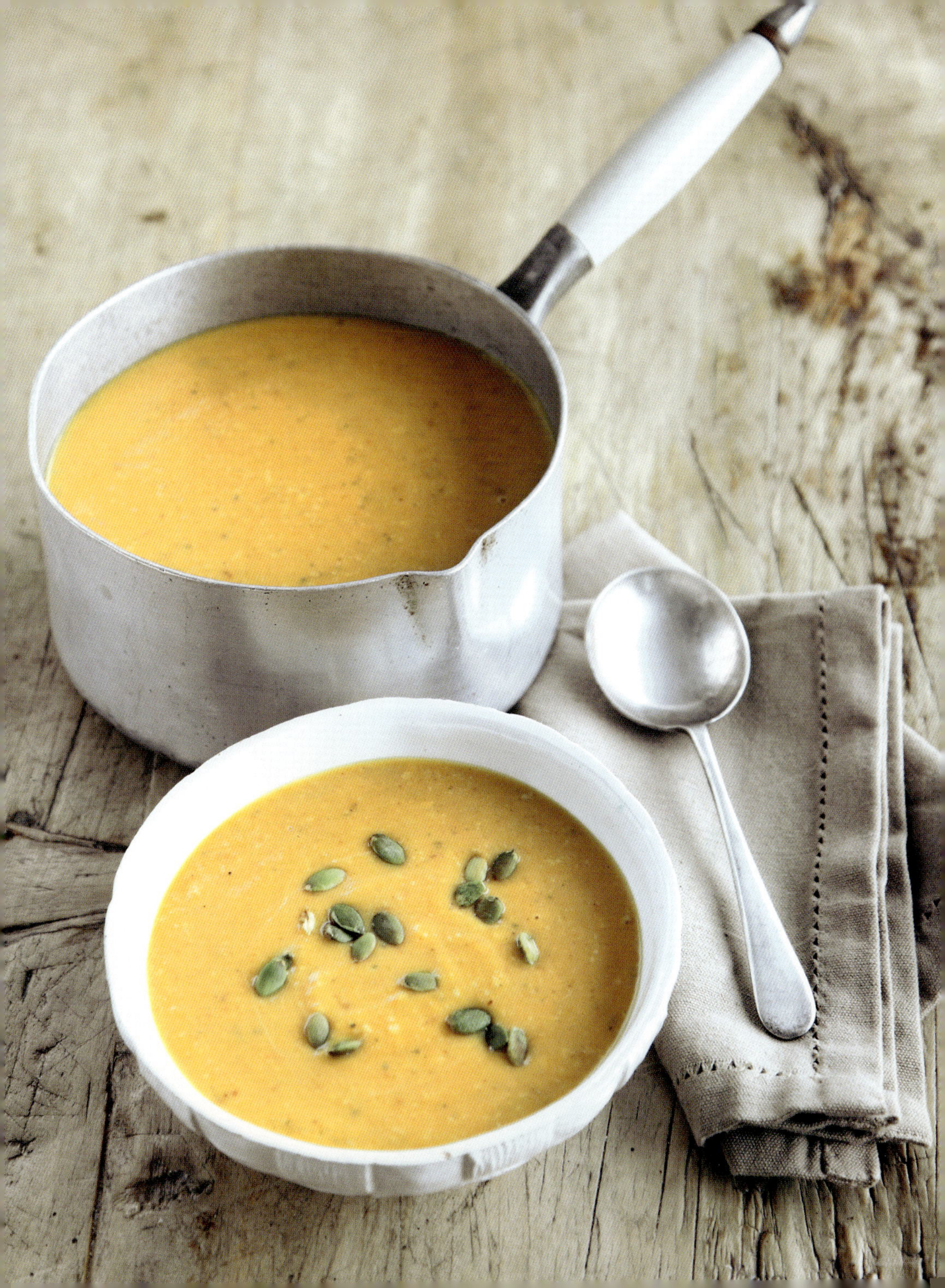

20 Gazpacho

Serves 4

4 red bell peppers, cored, seeded, and coarsely chopped
1 red onion, coarsely chopped
2 cucumbers, coarsely chopped
handful of basil leaves
handful of parsley leaves
2 garlic cloves
2 tablespoons sherry vinegar or balsamic vinegar
$\frac{2}{3}$ cup olive oil
2 cups chilled tomato juice
salt and black pepper

To serve

1 avocado, peeled, pitted, and chopped
1 soft-boiled egg, quartered

- Place the vegetables, herbs, and garlic in the food processor and process until finely chopped.
- Add the remaining ingredients, season to taste, and process again briefly. Cover and chill for 5 minutes.
- Serve in bowls topped with the chopped avocados and quartered eggs.

---

10 Mediterranean Pepper Salad

Bring a saucepan of water to a gentle simmer and stir with a large spoon to create a swirl. Break 2 eggs into the water and cook for 3 minutes. Remove with a slotted spoon and keep warm. Repeat with another 2 eggs. Toss together 1 bunch of watercress or 2 cups arugula, 1 sliced red onion, ½ chopped cucumber, 2 peeled, pitted, and sliced avocados, 10–12 basil leaves, and a small handful of parsley leaves in a serving bowl. Cut 4 roasted red peppers from a jar into slices. Top the salad with the roasted peppers and poached eggs, then drizzle with salad dressing.

30 Red Pepper Tarts

Unroll a sheet of ready-to-bake puff pastry and cut into 4 rectangles. Place on a baking sheet and top each with ½ peeled, pitted, and mashed avocado, 2–3 basil leaves, ½ sliced tomato, and ½ cup sliced roasted red peppers from a jar. Sprinkle with 2 tablespoons pine nuts and 2 tablespoons grated Parmesan cheese. Bake in a preheated oven, at 400°F, for 20 minutes, until the pastry is golden. Serve with arugula salad.

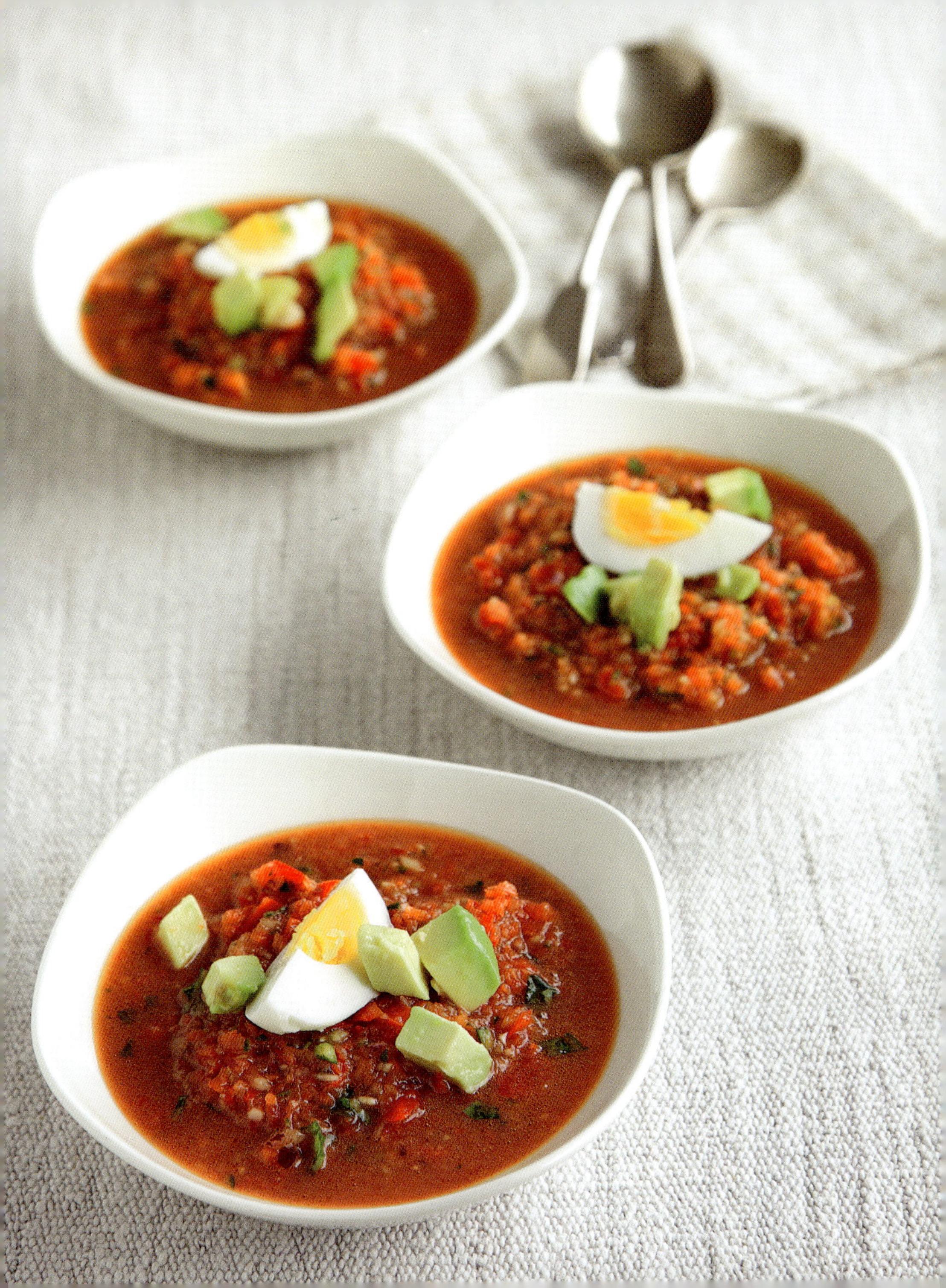

10 Warm Lentil, Tomato, and Muenster Cheese Salad

Serves 4

8 oz Muenster cheese, cut into chunks
½ red onion, sliced
16 cherry tomatoes, halved
1 (15 oz) can lentils, rinsed and drained, or 2 cups cooked lentils
1 garlic clove, crushed
juice of ½ lemon
2 tablespoons extra virgin olive oil
small handful of cilantro leaves, coarsely chopped
small handful of mint leaves, coarsely chopped

- Heat a nonstick skillet over a medium heat and dry-fry the Muenster cheese for a few minutes, turning frequently, until golden.

- Meanwhile, toss together the remaining ingredients in a bowl. Stir in the cooked cheese and serve immediately.

20 Lentil and Tomato Soup

Heat 1 tablespoon olive oil in a saucepan, add 1 chopped onion, 2 peeled and chopped carrots, and 2 sliced celery sticks, and cook for 5–6 minutes. Add 1 crushed garlic clove, 1 teaspoon ground cumin, and 1 cup lentils. Pour in 5 cups hot vegetable stock, 1 (14½ oz) can diced tomatoes, and 2 teaspoons tomato paste and bring to a boil, then simmer for 15–17 minutes, until the lentils are cooked. Using a handheld blender, blend the soup until smooth, then season. Serve with swirls of plain yogurt, sprinkled with chopped cilantro.

30 Lentil and Tomato Flatbreads

Mix together 7 cups all-purpose flour and 1 cup baking powder in a large bowl, then add 3½ sticks diced, chilled butter and rub in with the fingertips until the mixture resembles fine bread crumbs. Add 1 (15 oz) can lentils, rinsed and drained (or 2 cups cooked lentils), 1¾ cups milk, and 1 teaspoon salt and mix well. Using your hands, roughly shape the mixture into four 9-inch circles. Place the circles on a baking sheet and top with 2 thinly sliced tomatoes, a small handful of coarsely torn basil leaves, and a drizzle of olive oil. Bake in a preheated oven, at 400°F, for 15–20 minutes.

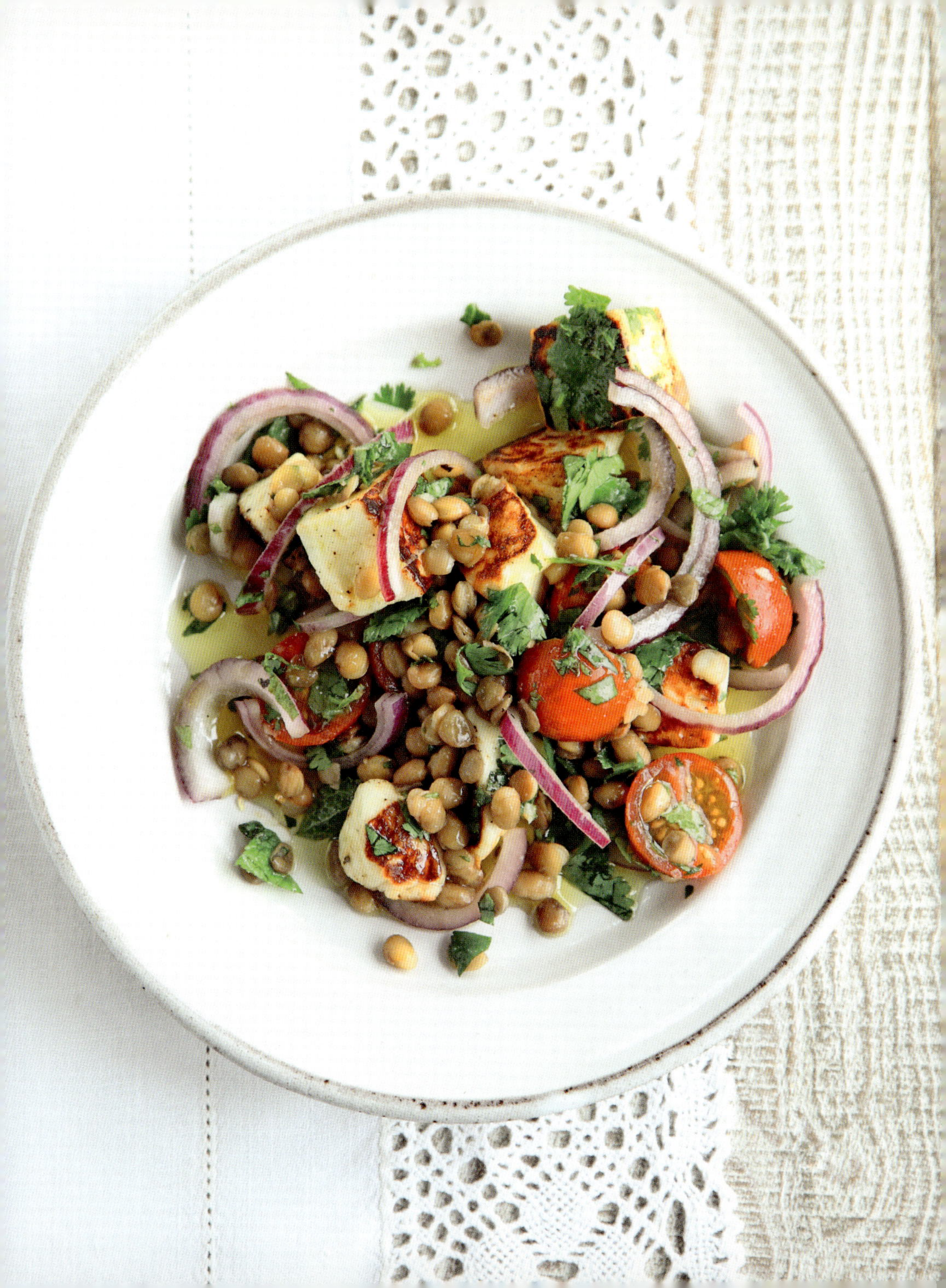

Peach, Feta, and Watercress Salad

Serves 4

2 tablespoons pumpkin seeds
juice of ½ lemon
2 tablespoons extra virgin olive oil
½ teaspoon Dijon mustard
1 teaspoon honey
1 tablespoon chopped oregano
1½ bunches of watercress
3 peaches, halved, pitted, and sliced
4 scallions, sliced
1¼ cups crumbled feta cheese
black pepper

- Heat a nonstick skillet over medium-low heat and dry-fry the pumpkin seeds for 2–3 minutes, stirring frequently, until slightly golden and toasted. Set aside.
- Whisk together the lemon juice, oil, mustard, honey, oregano, and black pepper in a small bowl.
- Divide the watercress among 4 plates, top with the peach slices and scallions, then sprinkle with the feta cheese.
- Serve sprinkled with the toasted pumpkin seeds and drizzled with the dressing.

Peach, Feta, and Watercress Bruschetta

Cut 2 baguettes into ¾ inch slices. Place the slices on a baking sheet and drizzle with 2 tablespoons olive oil. Bake in a preheated oven, at 400°F, for 10–12 minutes, until golden. Rub one side of each slice with a garlic clove. Halve, pit, and slice 4 peaches. Top the toasts with a few sprigs of watercress, the peach slices, and 1 cup crumbled feta cheese. Serve drizzled with balsamic glaze.

Roasted Feta-Topped Peach and Watercress Salad

Halve and pit 4 peaches and place in a roasting pan. Sprinkle with 1⅓ cups crumbled feta cheese, 1 tablespoon olive oil, and 1 teaspoon cumin seeds. Season with black pepper. Place in a preheated oven, at 400°F, for 15–18 minutes, until the peaches are soft and the cheese is melted. Meanwhile, whisk together 3 tablespoons olive oil, 1 tablespoon balsamic vinegar, ½ teaspoon whole-grain mustard, and ½ teaspoon granulated sugar in a small bowl. Divide 1½ bunches of watercress among 4 shallow bowls and sprinkle with 1 small, diced red onion and 6 quartered cherry tomatoes. Top with the roasted peach halves. Pour any juices from the can into the dressing and whisk together, then drizzle it over the salad to serve.

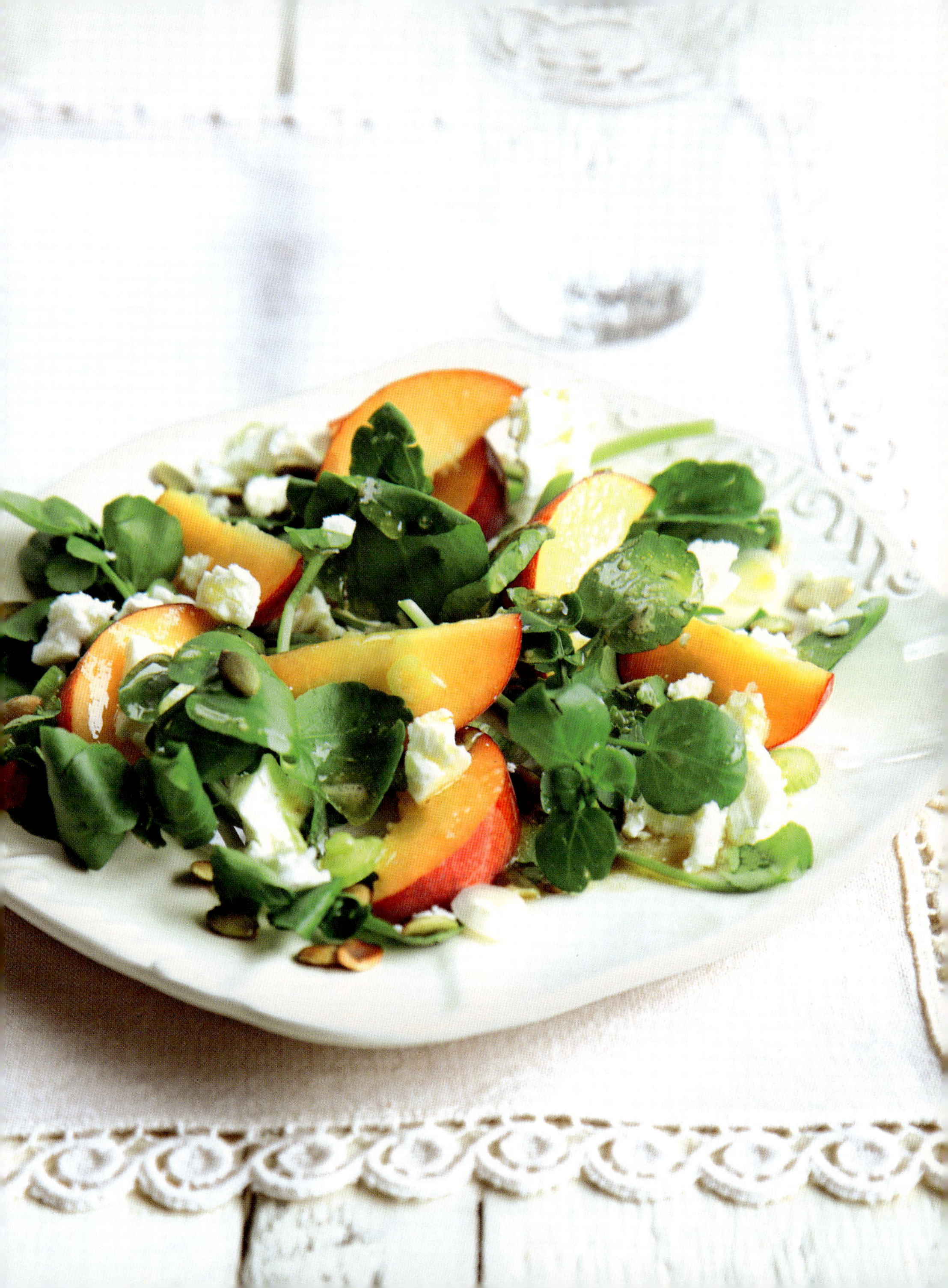

Avocado, Red Pepper, and Olive Salad

Serves 4

1 tablespoon sesame seeds
2 avocados, peeled, pitted, and chopped
juice of 1 lime
1 red bell pepper, cored, seeded, and chopped
1 yellow bell pepper, cored, seeded, and chopped
½ cucumber, finely chopped
2 carrots, peeled and chopped
2 tomatoes, chopped
4 scallions, sliced
10 pitted right black olives, halved
1 romaine lettuce, coarsely torn
¼ cup salad dressing
1 tablespoon chopped mint

- Heat a nonstick skillet over medium-low heat and dry-fry the sesame seeds for 2 minutes, stirring frequently, until golden brown and toasted. Set aside.
- Meanwhile, place the avocados in a large bowl and toss with the lime juice to prevent discoloration. Gently toss together with the remaining ingredients except the sesame seeds.
- Sprinkle the salad with the toasted sesame seeds and serve.

Muenster Cheese with Avocado, Red Pepper, and Olive Salsa Halve, core, and seed 2 red bell peppers and cook, skin side up, under a preheated hot broiler for 10–12 minutes, until blackened. Place in a bowl, cover with plastic wrap, and let cool for 5 minutes. Meanwhile, slice 8 oz Muenster cheese and dry-fry in a nonstick skillet for a few minutes on each side until golden. Peel the skin from the roasted red peppers, then cut into slices. Place 1 (5 oz) package baby spinach leaves on a serving plate, top with 2 sliced beefsteak tomatoes, 6 sliced scallions, 2 peeled, pitted, and sliced avocados, the Muenster slices, and 12–16 pitted, ripe, black olives. Serve drizzled with store-bought salad dressing.

Peperonata with Avocado and Olives Heat 3 tablespoons olive oil in a skillet, add 2 sliced garlic cloves and 3 sliced onions, and cook for 1–2 minutes. Core, seed, and slice 2 red bell peppers and 2 yellow bell peppers, then add to the skillet and cook for 10 minutes. Add 3 chopped, ripe tomatoes and cook for another 12–15 minutes, until the bell peppers are soft. Stir in 1 peeled, pitted, and chopped avocado, 12 halved, pitted, ripe, black olives, and a small handful of basil leaves. Serve with crusty bread.

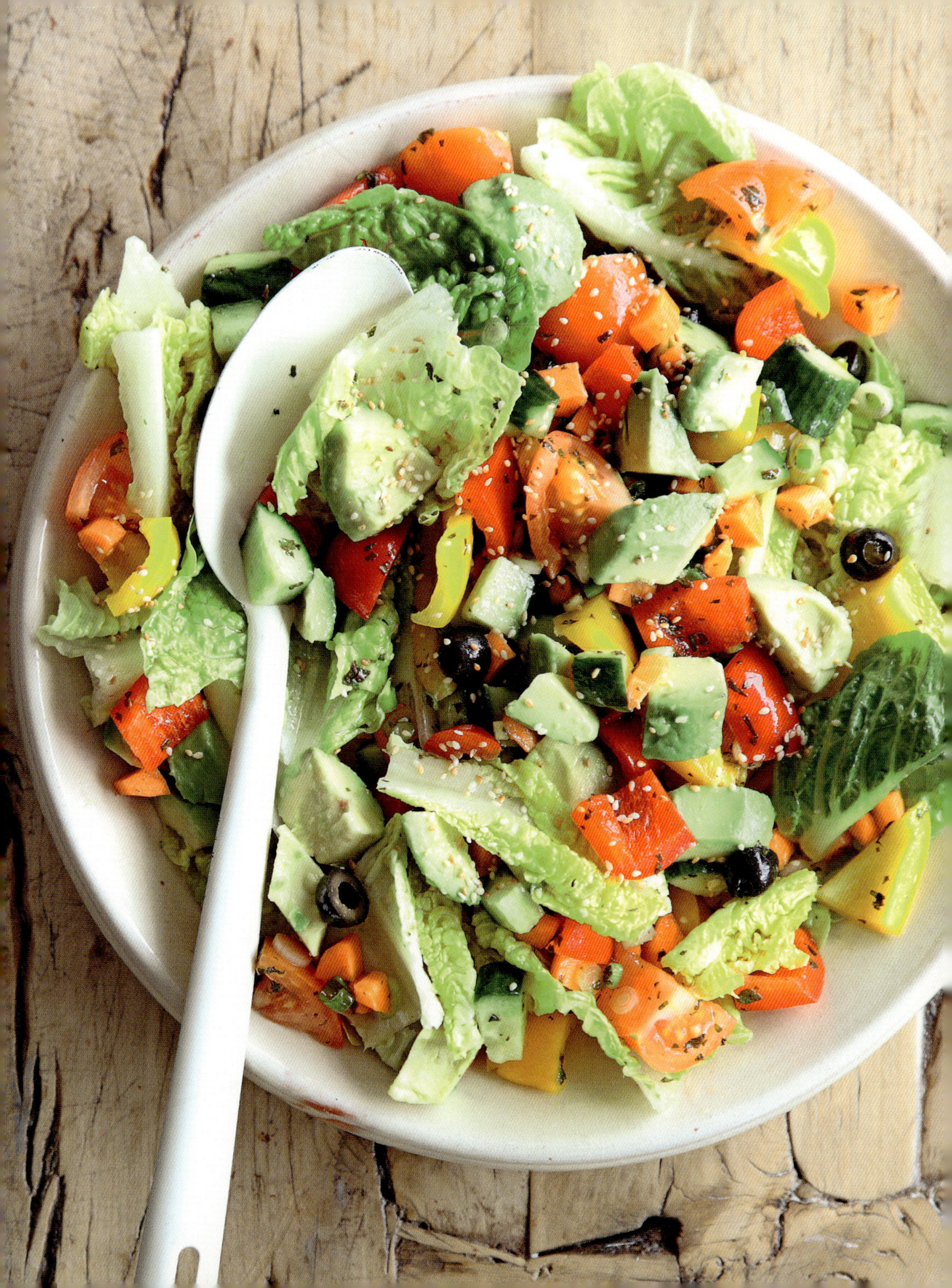

Salmon and Chickpea Salad

Serves 4

1¼ lb salmon fillet, skinned
1 orange
grated rind of ½ lemon
2 tablespoons extra virgin olive oil
1 (15 oz) can chickpeas, rinsed and drained
1 bunch of watercress or 1½ cups argula
2 tablespoons caper berries, rinsed and drained
small handful of mint leaves, coarsely torn
salt and black pepper

- Cook the salmon under a preheated hot broiler for 8–9 minutes, turning once, or until cooked through.
- Meanwhile, grate the rind of the orange into a bowl, then peel and segment the orange, catching the juice in the bowl. Whisk together the orange juice and rind, grated lemon rind, oil, and salt and black pepper.
- Flake the salmon in large pieces into a serving bowl. Toss together with the remaining ingredients, the orange segments, and dressing, then serve.

---

20 Broiled Salmon with Chickpea Curry

Heat 1 tablespoon olive oil in a saucepan, add 1 chopped onion, 1 tablespoon peeled and grated fresh ginger root, and 2 crushed garlic cloves, and cook for 1–2 minutes. Stir in 1 teaspoon each of ground cumin, ground coriander, turmeric, and chili powder, then add 3 chopped tomatoes and 2 (15 oz) cans chickpeas, rinsed and drained. Pour in ⅔ cup water and simmer for 12–14 minutes. Stir in 2 tablespoons chopped cilantro. Meanwhile, cook 4 (5 oz) salmon fillets under a preheated hot broiler for 4–5 minutes on each side. Serve with the curry.

30 Salmon en Papillote with Warm Chickpea Salad

Toss 2 red onions, cut into wedges, with 1 tablespoon olive oil in roasting pan. Place in a preheated oven, at 400°F, for 25 minutes. Meanwhile, place 4 (5 oz) skinless salmon fillets in the center of square sheets of wax paper and add ½ tablespoon olive oil, a splash of white wine, and a few cilantro sprigs to each. Fold up to make packages and place on a baking sheet. Bake in the oven for 6–8 minutes or until cooked through. While the fish is cooking, cook 3 cups broccoli florets in a saucepan of boiling water for 4–5 minutes, until tender, then drain, refresh under cold running water, and drain again. Heat 1 (15 oz) can chickpeas, rinsed and drained, in a saucepan until warmed through, then toss with the red onion and broccoli. Serve the salmon packages with the warm salad.

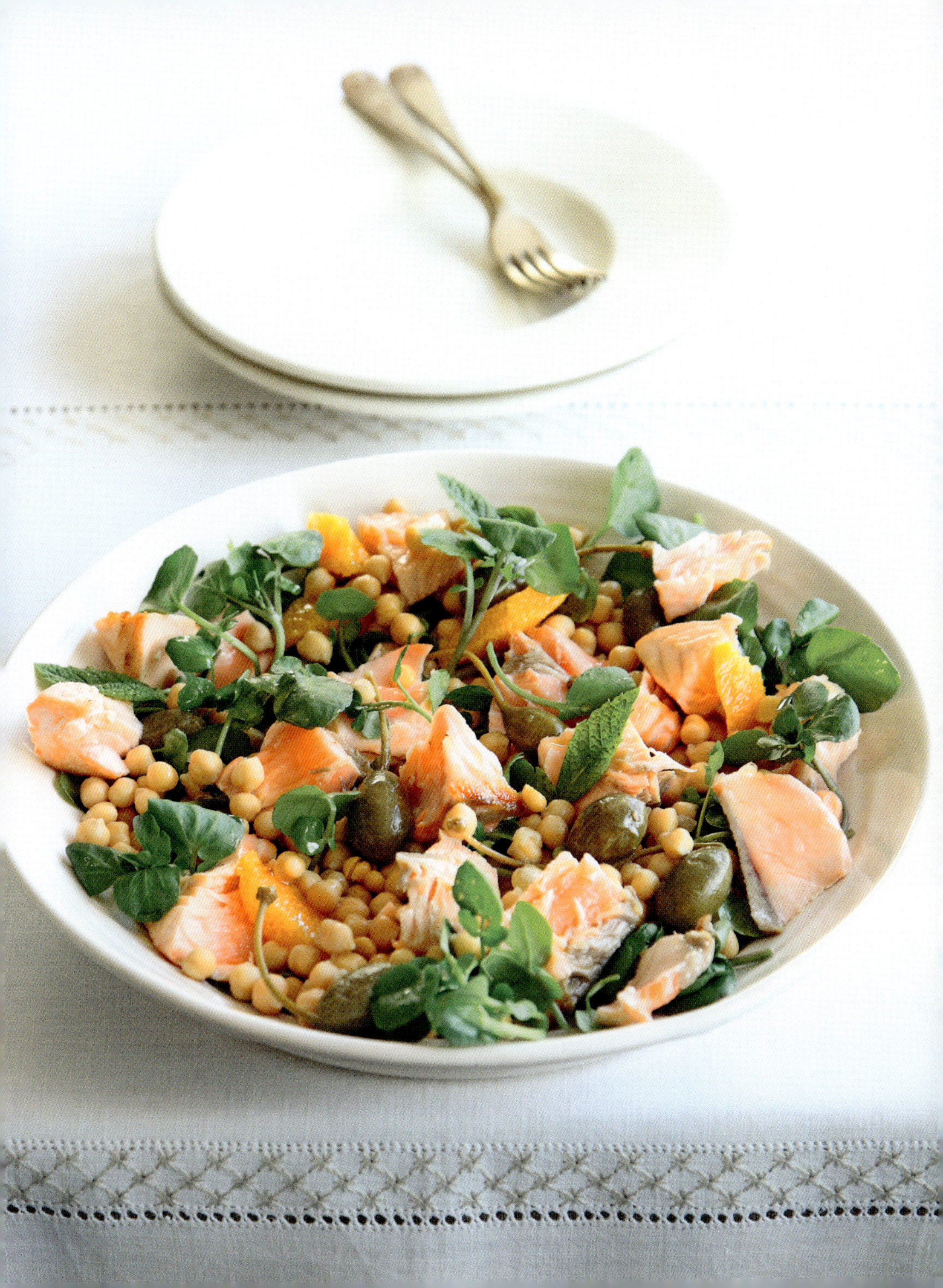

10 Warm Smoked Duck and Asparagus Salad

Serves 4

2 smoked duck breasts, sliced
1 lb asparagus, trimmed
20 radishes, quartered
2 tablespoons walnut pieces
3 tablespoons olive oil
1 tablespoon balsamic vinegar
3 stored-bought, cooked fresh beets, diced

- Cook the duck in a dry skillet for 3–4 minutes, until the fat is released. Remove from the skillet, using a slotted spoon, and keep warm.

- Meanwhile, cook the asparagus in a saucepan of boiling water for 2–3 minutes, then drain and halve widthwise. Add to the fat in the skillet and cook for 1–2 minutes, until lightly browned, then stir in the radishes and cook for 1 minute.

- While the asparagus is cooking, heat a nonstick skillet over medium-low heat and dry-fry the walnuts for 3–4 minutes, stirring frequently, until slightly golden. Whisk together the oil and vinegar in a bowl.

- Toss together the duck, asparagus and radishes, toasted walnuts, and beets. Serve drizzled with the dressing.

20 Pan-Fried Duck Breasts with Grilled Asparagus

Using a sharp knife, make 3 slashes through the skin of 4 duck breasts. Rub each one with ¼ teaspoon Chinese five spice powder. Heat ½ tablespoon olive oil in a large skillet until very hot, then add the duck, skin side down, and cook for 8–10 minutes, until the skin is crisp and brown. Pour out the excess fat and add 2 star anise to the skillet. Turn the duck over and cook for another 5 minutes, or until cooked to your liking. Meanwhile, toss 1 lb asparagus, trimmed, with 1 tablespoon olive oil, then cook in a preheated, hot grill pan for 3–4 minutes, turning once. Remove the duck from the pan and let rest for 2–3 minutes. Add 4 chopped scallions, 2 tablespoons soy sauce, ½ cup chicken stock, and 2 teaspoons honey to the duck pan and simmer for 2 minutes. Serve the duck with the sauce and asparagus.

30 Smoked Duck and Asparagus Tarts

Cook 1 lb asparagus, trimmed, in a saucepan of boiling water for 2 minutes, then drain. Unroll a sheet of ready-to-bake puff pastry and cut into 4 rectangles. Place on a baking sheet and spread each rectangle with 2 tablespoons cream cheese, leaving a ¾ inch border. Top with the asparagus and 1 sliced smoked duck breast. Season with black pepper and drizzle with 1 tablespoon olive oil. Cook in a preheated oven, at 400°F, for 20–25 minutes, until golden. Serve sprinkled with Parmesan cheese shavings.

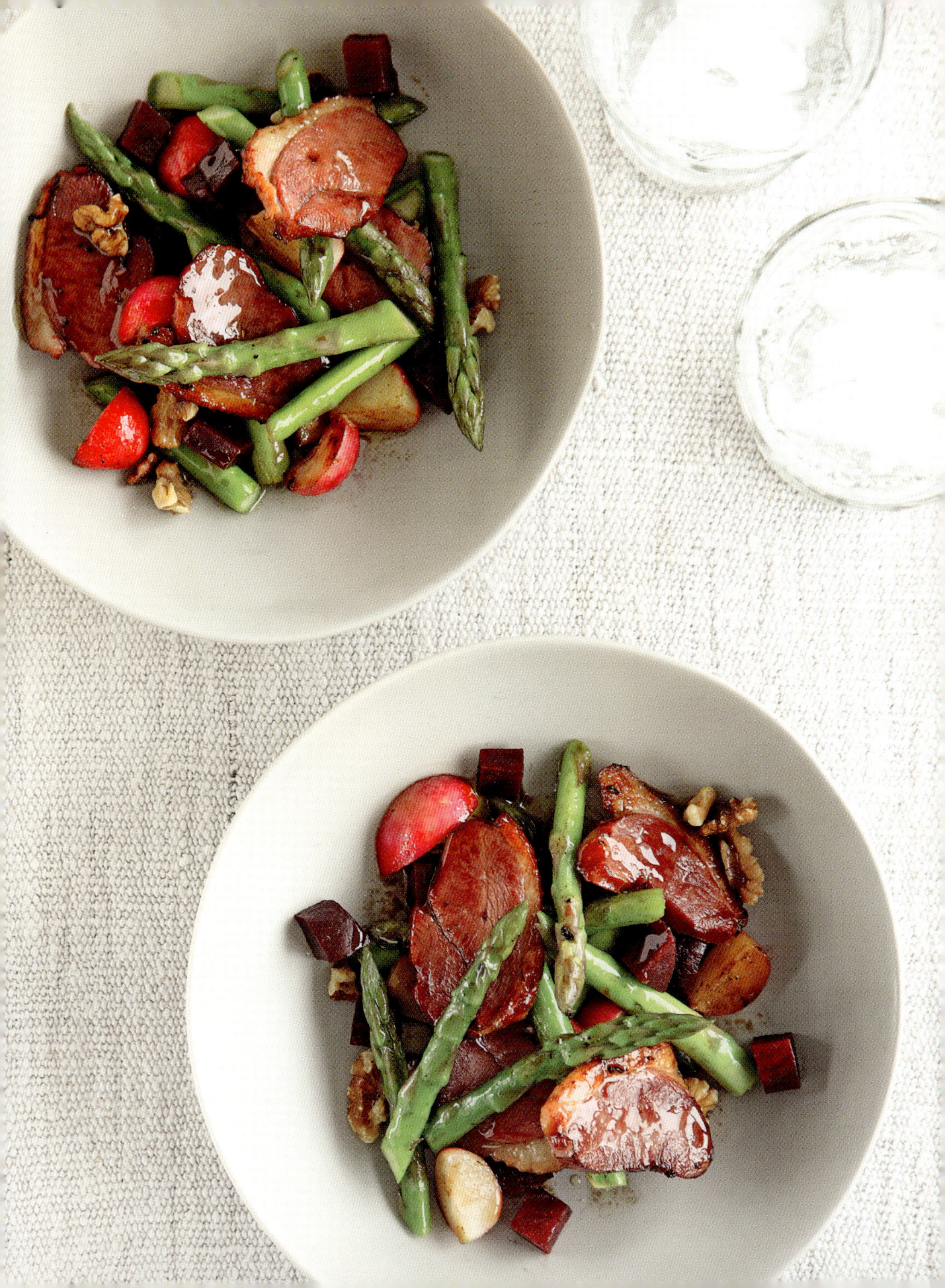

30 Smoked Mackerel Superfood Salad

Serves 4

½ (2 lb) butternut squash, peeled, seeded, and cut into ½ inch cubes
¼ cup olive oil
1 teaspoon cumin seeds
1 head of broccoli, cut into florets
1⅓ cups frozen or fresh peas
3 tablespoons quinoa
¼ cup mixed seeds
2 smoked mackerel fillets
juice of 1 lemon
½ teaspoon honey
½ teaspoon Dijon mustard
1 cup shredded red cabbage
4 tomatoes, chopped
4 cooked beets, cut into wedges
¾ cup radish sprouts

- Place the squash in a roasting pan and sprinkle with 1 tablespoon of the olive oil and the cumin seeds. Place in a preheated oven, at 400°F, for 15–18 minutes, until tender. Let cool slightly.

- Meanwhile, cook the broccoli in boiling water for 4–5 minutes, until tender, adding the peas 3 minutes before the end of the cooking time. Remove with a slotted spoon and refresh under cold running water, then drain. Cook the quinoa in the broccoli water for 15 minutes, then drain and let cool slightly.

- Heat a nonstick skillet over medium-low heat and dry-fry the seeds, stirring frequently, until golden brown and toasted. Set aside. Heat the mackerel fillets according to the package directions, then skin and break into flakes.

- Whisk together the remaining olive oil, lemon juice, honey, and mustard in a small bowl. Toss together all the ingredients, except the sprouts, with the dressing in a serving bowl. Serve topped with the sprouts.

10 Smoked Mackerel Superfood Toasts

Mash together the flesh of 2 peeled and pitted avocados, 1 crushed garlic clove, the juice of ½ lime, and 2 chopped tomatoes in a bowl. Toast 4 slices of whole-grain bread under a preheated hot broiler for 2–3 minutes on each side, then spread one side of each slice with 1 teaspoon creamed horseradish. Top each with ¼ bunch of watercress or 1 cup arugula, 1 sliced, small, cooked fresh beet, and ½ skinned and flaked smoked mackerel fillet. Top with the avocado mixture, a sprinkling of pumpkin seeds, toasted as above, and a small handful of alfalfa sprouts.

20 Smoked Mackerel Superfood Soup

Heat 1 tablespoon oil in a saucepan and sauté 1 chopped onion and 1 crushed garlic clove for 3–4 minutes. Add ½ (2 lb) butternut squash, peeled, seeded, and diced, 1 cup broccoli florets, 2 tablespoons quinoa, 2½ cups vegetable stock, and ⅔ cup orange juice and simmer for 15 minutes. Blend until smooth. Stir in 2 skinned, flaked smoked mackerel fillets and cook for 1 minute. Sprinkle with 2 tablespoons toasted pumpkin seeds and serve.

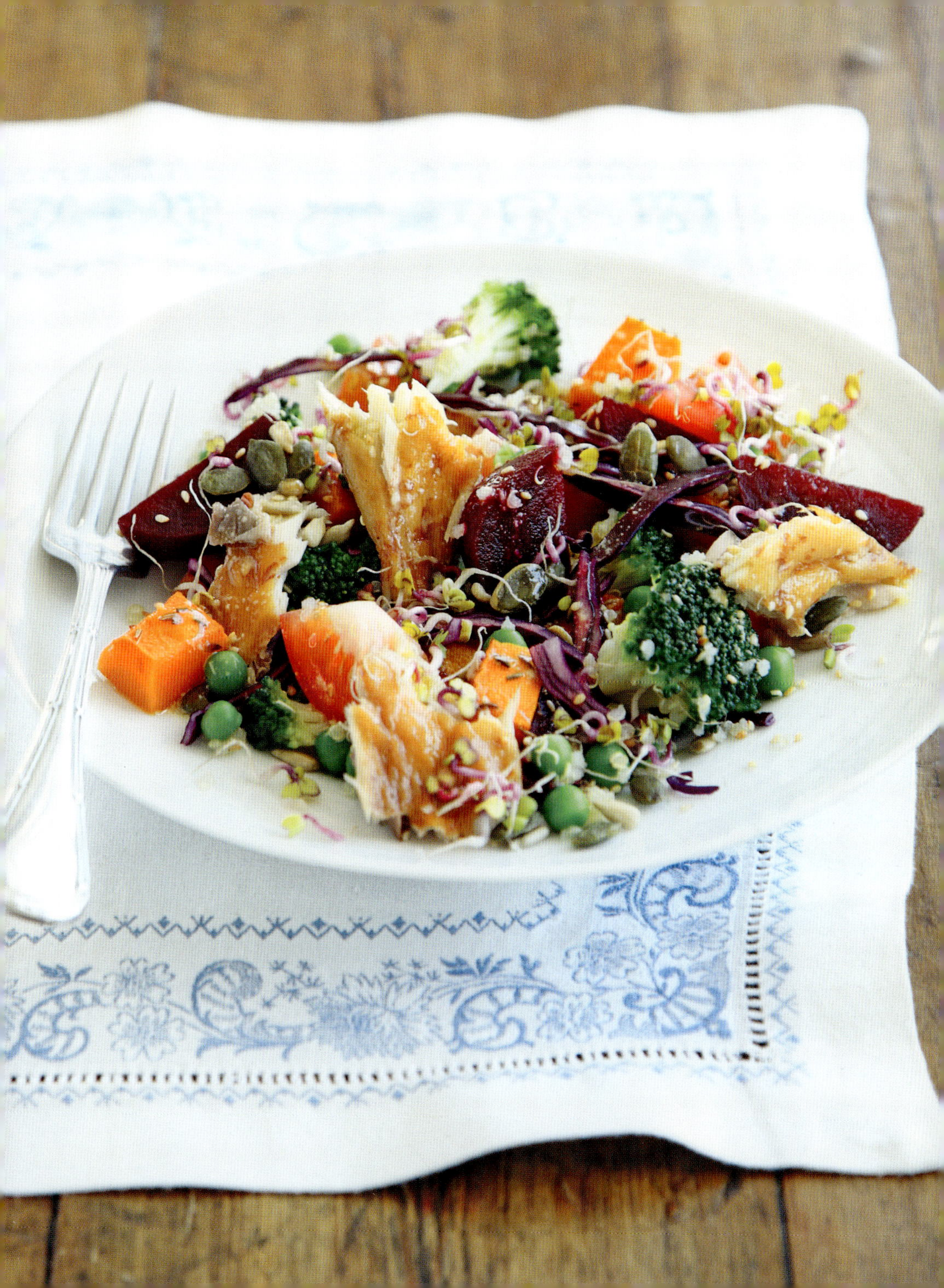

10 Beet and Goat Cheese Salad

Serves 4

2 tablespoons olive oil
3 raw beets, peeled and grated
¼ cup balsamic vinegar
2 tablespoons sunflower seeds
8 oz goat cheese
3 cups arugula leaves
2 tablespoons extra virgin olive oil
black pepper

- Heat the olive oil in a skillet, add the beet, and cook for 3–4 minutes. Season well with black pepper, then stir in the vinegar and cook over high heat for 30 seconds.

- Meanwhile, heat a nonstick skillet over medium-low heat and dry-fry the sunflower seeds for 2 minutes, stirring frequently, until golden and toasted. Set aside.

- Divide the beets among 4 plates. Crumble the cheese over the beets and top with the arugula.

- Serve drizzled with the extra virgin olive oil and sprinkled with the toasted sunflower seeds.

2 Beet Soup with Goat Cheese

Heat 1 tablespoon olive oil in a saucepan, add 1 chopped onion, and cook for 2–3 minutes. Add 3 grated, raw beets, 2½ cups hot vegetable stock, and 1 (14½ oz) can diced tomatoes and bring to a boil. Reduce the heat and simmer for 8–10 minutes, until the beets are tender. Using a handheld blender, blend the soup until smooth, then season to taste. Ladle into bowls, crumble 4 oz goat cheese over the soup, and serve.

3 Roasted Beet and Goat Cheese Salad

Place 8 oz halved, raw baby beets and 8 oz halved baby carrots in a roasting pan, sprinkle with 2 tablespoons cumin seeds, and drizzle with 2 tablespoons olive oil. Place the pan in a preheated oven, at 400°F, for 20–25 minutes. Meanwhile, dry-fry 2 tablespoons walnuts in a nonstick skillet for 3–4 minutes, stirring frequently, until slightly golden. Set aside. Mix together 3 tablespoons olive oil, the juice of ½ lemon, 1 teaspoon whole-grain mustard, and 1 teaspoon honey in a small bowl. Place 1 (7 oz) package salad greens on a large serving plate. Cook four 4 oz slices of goat cheese under a preheated medium-hot broiler for 4–5 minutes, until golden. Toss together the roasted vegetables, dressing, and salad greens and divide among 4 plates. Top with the broiled goat cheese and sprinkle with the toasted walnuts.

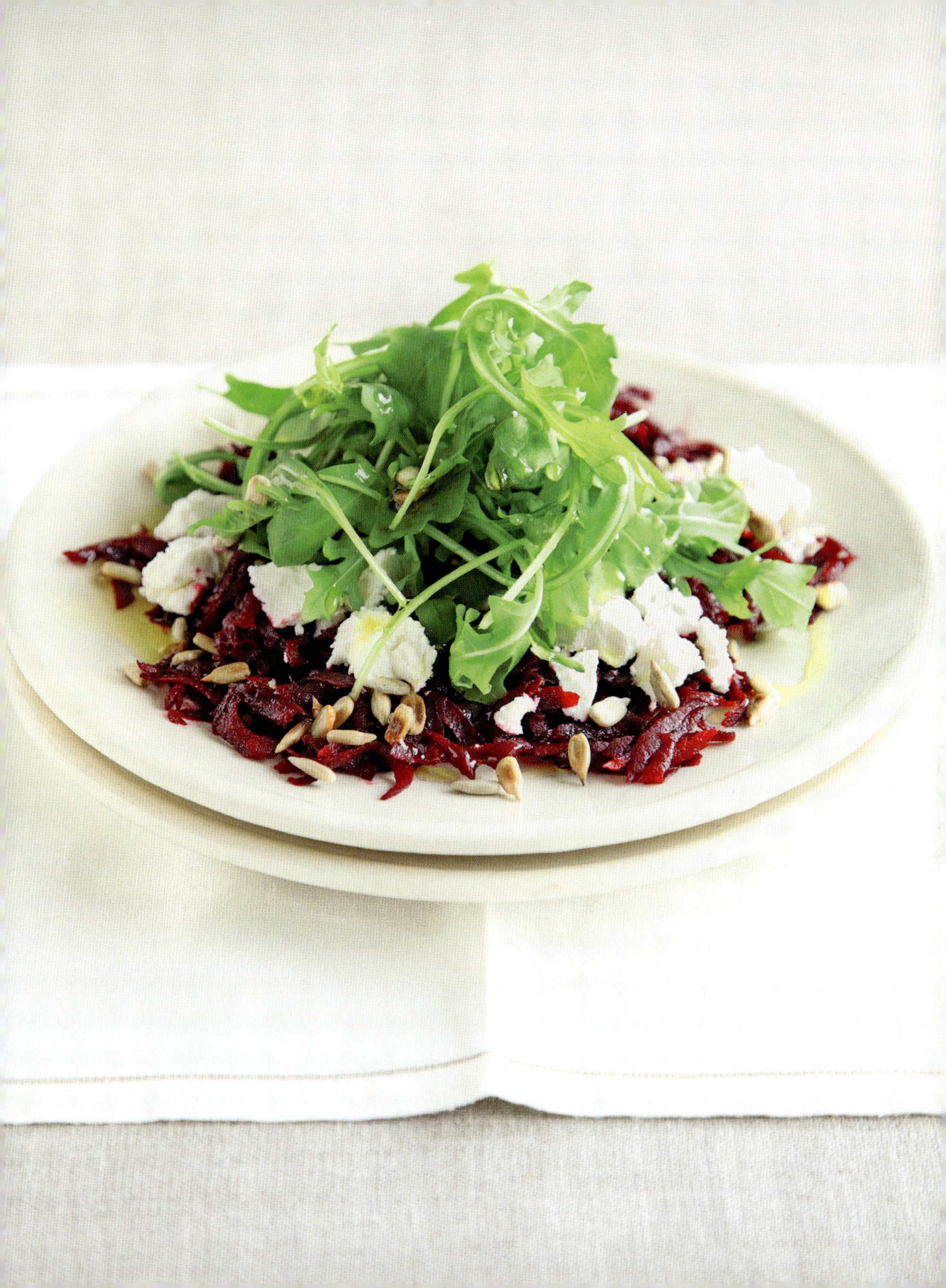

Mini Smoked Trout Quiches

Serves 4

½ tablespoon canola oil
1 (12 oz) package baby spinach leaves
6 extra-large eggs
½ cup milk
3 tablespoons grated Parmesan cheese
2 tablespoons finely chopped chives
5 oz smoked trout fillets, flaked
4 cherry tomatoes, halved
salt and black pepper

- Line 8 cups of a muffin pan with 6 inch-square sheets of wax paper.
- Heat the oil in a skillet, add the spinach, and cook briefly until wilted. Remove from the heat.
- Beat together the eggs, milk, and cheese in a small bowl and season to taste, then stir in the chives and trout.
- Divide the spinach among the muffin liners, then pour in the egg mixture. Top each one with half a tomato.
- Bake in a preheated oven, at 350°F, for 12–15 minutes, until just set.

Smoked Trout Baked Eggs

Brush 4 ramekins with melted butter, then add 2 oz flaked smoked trout fillet to each dish. Carefully break 2 eggs into each ramekin, top with 2 tablespoons shredded cheddar cheese, and season. Place the ramekins in a roasting pan with enough boiling water to come three-quarters of the way up the sides of the dishes. Bake in a preheated oven, at 400°F, for 8–9 minutes, until the cheese has melted and the egg is cooked but still soft. Serve with toast.

Smoked Trout Phyllo Quiche

Heat 2 tablespoons butter in a skillet, add 1 trimmed and sliced leek, and cook for 2–3 minutes. Meanwhile, lay 1 sheet of phyllo pastry in a 9-inch fluted tart pan and fold over any overhang. Repeat with another sheet to cover the bottom, then brush with melted butter. Repeat with another 6 sheets, turning the pan to make sure all sides are covered with pastry. Sprinkle the pastry bottom with 3 cups shredded cheddar cheese and 8 oz flaked smoked trout fillets, then add the leeks. Beat together 3 eggs, ½ cup heavy cream, and ½ cup plain yogurt, then pour into the shell. Top with 2 sliced tomatoes. Bake in a preheated oven, at 375°F, for 25 minutes, until golden.

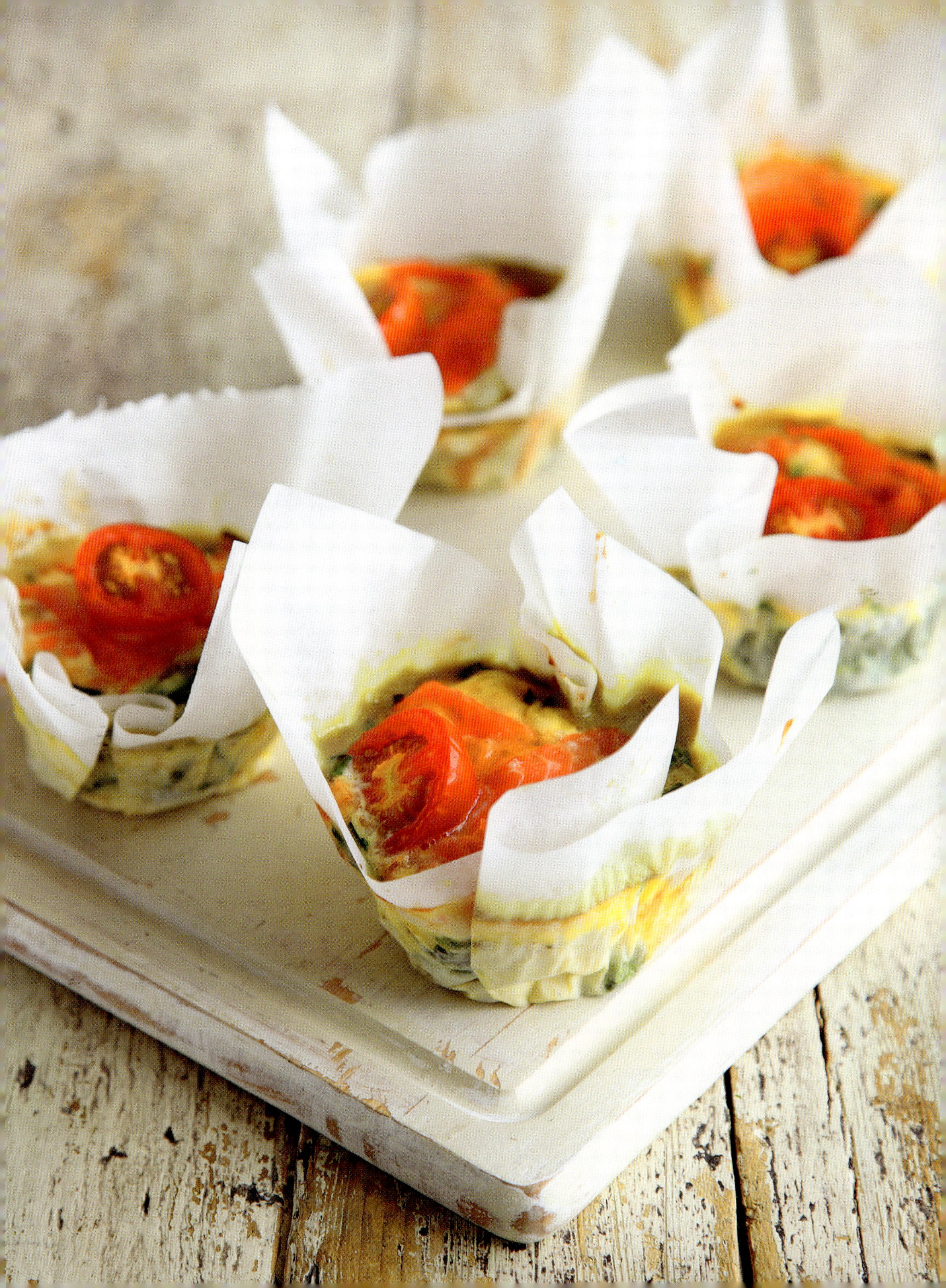

30 Rosemary Oatcakes

Makes 20–24

2 cups rolled oats
3 rosemary sprigs, leaves stripped
1 cup all-purpose flour, plus extra for dusting
¾ teaspoon baking powder
pinch of salt
6 tablespoons chilled unsalted butter, diced
½ cup milk

- Place the oats and rosemary in a food processor and process until they resemble bread crumbs. Add the flour, baking powder, and salt and process again. Add the butter, then process until it is mixed in. With the motor still running, pour in the milk through the feed tube until the dough forms a ball.

- Turn the dough out onto a floured surface and roll out to about ¼ inch thick. Cut out 20–24 circles, using a 2–2½ inch plain cookie cutter, rerolling the leftover dough as necessary.

- Place on a baking sheet and bake in a preheated oven, at 375°F, for 12–15 minutes, until golden at the edges. Transfer to a wire rack to cool. Store in an airtight container.

1 Mixed Salad with Rosemary Dressing

Whisk together 1 tablespoon balsamic vinegar, 3 tablespoons olive oil, 2 teaspoons Dijon mustard, 1 teaspoon finely chopped rosemary, and 1 teaspoon honey in a small bowl and season with salt and black pepper. Toss together 1 (7 oz) package salad greens, 1 cored, seeded, and chopped yellow bell pepper, 1 sliced red onion, and the dressing in a serving bowl. Serve with broiled fish or chicken.

2 Rosemary Scones

Sift together 1¾ cups all-purpose flour, 2¾ teaspoons baking powder, and a pinch of salt and black pepper in a bowl. Add 3 tablespoons diced, chilled butter and rub in with the fingertips until the mixture resembles fine bread crumbs. Stir in 1½ tablespoons chopped rosemary and ½ cup shredded cheddar cheese. Add ⅔ cup milk and mix with a spatula to a soft dough. Turn out onto a lightly floured surface and press or roll out to ¾ inch thick. Cut out 12 circles, using a 1½–2 inch cutter, rerolling the leftover dough as necessary, and place on a baking sheet. Sprinkle the tops with ½ cup shredded cheddar. Bake in a preheated oven, at 425°F, for 8–10 minutes, until golden. Transfer to a wire rack to cool.

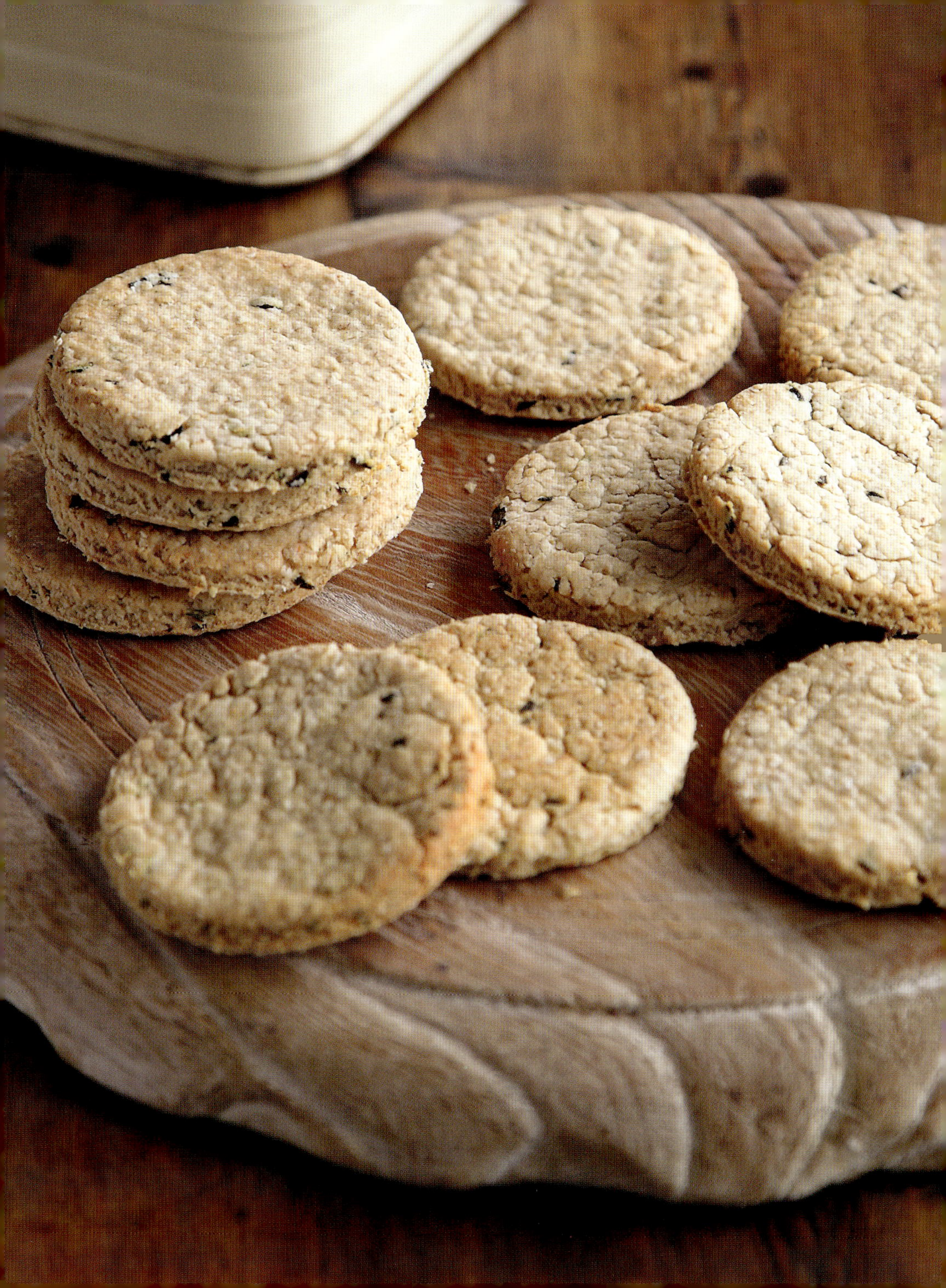

Whole-Wheat Cheese Straws

Makes 12–16

¾ cup whole-wheat flour, plus extra for dusting
2 teaspoons paprika
1¼ cup shredded sharp cheddar cheese
1 stick chilled unsalted butter, diced
2 teaspoons baking powder
2 egg yolks

- Mix together the flour and paprika in a bowl, then stir in the cheese. Add the butter and rub in with the fingertips until the mixture resembles fine bread crumbs. Stir in the baking powder, then add the egg yolks and mix to a stiff dough.

- Turn the dough out onto a floured surface and press or roll out to about ¼ inch thick. Cut into ½ inch-wide straws and place on a baking sheet.

- Bake in a preheated oven, at 425°F, for 10–12 minutes, until golden. Transfer to a wire rack to cool.

Cheese and Pickle Toasts Toast 4 slices of thick whole-grain bread under a preheated hot broiler for 2–3 minutes on each side. Meanwhile, mix together 1¾ cups shredded cheddar cheese, 4 sliced scallions, and 2 diced tomatoes in a bowl. Spread one side of each toast with 1 tablespoon chopped pickle, then spoon the cheese mixture over the top and broil for 2–3 minutes, until bubbling and golden.

Cheese Soda Bread Sift together $3^{2}/_{3}$ cups all-purpose flour and 1 teaspoon baking soda in a bowl. Stir in 1 teaspoon salt and ½ cup shredded cheddar cheese. Make a well in the center and pour in 1¾ cups buttermilk. Using your hands, mix together to form a soft dough. Turn the dough out onto a floured surface and roll out to 14 x 8 inches. Transfer to an oiled baking sheet and brush the top with 1 tablespoon olive oil. Sprinkle with ¾ cup shredded cheddar cheese and bake in a preheated oven, at 425°F, for 10 minutes, then reduce the temperature to 400°F and cook for another 8–12 minutes, until golden and firm. Transfer to a wire rack to cool. Serve cut into squares.

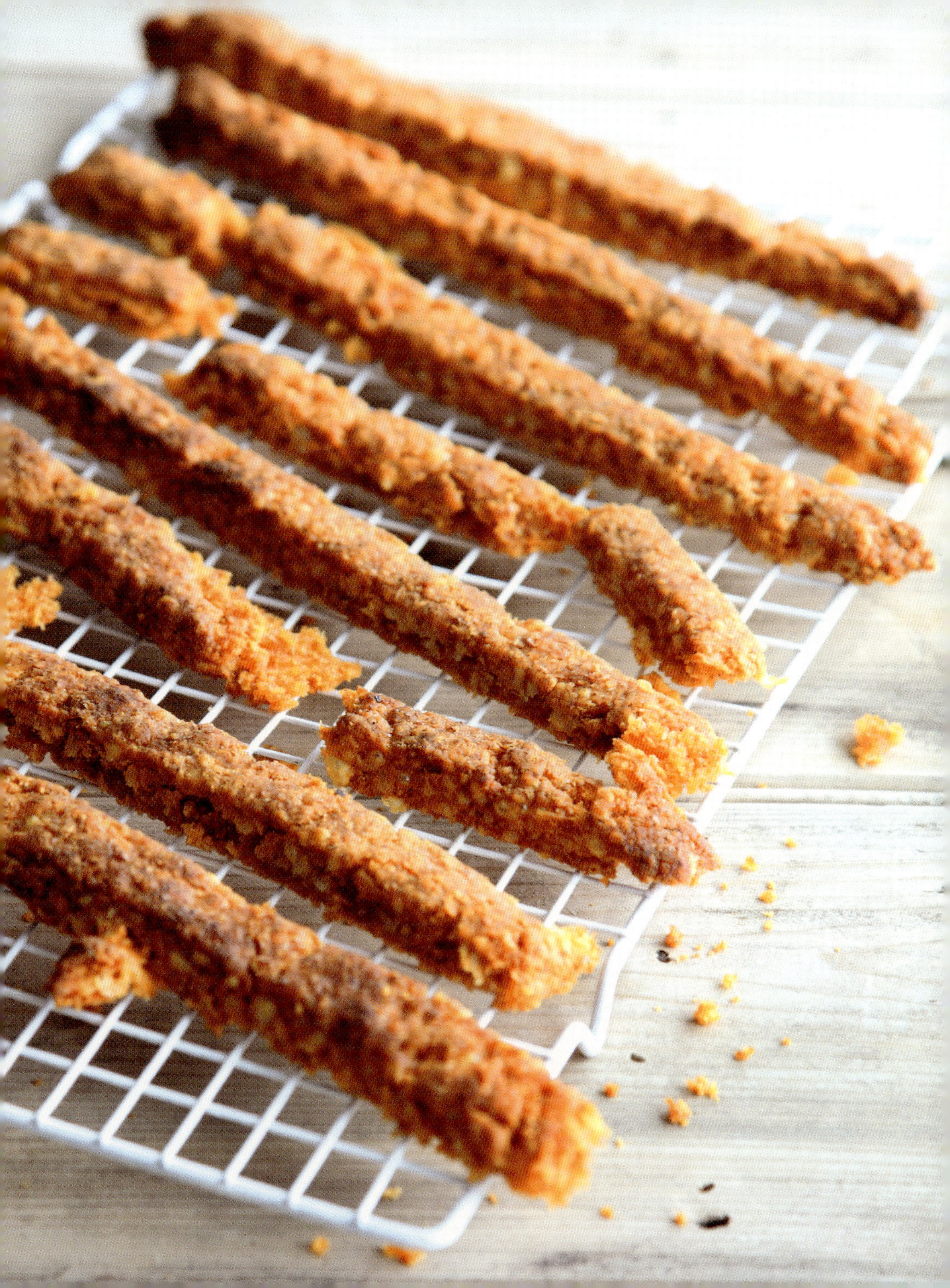

30 Cheese, Cumin, and Apple Scones

Makes about 10

1 cup all-purpose flour, plus extra for dusting
¾ cup whole-wheat flour
1¾ teaspoons baking powder
3 tablespoons chilled butter, diced, plus extra to serve
1 teaspoon cumin seeds
¾ cup shredded cheddar cheese
1 Pippin apple, peeled, cored, and diced
⅔ cup milk
conserves, to serve

- Sift the flours and baking powder into a large bowl, add the butter, and rub in with the fingertips until the mixture resembles fine bread crumbs. Stir in the cumin seeds, two-thirds of the cheese, and the apple, then add the milk and mix with a spatula to a soft dough.
- Turn the dough out onto a floured surface and press out to ¾ inch thick. Cut out about 10 circles, using a 2 inch plain cookie cutter or glass, using the leftover dough as necessary.
- Place the scones on a baking sheet and sprinkle with the remaining cheese. Bake in a preheated oven, at 425°F, for 15–18 minutes, until risen and golden. Transfer to a wire rack to cool or serve warm, spread with butter and conserves.

1 Cheese, Cumin, and Apple Toasts

Toast 4 slices of whole-grain bread under a preheated hot broiler for 2–3 minutes on each side. Spread one side of each toast with 2 teaspoons of a conserve or chutney. Core and thinly slice 2 Pippin apples and arrange over the toasts. Sprinkle with ½ teaspoon cumin seeds, then top each one with ¾ cup shredded cheddar cheese. Broil for 1–2 minutes, until the cheese is bubbling and golden. Serve with a crisp green salad.

2 Cheese, Cumin, and Apple Salad

Dry-fry ½ cup walnut pieces in a nonstick skillet for 3–4 minutes, stirring frequently, until slightly golden. Set aside. Whisk together ¼ cup plain yogurt, 1 tablespoon lemon juice, and ½ teaspoon ground cumin in a small bowl. In a separate bowl, mix together 3 cored and sliced Pippin apples, 2 sliced celery sticks, ⅓ cup raisins, and 1 bunch of watercress or 2 cups arugula. Add the yogurt dressing and toss until the salad is coated. Cook four 4 oz slices of goat cheese under a preheated medium-hot broiler for 4–5 minutes or until golden. Divide the salad among 4 plates or shallow bowls and top each one with a goat cheese slice. Serve sprinkled with the toasted walnuts.

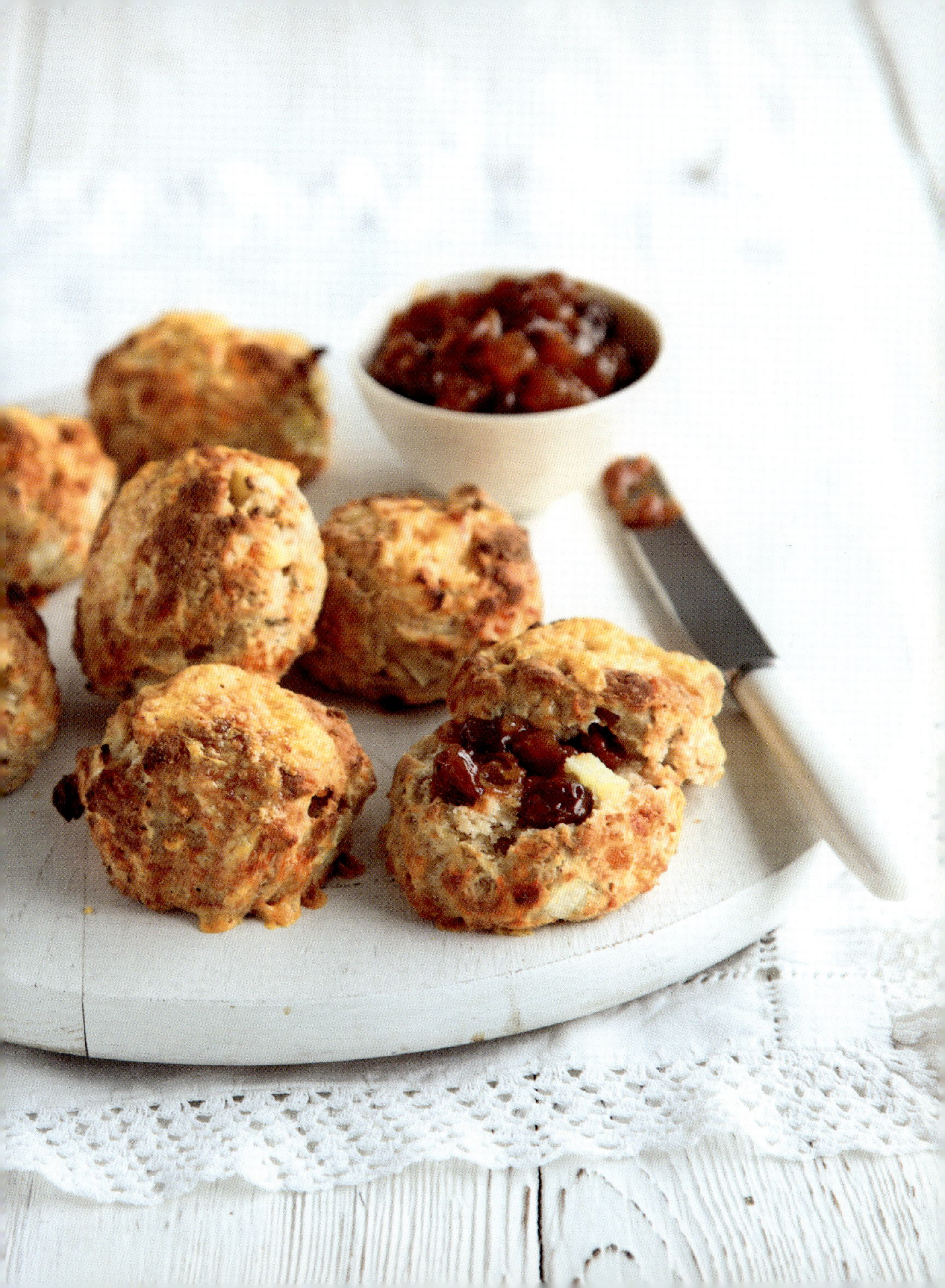

10 Mediterranean Beans

Serves 4

2 tablespoons extra virgin olive oil
1 red onion, diced
1 garlic clove, crushed
½ teaspoon cumin seeds
1 (15 oz) can cannellini beans, rinsed and drained
6 cherry tomatoes, quartered
2 teaspoons chopped sage
4 slices of crusty bread
salt and black pepper
¼ cup grated Manchego cheese or pecorino Romano cheese, to serve

- Heat the oil in a large skillet, add the onion, and cook for 1–2 minutes. Add the garlic and cumin seeds and cook for another 2–3 minutes.

- Add the beans and mix well to let them soak up the flavors, then add the tomatoes. Stir in the sage, season with salt and black pepper, and heat through.

- Meanwhile, toast the bread under a preheated hot broiler for 2–3 minutes on each side. Serve topped with the beans and a sprinkling of cheese.

20 Bean and Garlic Stew

Heat 2 tablespoons olive oil in a large saucepan, add 1 large chopped onion, and cook for 1–2 minutes. Add 2 peeled and thinly sliced carrots, 2 sliced celery sticks, and 7–8 sliced garlic cloves and cook for another 3 minutes. Add 2 (15 oz) cans cannellini beans, rinsed and drained, ½ head thickly shredded cabbage, and 3¾ cups hot vegetable stock, and season well, then bring to a simmer and cook for 12–15 minutes, stirring in 3 tablespoons ground almonds (almond meal) 2 minutes before the end of the cooking time.

30 Mixed Bean Goulash

Heat 1 tablespoon olive oil in a large skillet, add 1 large chopped onion and 2 crushed garlic cloves, and gently sauté for 5 minutes, until softened. Stir in 1½ cups chopped cremini mushrooms and cook for another 3–4 minutes. Add 1 tablespoon smoked paprika and continue to cook for 1–2 minutes. Stir in 1 (14½ oz) can diced tomatoes, 1 cup hot vegetable stock, and 2 cups rinsed and drained canned mixed beans (such as kidney beans, pinto beans, and chickpeas) and bring to a boil, then reduce the heat and simmer for 12–14 minutes, until thick and glossy. Serve with cooked rice, topped with a large spoonful of sour cream, if desired.

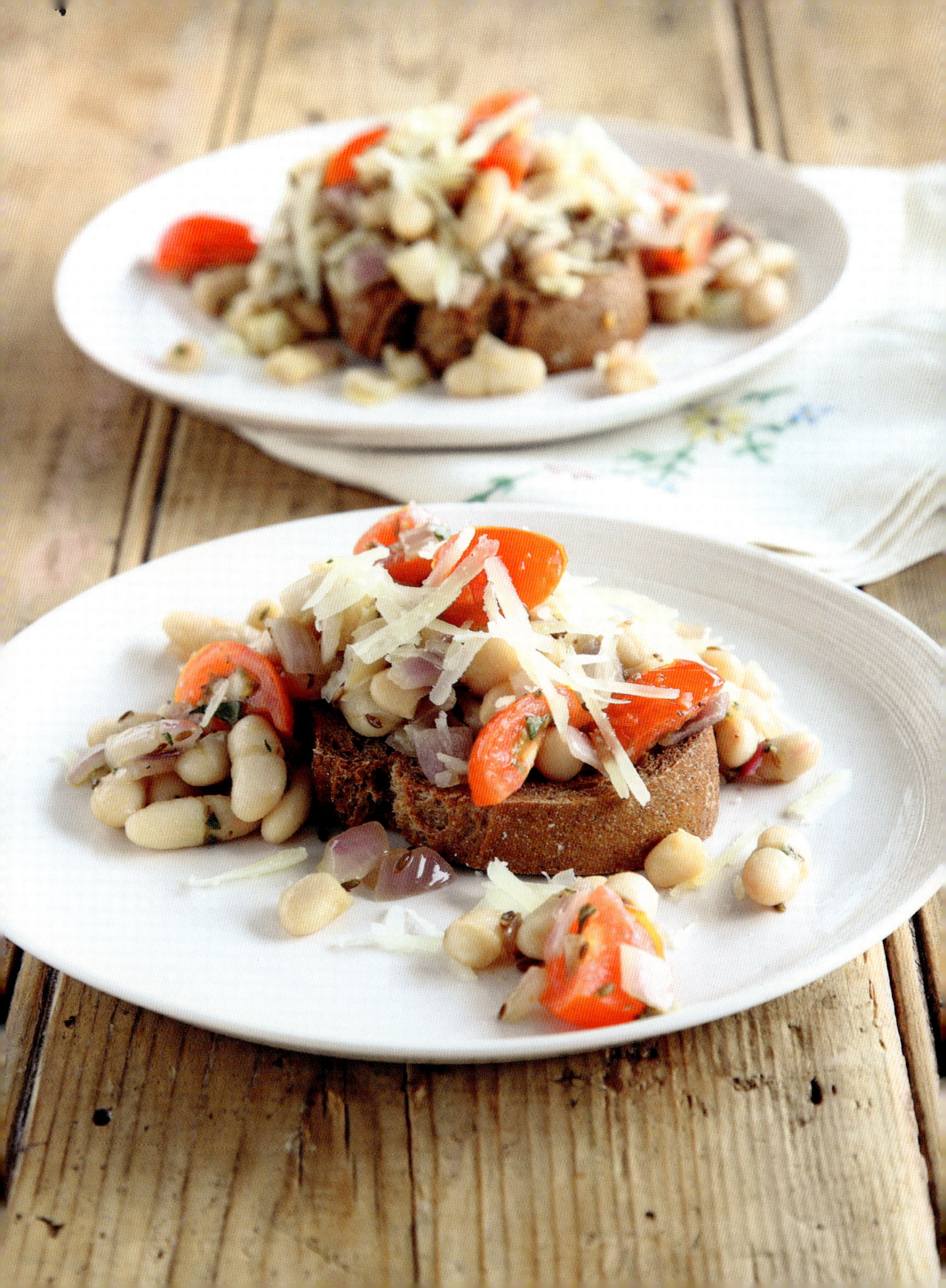

10 Chorizo and Olive Tapenade Toasts

Serves 4

1 baguette, cut into 8 thick slices
1 garlic clove, chopped
2 cups Kalamata olives, pitted
½ (2 oz) can anchovy fillets, drained
1 tablespoon capers, rinsed and drained
1 teaspoon chopped thyme
3 tablespoons lemon juice
¼ cup extra virgin olive oil
16 slices of chorizo

- Toast the bread under a preheated hot broiler for 2–3 minutes on each side.

- Meanwhile, place the garlic, olives, anchovies, capers, thyme, and lemon juice in a food processor or blender and process until combined. With the motor still running, slowly pour in the oil through the feed tube until the mixture forms a paste.

- Top each slice of toast with 2 slices of chorizo, then spoon the olive tapenade on top.

20 Chorizo and Olive Potatoes

Cook 6 Yukon gold peeled and chopped potatoes in a saucepan of boiling water for 15 minutes, until tender. Meanwhile, bring a saucepan of water to a gentle simmer and stir with a large spoon to create a swirl. Break 2 eggs into the water and cook for 3 minutes. Remove with a slotted spoon and keep warm. Repeat with another 2 eggs. Drain the potatoes, then mix with 1 cup chopped, pitted ripe black olives, 4 oz chopped chorizo, and 2 tablespoons olive oil. Season, then lightly crush with a fork. Serve topped with the poached eggs.

30 Chorizo, Onion, and Olive Tart

Heat 1 tablespoon olive oil in a skillet, add 2 large red onions, cut into wedges, and cook for 5 minutes, until softened. Stir in 2 tablespoons packed light brown sugar and 2 tablespoons balsamic vinegar and cook for another 5 minutes. Let cool for 2 minutes. Unroll a sheet of ready-to-bake puff pastry and place on a baking sheet. Score a ½ inch border around the outside, then spread the onion mixture within the border. Top with 10–12 slices of chorizo, then sprinkle with 4 oz goat cheese, crumbled, and 1¾ cups chopped, pitted ripe black olives. Season and drizzle with 1 tablespoon olive oil. Bake in a preheated oven, at 425°F, for 15 minutes, until golden. Serve with a crisp green salad.

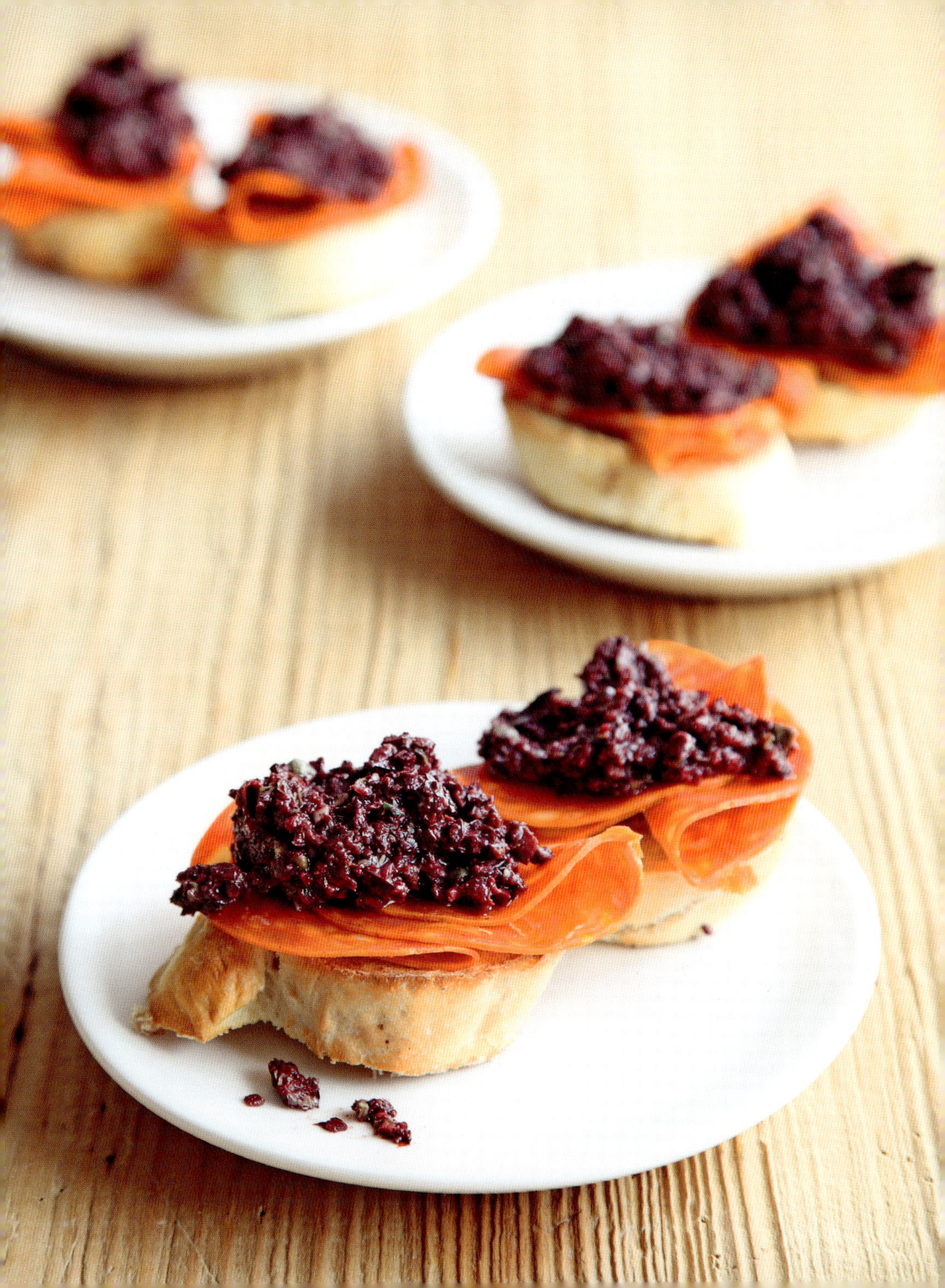

20 Grilled Zucchini Bruschetta

Serves 4

2 zucchini
1 tablespoon olive oil
2 cups button mushrooms
8–10 slices of whole-wheat or rye bread, ideally from a baguette
1 garlic clove
¼ cup canned diced tomatoes
black pepper

- Heat a ridged grill pan until very hot. Using a vegetable peeler, slice the zucchini into long, thin strips.
- Brush the hot grill pan with the oil, add the zucchini slices, in batches, and cook until charred with grill marks. Remove from the pan and keep warm.
- Place the mushrooms in the grill pan and cook for them 3–4 minutes, until softened.
- Meanwhile, toast the bread under a preheated hot broiler for 2–3 minutes on each side, then rub one side of each slice with the garlic clove.
- Spread the toasts with a little diced tomato, then divide the zucchini strips and mushrooms among them. Season with black pepper and serve.

10 Quick Zucchini Pasta

Cook 1 b farfalle pasta in a saucepan of boiling water according to the package directions until "al dente." Meanwhile, heat 2 tablespoons olive oil in a large skillet, add 3 large shredded zucchini, 2 crushed garlic cloves, and 1 seeded and diced red chile, and cook for 5–6 minutes, until softened. Drain the pasta, stir into the zucchini mixture, and toss together. Add a squeeze of lemon juice, season with black pepper, and serve sprinkled with grated Parmesan cheese.

30 Zucchini Lasagna

Heat 1 tablespoon olive oil in a skillet, add 1 chopped onion, and cook for 2–3 minutes, then add 6 shredded zucchini and 2 crushed garlic cloves and cook for another 2–3 minutes. Stir in 1 cup ricotta cheese and ¼ cup shredded cheddar cheese. Heat 1⅓ cups store-bought tomato sauce in a microwave. Cook 10 lasagna noodles in a saucepan of boiling water for 5 minutes, until softened, then drain. Layer the zucchini mixture, pasta, and tomato sauce in an ovenproof dish, finishing with a layer of lasagna. Dot with ¼ cup ricotta and sprinkle with ⅓ cup shredded cheddar. Bake in a preheated oven, at 425°F, for 10 minutes, until golden.

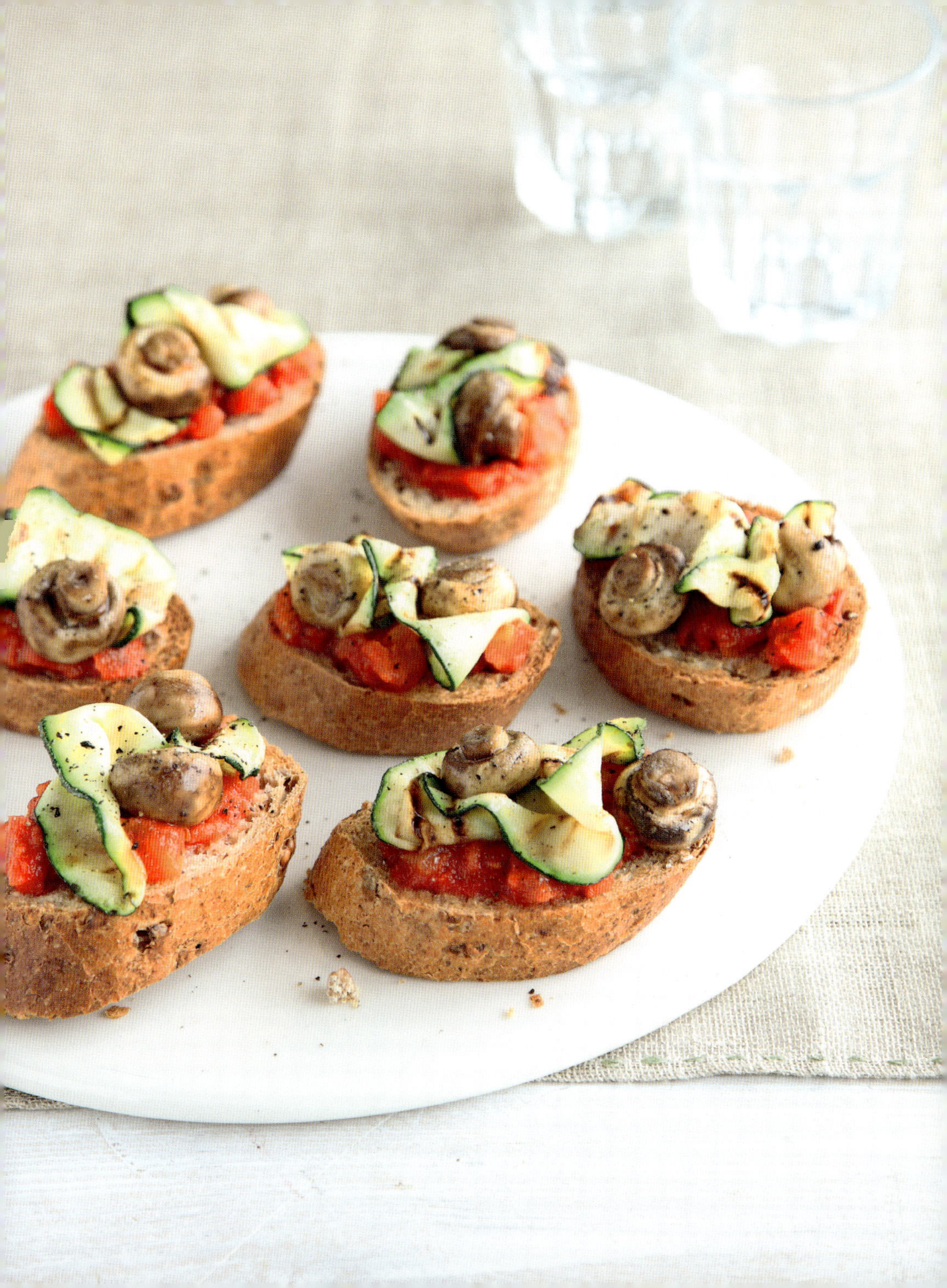

10 Tuna Open Sandwiches

Serves 4

2 (5 oz) cans chunk light tuna in oil or water, drained
¼ cup mayonnaise
2 tablespoons sliced celery
¼ teaspoon smoked paprika
¼ teaspoon cayenne pepper
1 tablespoon minced red onion
juice of ½ lemon
¼ cucumber, thinly sliced
4 slices of pumperknickel bread
sprigs of watercress or parsley
lemon wedges, to serve

- Flake the tuna in a bowl, then mix together with the mayonnaise, celery, paprika, cayenne pepper, onion, and lemon juice.

- Arrange the slices of cucumber on the pumpernickel, then top with the tuna mixture. Top with a few sprigs of watercress or parsley.

- Serve with lemon wedges.

---

20 Tuna Salad Niçoise

Dust a 1 lb tuna steak with 2 teaspoons each of ground cumin and ground coriander. Let stand for about 10 minutes. Heat 1 tablespoon olive oil in a dutch oven or ovenproof skillet until hot, add the tuna, and cook for 30 seconds on each side, until browned, then transfer to a preheated oven, at 425°F, for 5–6 minutes, or until cooked to your liking. Let rest. Meanwhile, using a mortar and pestle, pound together ½ garlic clove, 1 (2 oz) can anchovy fillets in oil, drained, and 1 egg yolk. Add the juice of ½ lemon, ¼–⅓ cup olive oil, and 1 teaspoon Dijon mustard and mix well. Set aside. Cook 8 oz halved new potatoes in a saucepan of boiling water for 12 minutes, adding 1 cup green beans 3–4 minutes before the end of the cooking time. Drain. Meanwhile, hard boil 4 eggs in a separate saucepan of boiling water, then refresh under cold running water, peel, and cut in half. Place the potatoes, beans, and eggs in a bowl, flake the tuna, and place on top. Pour the dressing over the salad and serve.

30 Spicy Tuna Pasta Casserole

Cook 1 lb rigatoni in boiling water for 8–9 minutes. Meanwhile, melt 4 tablespoons butter in a saucepan, then stir in ⅓ cup all-purpose flour. Cook for 1–2 minutes, then gradually whisk in 2½ cups milk and cook, stirring, until thick and smooth. Remove from the heat and stir in 1 teaspoon mustard and 1 cup shredded cheddar cheese. Drain the pasta and mix with the sauce, 1 (11 oz) can corn kernels, drained, 2 (5 oz) cans chunk light tuna in oil or water, drained, 1 teaspoon dried red pepper flakes, and a handful of chopped parsley. Season. Spoon into an ovenproof dish and top with 1 cup shredded cheddar. Bake in a preheated oven, at 400°F, for 15 minutes.

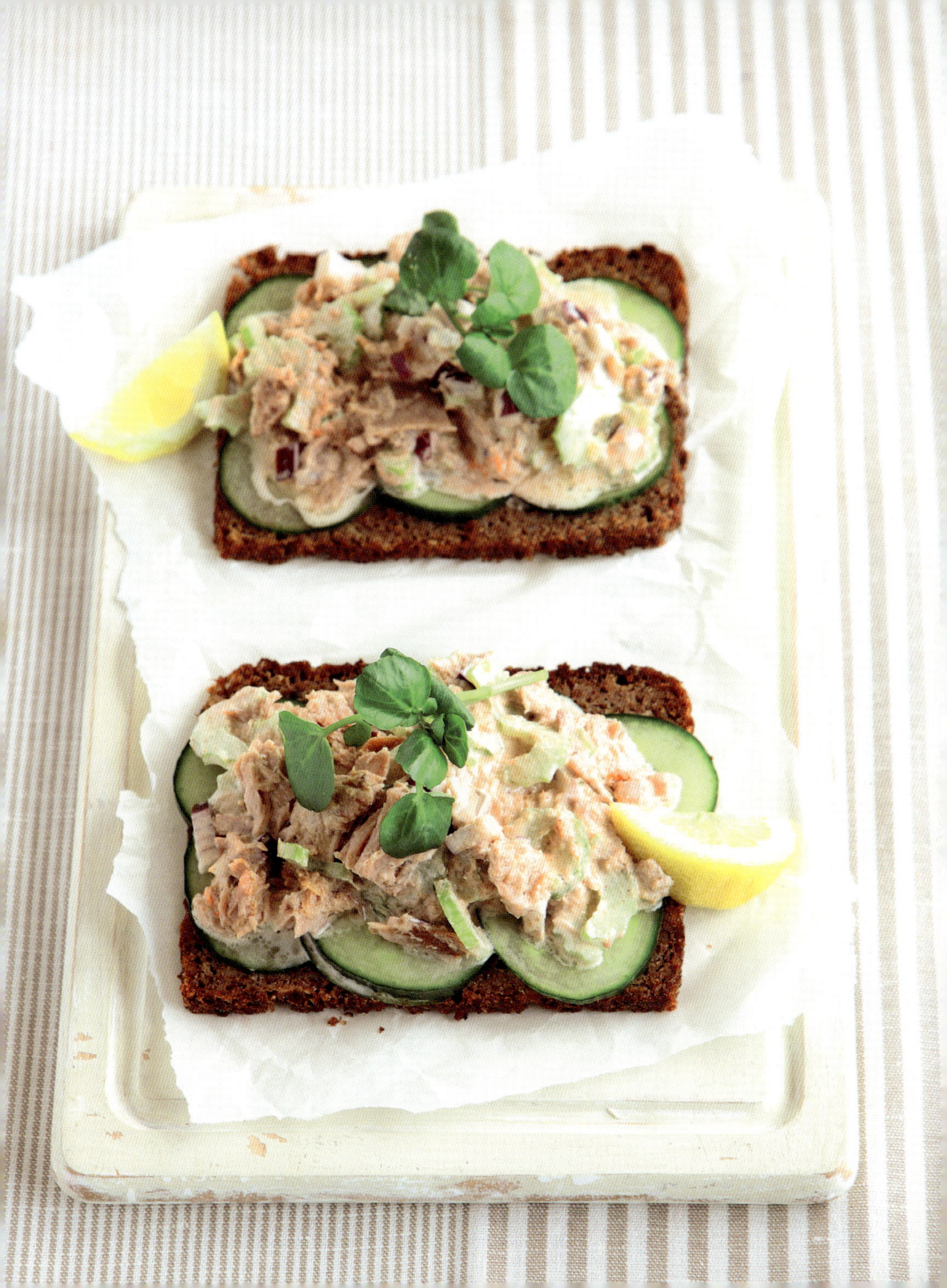

Spicy Barbecue Beans on Toast

Serves 4

1 tablespoon olive oil
1 red onion, diced
2 garlic cloves, chopped
1 tablespoon red wine vinegar
1 tablespoon packed dark brown sugar
1 (15 oz) can cannellini beans, rinsed and drained
1 tablespoon raisins
2 tablespoons slivered almonds
1¾ cups tomato puree or tomato sauce
1 teaspoon Worcestershire sauce
2 tablespoons chopped parsley
4 slices of whole-grain bread
salt and black pepper
2 tablespoons grated Manchego cheese or pecorino Romano cheese, to serve

- Heat the oil in a saucepan, add the onion and sauté for 3–4 minutes, until golden. Stir in the garlic and cook for 1 minute, then add the vinegar and sugar and cook for another 3–4 minutes.
- Stir in the beans, raisins, almonds, tomato puree or sauce, and Worcestershire sauce and season to taste. Simmer for 10–11 minutes, until thickened. Stir in the chopped parsley.
- Meanwhile, toast the bread under a preheated hot broiler for 2–3 minutes on each side.
- Spoon the beans over the toast and serve sprinkled with the cheese.

Boston Baked Beans

Heat 1 tablespoon olive oil in a saucepan, add 1 diced onion and 2 chopped garlic cloves, and cook for 3–4 minutes, until softened. Stir in 1 teaspoon paprika, 1 tablespoon mango chutney, and 1 (15 oz) can baked beans, and simmer for 2–3 minutes, until heated through. Meanwhile, toast 4 slices of whole-wheat bread under a preheated hot broiler for 2–3 minutes on each side, then spoon the beans on top to serve.

Spicy Bean Quesadillas

Mix together 1 (15 oz) can black-eyed peas, rinsed and drained, ½ teaspoon ground cumin, 1 teaspoon dried red pepper flakes, 2 sliced scallions, 1 cored, seeded, and diced red bell pepper, and ¾ cup shredded cheddar cheese in a bowl, then season. Rub 1 garlic clove over 2 flour tortillas. Spoon the bean mixture over the tortillas and spread to the edges. Top each one with another tortilla. Heat 1 tablespoon olive oil in a skillet, slide in 1 quesadilla, and cook for 3–4 minutes on each side, turning it over gently, until golden and the filling has melted. Remove from the skillet and keep warm. Repeat with the remaining quesadilla. Meanwhile, mix together 2 peeled, pitted, and diced avocados, the juice of 1 lime, and 2 tablespoons chopped cilantro in a bowl. Serve the quesadilla cut into wedges, with the avocado salsa on the side.

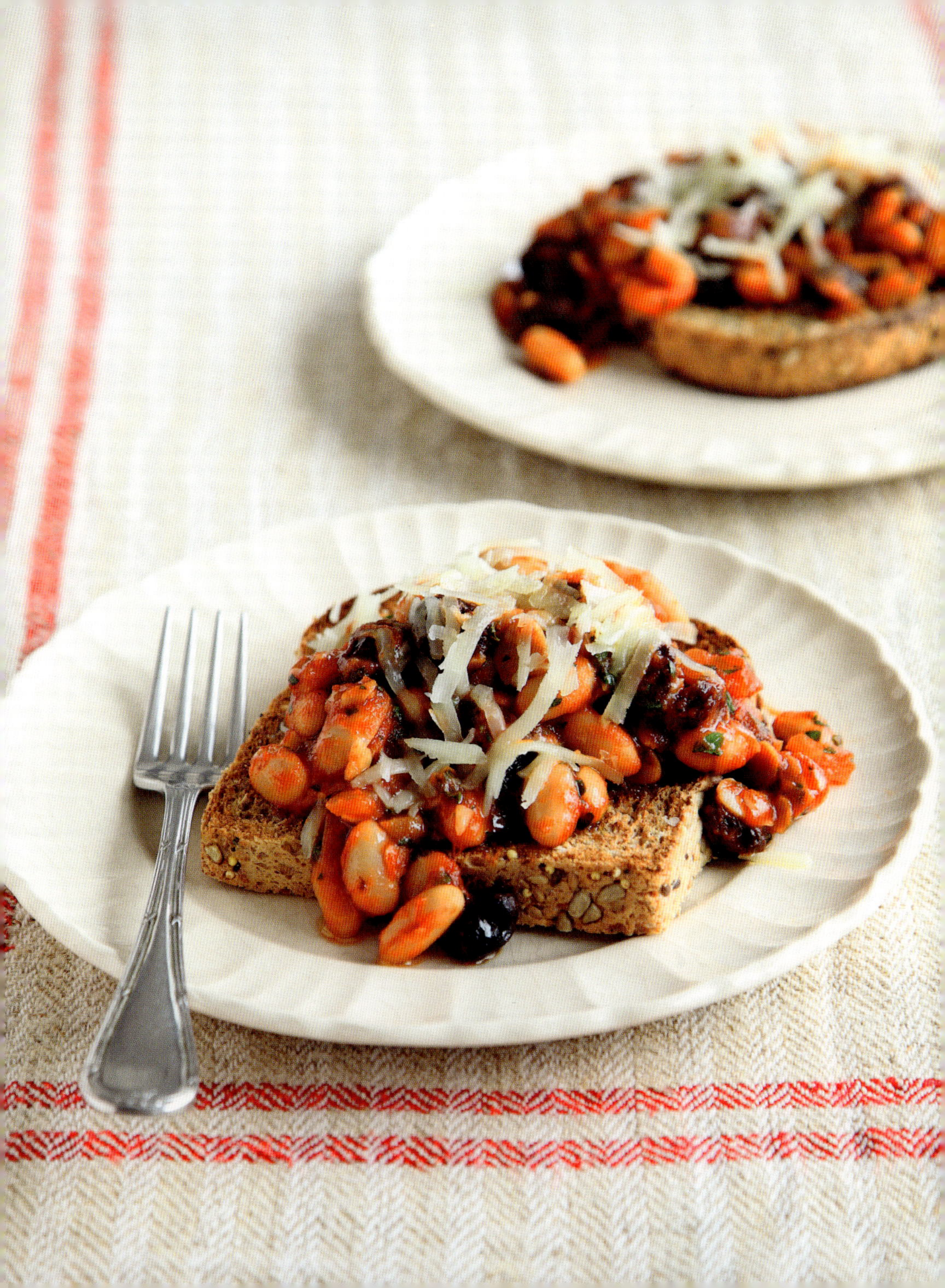

30 Salmon and Sesame Skewers

Serves 4

1 tablespoon soy sauce
2 teaspoons honey
1 lb salmon fillet, skinned and cut into strips
4 teaspoons sesame oil
juice of 1 lime
1 cucumber
6 scallions, finely sliced
16 cherry tomatoes, halved
3 tablespoons sesame seeds

- Mix together the soy sauce and honey in a shallow bowl. Add the salmon and mix well, then cover and let marinate in the refrigerator for 12–15 minutes. Meanwhile, soak 8 wooden skewers in water for 10 minutes.

- Mix together the sesame oil and lime juice in a large bowl. Using a vegetable peeler, slice the cucumber into long, thin strips and place in the bowl with the scallions and cherry tomatoes. Toss in the dressing.

- Thread the salmon onto the skewers, then roll in the sesame seeds to coat. Cook in a preheated hot grill pan or under a preheated hot broiler for 2–3 minutes on each side or until cooked through.

- Serve the salmon skewers with the cucumber salad.

10 Pan-Fried Sesame-Crusted Salmon

Place ¼ cup sesame seeds on a plate. Brush the skin of four 5 oz salmon fillets with 1 egg white, then dip into the seeds. Heat 1 tablespoon olive oil in a skillet, add the salmon, skin side down, and cook for 4–5 minutes, then turn and cook for another 3 minutes. Meanwhile, mix together 2 tablespoons soy sauce, 1 tablespoon sherry, ½ teaspoon packed brown sugar, 2 teaspoons peeled and grated fresh ginger root, and 1 crushed garlic clove. Pour into the skillet and simmer for 2 minutes. Serve the salmon with steamed vegetables and the sauce spooned over the top.

20 Broiled Salmon with Sesame Salad

Mix together 3 tablespoons soy sauce, 2 teaspoons honey, 1 teaspoon sesame oil, 2 tablespoons olive oil, and the juice of ½ lime in a nonmetallic bowl. Add 4 (5 oz) salmon fillets and let marinate for 5 minutes. Meanwhile, dry-fry 2 tablespoons sesame seeds in a nonstick skillet for 2 minutes, stirring frequently, until golden. Toss together 2 cups arugula leaves, 1 chopped cucumber, 6 quartered cherry tomatoes, 6 sliced scallions, and the toasted sesame seeds. Cook the salmon under a preheated hot broiler for 4–5 minutes on each side or until cooked through. Toss the remaining marinade into the salad and serve with the salmon.

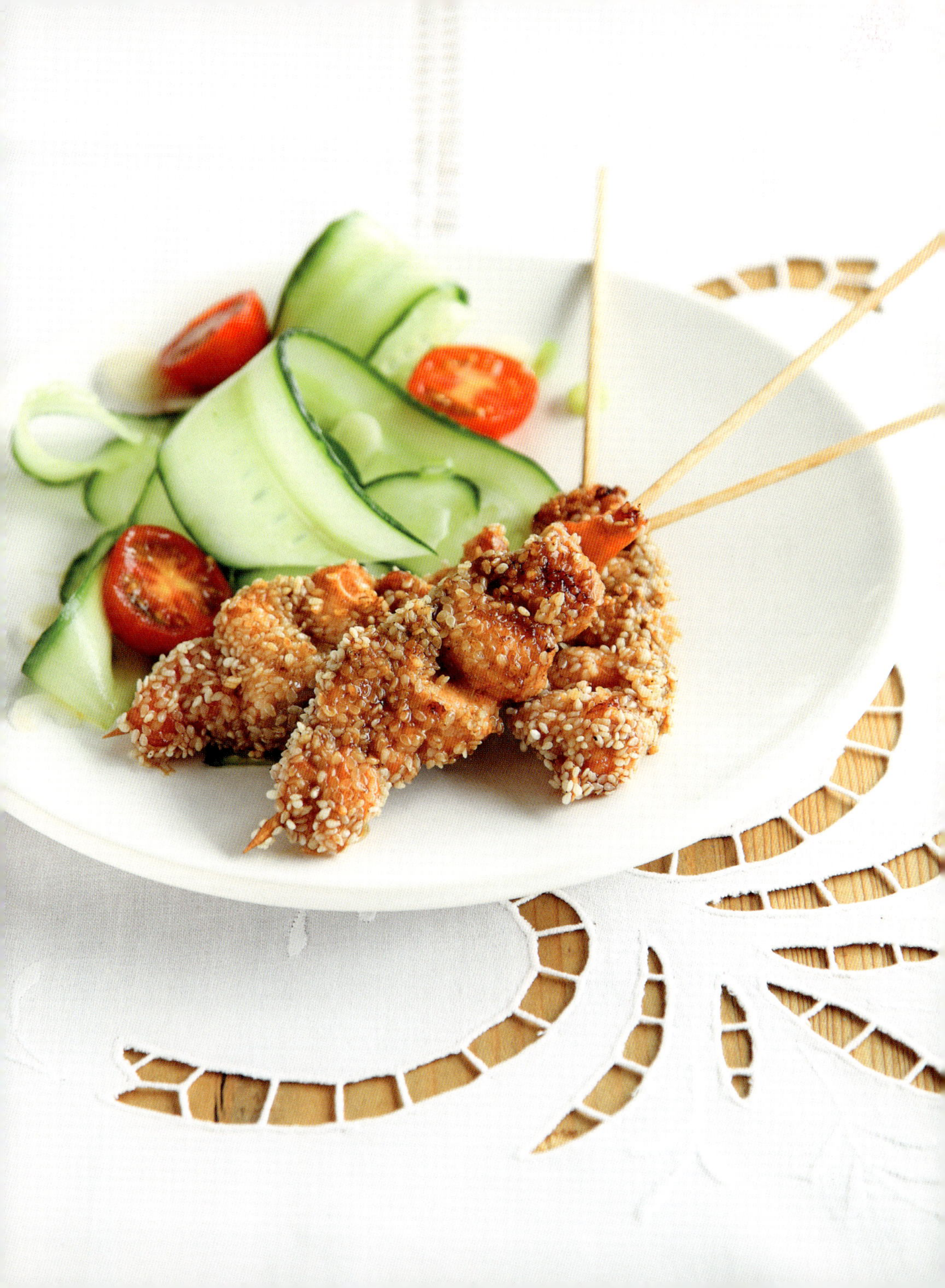

10 Pancetta and Cannellini Bean Bruschetta

Serves 4

1 small baguette, cut into 8 slices
8 slices of pancetta
1 garlic clove
½ (15 oz) can cannellini beans, rinsed and drained (about ¾ cup)
2 tablespoons chopped chives
juice of ½ lemon
olive oil, for drizzling
4 cherry tomatoes, halved
black pepper

- Toast the bread and pancetta under a preheated hot broiler for 2–3 minutes on each side, until the bread is toasted and the pancetta crisp. Rub one side of each slice of toast with the garlic clove.

- Meanwhile, place the beans, chives, lemon juice, and black pepper to taste in a bowl, then mash together lightly, leaving some of the beans whole.

- Spoon a little of the bean mixture onto the toasts, then drizzle with oil and top each with a crisp pancetta slice and a piece of tomato. Serve immediately.

---

20 Pancetta and Cannellini Bean Spaghetti

Cook 1 lb spaghetti in a large saucepan of boiling water according to the package directions, until "al dente." Meanwhile, heat 1 tablespoon olive oil in a skillet, add 2 crushed garlic cloves, 6 oz diced pancetta, and a pinch of dried red pepper flakes, and cook for 1 minute. Add ½ (14½ oz) can diced tomatoes (about 1¾ cups) and ½ (15 oz) can cannellini beans, rinsed and drained (about ¾ cup), and cook for 2–3 minutes, then stir in 1 cup pitted ripe black olives and 1 tablespoon capers, rinsed and drained. Drain the pasta, then toss into the sauce with 2 tablespoons chopped parsley.

30 Pancetta-Wrapped Asparagus with Cannellini Bean Salad

Place ½ cup couscous in a heatproof bowl and just cover with boiling water. Let stand for 15 minutes, then fluff up with a fork. Meanwhile, finely slice 1 fennel bulb and stir into the couscous with ½ (15 oz) can cannellini beans, rinsed and drained (about ¾ cup), ⅓ cup toasted pine nuts, ⅓ cup golden raisins, 2 tablespoons pitted green olives, and 1 tablespoon chopped dill. Mix together the juice and grated rind of 1 lemon, 2 tablespoons chopped parsley, and 1 chopped garlic clove in a small bowl, then stir into the salad with 1 tablespoon extra virgin olive oil. Season well. Wrap 12 trimmed asparagus spears in 12 slices of pancetta. Heat 1 tablespoon olive oil in a ridged grill pan, add the asparagus and cook for 4–5 minutes, turning occasionally, until chargrilled on all sides. Serve with the bean salad.

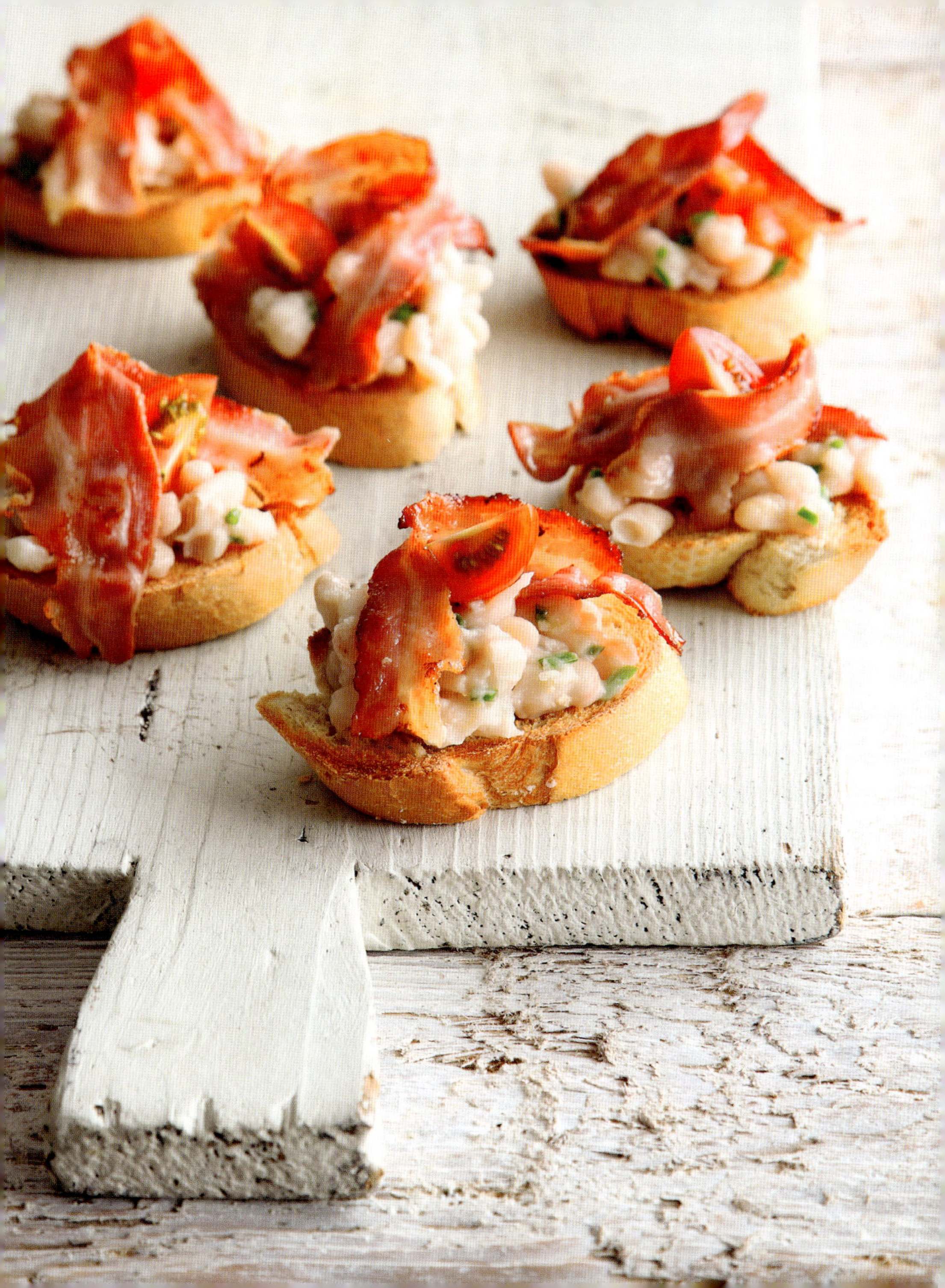

Chickpea and Bean Sprout Patties

Serves 4
½ red onion, diced
1 (15 oz) can chickpeas, rinsed and drained
¼ teaspoon cumin seeds
⅓ cup sun-dried tomatoes
2 tablespoons bean sprouts
2 tablespoons olive oil
salt and black pepper

To serve
mango chutney
crisp green salad

- Place the onion and chickpeas in a food processor or blender and process until the chickpeas are broken down. Add all the remaining ingredients except the olive oil, season with salt and black pepper, and process again until the mixture comes together.
- Using wet hands, form the mixture into small patties. Cover and chill for 5 minutes.
- Heat the oil in a large skillet, add the patties, and cook for 4–5 minutes on each side, until golden.
- Serve with a little mango chutney and a crisp green salad.

Chickpea and Alfalfa Sprout Salad Toss together 1 bunch of watercress or 2 cups arugula, 1 cored, seeded, and sliced red bell pepper, 1 cored, seeded, and sliced yellow bell pepper, 1 sliced small red onion, 6 halved cherry tomatoes, 1 (15 oz) can chickpeas, rinsed and drained, and 1¼ cups crumbled feta cheese in a serving bowl. Whisk together the juice of ½ lemon, 3 tablespoons olive oil, 1 seeded and finely diced chile, ½ teaspoon Dijon mustard, and ½ teaspoon honey in a small bowl, then toss with the salad. Sprinkle with 1⅓ cups alfalfa sprouts and serve.

Chickpea and Bean Sprout Curry Heat 2 tablespoons coconut oil in a wok or large saucepan, add 2 chopped onions and 2 garlic cloves, and cook over medium-low heat for 9–10 minutes, until starting to caramelize. Increase the heat, add 1 teaspoon ground cumin, ½ teaspoon each of ground coriander, turmeric, and chili powder, and a pinch of garam masala, and stir-fry for 1–2 minutes, then add 4 chopped tomatoes and cook for 6–8 minutes, until the sauce starts to thicken. Add ⅔ cup water and mix well, then add 2 (15 oz) cans chickpeas, rinsed and drained and cook for 5 minutes, mashing a few chickpeas while cooking. Stir in a 1½-inch piece of fresh ginger root, peeled and grated, 2 tablespoons bean sprouts, and 2 tablespoons chopped cilantro. Serve with cooked long-grain rice.

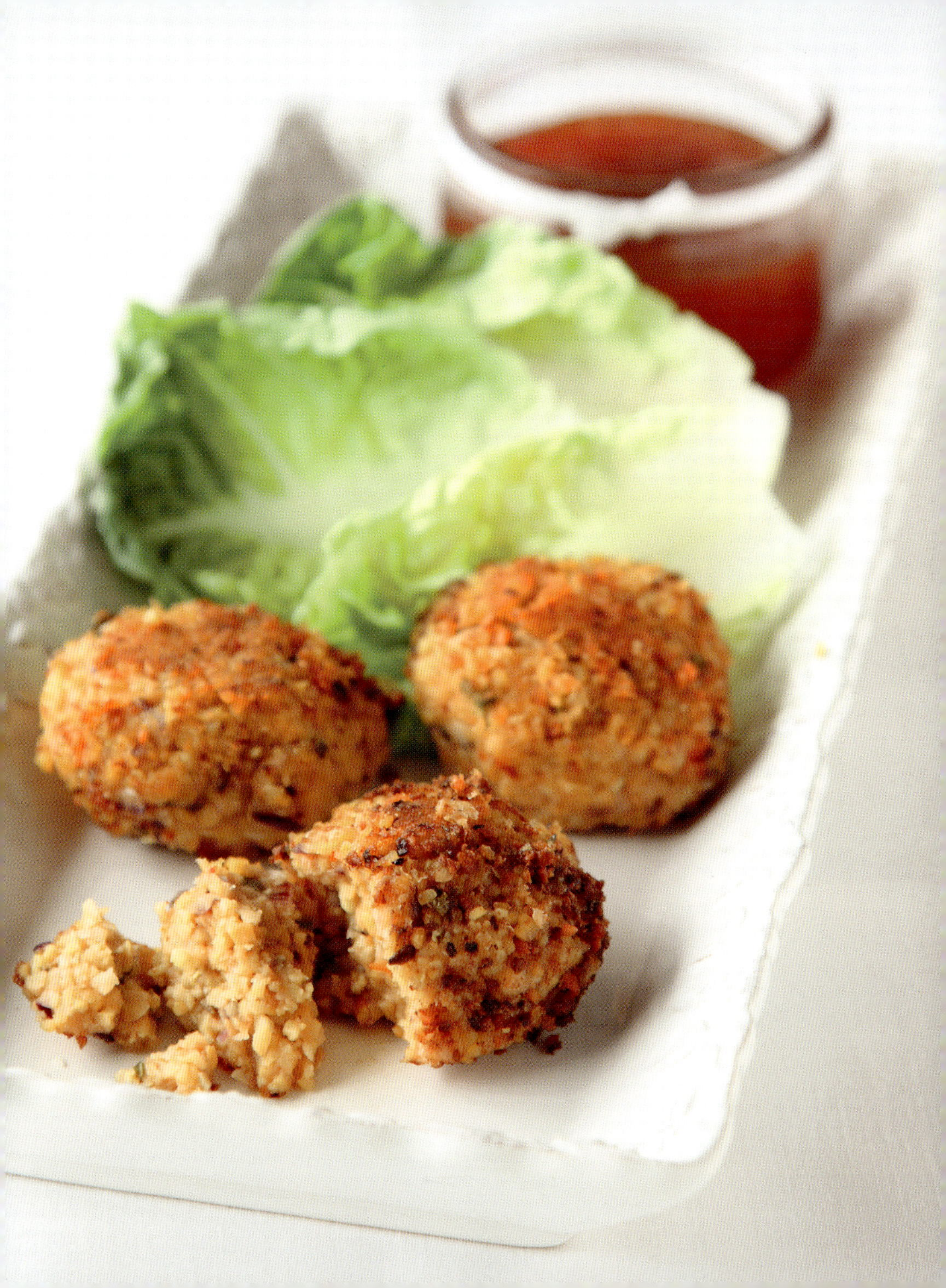

10 Shrimp and Zucchini Spring Rolls

Serves 4

3 large zucchini
1 large carrot, cut into matchsticks
4 scallions, shredded
¼ cup bean sprouts
1 red bell pepper and 1 yellow bell pepper, cored, seeded, and thinly sliced
4 oz peeled, cooked shrimp
12–15 mint leaves
12–15 cilantro leaves

To serve

2 cups arugula leaves
1 cup store-bought salsa

- Using a vegetable peeler, thinly slice the zucchini into long, wide ribbons. Place the slices on a clean surface.
- Place a few pieces of each vegetable, 1 teaspoon of the shrimp, and a few herbs onto the end of each zucchini slice, then roll up to enclose the filling.
- Place the rolls in a steamer and steam for 6–8 minutes, until tender.
- Serve with arugula leaves and salsa.

---

20 Vietnamese Shrimp Spring Rolls

Mix together 1 diced lemon grass stalk, 2 crushed garlic cloves, 1 teaspoon each of soy sauce and sugar, and 2 teaspoons Thai fish sauce. Add 1 lb raw, peeled shrimp, cover, and marinate for 6–8 minutes. Heat a wok, and stir-fry the shrimp for 5–6 minutes. Set aside. Cut 1 cucumber, 2 carrots, and 1 cored and seeded red bell pepper into matchsticks. Dip 1 rice paper wrapper into warm water for 2 seconds, then fold in half on a dry surface. Add 1 tablespoon each of the shrimp and vegetables and 1 basil and 1 mint leaf, then roll up to enclose the filling. Repeat to make 16. Serve with dipping sauce.

30 Shrimp, Chicken, and Vegetable Spring Rolls

Heat 1 tablespoon peanut oil in a wok or skillet, add 8 oz diced chicken breast and 1 cup chopped cremini mushrooms, and cook for 2–3 minutes. Stir in 1 tablespoon soy sauce and 1 teaspoon Chinese five-spice powder. Remove from the heat and add 4 oz cooked, peeled shrimp, 1 teaspoon peeled and grated fresh ginger root, ¾ cup bean sprouts, 2 diced scallions, 1 grated zucchini, and 1 small carrot, peeled and cut into matchsticks. Lay 2 spring roll wrappers on top of each other and spoon 2 tablespoons of the filling into the center. Brush the corners of the wrapper with beaten egg and fold in the edges, then roll up to enclose the filling. Repeat with the remaining ingredients to make 12 spring rolls. Place on a large baking sheet and brush with 2 tablespoons melted butter. Bake in a preheated oven, at 400°F, for 10–12 minutes, until golden and heated through. Serve immediately with sweet chili dipping sauce.

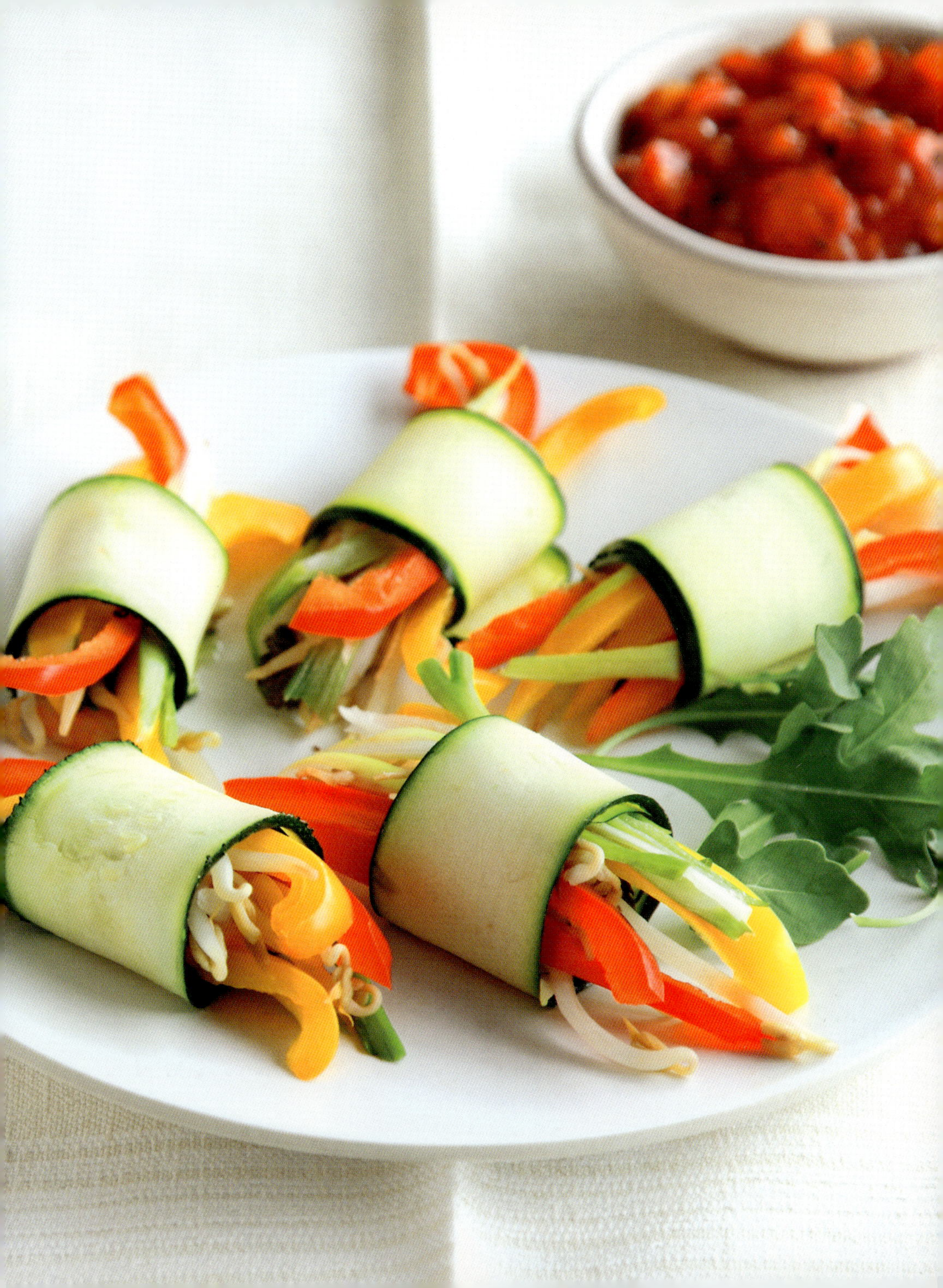

QuickCook

Meat and Poultry

Recipes listed by cooking time

30

Recipe	Page
Spicy Pancetta-Wrapped Chicken with Eggplant Dip	90
Mint-Crusted Rack of Lamb	92
Roasted Chicken Breasts with Pesto Pasta	94
Chicken and Apricot Stew	96
Beef and Lentil Casserole	98
Chicken and Tarragon Risotto	100
Apple and Ginger Pork	102
Lamb Racks with Rosemary and Garlic	104
Chicken with Orange and Olives	106
Harissa Hamburgers	108
Ginger Chicken Stir-Fry	110
Bacon and Leek Tortilla	112
Spicy Chicken with Cucumber and Radish Salad	114
Horseradish Beef with Quinoa	116
Chicken, Vegetable, and Noodle Stir-Fry	118
Roasted Pork Loin with Creamy Cabbage and Leeks	120
Nectarine-Glazed Chicken Kebabs	122
Calf Liver with Caramelized Shallot Sauce	124
Coconut Chicken with Avocado Salsa	126
Beef and Leek Phyllo Pie	128
Chicken Livers with Mustard Mashed Potatoes	130

20

Recipe	Page
Spicy Chicken Breasts with Hummus	90
Lamb Koftas with Mint Yogurt	92
Chicken Pasta Salad with Pesto Dressing	94
Chicken and Apricot Kebabs	96
Beef and Lentil Chili	98
Chicken and Tarragon Tagliatelle	100
Pork, Apple, and Ginger Stir-Fry	102
Lamb Cutlets with Pea and Rosemary Mashed Potatoes	104
Grilled Chicken, Orange, and Olive Salad	106
Harissa Beef Salad	108
Ginger Chicken Soup	110
Bacon and Leek Penne	112
Spicy Chicken with Cucumber and Radish Stir-Fry	114
Steak and Chickpea Salad with Horseradish Dressing	116

Chicken and Asian Vegetable Stir-Fry		118
Pork Cutlets with Cabbage and Leek Potato Cakes		120
Chicken Satay with Nectarine Salad		122
Calf Liver with Caramelized Onions		124
Chicken Kebabs with Avocado Dip		126
Steak and Caramelized Leek Sandwiches		128
Chicken Liver and Mustard Pâté		130

Chicken Dippers with Homemade Hummus		90
Lamb Chops with Cucumber and Mint Salad		92
Chicken Pesto Baguettes		94
Chicken and Apricot Wraps		96
Quick Spaghetti with Lentil Meat Sauce		98
Chicken and Tarragon Double-Decker Sandwiches		100
Broiled Pork Cutlets with Apple and Ginger Coleslaw		102
Rosemary Lamb Cutlets with Summer Salad		104
Chicken, Orange, and Olive Sandwiches		106
Harissa Beef Fajitas		108
Ginger Chicken Wraps		110
Leek, Butternut, and Bacon Soup		112
Chicken, Cucumber, and Radish Pita Breads		114
Horseradish Steak Sandwiches		116
Chicken and Vegetable Stir-Fry		118

Broiled Pork Chops with Cabbage and Leek Mashed Potatoes		120
Chicken and Nectarine Salad		122
Calf Liver Pâté with Caramelized Onion		124
Curried Chicken with Avocado Salad		126
Stir-Fried Beef and Leeks		128
Chicken Liver Salad with Mustard Dressing		130

10 Chicken Dippers with Homemade Hummus

Serves 4

1 tablespoon all-purpose flour
1 tablespoon chopped parsley
1 tablespoon chopped cilantro
12 oz chicken breast strips
2 tablespoons butter
1 tablespoon olive oil

For the hummus
1 garlic clove, finely diced
1 (15 oz) can chickpeas, rinsed and drained
juice of ½ lemon
2 tablespoons tahini paste
3–4 tablespoons extra virgin olive oil

- Mix together the flour and herbs on a plate, then toss the chicken strips in the herbed flour.

- Heat the butter and olive oil in a large skillet, add the chicken, and cook for 3–4 minutes on each side or until golden and cooked through.

- Meanwhile, make the hummus. Place the garlic, chickpeas, lemon juice, and tahini in a food processor or blender and blend until nearly smooth. With the motor still running, pour in the extra virgin olive oil through the feed tube and blend to the desired consistency.

- Serve the chicken with hummus for dipping.

---

20 Spicy Chicken Breasts with Hummus
Mix together 1 crushed garlic clove and ½ tablespoon each of paprika, dried thyme, cayenne pepper, and ground black pepper in a small bowl, then rub over 4 (5 oz) boneless, skinless chicken breasts. Cook the chicken breasts under a preheated hot broiler for 6–8 minutes on each side or until cooked through. Spoon 1¼ cups store-bought hummus into a bowl. Serve the chicken with the hummus and an arugula salad.

30 Spicy Pancetta-Wrapped Chicken with Eggplant Dip
Place 4 (5 oz) boneless, skinless chicken breasts between 2 sheets of plastic wrap and bash with a meat mallet or rolling pin until about ¼ inch thick. Lay each piece on 2 slices of pancetta, spread each with 1 tablespoon harissa paste and ¼ cup chopped mozzarella cheese, and roll up. Place on a baking sheet, drizzle with a little olive oil, and cook in a preheated oven, at 400°F, for 20–25 minutes or until cooked through. Meanwhile, prick 1 extra-large eggplant all over with a fork and cook over an open gas (or barbecue) flame, turning frequently, for 15–20 minutes, until blackened and cooked through. Peel off and discard the skin while warm, then put the flesh into a bowl. Mash with a fork, then add ½ cup tahini paste and the juice of 2–3 lemons and season to taste. Slice the chicken and serve with the eggplant dip and steamed green beans.

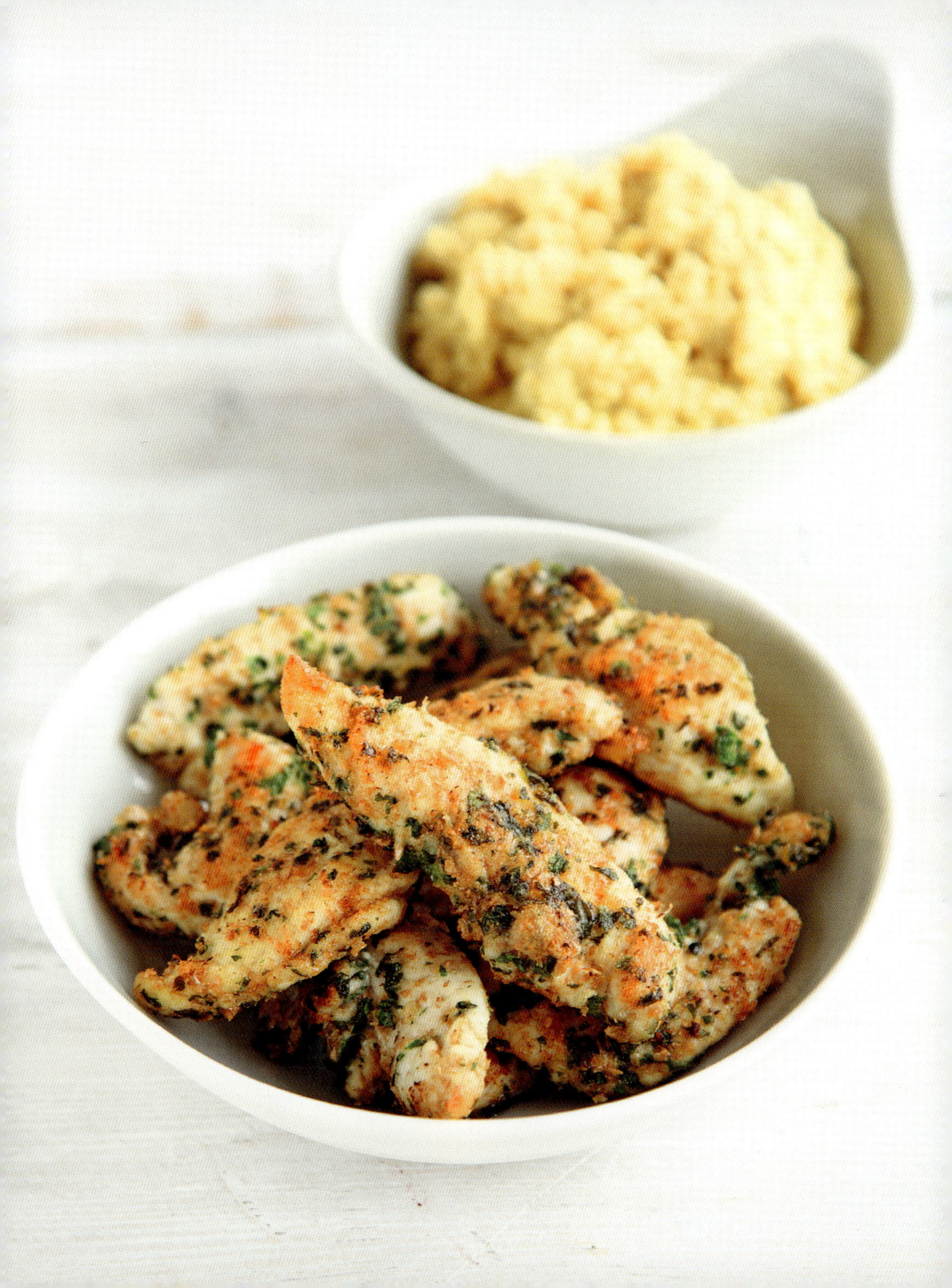

Lamb Koftas with Mint Yogurt

Serves 4

1 lb ground lamb
1 teaspoon ground cumin
1 teaspoon ground coriander
1 teaspoon turmeric
3 tablespoons chopped cilantro
1 red chile, seeded and diced
4 garlic cloves, crushed
1 medium egg, beaten
1 tablespoon olive oil
salt and black pepper
salad greens, to serve

For the mint yogurt

1 cup Greek yogurt
1 tablespoon chopped mint
½ cucumber, grated
juice of ½ lemon

- Place the lamb, spices, fresh cilantro, chile, garlic, salt and black pepper, and egg into a food processor and process together. Using wet hands, roll the mixture into walnut-size balls, then shape the balls around 8 metal skewers.
- Heat the oil in a dutch oven or ovenproof skillet, add the skewers, and cook for 2–3 minutes on all sides, then transfer to a preheated oven, at 425°F, for another 6–8 minutes, until cooked through.
- Meanwhile, to make the mint yogurt, mix together all the ingredients in a bowl.
- Serve the koftas with a few salad greens and the mint yogurt.

Lamb Chops with Cucumber and Mint Salad

Cook 8 lamb cutlets under a preheated hot broiler for 3–4 minutes on each side, or until cooked to your liking. Meanwhile, using a vegetable peeler, slice 2 cucumbers into long, thin strips. Place in a bowl and mix together with 2 tablespoons shredded mint, the seeds of 1 pomegranate, and 1 bunch of watercress or 2 cups arugula. Whisk together 3 tablespoons olive oil, 1 tablespoon sherry vinegar, ½ teaspoon mustard, and ½ teaspoon honey in a bowl, then toss with the salad. Serve with the lamb.

Mint-Crusted Rack of Lamb

Heat 4 tablespoons butter and 1 tablespoon olive oil in a dutch oven or ovenproof skillet, add 2 racks of French-trimmed lamb, and cook for 2–3 minutes on each side to brown. Cover the bones with aluminum foil, then transfer to a preheated oven, at 340°F, and cook for 4–5 minutes. Let rest for 5 minutes. Meanwhile, place 3 tablespoons chopped mint, 2 crushed garlic cloves, and 1½ cups fresh whole-wheat bread crumbs in a food processor and process to a paste. Brush the lamb with 2 tablespoons Dijon mustard and press on the paste. Return to the oven for 5–10 minutes, or until cooked to your liking. Let rest for 3 minutes. Serve with steamed broccoli.

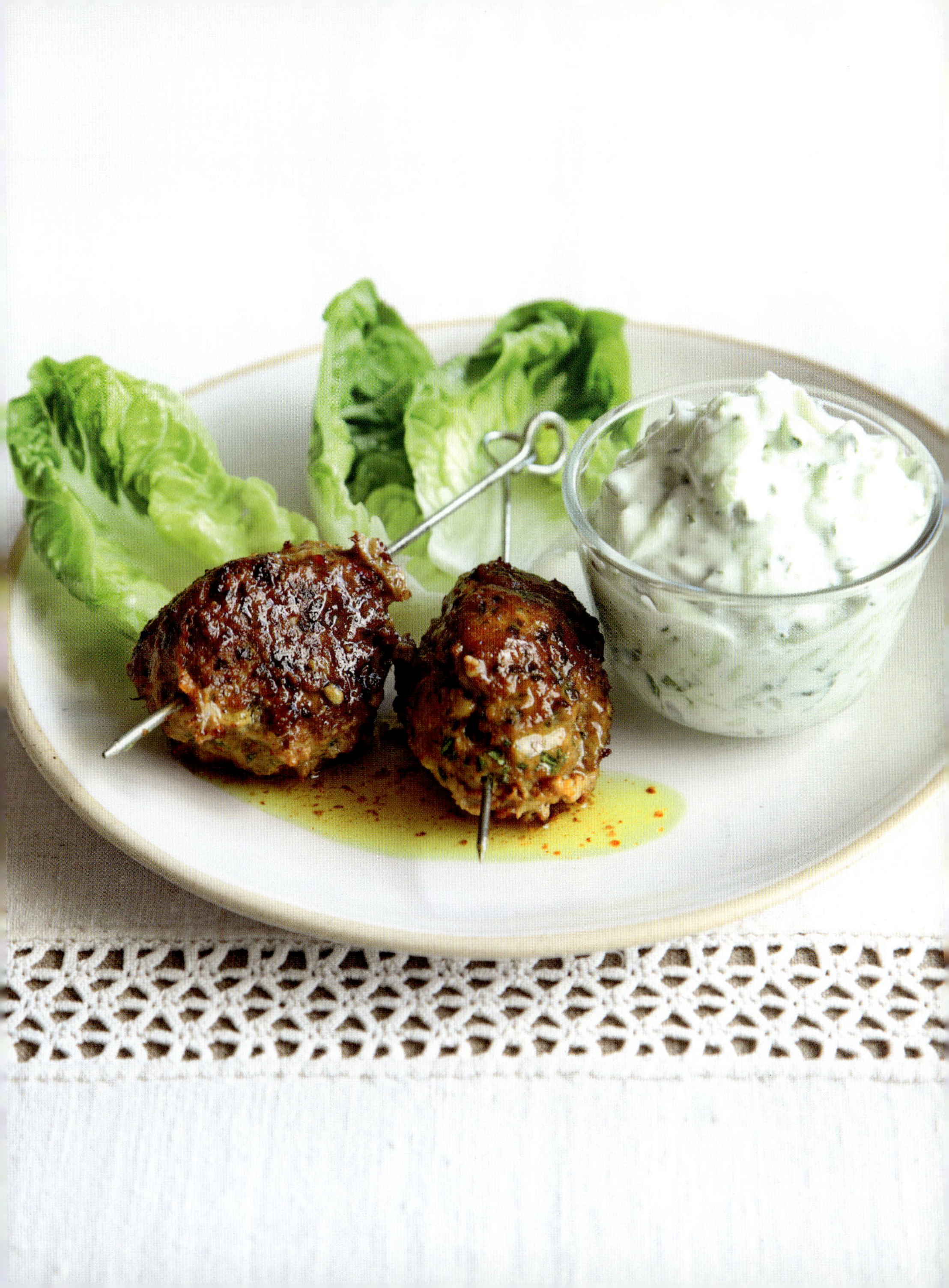

Chicken Pasta Salad with Pesto Dressing

Serves 4

2 boneless, skinless chicken breasts
½ tablespoon olive oil
6 oz conchiglie pasta
¼ cup walnut halves
1 small red onion, sliced
1½ cups halved baby plum tomatoes, halved
½ cucumber, cut into chunks
2 bunches of watercress or 4 cups arugula
2 tablespoons Parmesan cheese shavings, to serve

For the dressing

1½ tablespoons olive oil
2 tablespoons store-bought pesto
1 tablespoon balsamic vinegar

- To make the pesto dressing, whisk together all the ingredients in a small bowl and set aside.

- Brush the chicken breasts with the oil, then cook in a preheated hot ridged grill pan for 12–15 minutes, turning once, until cooked through.

- Meanwhile, cook the pasta in a saucepan of boiling water according to the package directions, until "al dente." Drain, then refresh under cold running water and drain again.

- Heat a nonstick skillet over medium-low heat and dry-fry the walnuts for 3–4 minutes, stirring frequently, until slightly golden.

- Thinly slice the chicken, then place in a large bowl with the pasta, toasted walnuts, onion, tomatoes, cucumber, and watercress or arugula.

- Toss with the pesto dressing and serve sprinkled with the Parmesan cheese shavings.

Chicken Pesto Baguettes

Halve 4 baguettes horizontally and spread the bottoms of each with ½ tablespoon store-bought pesto. Divide 1 bunch of watercress or 2 cups arugula among the baguettes and top with 4 sliced tomatoes, ¼ sliced cucumber, ½ sliced red onion, and 2 sliced store-bought cooked chicken breasts. Top each with a spoonful of mayonnaise, then add the tops.

Roasted Chicken Breasts with Pesto Pasta

Rub 4 boneless, skinless chicken breasts with olive oil and season, then cook in a preheated hot ovenproof ridged grill pan for 2–3 minutes on each side. Transfer to a preheated oven, at 400°F, for 16–18 minutes or until cooked through. Meanwhile, cook 1 lb linguine in a saucepan of boiling water according to the package directions, until "al dente." Drain, then return to the pan and toss together with ¼ cup store-bought pesto, 1 bunch of chopped watercress or 2 cups arugula, and 4 halved cherry tomatoes. Serve topped with the roasted chicken breasts and 2 tablespoons grated pecorino cheese.

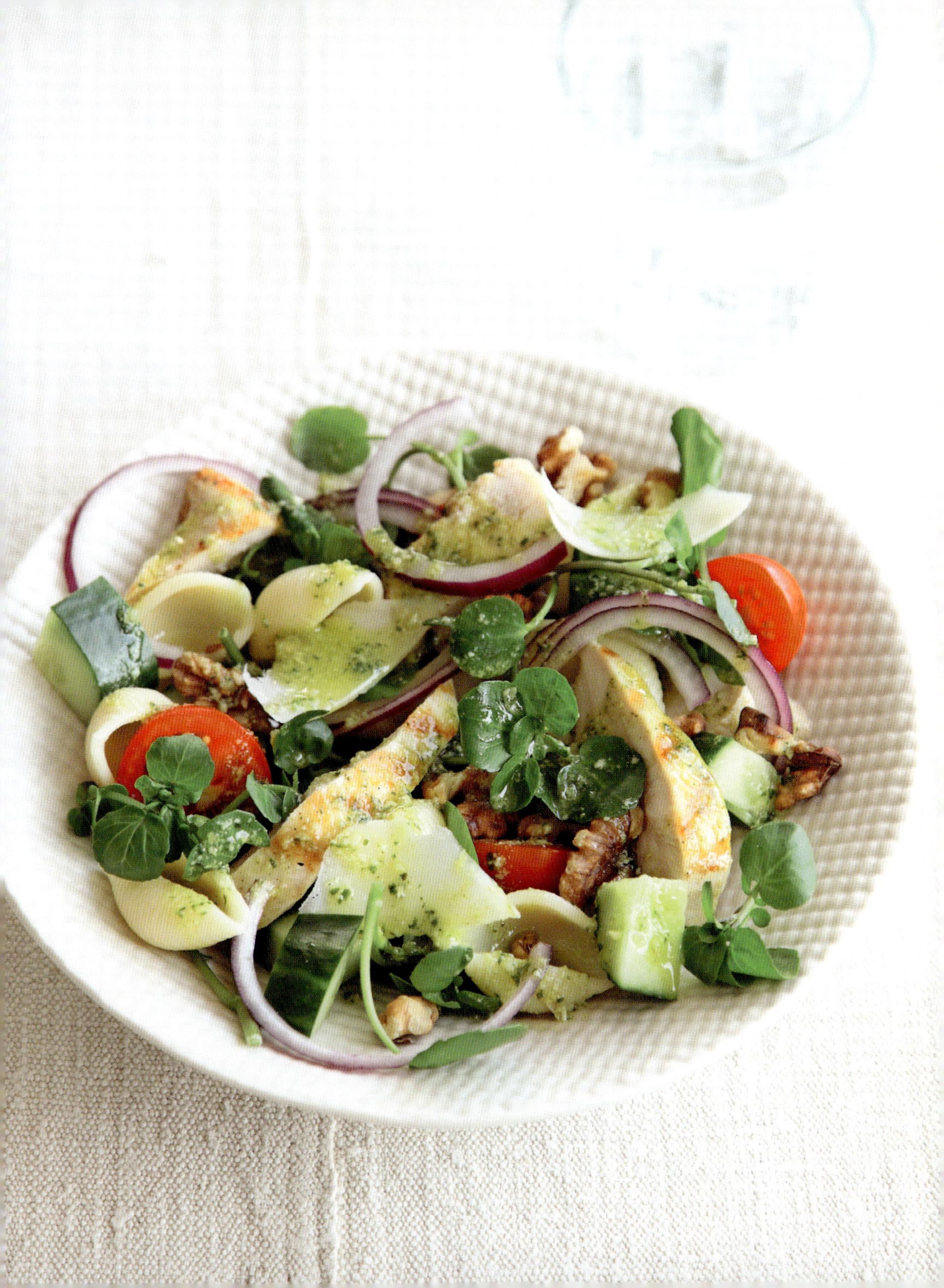

30 Chicken and Apricot Stew

Serves 4

1 tablespoon olive oil
2 garlic cloves, crushed
1 tablespoon peeled and grated fresh ginger root
1 large onion, chopped
1¼ lb skinless, boneless chicken breasts, cubed
½ cup red lentils
1 teaspoon ground cumin
¼ teaspoon ground cinnamon
¼ teaspoon turmeric
¼ teaspoon ground coriander
12 dried apricots
juice of 1 lemon
3 cups hot chicken stock
1 tablespoon chopped mint
1 tablespoon chopped cilantro
seeds of 1 pomegranate
2 tablespoons toasted slivered almonds
couscous, to serve

- Heat the oil in a large saucepan, add the garlic, ginger, and onion, and cook for 1–2 minutes. Add the chicken and cook for another 5 minutes, stirring occasionally.

- Stir in the lentils, spices, apricots, and lemon juice and stir well. Pour in the stock and bring to a boil, then reduce the heat and simmer for 15 minutes.

- Stir in the herbs and pomegranate seeds, then sprinkle with the almonds. Serve in bowls with couscous.

10 Chicken and Apricot Wraps

Spread 4 tortilla wraps with 2 tablespoons mayonnaise. Top each with the leaves of ½ Boston lettuce, ½ cored, seeded, and sliced red bell pepper, 2 chopped dried apricots, a few cilantro leaves, 4 oz store-bought cooked chicken breasts, diced, and 2 teaspoons mango chutney. Roll up the wraps and serve.

20 Chicken and Apricot Kebabs

Mix together 2 tablespoons olive oil, the juice and grated rind of 1 orange, and 1 teaspoon each of ground cumin and dried red pepper flakes in a large nonmetallic bowl. Add 1 lb cubed boneless, skinless chicken breasts, 12 dried apricots, and 2 cored, seeded, and chopped red bell peppers and mix well to coat. Let marinate for 3–4 minutes. Thread the chicken, apricots, and red bell pepper onto 8 metal skewers, then cook under a preheated hot broiler or on a barbecue grill for 10–12 minutes, turning occasionally, until the chicken is cooked through. Sprinkle with chopped cilantro and serve with cooked brown rice or quinoa.

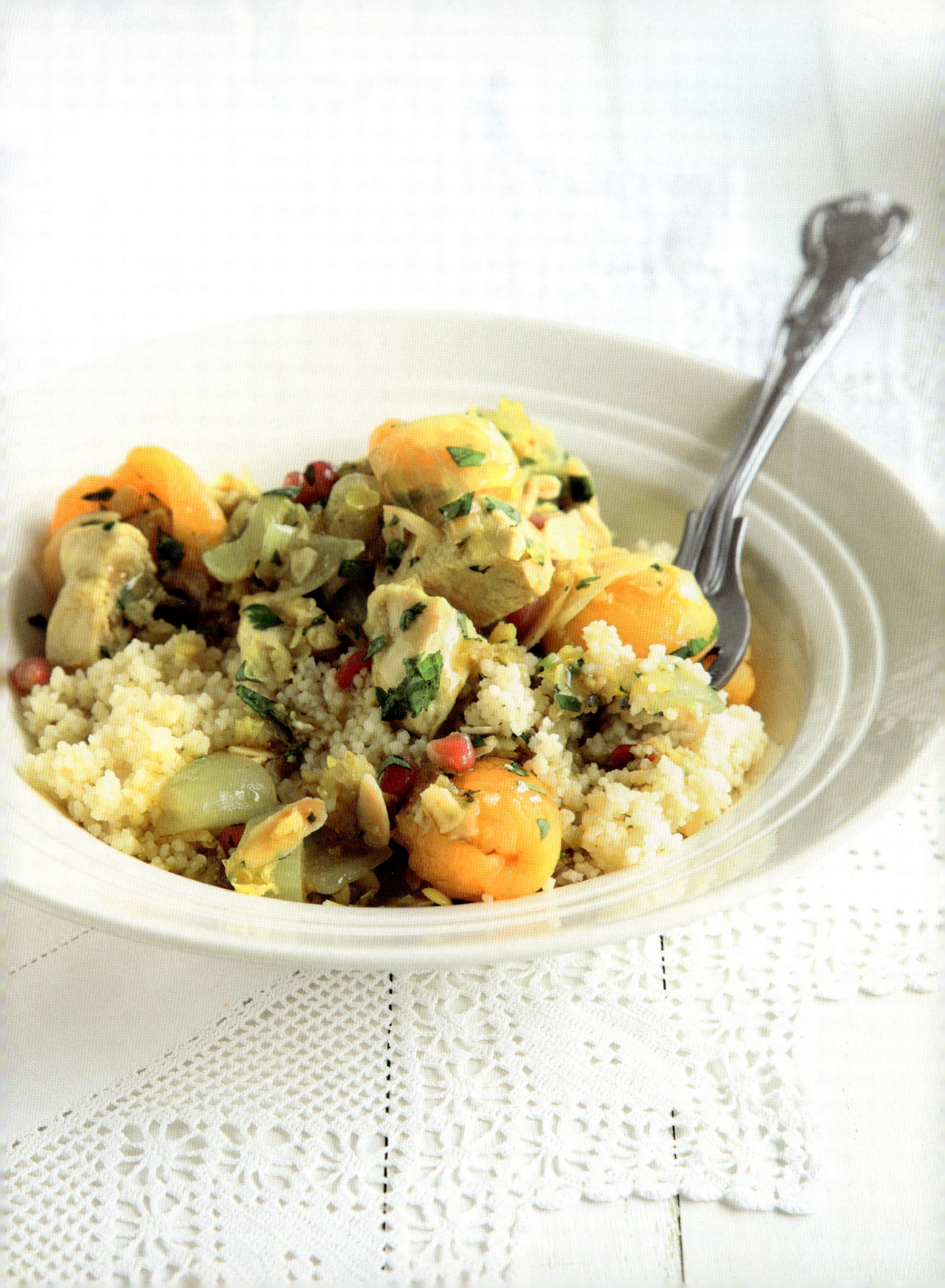

Beef and Lentil Chili

Serves 4

1 tablespoon olive oil
1 large onion, diced
2 garlic cloves, crushed
1 red bell pepper, cored, seeded, and diced
1 teaspoon chili powder
1 teaspoon paprika
1 teaspoon ground cumin
8 oz ground beef
1 (15 oz) can lentils, rinsed and drained, or 2 cups cooked lentils
1 cup water
1 (14½ oz) can tomatoes
½ teaspoon sugar
2 tablespoons tomato paste
1 (15 oz) can kidney beans, rinsed and drained
cooked long-grain rice, to serve

- Heat the oil in a saucepan, add the onion, and cook for 1 minute. Add the garlic and red bell pepper and cook for 1 minute, then stir in the spices. Add the beef and cook, stirring occasionally, for another 4 minutes, until browned.

- Stir in the lentils, measured water, tomatoes, sugar, and tomato paste into the mixture. Bring to a simmer and cook for 10–12 minutes, breaking the tomatoes up with a wooden spoon. Stir in the kidney beans and cook for 2 minutes, until heated through.

- Serve the chili with cooked rice.

Quick Spaghetti with Lentil Meat Sauce Cook 1 lb spaghetti in a saucepan of boiling water according to the package directions. Meanwhile, heat 1 tablespoon olive oil in a saucepan, add 8 oz ground beef, and cook until browned. Stir in 1 (15 oz) can lentils, rinsed and drained, or 2 cups cooked lentils, and 1¼ cups store-bought spaghetti sauce. Simmer for 8 minutes. Drain the spaghetti and stir into the sauce. Serve sprinkled with Parmesan cheese shavings.

Beef and Lentil Casserole Heat 1 tablespoon olive oil in a large skillet, add 1 chopped onion, 1 crushed garlic clove, 2 diced celery sticks, and 2 peeled and diced carrots, and cook for 1–2 minutes. Add 8 oz ground beef and cook for 5 minutes. Stir in 1 (15 oz) can lentils, rinsed and drained, or 2 cups cooked lentils, 1 (14½ oz) can diced tomatoes, 1¼ cups beef stock, 1 teaspoon dried mixed herbs, and a dash of Worcestershire sauce. Season and simmer for 15 minutes. Meanwhile, cook 6 peeled and chopped russet potatoes in a saucepan of boiling water for 10–12 minutes, until tender. Drain and mash in the pan with 2 tablespoons butter, 2 tablespoons milk, and 2 teaspoons whole-grain mustard. Spoon the beef mixture into an ovenproof dish and top with the mashed potatoes. Cook in a preheated oven, at 400°F, for 10 minutes, until golden.

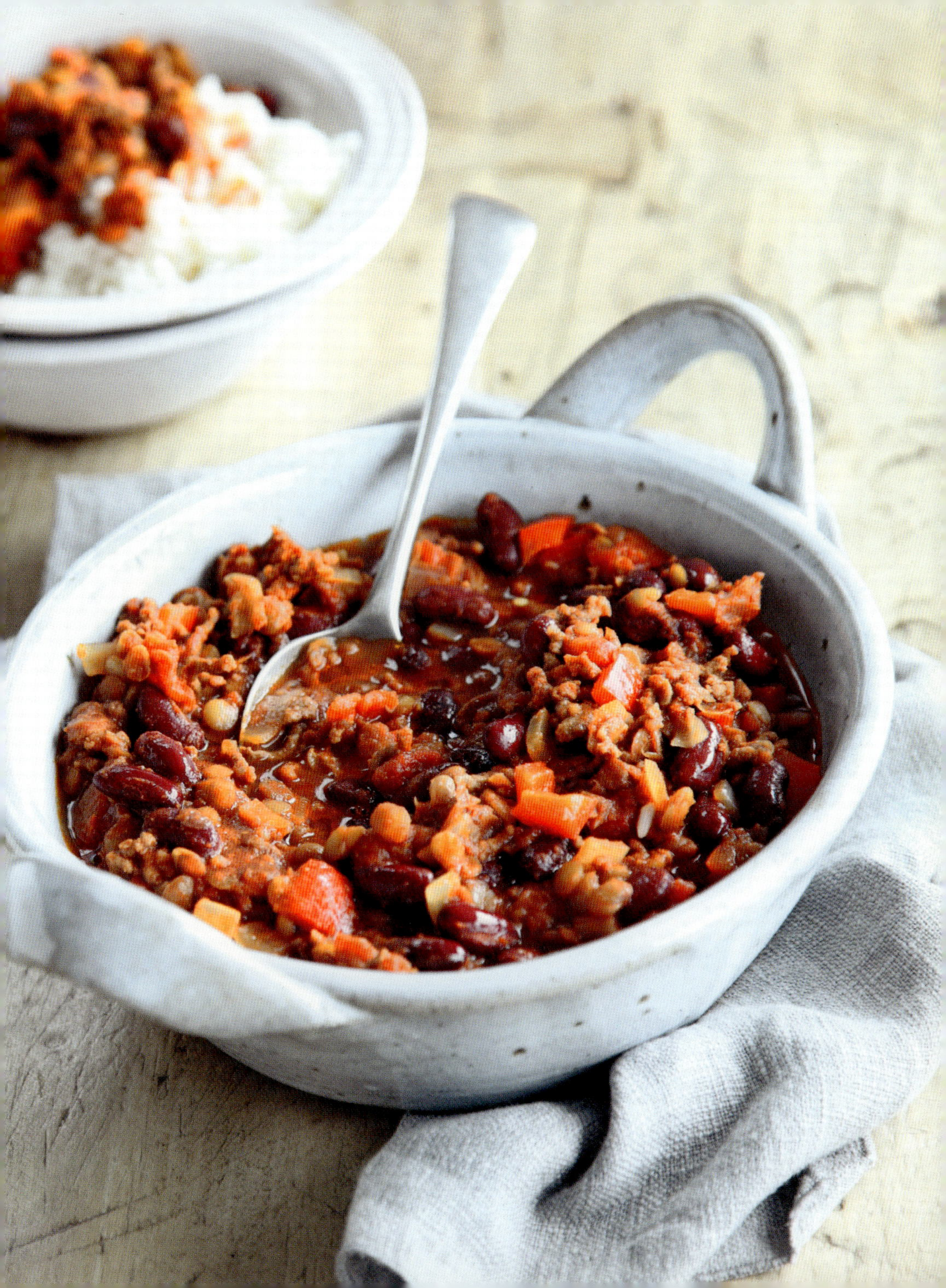

30 Chicken and Tarragon Risotto

Serves 4

2 tablespoons olive oil
4 (5 oz) boneless, skinless chicken breasts, seasoned
4 tablespoons butter
1 onion, finely chopped
2 garlic cloves, crushed
2 cups risotto rice
splash of white wine
4 cups hot chicken stock
8 oz asparagus tips
1 tablespoon chopped tarragon
¼ cup grated Parmesan cheese
salt and black pepper

- Heat half the oil in a heatproof skillet, add the chicken, and cook for 4–5 minutes on each side, until browned. Transfer to a preheated oven, at 400°F, and cook for 15–18 minutes or until cooked through.

- Meanwhile, heat the remaining oil and butter in a saucepan, add the onion and garlic, and cook for 2–3 minutes. Stir in the rice, then add the wine and simmer until absorbed. Add a ladle of stock and cook, stirring, until absorbed. Continue adding more stock for 18–20 minutes, until the rice is cooked "al dente."

- While the risotto is cooking, steam the asparagus for 3–4 minutes, until tender, then cut in half. Stir the asparagus, tarragon, and half the cheese into the risotto, then season.

- Slice the chicken breasts diagonally. Serve the risotto topped with the chicken and sprinkled with the remaining Parmesan.

---

10 Chicken and Tarragon Double-Decker Sandwiches Mix 1 tablespoon chopped tarragon with 2 tablespoons mayonnaise. Toast 12 slices of whole-wheat bread under a preheated hot broiled for 2–3 minutes on each side, then spread 4 slices with the mayonnaise. Divide 4 sliced tomatoes and 2–3 leaves of iceburg lettuce among the slices, then top each with another slice of toast. Spread each of these with 2 teaspoons mango chutney, then add slices of cooked chicken and cucumber. Top with the remaining toast, cut into quarters, and serve.

20 Chicken and Tarragon Tagliatelle Heat 1 tablespoon olive oil in a skillet, add 2 chopped skinless, boneless chicken breasts, and cook for 5–6 minutes. Pour in 2 tablespoons white wine and simmer for 4–5 minutes, until the liquid has reduced. Stir in 2 chopped garlic cloves, 1 cup plain yogurt, and 3 tablespoons coarsely chopped tarragon and simmer for 5–6 minutes or until the chicken is cooked through. Meanwhile, cook 1 lb tagliatelle in a saucepan of boiling water according to the package directions, until "al dente." Drain, then toss in the pan with 4 cups baby spinach leaves until the leaves are wilted. Mix in the chicken, season well, and serve sprinkled with Parmesan cheese shavings.

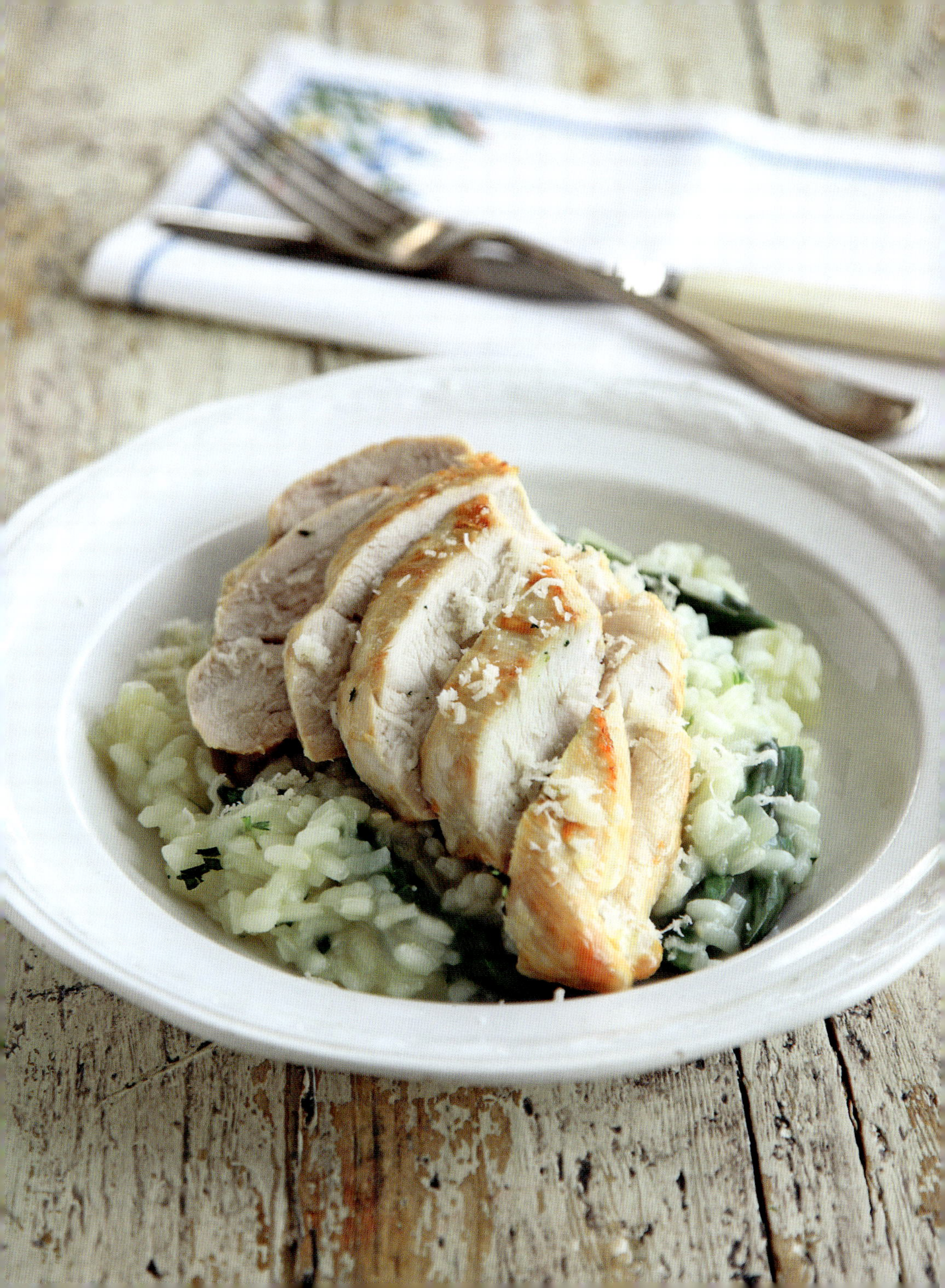

Pork, Apple, and Ginger Stir-Fry

Serves 4

2 tablespoons sesame seeds
1 tablespoon coconut oil
12 oz pork tenderloin strips
2 garlic cloves, chopped
2-inch fresh ginger root, peeled and cut into matchsticks
1 green chile, seeded and chopped
2 apples, cored and cut into wedges
2 carrots, cut into matchsticks
1½ cups broccoli florets
12 oz ribbon rice noodles
juice of 1 lime

- Heat a nonstick skillet over medium-low heat and dry-fry the sesame seeds for 2 minutes, stirring frequently, until golden and toasted. Set aside.

- Heat the oil in a wok or large skillet, add the pork, and stir-fry for 6–8 minutes, until lightly browned. Add the garlic, ginger, chile, apples, and vegetables and stir-fry for another 4–5 minutes or until the pork is cooked through.

- Meanwhile, cook the noodles according to the package directions, then add to the stir-fry with the lime juice and toss all the ingredients together.

- Serve sprinkled with the toasted sesame seeds.

Broiled Pork Cutlets with Apple and Ginger Coleslaw Cook 4 (5 oz) pork cutlets under a preheated hot broiler for 3–4 minutes on each side or until cooked through. Meanwhile, finely slice 1 small green cabbage, 2 celery sticks, and 1 cored and seeded red bell pepper and place in a bowl. Add 2 peeled and shredded carrots and 2 peeled, cored, and grated apples and mix well. Mix together 2 tablespoons plain yogurt, a 1-inch piece of fresh ginger root, peeled and grated, and 1 tablespoon mayonnaise in a small bowl, then stir into the coleslaw with 2 tablespoons chopped cilantro. Serve with the pork.

Apple and Ginger Pork Toss 1 lb chopped pork tenderloin in seasoned flour. Heat 1 tablespoon olive oil in a large skillet, add the pork, and cook for 4–6 minutes, until browned. Remove with a slotted spoon and set aside. Add 2 peeled, cored, and sliced apples to the skillet and cook for 3 minutes, until slightly browned. Stir in 2 chopped garlic cloves, 1 tablespoon peeled and chopped fresh ginger root, and 1 teaspoon each of ground coriander, ground cumin, and mustard seeds and cook, stirring, for another 2–3 minutes. Pour in 1 cup hot chicken stock and add the reserved pork. Bring to a simmer and cook for 10 minutes, until the pork is cooked through and the sauce has started to thicken. Serve with cooked long-grain rice and sprinkle with chopped cilantro.

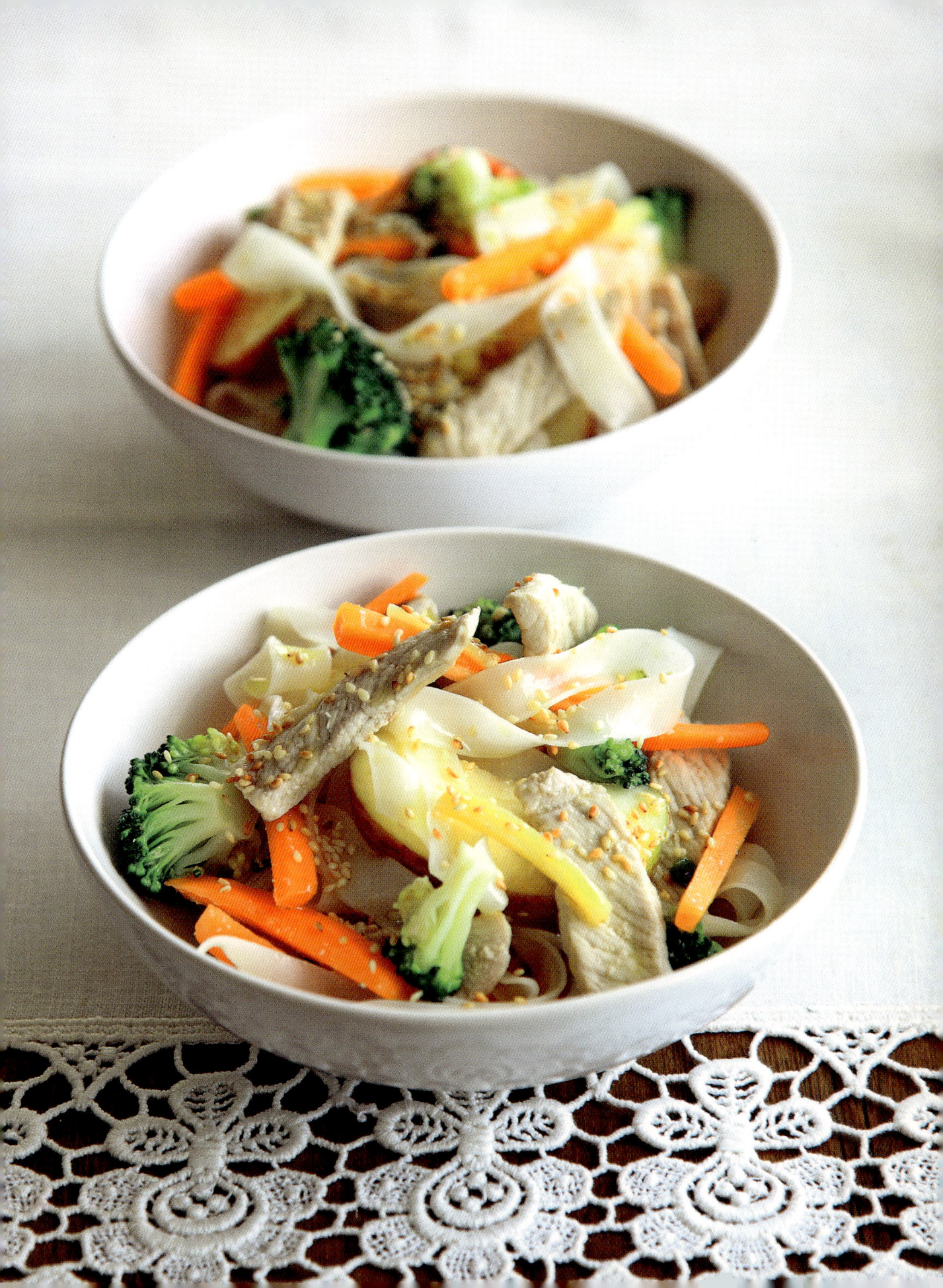

Lamb Cutlets with Pea and Rosemary Mashed Potatoes

Serves 4

6 russet potatoes, peeled and chopped
2⅓ cups frozen or fresh peas
1 tablespoon chopped rosemary
8 lamb cutlets
2 tablespoons butter
salt and black pepper

- Cook the potatoes in a saucepan of boiling water for 12–15 minutes, until tender, adding the peas 2 minutes before the end of the cooking time.

- Meanwhile, sprinkle half the rosemary over the lamb cutlets, then cook them under a preheated hot broiler for 3–4 minutes on each side, or until cooked to your liking. Let rest.

- Drain the potatoes and peas, then return to the pan and lightly mash with the remaining rosemary, the butter, and salt and black pepper to taste. Serve the lamb cutlets accompanied by the pea and rosemary mashed potatoes.

Rosemary Lamb Cutlets with Summer Salad Mix together 2 tablespoons chopped rosemary and 1 tablespoon olive oil in a small bowl, then rub over 8 lamb cutlets. Cook under a preheated hot broiler for 3–4 minutes on each side, or until cooked to your liking. Meanwhile, cook ⅔ cup fresh or frozen peas, ½ cup fava beans, and 4 oz asparagus tips in a saucepan of boiling water for 2–3 minutes. Drain, refresh under cold running water, and drain again, then toss together with 2 carrots, peeled and cut into matchsticks, 12 baby corn, the torn leaves of 1 romaine lettuce, a small handful of mint leaves, and 12 cherry tomatoes in a serving bowl. Drizzle with 2 tablespoons extra virgin olive oil and the juice of 1 lemon. Serve with the lamb.

Lamb Racks with Rosemary and Garlic Cut small slits into 4 (3-cutlet) racks of lamb and insert 2 sliced garlic cloves and 4 rosemary sprigs into the slits. Whisk together 1 tablespoon honey, 2 tablespoons whole-grain mustard, and 1 tablespoon store-bought mint sauce in a bowl, then brush over the lamb. Let marinate for 10 minutes. Place in a roasting pan and cook in a preheated oven, at 400°F, for 18 minutes, or until cooked to your liking, basting with the marinade 2 or 3 times. Serve the lamb with cooked asparagus and mashed potatoes.

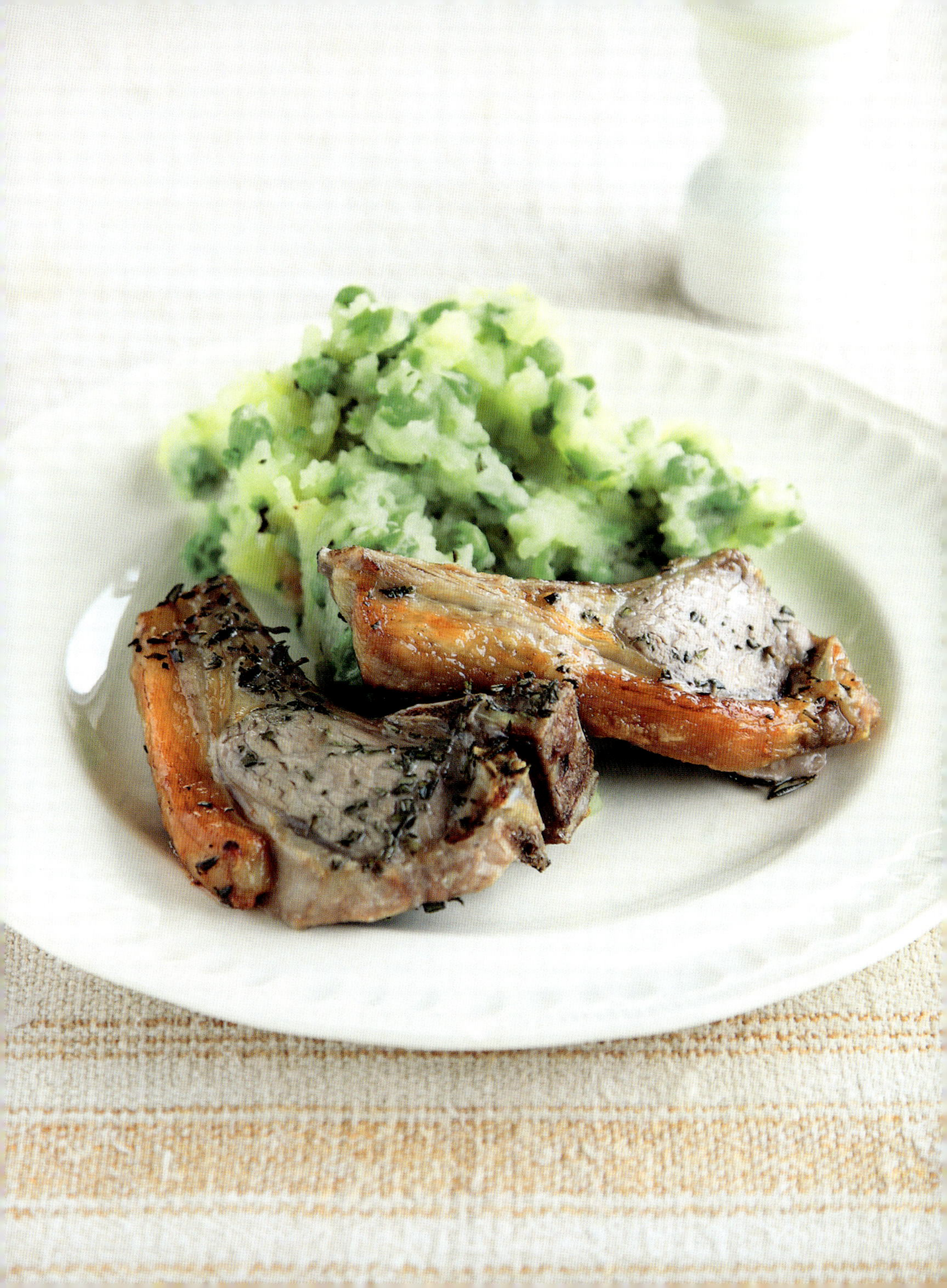

Chicken with Orange and Olives

Serves 4

2 tablespoons olive oil
4 (5 oz) boneless, skinless chicken breasts
3 cups chicken stock
a few thyme sprigs
12 ripe black olives, pitted
2 oranges, segmented
1⅔ cups bulgur wheat
3 tablespoons toasted slivered almonds
2 tablespoons chopped parsley
salt and black pepper

- Heat the oil in a large skillet, add the chicken, and cook for 3–4 minutes on each side, until browned. Pour in 2 cups of the stock, then stir in the thyme, olives, and orange segments. Cover and simmer for 15–16 minutes, until cooked through.

- Meanwhile, place the bulgur wheat in a saucepan with the remaining stock, season to taste, and simmer for 8–10 minutes, until most of the water is absorbed. Remove the pan from the heat and stir in the almonds, then cover and let stand.

- Remove the chicken from the skillet and keep warm. Simmer the sauce for 4–5 minutes, until reduced by half. Stir in the chopped parsley.

- Serve the chicken with the bulgur wheat, drizzled with the thyme, olive, and orange sauce.

Chicken, Orange, and Olive Sandwiches
Toast 8 slices of whole-wheat bread under a preheated hot broiler for 2–3 minutes on each side. Spread 4 of the slices with 2 teaspoons store-bought pesto each, then top each with a small handful of salad greens, a few orange segments, 2–3 slices of store-bought cooked chicken, 1 sliced tomato, and 2–3 sliced pitted olives. Top with the remaining toast and serve.

Grilled Chicken, Orange, and Olive Salad
Mix together 2 crushed garlic cloves, 2 tablespoons olive oil, and 2 tablespoons chopped basil in a dish, then add 4 (5 oz) boneless, skinless chicken breasts and let marinate for 2–3 minutes. Heat a ridged grill pan until hot, add the chicken breasts, and cook for 6–8 minutes on each side or until cooked through. Meanwhile, toss together 1 coarsely torn romaine lettuce, 1 cup arugula leaves, 1 sliced red onion, 12 pitted ripe black olives, and 6 halved cherry tomatoes in a serving bowl. Segment 2 oranges over a bowl to catch the juice, then add the segments to the salad. Whisk together the reserved juice, 3 tablespoons olive oil, and ½ teaspoon each of sugar and mustard. Cut the chicken into thick slices and add to the salad. Serve sprinkled with the dressing.

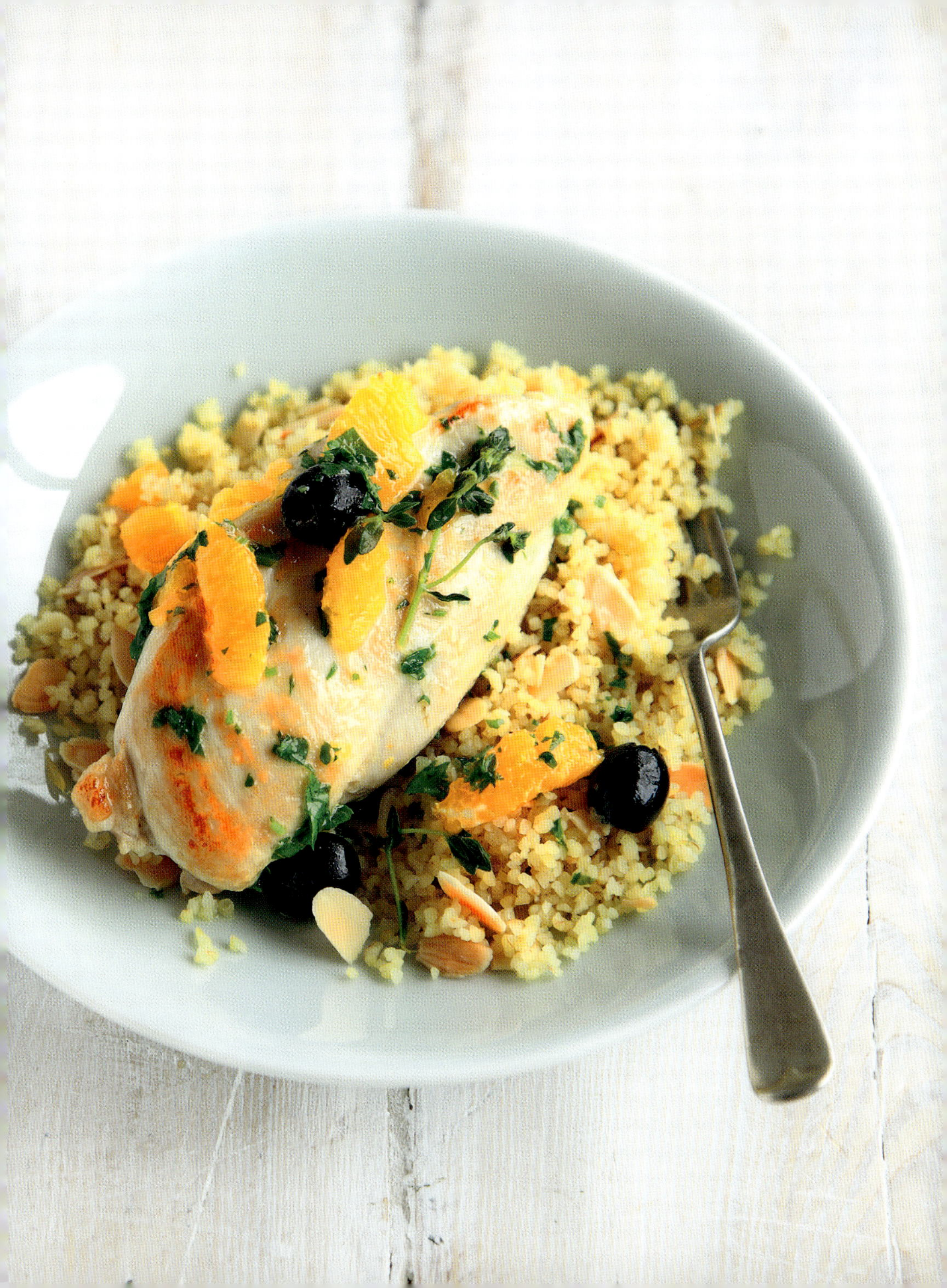

Harissa Beef Fajitas

Serves 4

3 teaspoons harissa paste
½ teaspoon paprika
2 tablespoons olive oil
1 lb top sirloin steak, cut into thick strips
8 tortilla wraps
½ iceburg lettuce, shredded
¼ cup sour cream
¼ cup store-bought guacamole
¼ cup store-bought tomato salsa
¼ cup shredded cheddar cheese

- Mix together the harissa, paprika, and oil in a nonmetallic bowl. Add the steak and mix to coat, then cover and let marinate for 5 minutes.

- Heat a ridged grill pan until hot, add the steak, and cook for 20 seconds on each side, or until cooked to your liking. Remove from the pan and keep warm.

- Heat the tortillas in a microwave according to the package directions. Sprinkle some shredded lettuce in the center of each tortilla and layer the steak on top. Spoon a little sour cream, guacamole, and salsa over the steak, then sprinkle with the cheese. Roll up the wraps and serve.

Harissa Beef Salad

Mix together 3 teaspoons harissa paste and 2 tablespoons olive oil in a bowl, then rub over 3 (5 oz) top sirloin steaks. Cover and let marinate for 10 minutes. Meanwhile, toss together 1 chopped cucumber, 4 chopped tomatoes, 4 scallions, ½ thickly shredded iceburg lettuce, and a handful each of fresh mint and cilantro leaves in a bowl. Whisk together 2 teaspoons sugar, 2 tablespoons Thai fish sauce, the juice of 1 lime, and 2 tablespoons olive oil, then pour the dressing over the salad. Heat a ridged grill pan until hot, add the steaks, and cook for 2–3 minutes on each side, or until cooked to your liking. Let rest for 2–3 minutes. Slice the steak across the grain and add to the salad. Serve sprinkled with 2 tablespoons chopped peanuts.

Harissa Hamburgers

Place 1 lb ground chuck beef, 2 tablespoons chopped cilantro, 1 tablespoon harissa paste, 1 chopped onion, 1 egg yolk, 1 tablespoon olive oil, and salt and black pepper in a food processor and blend together. Shape into 4 equal patties, cover, and chill for 10 minutes. Cook the patties under a preheated medium broiler for 15 minutes, turning once. Toast 4 halved burger buns. Place a burger on each bottom and top with iceburg lettuce, sliced tomatoes, sliced red onion, and a spoonful of mayonnaise or sour cream. Top with the lids and serve.

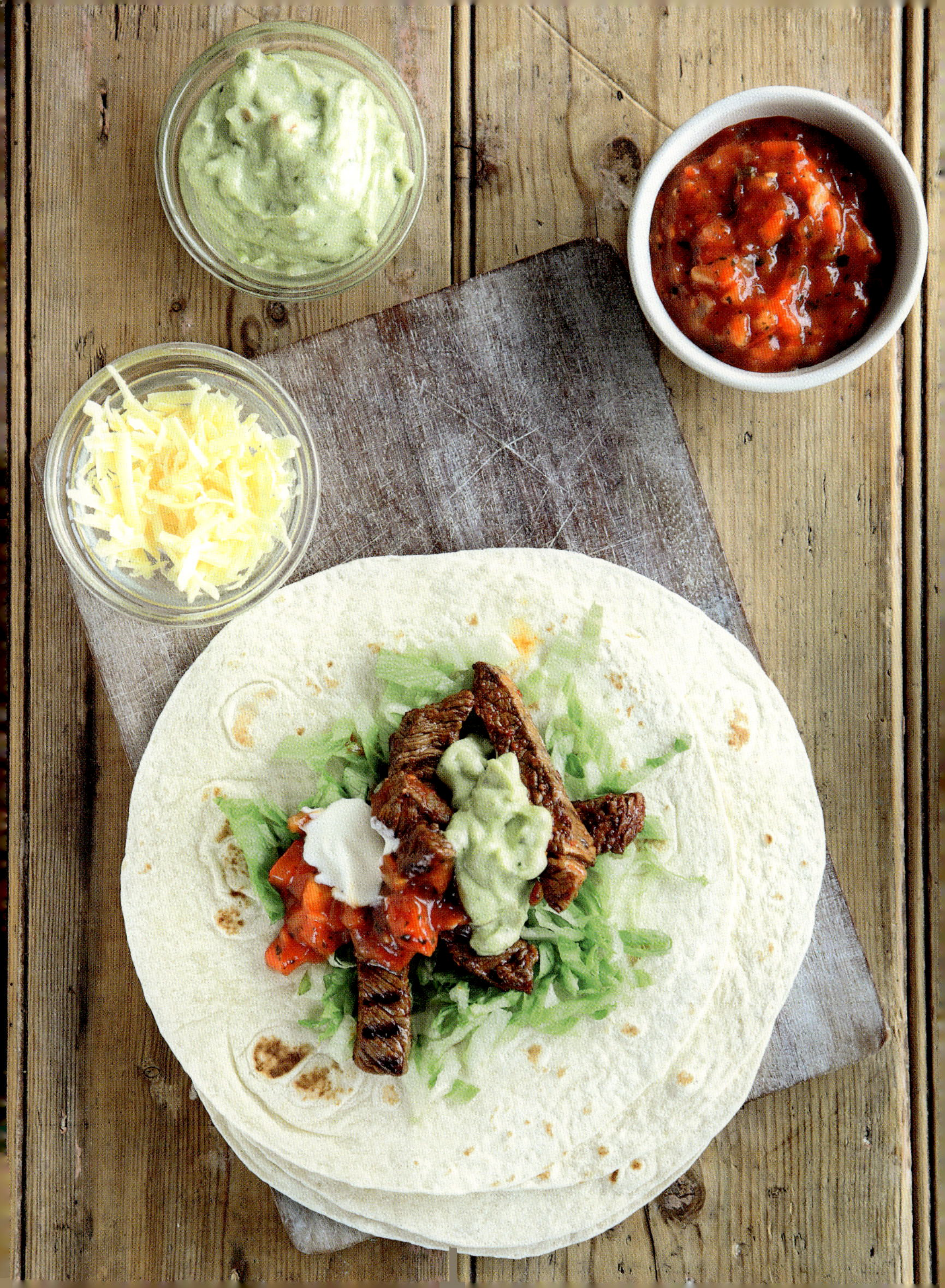

Ginger Chicken Soup

Serves 4

1 tablespoon peanut oil
1-inch piece of fresh ginger root, peeled and grated
10 oz chicken breast strips
4 cups hot chicken stock
4 bok choy, sliced
8 oz dried egg noodles
2 tablespoons sesame seeds

- Heat the oil in a wok or large saucepan, add the ginger, and stir-fry for 1 minute, then stir in the chicken and ½ cup of the stock. Bring to a boil, then cook over high heat for 5 minutes or until the chicken is cooked through.

- Add the remaining stock and bring to a simmer. Stir in the bok choy and noodles and simmer for 5 minutes, until the noodles are cooked.

- Meanwhile, heat a nonstick skillet over medium-low heat and dry-fry the sesame seeds for 2 minutes, stirring frequently, until golden brown and toasted.

- Ladle the soup into bowls and serve sprinkled with the toasted sesame seeds.

Ginger Chicken Wraps Heat 1 tablespoon olive oil in a skillet, add 1 lb thinly sliced skinless, boneless chicken breasts, 1 tablespoon peeled and grated fresh ginger root, 2 diced garlic cloves, and 6 sliced scallions, and sauté, stirring, for 5–6 minutes or until the chicken is cooked through. Divide the chicken among 4 tortilla wraps, then top with 1 red and 1 yellow bell pepper, both cored, seeded, and sliced, and ½ shredded romaine lettuce. Roll up the wraps and serve.

Ginger Chicken Stir-Fry Heat 1 tablespoon olive oil or coconut oil in a wok, add 2 crushed garlic cloves, a 2-inch piece of fresh ginger root, peeled and grated, and 1 lb sliced skinless, boneless chicken breasts, and stir-fry for 3–4 minutes. Add 4 chopped scallions, 2 peeled and sliced carrots, and 4 halved baby corn and stir-fry for another 4–5 minutes. Add 2 tablespoons soy sauce, 2 tablespoons oyster sauce, and ½ cup water and simmer for 15 minutes. Stir in 2 chopped bok choy and ½ cup bean sprouts and cook for 2–3 minutes, until heated through. Serve with cooked long-grain rice.

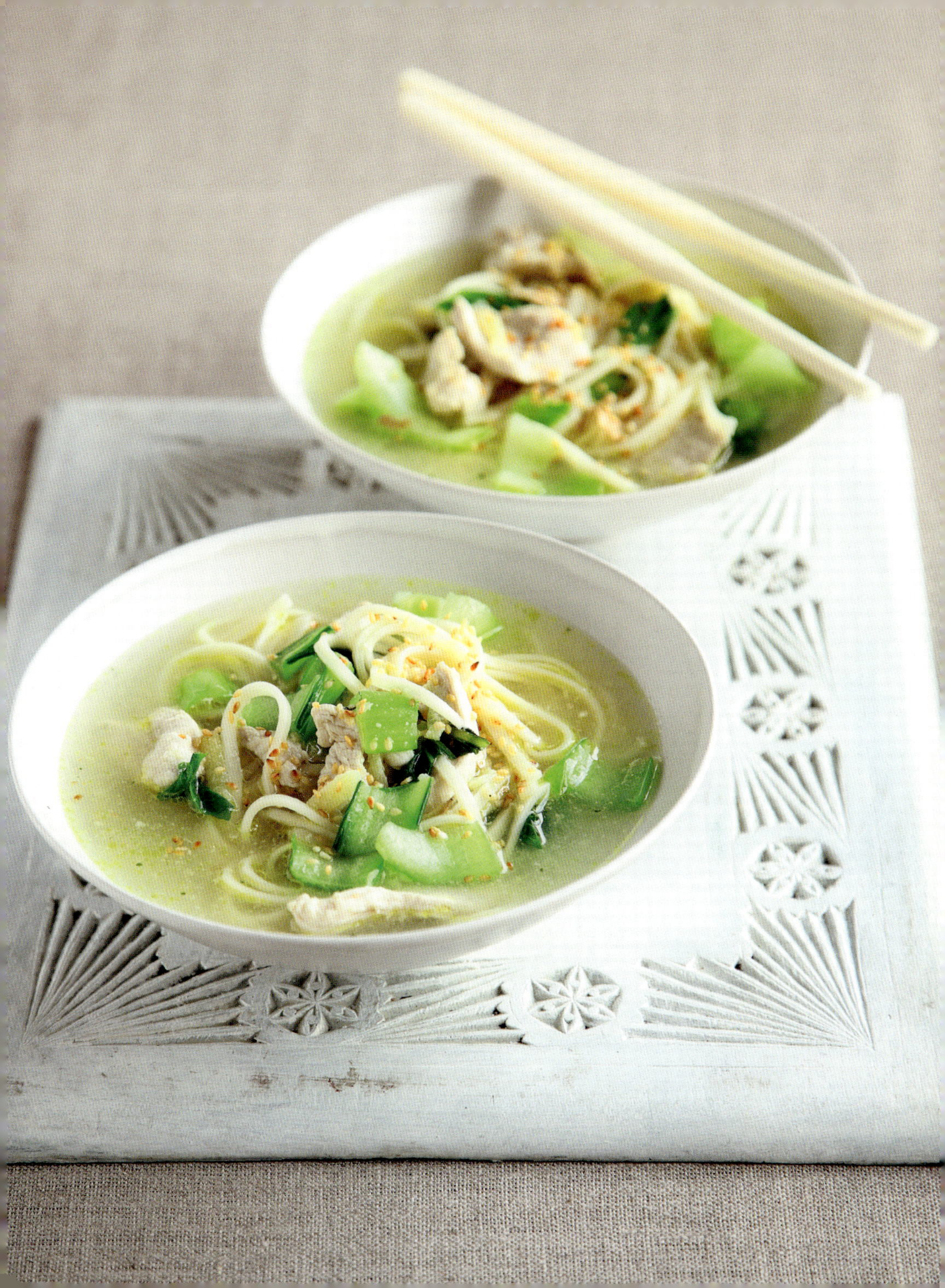

30 Bacon and Leek Tortilla

Serves 4–6

¼ cup olive oil
2 leeks, trimmed and thickly sliced
11 oz new potatoes, sliced
4 bacon slices, chopped
6 extra-large eggs
¾ cup shredded sharp cheddar cheese
salt and black pepper

- Heat the oil in a large flameproof skillet, add the leeks and potatoes, and sauté for 8–10 minutes, stirring frequently, until golden and tender. Add the bacon and cook for another 4–5 minutes.

- Meanwhile, beat the eggs in a large bowl and add the cheese. Season well.

- Stir the potato mixture into the beaten eggs, then return to the skillet and cook over low heat for 8–10 minutes, making sure the bottom does not overcook.

- Place the skillet under a preheated hot broiler and cook for another 3–4 minutes, until the tortilla is cooked through and golden.

- Serve cut into wedges.

10 Leek, Butternut, and Bacon Soup

Heat 2 tablespoons olive oil in a saucepan, add 3 trimmed and diced leeks and 3 cups peeled, seeded, and diced butternut squash and cook for 3 minutes. Pour in 4 cups hot vegetable stock and bring to a boil, then reduce the heat and simmer for 4–5 minutes, until the vegetables are soft. Meanwhile, cook 4 bacon slices under a preheated hot broiler until crisp, then coarsely chop. Stir 1¼ cups soy milk into the soup, then, using a handhand blender, blend the soup until smooth. Season to taste. Serve sprinkled with the bacon.

20 Bacon and Leek Penne

Cook 1 lb penne in a saucepan of boiling water according to package directions, until "al dente." Meanwhile, heat 2 tablespoons olive oil in a skillet, add 4 oz chopped bacon, and cook for 2–3 minutes. Add 2 trimmed and sliced leeks and 2 crushed garlic cloves and cook for another 6–8 minutes, then stir in 2 chopped tomatoes and 2 tablespoons chopped parsley. Drain the pasta and toss in the pan with the bacon mixture. Season and serve sprinkled with grated Parmesan cheese.

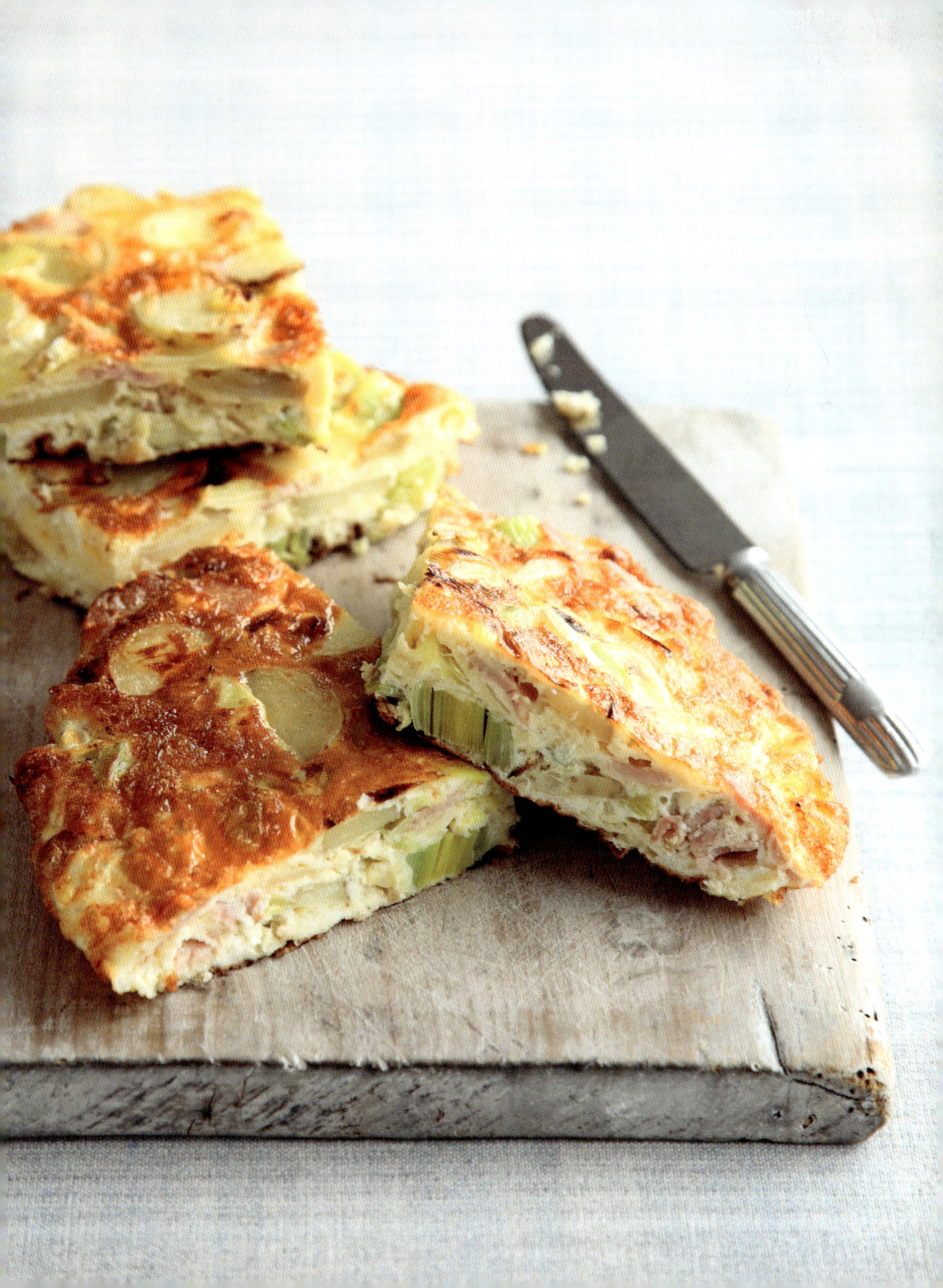

30 Spicy Chicken with Cucumber and Radish Salad

Serves 4

¼ cup honey
2 tablespoons soy sauce
juice of ½ lemon
a few drops of Tabasco
2 garlic cloves, crushed
4 (5 oz) chicken breasts
2 tablespoons sesame seeds, toasted

For the salad

1 cucumber
1 tablespoon sea salt
2 tablespoons sugar
1 tablespoon boiling water
¼ cup white wine vinegar
1 teaspoon black pepper
a handful of dill, finely chopped
6 radishes, thinly sliced

- Mix together the honey, soy sauce, lemon juice, Tabasco, and garlic in a nonmetallic bowl, then brush the marinade over the chicken breasts. Cover and let marinate in the refrigerator for 10 minutes. Cook under a preheated hot broiler for 6–8 minutes on each side, brushing frequently with the marinade, until cooked through.

- Meanwhile, make the salad. Using a vegetable peeler or mandolin, thinly slice the cucumber. Place in a colander and toss with the salt. Let stand for 10 minutes to let the juices run out.

- Place the sugar and water into a bowl and stir until the sugar is dissolved. Add the vinegar, black pepper, and dill. Chill for 2 minutes.

- Wrap the cucumber in a clean dish towel and squeeze gently to remove any excess water, then stir into the dill mixture with the radishes. Cover and chill until ready to serve.

- Divide the salad among 4 plates. Slice the chicken breasts and add to the salad. Serve sprinkled with the sesame seeds.

---

10 Chicken, Cucumber, and Radish Pita Breads

Toast 4 whole-wheat pita breads under a preheated broiler until warmed through, then cut down 1 long edge to form pockets. Meanwhile, mix together ½ sliced cucumber, 6 sliced radishes, 1 tablespoon chopped dill, and 2 cups baby spinach leaves in a bowl, then gently toss with 12 oz store-bought cooked chicken slices and ¼ cup Caesar salad dressing. Stuff into the pitas and serve.

20 Spicy Chicken with Cucumber and Radish Stir-Fry

Mix together 2 tablespoons honey, the juice of 2 limes, 2 tablespoons Chinese five-spice powder, and 1 teaspoon sesame oil in a bowl, then spread over 8 chicken drumsticks. Place in an ovenproof dish and bake in a preheated oven, at 400°F, for 16–18 minutes or until cooked through. Meanwhile, mix together 4 chopped bok choy, 1 peeled and thinly sliced carrot, ½ cup bean sprouts, ¼ seeded and sliced cucumber, 6 sliced radishes, 2 tablespoons soy sauce, a 1-inch piece of peeled and chopped fresh ginger root, and a pinch of dried red pepper flakes in a bowl. Heat 1 tablespoon peanut oil in a wok, add the vegetables, and stir-fry for 5–6 minutes, until starting to wilt. Serve hot with the crispy chicken.

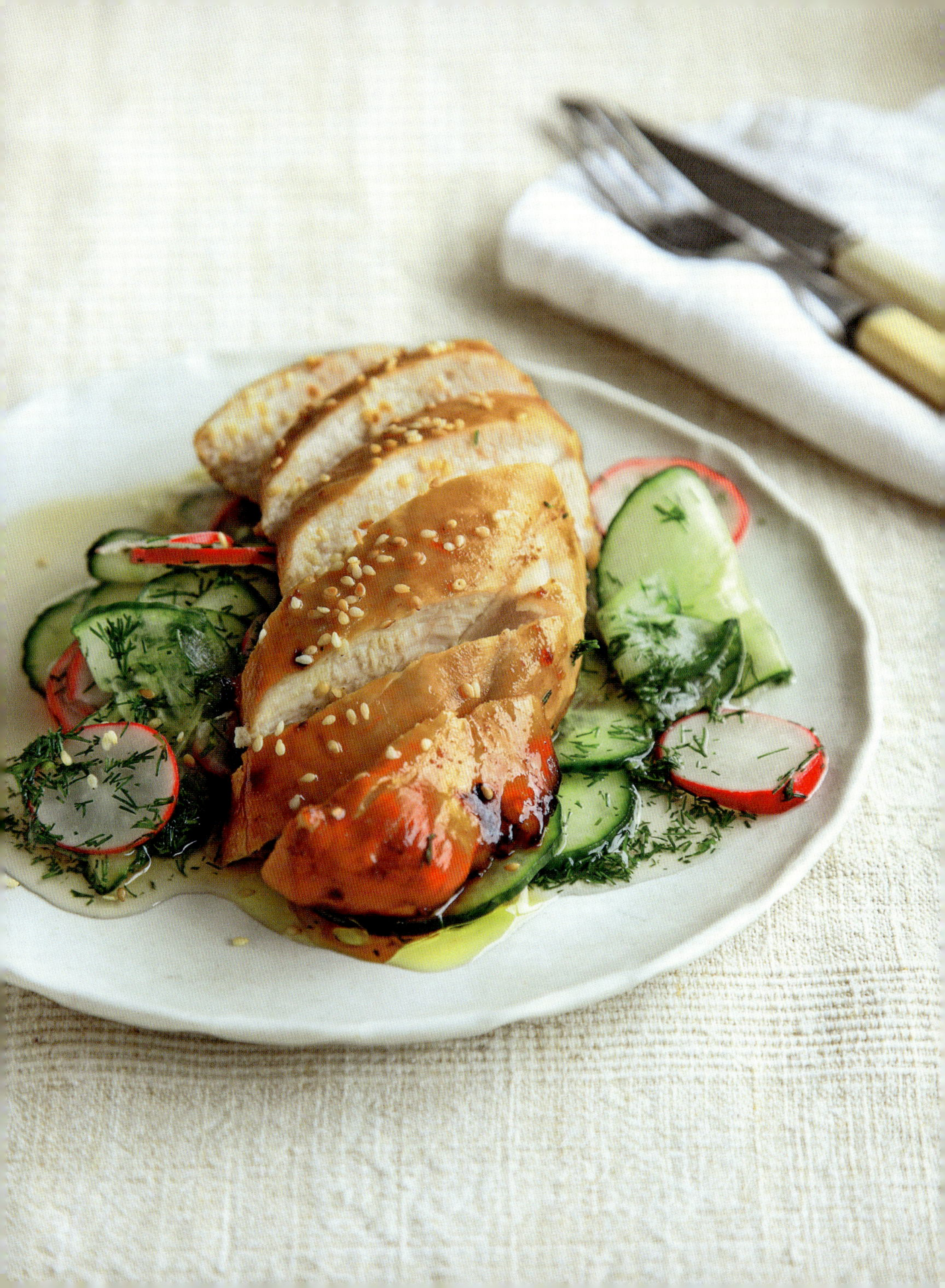

30 Horseradish Beef with Quinoa

Serves 4

1¼ lb London broil or flank steak, rolled and tied
1 tablespoon creamed horseradish
2 tablespoons olive oil
2 cups quinoa
1 red onion, thinly sliced
2 cups sliced cremini mushrooms
1 tablespoon chopped parsley
1 tablespoon chopped mint
2 cups arugula leaves
3 tablespoons balsamic glaze

- Brush the beef with the horseradish. Heat 1 tablespoon of the oil in a skillet over high heat, add the beef, and sear on all sides until browned. Transfer to a roasting pan and place in a preheated oven, at 400°F, for 20 minutes. Cover with aluminum foil and let rest for 5–6 minutes, then slice.

- Meanwhile, cook the quinoa in a saucepan of boiling water for 8–9 minutes, or according to the package directions.

- Heat the remaining oil in a large skillet, add the onion, and cook for 2 minutes, then add the mushrooms and cook for another 5–6 minutes, until softened. Remove from the heat and stir in the chopped herbs.

- Drain the quinoa and stir into the mushroom mixture. Divide among 4 warm plates and top with the arugula and sliced beef. Serve drizzled with the balsamic glaze.

10 Horseradish Steak Sandwiches

Drizzle 1 tablespoon olive oil over 4 (6 oz) top sirloin steaks and season. Heat a ridged grill pan to hot and cook the steaks for 3 minutes on each side, or to your liking, then let rest. Reduce the heat to medium and cook 1 onion, sliced into rings, for 1 minute on each side. Meanwhile, toast 4 split ciabatta rolls under a preheated hot broiler. Mix ¼ cup mayo with 2 teaspoons creamed horseradish, then spread over the bottoms. Top with the torn leaves of ½ romaine lettuce, the onion, the sliced steak, and 4 sliced tomatoes. Add the lids and serve.

20 Steak and Chickpea Salad with Horseradish Dressing

Toss together 2 (15 oz) cans chickpeas, rinsed and drained, 1 sliced red onion, 12 halved cherry tomatoes, and a small handful of chopped parsley in a serving bowl. Season a 1 lb top sirloin steak. Heat a ridged grill pan until piping hot, add the steak, and cook for 3 minutes on each side, or until cooked to your liking, then let rest. Whisk together 1 cup plain yogurt, 1 tablespoon creamed horseradish, 1 tablespoon olive oil, and the juice of ½ lemon in a bowl. Slice the steak, toss with the chickpeas, and drizzle with the yogurt dressing.

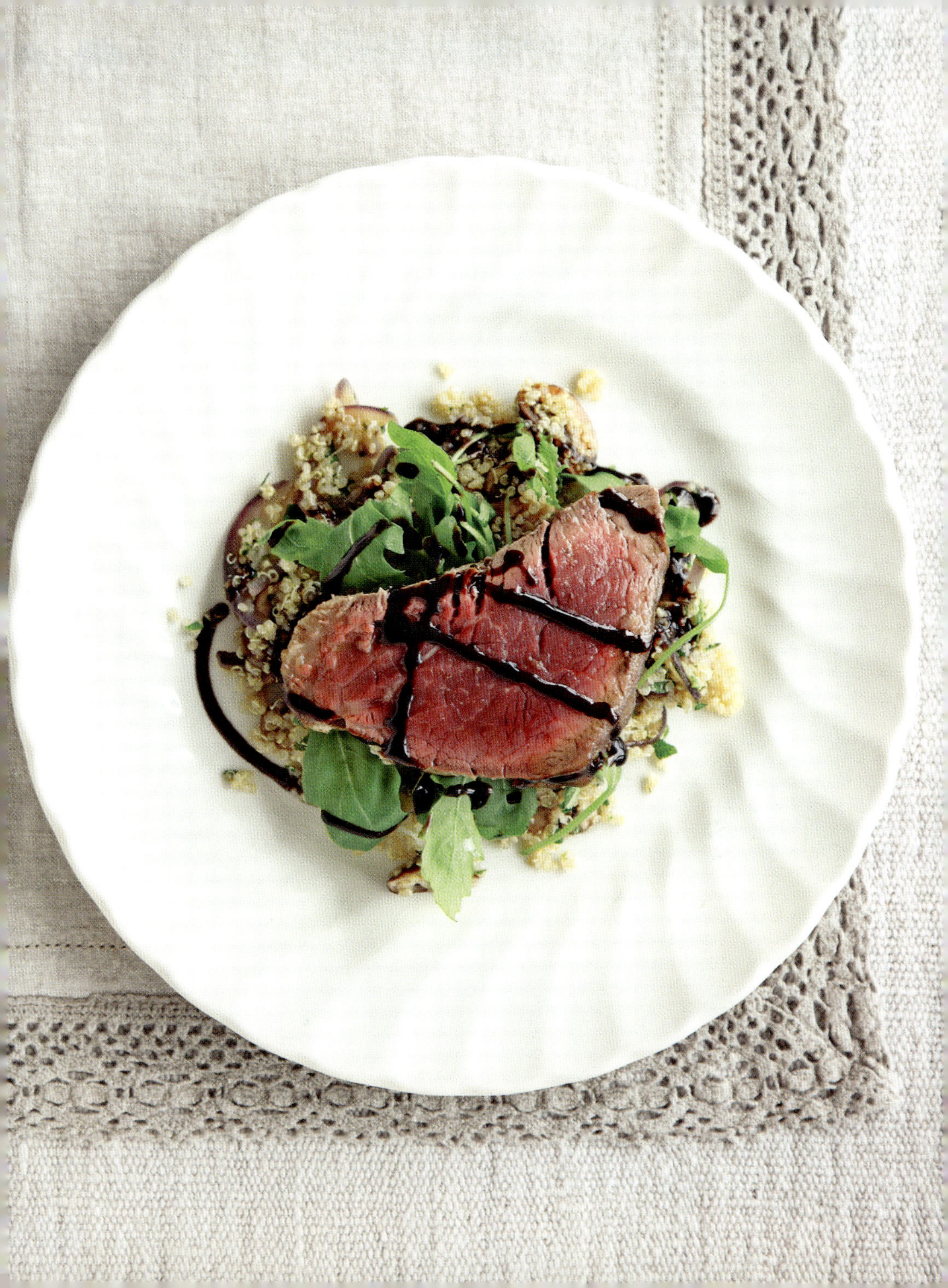

10 Chicken and Vegetable Stir-Fry

Serves 4

2 tablespoons coconut oil
1¼-inch piece of fresh ginger root, peeled and finely diced
2 garlic cloves, crushed
1 onion, chopped
1 lb chicken breast strips
2 cups quartered mushrooms
3 cups broccoli florets
2 cups chopped curly kale
1–2 tablespoons soy sauce
2 tablespoons sesame seeds

- Heat the oil in a wok or large skillet until hot, add the ginger, garlic, and onion, and stir-fry for 30 seconds. Add the chicken and stir-fry for another 2–3 minutes.

- Add the vegetables, then sprinkle with the soy sauce. Stir-fry for 1–2 minutes, then cover and steam for another 4–5 minutes, until the vegetables are tender and the chicken is cooked through.

- Serve sprinkled with the sesame seeds.

20 Chicken and Asian Vegetable Stir-Fry

Heat 2 tablespoons coconut oil in a wok until hot, add 6 chopped scallions, 2 crushed garlic cloves, and 1 tablespoon peeled and grated ginger root, and stir-fry for 2 minutes. Add 1 lb chicken breast strips and stir-fry for 2–3 minutes. Add 8 baby corn and 1 cored, seeded, and sliced red bell pepper and stir-fry for another 3–4 minutes. Stir in 4 oz shiitake mushrooms, chopped, ½ cup bean sprouts, and 2 chopped bok choy and stir-fry for 4–5 minutes. Stir in 2 tablespoons oyster sauce and 1 teaspoon soy sauce and cook for another 4–5 minutes. Serve sprinkled with 2 tablespoons toasted sesame seeds.

30 Chicken, Vegetable, and Noodle Stir-Fry

Mix together 3 tablespoons soy sauce, 2 tablespoons red wine, 2 crushed garlic cloves, 2 teaspoons honey, and 1 teaspoon Dijon mustard in a nonmetallic bowl. Add 1 lb skinless, boneless chicken breasts, cut into thick strips, and toss in the marinade. Let marinate for about 15 minutes. Drain, reserving the marinade. Heat 2 teaspoons peanut oil in a wok or large skillet until hot, add half the drained chicken, and stir-fry for 2–3 minutes or until cooked through, then remove with a slotted spoon and keep warm. Repeat with the remaining chicken. Add 2 thinly sliced garlic cloves, a 1½-inch piece of fresh ginger root, peeled and cut into strips, and 2 carrots, peeled and cut into batons, to the wok and stir-fry for 3–4 minutes. Add 1 trimmed leek, cut into strips, and stir-fry for another 2 minutes, then add 1 lb udon noodles and the reserved marinade, cover, and cook for 2 minutes, until the noodles are softened. Add the reserved chicken to the wok, toss together well, and heat through.

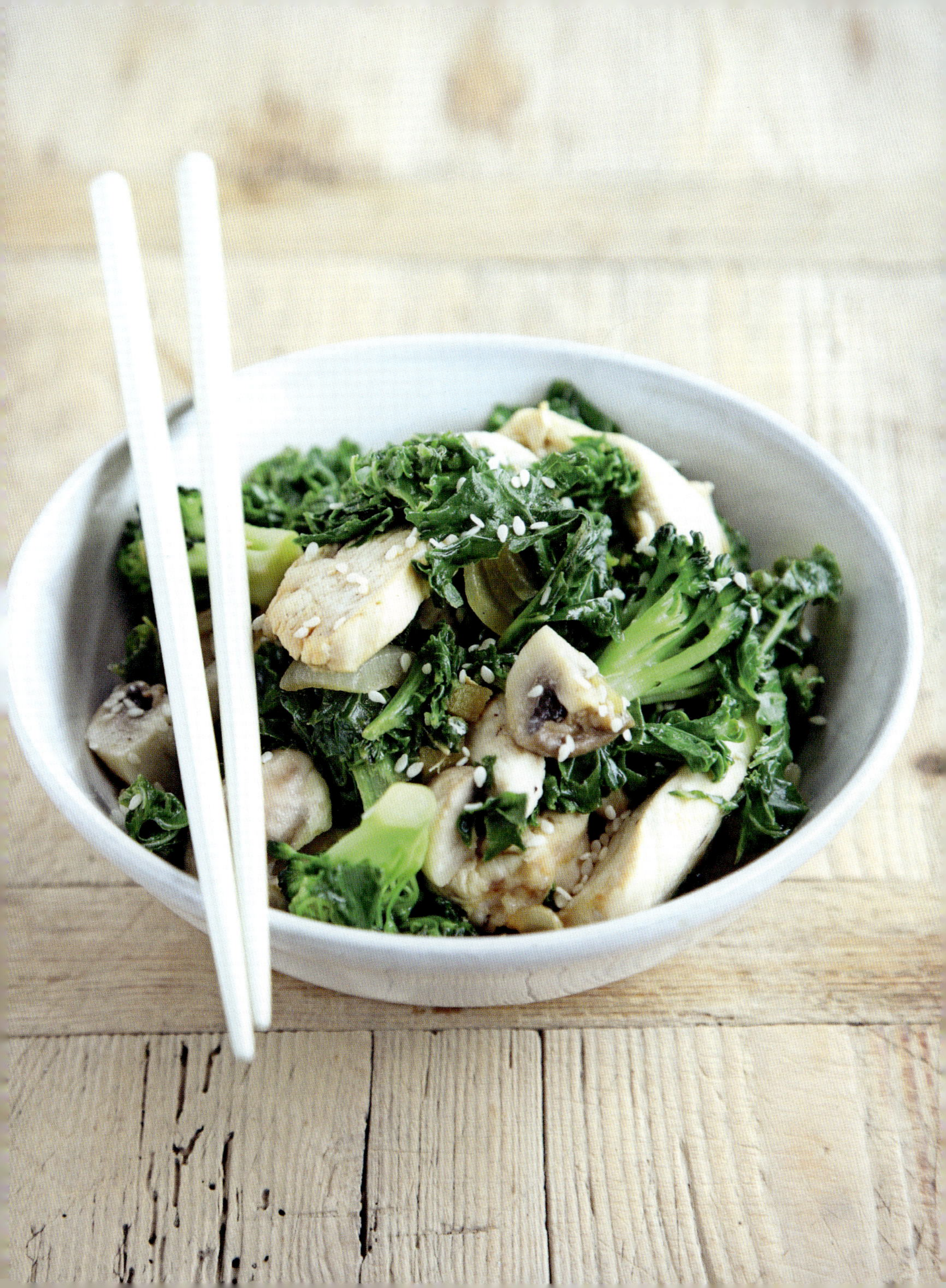

30 Roasted Pork Loin with Creamy Cabbage and Leeks

Serves 4

- 1 teaspoon ground cumin
- 1 teaspoon ground coriander
- 1 lb pork loin, trimmed of fat
- 3 tablespoons olive oil
- 2 sweet potatoes, peeled and chopped
- 3 cups shredded savoy cabbage
- 3 leeks, trimmed and sliced
- 3 tablespoons sour cream
- 2 teaspoons whole-grain mustard

- Mix together the spices in a bowl, then rub over the pork. Heat 1 tablespoon of the oil in an ovenproof skillet, add the pork, and cook until browned on all sides. Transfer to a preheated oven, at 350°F, and cook for 20–25 minutes or until cooked through. Let rest for 2 minutes.

- Meanwhile, cook the sweet potatoes in a saucepan of boiling water for 12–15 minutes, until tender, adding the cabbage and leeks 3–4 minutes before the end of the cooking time. Drain well.

- Heat the remaining oil in a skillet, add the vegetables, and cook for 7–8 minutes, until starting to turn golden. Stir in the cream and mustard.

- Slice the pork and serve on top of the vegetables.

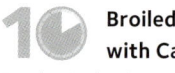

---

1 Broiled Pork Chops with Cabbage and Leek Mashed Potatoes

Cook 4 (5 oz) pork chops under a preheated hot broiler for 5 minutes on each side or until cooked through. Meanwhile, cook 4 peeled and finely diced russet potatoes, ½ finely shredded savoy cabbage, and 2 trimmed and finely sliced leeks in a saucepan of boiling water for 8 minutes, until tender. Drain, then mash in the pan with 2 tablespoons plain yogurt and salt and black pepper. Serve with the pork.

2 Pork Cutlets with Cabbage and Leek Potato Cakes

Cook 4 peeled and diced russet potatoes in a saucepan of boiling water for 8–10 minutes, until tender. Meanwhile, heat 1 tablespoon olive oil in a skillet, add ½ finely shredded cabbage and 1 trimmed and diced leek, and cook for 3–4 minutes, until soft. Drain the potatoes, return to the pan, and mash. Stir in the cabbage and leeks and transfer to a bowl to cool slightly. Shape into 8 patties, then dredge with a little flour. Melt 4 tablespoons butter with the juice of ½ lemon and 1 crushed garlic clove in a skillet. Brush 4 (5 oz) pork cutlets with the butter, then cook under a preheated hot broiler for 3–4 minutes on each side or until cooked through. Meanwhile, heat 2 tablespoons olive oil in a separate skillet, add the potato cakes, and cook for 2–3 minutes on each side. Serve with the pork.

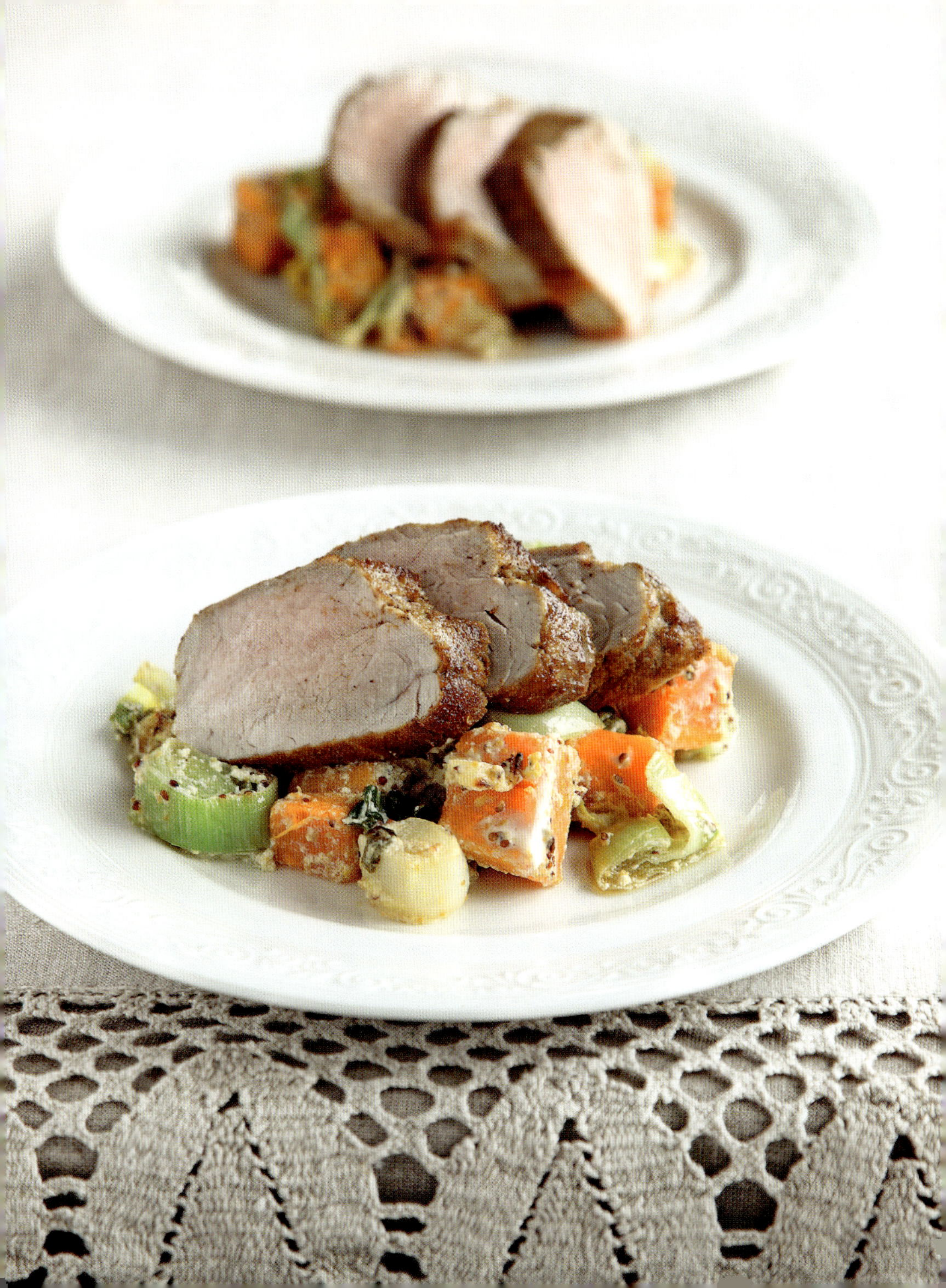

30 Nectarine-Glazed Chicken Kebabs

Serves 4

2 nectarines, halved, pitted, and coarsely chopped
1½-inch piece of fresh ginger root, peeled and coarsely chopped
2 garlic cloves, chopped
1 teaspoon soy sauce
1 teaspoon Worcestershire sauce
2 teaspoons olive oil
1¼ lb skinless, boneless chicken breasts, cut into bite-size pieces
1 red bell pepper, cored, seeded, and cut into bite-size pieces
1 yellow bell pepper, cored, seeded, and cut into bite-size pieces
crisp green salad, to serve

- Place the nectarines, ginger, garlic, soy sauce, Worcestershire sauce, and oil in a small food processor or blender and process until completely smooth.
- Place the chicken and bell peppers in a nonmetallic bowl and pour over the marinade. Cover and let marinate in the refrigerator for 5 minutes.
- Thread the pieces of chicken and bell pepper onto metal skewers and cook under a preheated medium broiler or on a barbecue grill for 12–15 minutes, turning frequently, or until the chicken is cooked through.
- Serve with a crisp green salad.

1 Chicken and Nectarine Salad

Whisk together 1 tablespoon white wine vinegar, 3 tablespoons olive oil, 1 tablespoon chopped mint, 1 teaspoon honey, and ½ teaspoon Dijon mustard in a bowl. Toss together 3 halved, pitted, and sliced nectarines, 1 lb store-bought cooked chicken breast, cubed, 1 chopped cucumber, ½ sliced red onion, and 2 cups arugula leaves in a serving bowl. Toss with the dressing and serve with crusty bread.

2 Chicken Satay with Nectarine Salad

Soak 16 wooden skewers in water for 10 minutes. Meanwhile, cut 1 lb skinless, boneless chicken breasts into strips, then lay on a board, cover with plastic wrap, and bash with a meat mallet or rolling pin to flatten slightly. Mix together 3 tablespoons soy sauce, 1 tablespoon vegetable oil, 1 tablespoon lime juice, 1 teaspoon each of ground cumin and ground coriander, and 2 crushed garlic cloves in a nonmetallic bowl. Add the chicken and mix to coat well, then cover and marinate in the refrigerator for 5 minutes. Mix together 1 tablespoon oyster sauce, 1 tablespoon chunky peanut butter, 3 tablespoons sweet chili sauce, and the juice of ½ lime in a small bowl. Using a vegetable peeler, slice 1 cucumber into long, thin strips and place on a serving plate with 2 halved, pitted, and thinly sliced nectarines. Thread the chicken strips onto the skewers, then cook under a preheated hot broiler or on a barbecue grill for 2 minutes on each side or until cooked through. Serve with the cucumber salad and the peanut sauce for dipping.

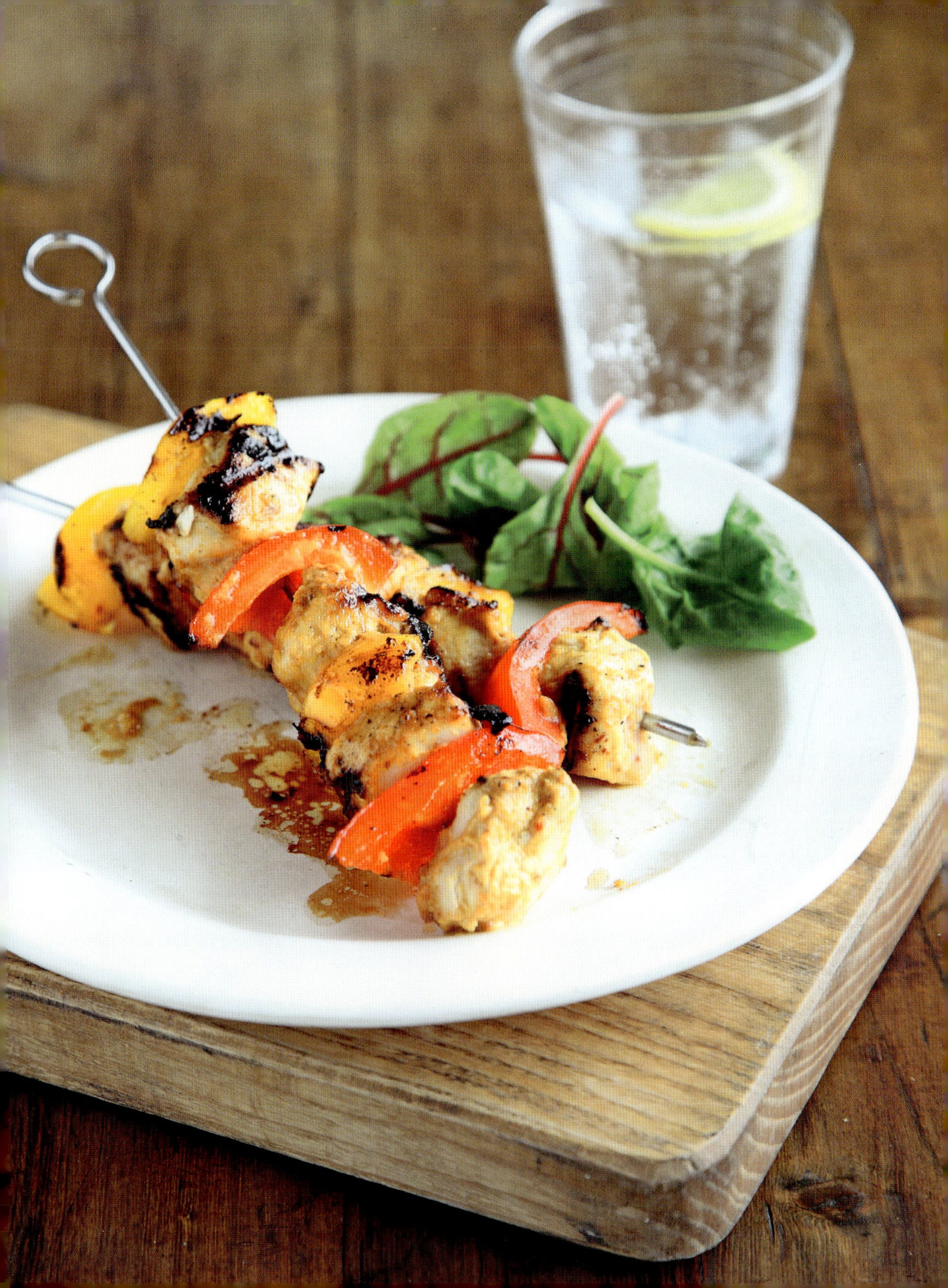

20 Calf Liver with Caramelized Onions

Serves 4

3 tablespoons olive oil
1 large onion, finely sliced
4 teaspoons balsamic vinegar
1 teaspoon sugar
6 russet potatoes, peeled and chopped
3 sweet potatoes, peeled and chopped
2 tablespoons all-purpose flour
½ tablespoon freshly ground black pepper
1 lb calf liver, cut into strips
2 tablespoons butter
1 cup arugula leaves
salt and black pepper

- Heat 1 tablespoon of the oil in a skillet, add the onion, and sauté over medium heat for about 5 minutes. Add the vinegar and sugar and cook for another 15 minutes, stirring occasionally, until caramelized.

- Meanwhile, cook the potatoes and sweet potatoes in a saucepan of boiling water for 12–15 minutes, until tender.

- Mix together the flour and freshly ground black pepper on a plate. Toss the liver in the flour to coat. Heat the remaining oil in a separate skillet, add the liver, and cook over high heat for 2–3 minutes on each side until golden, being careful to avoid overcooking it.

- Drain the potatoes, then return to the pan and mash with the butter and salt and black pepper. Stir in the arugula, then serve with the liver and onions.

10 Calf Liver Pâté with Caramelized Onion

Heat 1½ sticks butter in a skillet, add 1 large chopped onion and 2 crushed garlic cloves, and cook for 2–3 minutes. Add 12 oz chopped calf liver and 4 finely chopped bacon slices and cook over medium heat for 4–5 minutes. Transfer to a food processor with a dash of Worcestershire sauce, a pinch of nutmeg, and 2 teaspoons thyme leaves and process until smooth. Serve on toasted slices of baguette with store-bought caramelized onion.

30 Calf Liver with Caramelized Shallot Sauce

Melt 2 tablespoons butter in a skillet, add 2 finely chopped shallots, and cook over low heat for 10 minutes, then add 1 tablespoon capers, rinsed and drained, and ¾ cup sherry and simmer until reduced by half. Stir in 2 teaspoons sherry vinegar, ⅔ cup beef stock, and 2 tablespoons butter and whisk until starting to thicken. Stir in 1 tablespoon chopped sage. Meanwhile, cook 5 peeled and chopped russet potatoes in a saucepan of boiling water for 15–16 minutes, until tender. Heat 1 tablespoon olive oil in a separate large skillet, add 4 (6 oz) pieces of calf liver, and cook over high heat for 2–3 minutes on each side. Drain the potatoes, then mash in the pan with 1 tablespoon plain yogurt and salt and black pepper. Serve with the liver, with the sauce poured over the top.

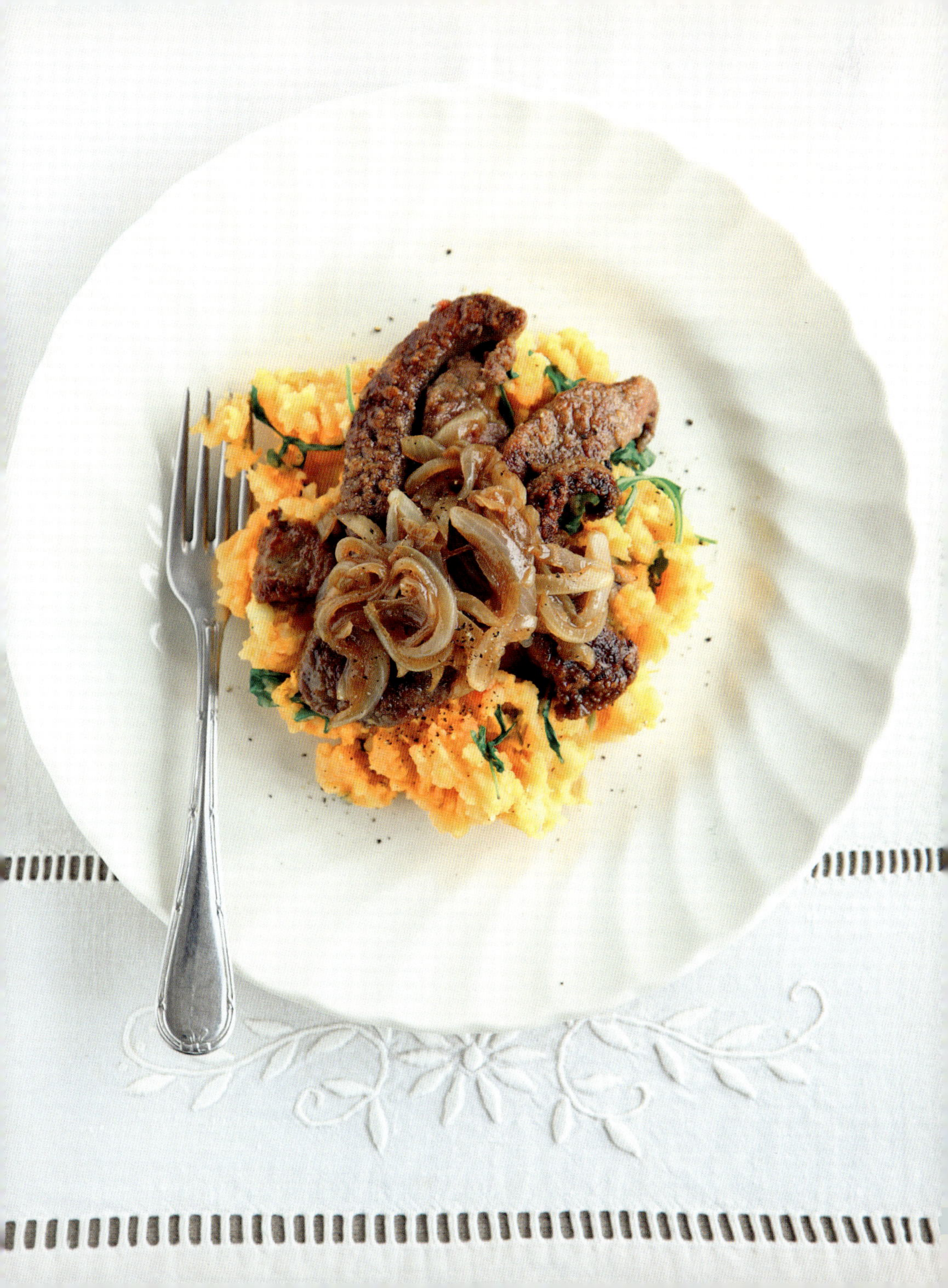

10 Curried Chicken with Avocado Salad

Serves 4

⅔ cup mayonnaise
1½ teaspoons mild curry powder
1 teaspoon ground allspice
1 red chile, seeded and diced
juice of ½ lime
⅓ cup mango chutney
⅓ cup Greek yogurt
1 lb cooked chicken, shredded
½ iceburg lettuce, leaves torn
¾ bunch of watercress
 or 1½ cups arugula
2 avocados, peeled and sliced
2 large beefsteak tomatoes, sliced
2 tablespoons toasted slivered almonds

- Mix together the mayonnaise, curry powder, allspice, chile, lime juice, chutney, and yogurt in a large bowl, then stir in the chicken.

- Place the lettuce on a serving plate, then top with the watercress or arugula, avocados, and tomatoes.

- Spoon the chicken over the salad and serve sprinkled with the almonds.

20 Chicken Kebabs with Avocado Dip

Grind 2 garlic cloves, 1 tablespoon grated ginger, and 3 chopped scallions to a paste. Stir in the juice of ½ lime, 1 tablespoon soy sauce, and 1 tablespoon oil. Place 1¼ lb cubed chicken breast and 20 small mushrooms in bowl, pour the marinade over them, and toss. Thread the chicken, mushrooms, and 20 cherry tomatoes onto metal skewers. Cook in a preheated hot grill pan for 7–8 minutes on each side, until cooked through. Mix together 2 peeled and mashed avocados, the juice of ½ lemon, 2 chopped tomatoes, and a pinch of dried red pepper flakes. Serve with the kebabs.

30 Coconut Chicken with Avocado Salsa

Mix together 2 peeled, pitted, and diced avocados, 2 diced tomatoes, ½ diced red onion, 1 tablespoon chopped cilantro, and the juice of ½ lime in a bowl, then let stand. Meanwhile, place 3 shallots, 3 garlic cloves, 1–2 halved and seeded red chiles, 1 lemon grass stalk, and 1 teaspoon each of turmeric and peeled and grated fresh ginger root in a food processor and process to a paste. Heat 2 tablespoons peanut oil in a wok or large skillet and cook the paste for 4–5 minutes. Pour in 1¾ cups coconut milk and bring to a simmer. Add 4 (5 oz) skinless, boneless chicken breasts and simmer for 10–12 minutes. Remove the chicken from the broth with a slotted spoon and cook on a barbecue grill or under a preheated hot broiler for 6–8 minutes, turning once, until cooked through. Serve with the broth, cooked rice, and the avocado salsa.

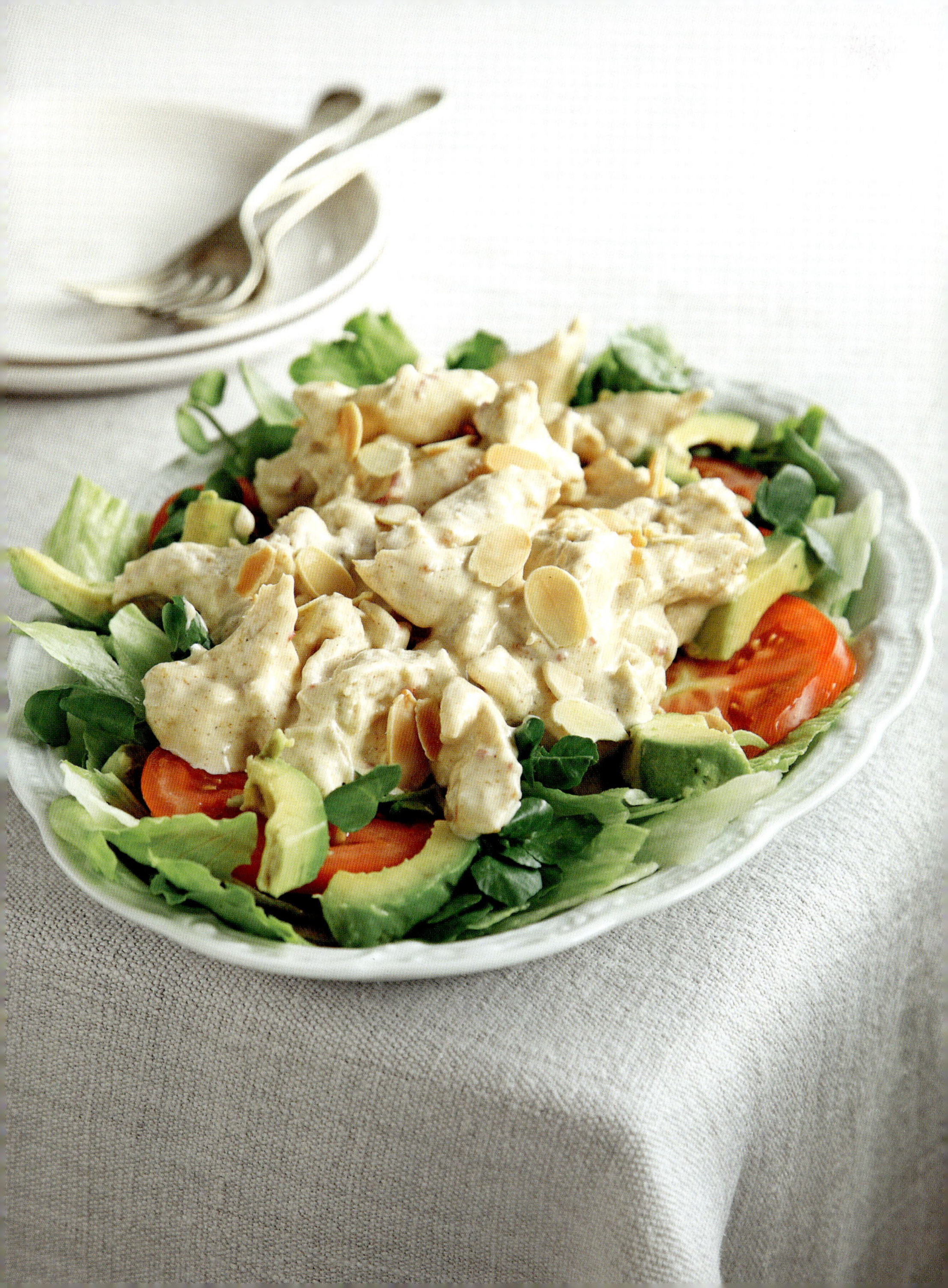

10 Stir-Fried Beef and Leeks

Serves 4

2 tablespoons sunflower oil
1 lb tenderloin steak, cut into strips
2 garlic cloves, crushed
1 teaspoon dried red pepper flakes
4 leeks, trimmed and thinly sliced
juice of 1 lemon
2 tablespoons crème fraîche
  or sour cream
salt and black pepper
steamed broccoli, to serve

- Heat the oil in a wok or large skillet until hot, add the beef, and stir-fry for 2 minutes. Remove from the pan with a slotted spoon.

- Add the garlic, dried red pepper flakes, and leeks to the wok and stir-fry for 3–4 minutes.

- Return the beef to the wok, stir in the lemon juice and crème fraiche or sour cream, and cook for 2 minutes, until heated through.

- Season to taste and serve with steamed broccoli.

20 Steak and Caramelized Leek Sandwiches

Heat 2 tablespoons butter and 1 tablespoon olive oil in a skillet, add 2 trimmed and sliced leeks, and cook over low heat for 10 minutes, stirring occasionally. Add 1 tablespoon brown sugar and 1 tablespoon white wine and cook for another 5 minutes. Meanwhile, heat a ridged grill pan until hot, add 4 (5 oz) sirloin steaks, and cook for 3–4 minutes on each side, or until cooked to your liking. Let rest. Toast 4 halved ciabatta rolls, then spread the bottoms with 1 teaspoon horseradish mixed with 1 tablespoon mayonnaise. Top each with a steak and the caramelized leeks, then add the lids and serve.

30 Beef and Leek Phyllo Pie

Heat 1 tablespoon olive oil in a skillet, add 1 lb chopped sirloin steak, and cook for 8 minutes. Stir in 3 trimmed and sliced leeks and cook for another 4 minutes. Sprinkle with 1 tablespoon all-purpose flour and cook for 1 minute, then pour in ½ cup white wine. Simmer for 4 minutes, then stir in ½ cup cream cheese and 2 tablespoons chopped parsley. Spoon into an ovenproof dish. Brush the edges of the dish with olive oil, then lay 1 sheet of phyllo pastry over the top. Brush with olive oil, then lay another sheet on top. Scrunch up the overhanging pastry onto the top of the pie and drizzle with a little more olive oil. Bake for 12 minutes in a preheated oven, 375°F, until golden. Serve with steamed vegetables.

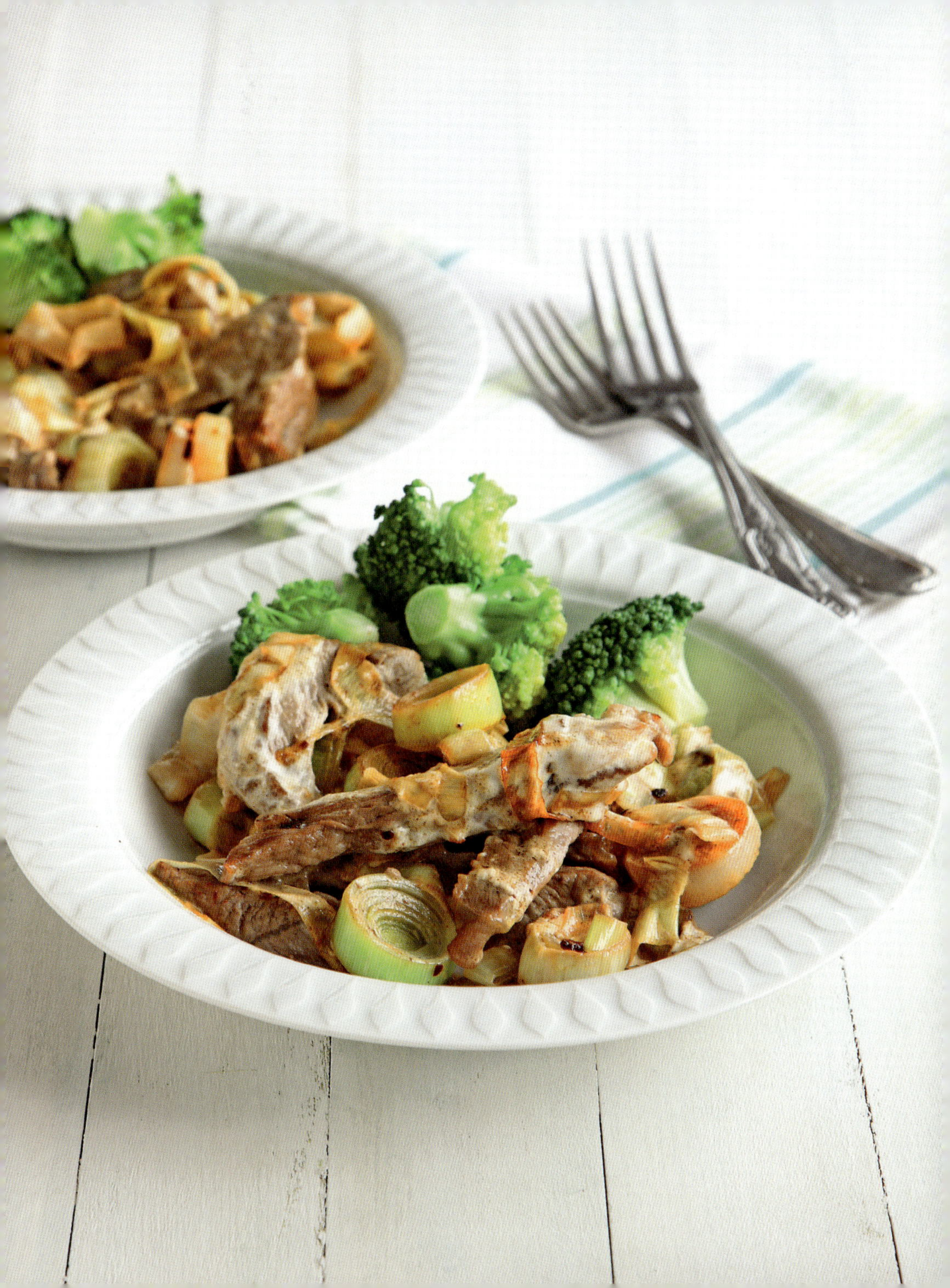

10 Chicken Liver Salad with Mustard Dressing

Serves 4

8 oz bacon slices
⅓ cup olive oil
7 slices crusty bread, cut into small cubes
1 lb chicken livers, halved and trimmed
½ bunch watercress or 1 cup arugula
2 cups mache
3 small, cooked fresh beets, cut into wedges
1 red onion, sliced
1 tablespoon raspberry vinegar
1 tablespoon Dijon mustard
1 teaspoon honey

- Cook the bacon under a preheated hot broiler for 6–8 minutes, until crisp.

- Meanwhile, heat 1 tablespoon of the oil in a skillet, add the bread, and cook for 3–4 minutes, turning frequently, until golden. Remove from the skillet with a slotted spoon and drain on paper towels.

- Heat another tablespoon of the oil in the skillet and cook the chicken livers for 2–3 minutes on each side, until golden brown but still slightly pink in the middle. Let cool slightly, then cut into bite-size pieces.

- Toss together the watercress or arugula, mache, beets, and onion in a serving bowl, then add the chicken livers and croutons. Top with the bacon.

- Whisk together the remaining oil, the vinegar, mustard, and honey in a small bowl and drizzle over the salad to serve.

20 Chicken Liver and Mustard Pâté

Heat 1 stick butter over medium heat, add 1 diced onion, and cook for 3–4 minutes. Add 1 crushed garlic clove and 1 lb trimmed and halved chicken livers and cook for 6–8 minutes, until cooked through. Stir in 1 tablespoon brandy and 1 teaspoon mustard powder and season well. Transfer to a food processor with 5 tablespoons melted butter and process until smooth. Pour into 4 small ramekins and let cool before serving.

30 Chicken Livers with Mustard Mashed Potatoes

Heat 1 tablespoon olive oil in a skillet, add 3 thinly sliced onions, and cook over low heat for 20 minutes, stirring occasionally. Pour in 2 tablespoons Madeira wine and 2 teaspoons sugar and cook for another 5–6 minutes, until caramelized. Meanwhile, cook 6 peeled and chopped russet potatoes in a saucepan of boiling water for 12–15 minutes, until tender. Heat 1 tablespoon olive oil in a separate skillet and cook 1 lb trimmed and halved chicken livers for 2–3 minutes on each side, until just cooked through. Drain the potatoes and mash in the pan with 2 tablespoons whole-grain mustard, 2 tablespoons butter, 1 tablespoon sour cream, and salt and black pepper. Serve the mashed potatoes topped with the chicken livers and caramelized onions.

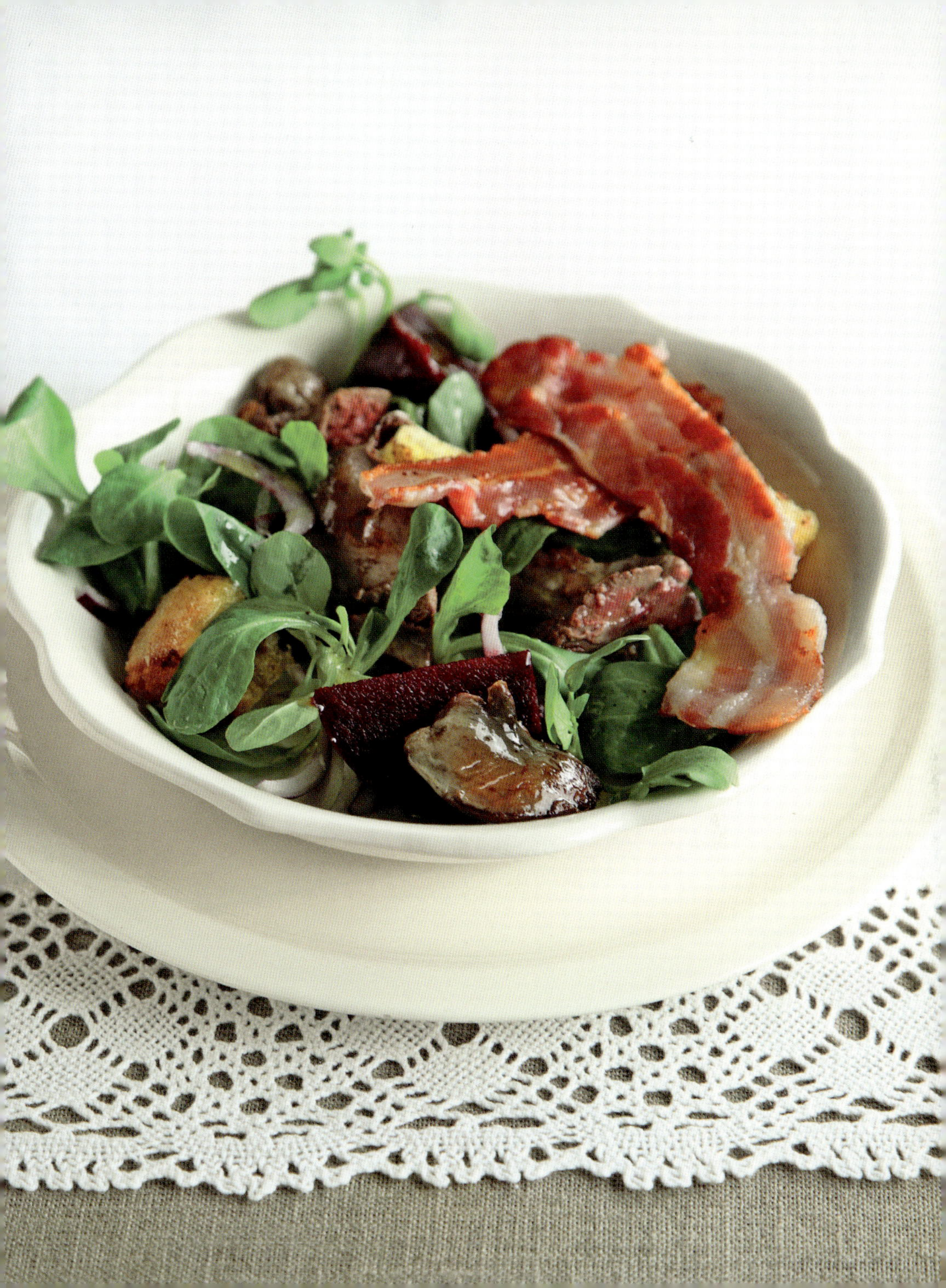

QuickCook
Fish and Seafood

Recipes listed by cooking time

30

Mussel and Watercress Linguine	136
Oysters Rockefeller	138
Marinated Salmon with Ginger Rice	140
Pan-Fried Mackerel with Crushed Potatoes	142
Salmon Ceviche	144
Baked Flounder with Mushrooms and Hazelnuts	146
Cod with Roasted Tomato Ratatouille	148
Baked Sole with Fennel Pesto	150
Shrimp and Spinach Soufflés	152
Lemony Sardine Fish Cakes	154
Smoked Haddock Omelets	156
Spicy Red Snapper with Lentil and Watercress Salad	158
Salmon with Grapefruit Dressing and Roasted Veg	160
Indian-Spiced Fish Cakes	162
Smoked Mackerel and Cheese Toasts	164
Jumbo Shrimp and Coconut Curry	166
Smoked Mackerel and Spring Vegetable Paella	168
Sea Bass with Spicy Leek and Lentil Casserole	170
Salmon Packages with Avocado Sauce	172
Fish Casserole	174
Shrimp and Cheese Gratin	176
Cod, Red Snapper, and Shrimp Casserole	178

20

Moules Marinières	136
Oysters Kilpatrick	138
Salmon and Rice Salad	140
Smoked Mackerel and New Potato Salad	142
Smoked Salmon and Potato Salad	144
Flounder with Mushroom Cream and Hazelnut Broccoli	146
Baked Cod, Tomatoes, and Leeks	148
Sole and Fennel Soup	150
Shrimp and Spinach Curry	152
Sardine and Lemon Spaghetti	154
Smoked Haddock with Soft-Boiled Eggs	156
Red Snapper with Warm Potato and Watercress Salad	158
Breaded Salmon with Grapefruit	160
Keralan Fish Curry	162
Smoked Haddock with a Cider and Cheese Sauce	164

10

Spicy Jumbo Shrimp Noodles 166	Smoked Mussel Bruschetta 136	Jumbo Shrimp Caesar Salad 166
Smoked Mackerel and Spring Vegetable Tabbouleh 168	Oysters with Shallot Vinaigrette 138	Smoked Mackerel and Spring Vegetable Salad 168
Pan-Fried Sea Bass with Warm Leek and Lentil Salad 170	Salmon and Rice Bhajis 140	Sea Bass, Leek, and Lentil Soup 170
	Smoked Mackerel Dip 142	
	Smoked Salmon Blinis 144	Salmon and Avocado Salad 172
Broiled Salmon with Avocado Salsa 172	Flounder with Caper Butter, Mushrooms, and Hazelnut Green Salad 146	Fish Pâté 174
Fish Soup 174		Shrimp and Goat Cheese Salad 176
Shrimp and Cheese Soufflés 176	Pan-Fried Cod with Grilled Tomatoes and Veg 148	Quick Cod, Red Snapper, and Shrimp Curry 178
Chunky Cod, Red Snapper, and Shrimp Stew 178	Broiled Sole with Fennel Coleslaw 150	
	Shrimp Skewers with Spinach Salad 152	
	Broiled Lemon and Mustard Sardines 154	
	Smoked Haddock with Poached Eggs 156	
	Red Snapper with Mango Salsa and Watercress 158	
	Salmon and Grapefruit Salad 160	
	Curried Fish Kebabs 162	
	Smoked Haddock and Tangy Cheese on Toast 164	

Moules Marinières

Serves 4

3 tablespoons butter
3 shallots, chopped
2 garlic cloves, crushed
¼ cup white wine
4 lb mussels, scrubbed and debearded
½ cup light cream
2–3 tablespoons chopped parsley
crusty bread, to serve

- Melt the butter in a large saucepan, add the shallots and garlic, and cook for 3–4 minutes, until softened. Pour in the wine and bring to a boil.
- Add the mussels (first discarding any that don't shut when tapped against a work surface), cover the pan, and cook for 3–4 minutes, shaking the pan once or twice, until all the shells are open. Discard any mussels that remain shut.
- Stir in the cream and parsley and heat through.
- Serve in deep bowls with crusty bread to mop up the juices.

Smoked Mussel Bruschetta

Cut 1 baguette into 8 thick slices. Drizzle with olive oil, then toast under a preheated hot broiler for 2–3 minutes on each side until golden. Meanwhile, toss together 2 diced tomatoes, a small handful of chopped watercress or arugula, 4 sliced scallions, and 4 oz smoked mussels in a bowl. Rub one side of each slice of toast with a garlic clove, then top with the mussels. Serve sprinkled with grated pecorino cheese.

Mussel and Watercress Linguine

Place ½ cup white wine and 3 lb scrubbed and debearded mussels (first discarding any that don't shut when tapped against a work surface) in a large saucepan, cover and cook for 3–4 minutes, until all the shells are open. Discard any mussels that remain shut. Drain, then remove the mussels from the shells. Heat 3 tablespoons olive oil in a skillet, add 2 diced shallots and 2 crushed garlic cloves, and cook for 2–3 minutes. Stir in 2 tablespoons store-bought pesto. Cook 1 lb linguine in a saucepan of boiling water according to the package directions, until "al dente." Add the mussels to the pesto mixture with 1¾ bunches of coarsely chopped watercress or 3 cups arugula. Drain the pasta, then toss in the sauce. Serve sprinkled with Parmesan cheese shavings.

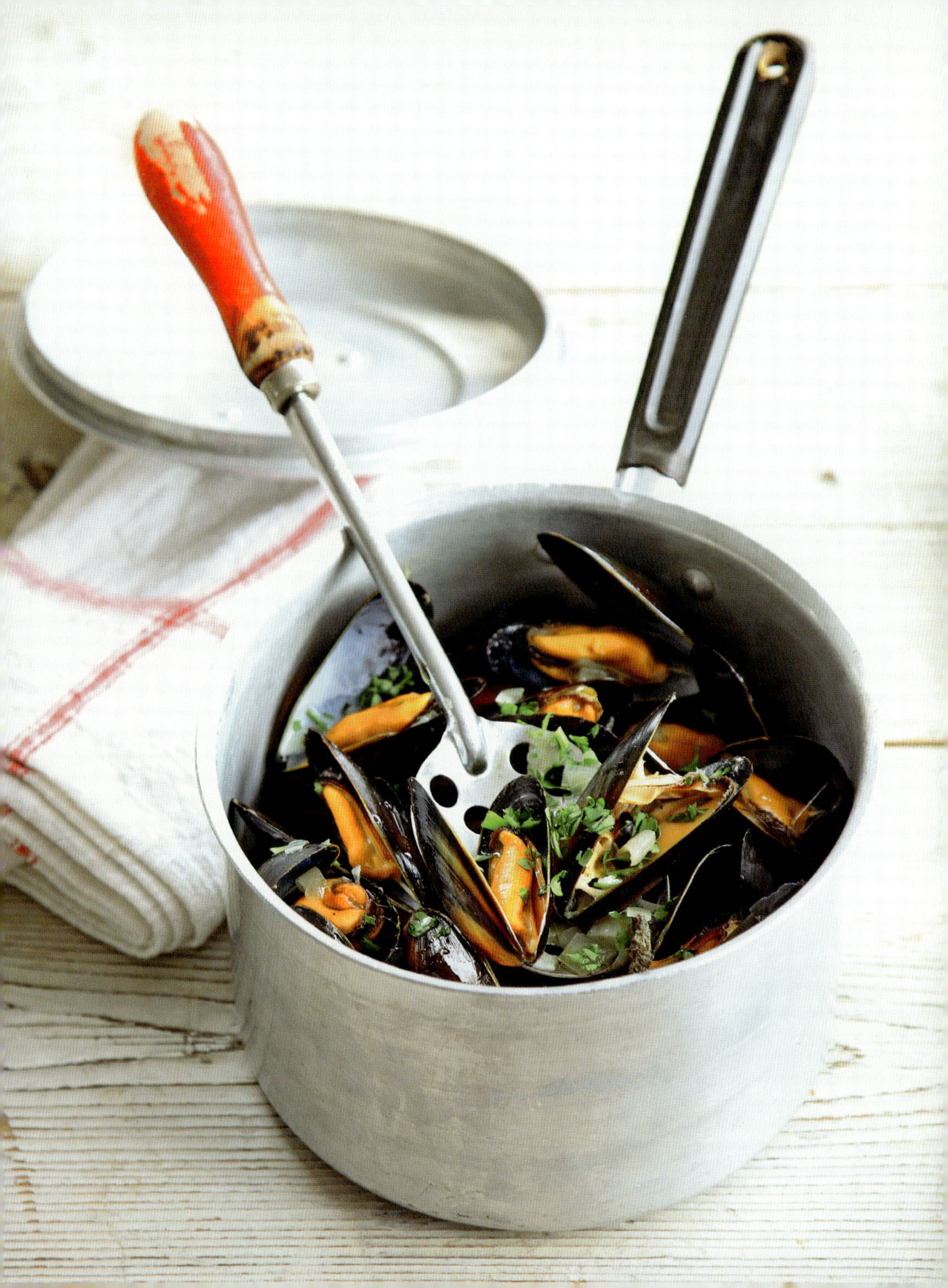

Oysters Rockefeller

Serves 4

3 tablespoons olive oil
1 shallot, diced
1 garlic clove, crushed
1 (6 oz) package baby spinach leaves
dash of Pernod (optional)
24 oysters, opened and in the half shells
2 cups fresh whole-wheat bread crumbs
1 cup grated Parmesan cheese
kosher salt

- Heat 2 tablespoons of the oil in a skillet, add the shallot and garlic, and cook for 2–3 minutes. Add the spinach and stir until wilted. Add the Pernod, if using, and cook until the liquid has been absorbed.

- Cover the bottom of a roasting pan with kosher salt, then arrange the oysters on top. Spoon the spinach mixture onto the oysters. Mix together the bread crumbs and cheese, then sprinkle it over the spinach.

- Drizzle with the remaining oil and bake in a preheated oven, at 400°F, for 10–15 minutes until lightly golden.

Oysters with Shallot Vinaigrette

Mix together 2 finely diced shallots, ¼ cup sherry vinegar, ¼ cup olive oil, the juice of 1 lemon, and 2 tablespoons chopped parsley in a bowl. Spoon over 24 shucked oysters and serve.

Oysters Kilpatrick

Heat ½ tablespoon olive oil in a skillet, add 4 oz chopped bacon, and cook for 3–4 minutes, until crisp. Remove from the skillet with a slotted spoon and drain on paper towels. Melt 2 tablespoons butter in the skillet, add 2 diced shallots, and sauté for 2 minutes, then remove the skillet from the heat and add 2 tablespoons Worcestershire sauce, 2 tablespoons ketchup, and a few drops of Tabasco. Shuck 24 oysters, return to the half shells, and place on a baking sheet. Spoon the sauce over the oysters and sprinkle with the bacon. Cook under a preheated hot broiler for 1–2 minutes, until just cooked through and sizzling. Serve with lemon wedges.

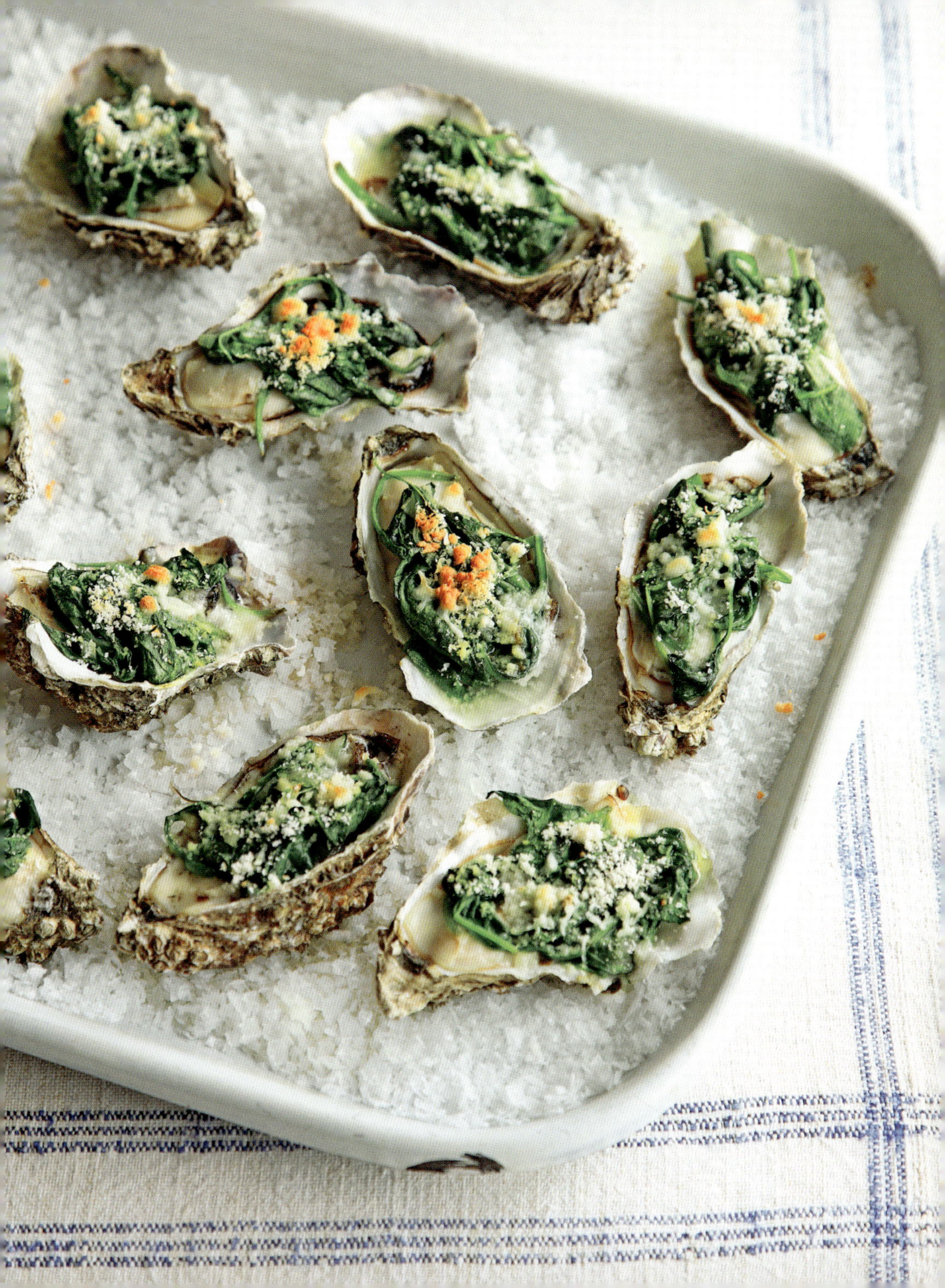

10 Salmon and Rice Bhajis

Serves 4

2 (6 oz) cans salmon, drained and flaked
1 small onion, sliced
½ teaspoon ground cumin
¼ teaspoon dried red pepper flakes
2 tablespoons chopped cilantro
½ cup cooked white rice
1 egg, beaten
1–2 tablespoons all-purpose flour
2 tablespoons canola oil
⅔ cup plain yogurt
½ cucumber, grated
1 tablespoon chopped mint
salt and black pepper

- Place the salmon, onion, spices, cilantro, and rice in a large bowl and mix well. Stir in the egg and season well. Mix in enough of the flour to form a stiff mixture. Using wet hands, shape into 20 small balls.

- Heat the oil in a large skillet, add the bhajis, and cook for 3–4 minutes, turning once, until golden.

- Meanwhile, mix together the yogurt, cucumber, and mint in a bowl. Serve with the bhajis.

---

20 Salmon and Rice Salad

Place 4 (5 oz) skinless salmon fillets in a shallow nonmetallic dish. Pour ⅓ cup sweet chili sauce and the juice of 1 lime over the salmon, cover, and marinate for 10 minutes. Meanwhile, cook 1 cup long-grain rice in boiling water according to the package directions, until tender. Drain, then stir in 2 tablespoons white wine vinegar and 1 tablespoon sugar. Cook the salmon under a preheated hot broiler for 4–5 minutes on each side. Flake into chunks in a serving bowl, then stir in the rice, 2 carrots, cut into matchsticks, 4 shredded scallions, and 1 seeded and shredded red chile. Serve with lime wedges.

30 Marinated Salmon with Ginger Rice

Mix together 2 tablespoons soy sauce, 1 tablespoon white wine vinegar, 1 tablespoon honey, ½ tablespoon mustard, and 2 crushed garlic cloves in a nonmetallic dish. Add 4 (5 oz) skinless salmon fillets, cover, and let marinate in the refrigerator for 20 minutes, turning the salmon after 10 minutes. Meanwhile, heat 1 tablespoon coconut oil in a skillet, add 2 sliced onions, and sauté for 3–4 minutes, until slightly browned. Stir in a 1-inch piece of fresh ginger root, peeled and chopped, and 1 thinly sliced garlic clove and cook for another minute. Stir in 1 cup long-grain rice, then pour over 2½ cups boiling water. Cover and cook for 10–12 minutes, until the rice is tender. Cook the salmon fillets under a preheated hot broiler for 4–5 minutes on each side or until just cooked through, basting with the marinade. Serve with the rice, sprinkled with a small handful of torn cilantro leaves.

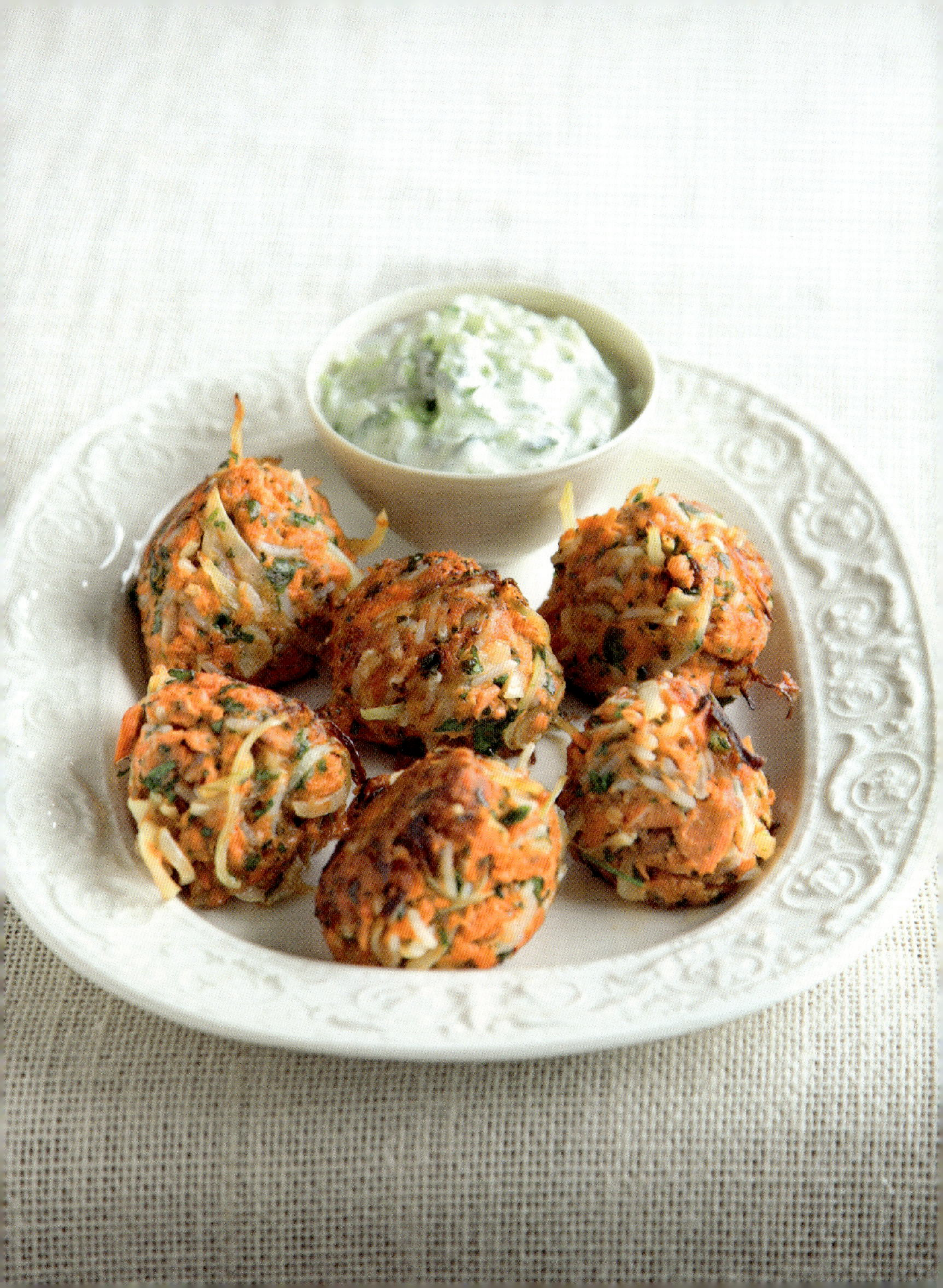

20 Smoked Mackerel and New Potato Salad

Serves 4

1½ lb new potatoes, halved if large
1 cup crème fraîche (or ½ cup sour cream mixed with ½ cup heavy cream)
2 teaspoons creamed horseradish
juice of 1 lemon
2 tablespoons pumpkin seeds
4 (4 oz) smoked mackerel fillets, skinned and flaked
3 bunches watercress or 6 cups arugula
salt and black pepper

- Cook the potatoes in a saucepan of boiling water for 15–16 minutes, until tender.
- Meanwhile, mix together the crème fraîche, horseradish, and lemon juice in a large serving bowl and season to taste.
- Heat a nonstick skillet over a medium-low heat and dry-fry the pumpkin seeds for 2–3 minutes, stirring frequently, until golden brown and toasted. Set aside.
- Drain the potatoes, then refresh under cold running water and drain again. Mix with the crème fraîche mixture. Gently toss in the mackerel and watercress or arugula.
- Serve sprinkled with the toasted pumpkin seeds.

---

10 Smoked Mackerel Dip Skin and flake 1 lb smoked mackerel fillets into a bowl. Mix in 6–7 chopped scallions, 1 cup crème fraîche, the juice of ½ lemon, and 2–3 teaspoons creamed horseradish. Season to taste with salt and black pepper and serve with vegetable crudités and toasted pita breads.

30 Pan-Fried Mackerel with Crushed Potatoes Cook 8 peeled and chopped russet potatoes in a saucepan of boiling water for 12–15 minutes, until tender. Drain the potatoes, then return to the pan and stir in a small handful of chopped parsley, 2 teaspoons creamed horseradish, 2 teaspoons whole-grain mustard, and 2 tablespoons chopped chives. Crush the potatoes lightly with a masher or the back of a fork. Cover and keep warm. Heat 1 tablespoon olive oil in a skillet, add 4 fresh mackerel fillets, and cook for 3–4 minutes on each side or until cooked through. Spoon the crushed potatoes onto 4 plates, top with the mackerel, and drizzle with 2 tablespoons olive oil.

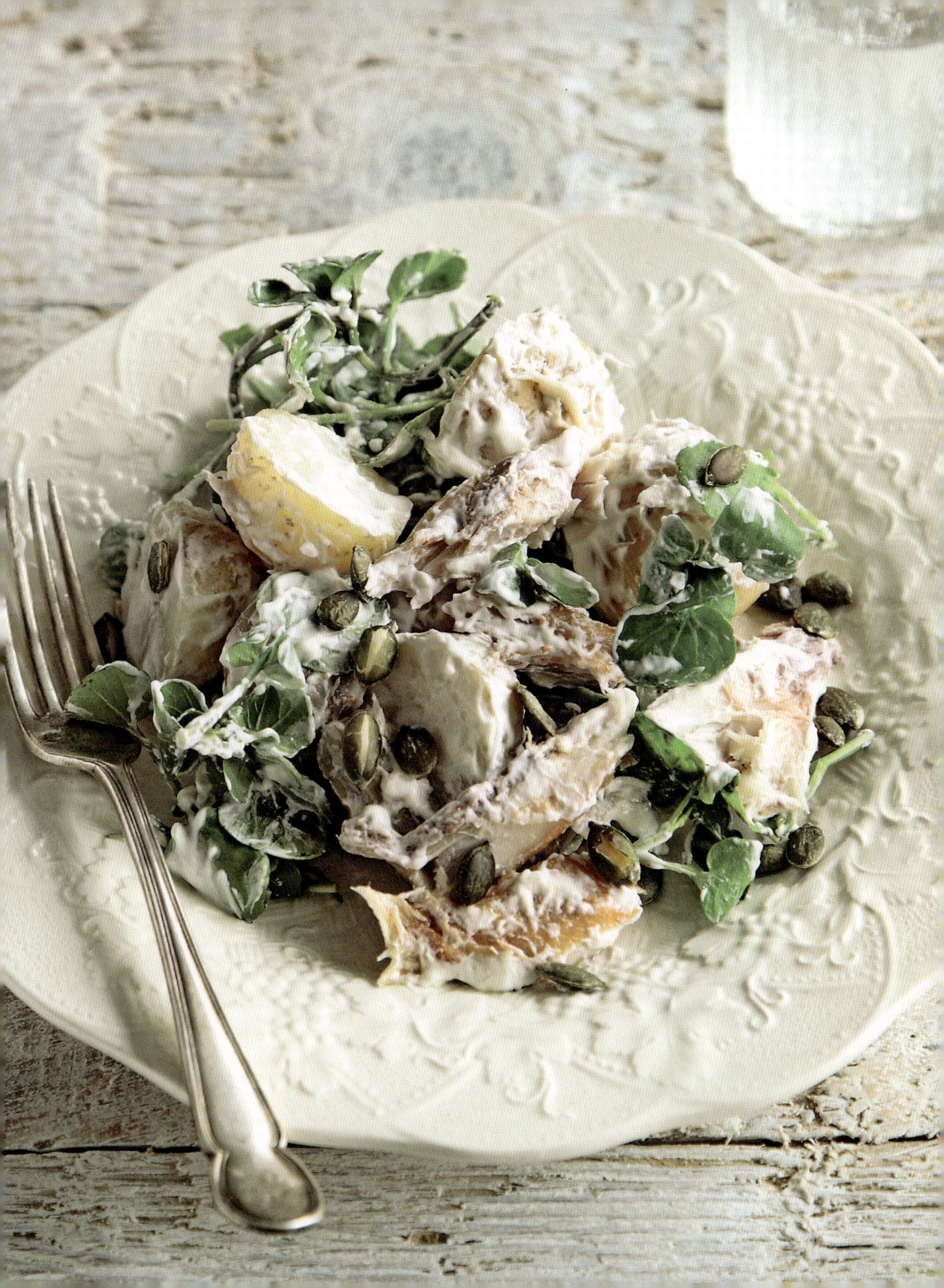

Salmon Ceviche

Serves 4

1 lb very fresh salmon fillet, skinned and thinly sliced
juice of 6–8 limes
4 scallions, finely chopped
2 celery sticks, finely sliced
1 tablespoon finely chopped cilantro
lime wedges, to serve

- Place the salmon in a nonmetallic bowl and cover with the lime juice. Cover and let marinate in the refrigerator for 20 minutes.

- Drain the lime juice from the salmon, then add the scallions, celery, and cilantro and mix well.

- Serve with lime wedges.

Smoked Salmon Blinis

Heat through 16 store-bought blinis according to the package directions. Meanwhile, mix together ⅓ cup crème fraîche or sour cream, and 1 tablespoon creamed horseradish in a bowl. Spoon a little of the horseradish cream onto each blini and top with ½ oz smoked salmon and a dill sprig. Season with black pepper and serve.

Smoked Salmon and Potato Salad

Cook 8 oz halved new potatoes in a saucepan of boiling water for 12 minutes, until tender, adding 4 oz asparagus tips 2 minutes before the end of the cooking time. Drain, refresh under cold running water, and drain again, then place in a large bowl. Whisk together the juice of 1 lemon, 3 tablespoons olive oil, 1 teaspoon each of whole-grain mustard and honey, and 1 seeded and diced red chile in a small bowl. Add 4 cups salad greens, 4 sliced scallions, 2 tablespoons chopped parsley, and 12 oz flaked smoked salmon fillets to the potatoes. Add the dressing and lightly toss together before serving.

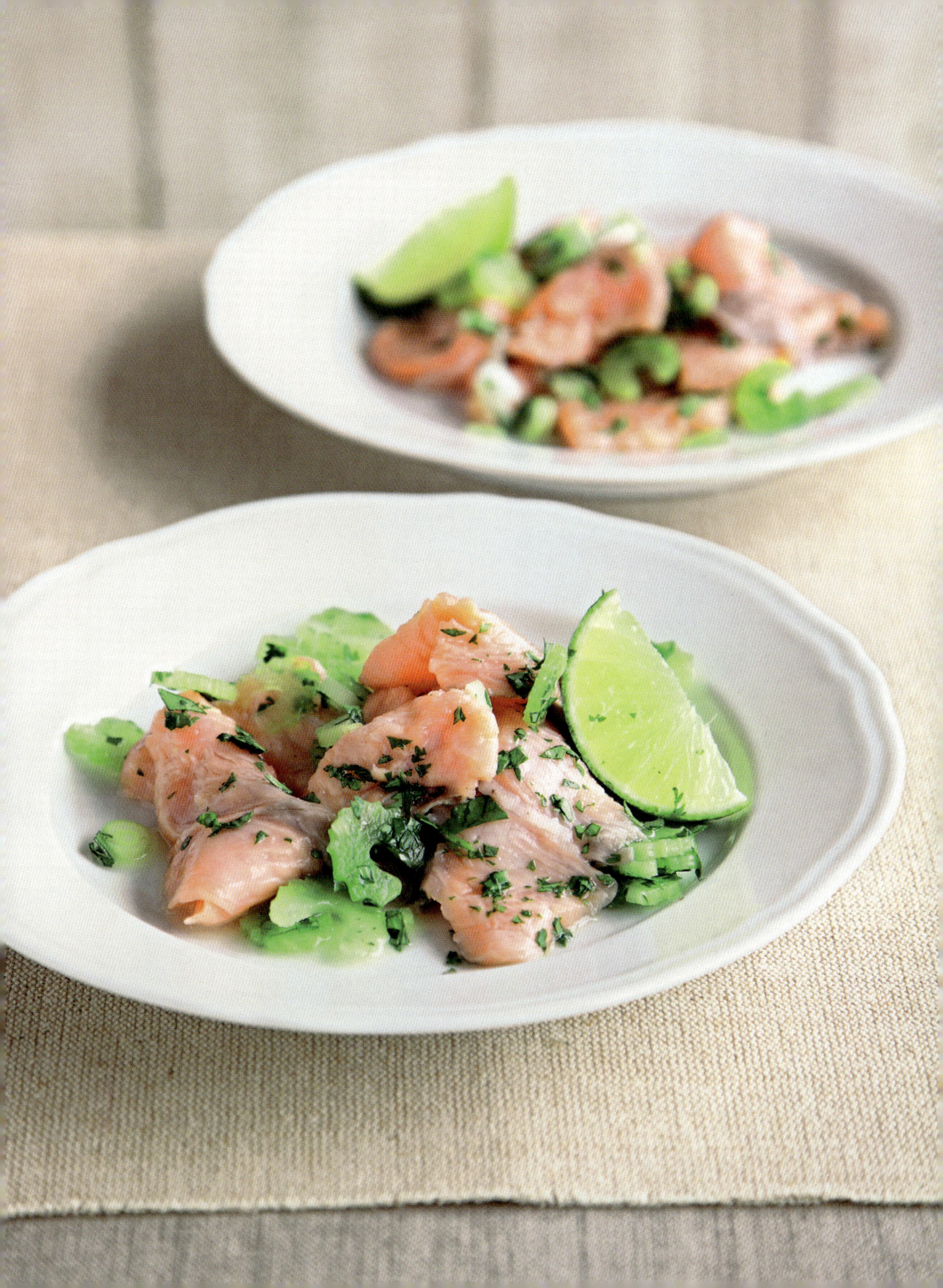

30 Baked Flounder with Mushrooms and Hazelnuts

Serves 4

2 tablespoons rapeseed oil
1 cup chopped cremini mushrooms
¾ cup roasted chopped hazelnuts
½ tablespoon chopped parsley
4 flounder fillets, skinned
¼ cup white wine
2 tablespoons butter
1 lb new potatoes, halved
1 tablespoon chopped mint
4 Boston lettuce, quartered
black pepper

- Heat 1 tablespoon of the oil in a skillet, add the mushrooms, and cook for 5 minutes, until softened. Stir in the hazelnuts, then remove from the heat and stir in the parsley.

- Lay the flounder on a clean surface and divide the mushroom mixture among them, then roll up to enclose the stuffing. Place each fillet on a piece of aluminum foil large enough to enclose it, sprinkle with the white wine, season with black pepper, add a pat of butter, and wrap well. Bake in a preheated oven, at 400°F, for 15 minutes or until cooked through.

- Heat the remaining oil in a skillet, add the lettuce, and sauté for 2–3 minutes on each side.

- Meanwhile, cook the potatoes in a saucepan of boiling water for 12–15 minutes, until tender. Drain and season, then add the mint and lightly crush with a fork. Serve the potatoes topped with the lettuce and flounder packages.

---

10 Flounder with Caper Butter, Mushrooms, and Hazelnut Green Salad Heat 2 tablespoons olive oil in a skillet and sauté 1½ cups thinly sliced mushrooms for 1–2 minutes. Remove from the skillet with a slotted spoon. Meanwhile, season 4 flounder fillets with salt and black pepper, then dust each with 1 tablespoon flour. Heat 1 tablespoon olive oil in a skillet, add the flounder fillets, skin side down, and cook for 3–4 minutes. Turn the fish over and cook for another 1–2 minutes, until cooked through. Remove from the skillet and keep warm. Heat 1 stick butter and the grated rind of 1 lemon in the skillet, stirring until the butter melts and becomes nutty brown. Remove from the heat and stir in the juice of 1 lemon, ¼ cup capers, rinsed and drained, and 3 tablespoons chopped parsley. Spoon the caper butter over the flounder fillets and serve with a crisp green salad tossed with the sautéed mushrooms and ¼ cup roasted chopped hazelnuts.

20 Flounder with Mushroom Cream and Hazelnut Broccoli Put 4 flounder fillets in an ovenproof dish and cover with 3 cups sliced mushrooms. Sprinkle with the juice of 1 lemon and season. Dot with 2 tablespoons butter and bake in a preheated oven, at 350°F, for 16–17 minutes, basting frequently. Pour ⅔ cup light cream over the fish and brown under a preheated hot broiler. Meanwhile, steam 3 cups broccoli florets for 3–4 minutes, until tender. Toss together with 2 tablespoons olive oil and 3 tablespoons chopped hazelnuts. Serve with the flounder.

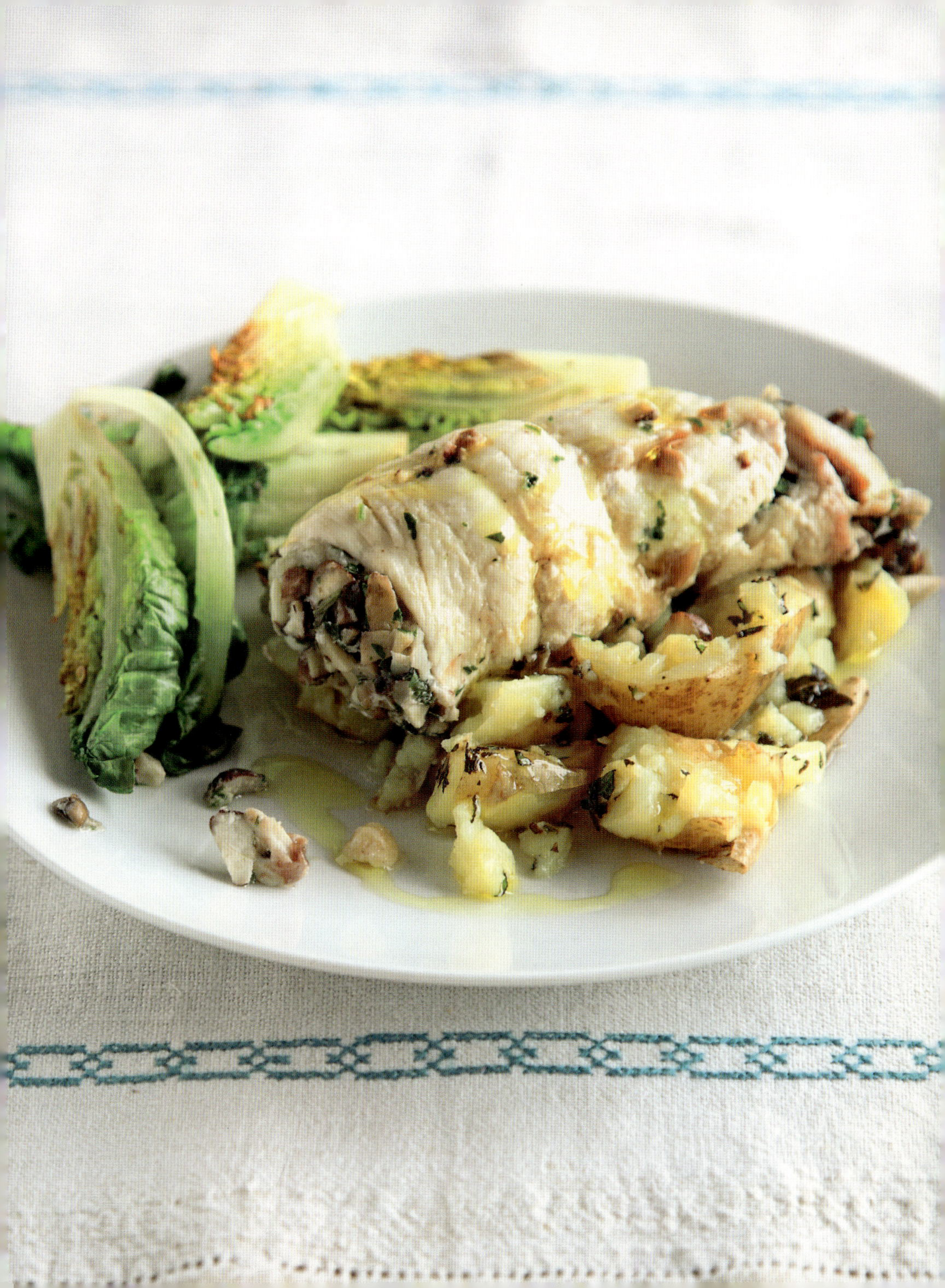

Cod with Roasted Tomato Ratatouille

Serves 4

3 zucchini, sliced
2 red bell peppers, cored, seeded, and chopped
2 red onions, cut into wedges
1 eggplant, chopped
4 garlic cloves, sliced
2 tablespoons olive oil
2 cups cherry tomatoes
small handful of basil leaves, torn
4 (5 oz) cod fillets
salt and black pepper

- Place the zucchini, red bell peppers, onions, and eggplant in a roasting pan and toss together with the garlic, oil, and salt and black pepper. Place in a preheated oven, at 425°F, for 16 minutes.

- Add the tomatoes and basil to the vegetables and toss together. Nestle the cod among the vegetables, then return to the oven for another 10–12 minutes or until the fish is cooked through.

---

10 Pan-Fried Cod with Grilled Tomatoes and Veg

Using a vegetable peeler, slice 3 zucchini into long, thin strips, then toss together with 1 tablespoon olive oil, 1 tablespoon chopped basil, 4 oz asparagus tips, and 8 halved cherry tomatoes in a bowl. Cook the vegetables in a preheated hot ridged grill pan or on a barbecue grill until slightly charred. Meanwhile, heat 1 tablespoon olive oil in a skillet, add 4 (5 oz) cod fillets, and cook for 3–4 minutes on each side or until cooked through. Serve with the chargrilled vegetables.

20 Baked Cod, Tomatoes, and Leeks

Place 4 (5 oz) cod fillets in an aluminum foil-lined ovenproof dish. Drizzle with 2 tablespoons olive oil and the juice of 1 lemon, then add 2 trimmed and sliced leeks and 6 halved cherry tomatoes, and season with salt and black pepper. Toss together gently, then seal the foil into a package. Place in a preheated oven, at 400°F, for 18–19 minutes or until the fish is cooked through. Meanwhile, cook 4 peeled and chopped russet potatoes in a saucepan of boiling water for 12–15 minutes, until tender. Drain, then mash in the pan with 1 tablespoon plain yogurt, ½ tablespoon olive oil, and 4 sliced scallions. Serve the cod with the mashed potatoes.

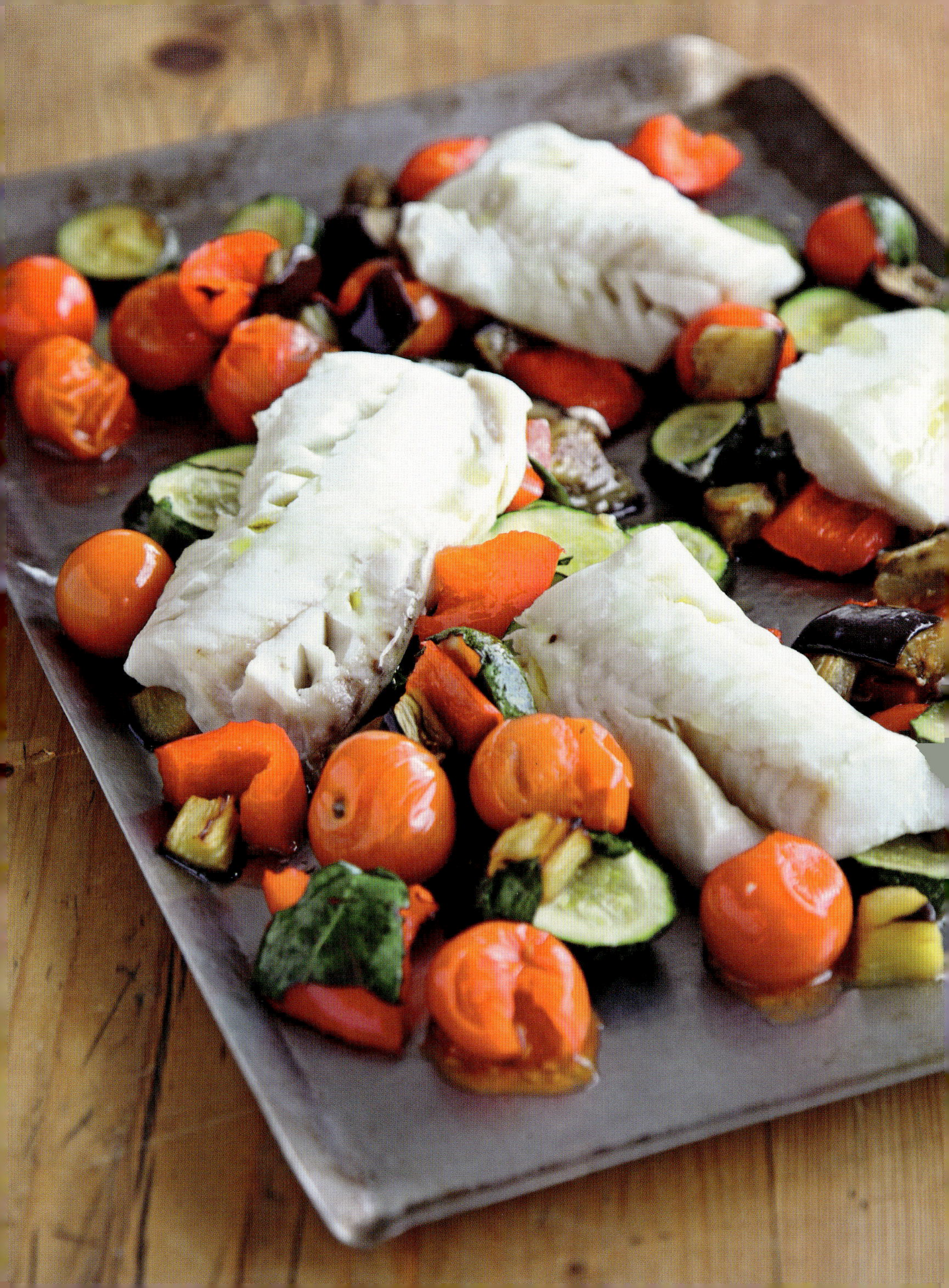

30 Baked Sole with Fennel Pesto

Serves 4

1 fennel bulb, coarsely chopped
2 tablespoons chopped dill
½ cup toasted pine nuts
2 tablespoons ground almonds (almond meal)
½ cup grated Parmesan cheese
juice of ½ lemon
½ cup olive oil, plus 1 tablespoon for drizzling
4 (6 oz) lemon sole fillets, skinned
2 zucchini
1 tablespoon olive oil
2 cups green beans
2 tomatoes, chopped

- Place the fennel in a food processor and blend to a puree. Add the dill, pine nuts, ground almonds, cheese, and lemon juice and process to combine. With the motor still running, slowly pour in the ½ cup olive oil through the feed tube until combined.

- Place the sole fillets on a board, skinned side up, and spread with the fennel pesto. Using a vegetable peeler, slice the zucchini into long, thin strips, then place 2–3 slices on each sole fillet. Roll up the fish and place in an ovenproof dish.

- Drizzle with the remaining oil, cover, and bake in a preheated oven, at 375°F, for 15 minutes, until cooked through.

- Meanwhile, steam the green beans, then toss with the tomatoes and divide among 4 plates. Top each with a sole fillet and serve.

---

10 Broiled Sole with Fennel Coleslaw

Cook 4 sole fillets under a preheated hot broiler for about 2–3 minutes on each side or until cooked through. Meanwhile, finely slice ½ red cabbage, 2 fennel bulbs, 1 celery stick, and 1 apple, then mix with the juice of 1 lemon in a large bowl. Dry-fry 2 tablespoons walnuts in a nonstick skillet for 3–4 minutes, stirring frequently, then add to the coleslaw with 2 tablespoons golden raisins, 2 tablespoons plain yogurt, and a pinch of cayenne pepper. Serve with the fish.

20 Sole and Fennel Soup

Heat 1 tablespoon olive oil in a large saucepan, add 1 chopped onion and 2 sliced garlic cloves, and cook for 2 minutes, until starting to soften. Add 2 thinly sliced fennel bulbs and cook for another 8 minutes. Stir in ½ cup white wine and cook for 2 minutes, then add 2 cups hot fish stock, 2 (14½ oz) cans diced tomatoes, and salt and black pepper. Bring to a boil, then reduce the heat and simmer for 5 minutes. Add 1¼ lb chopped skinned sole fillets and cook for 3 minutes or until cooked through. Stir in 2 tablespoons chopped parsley and serve with crusty bread.

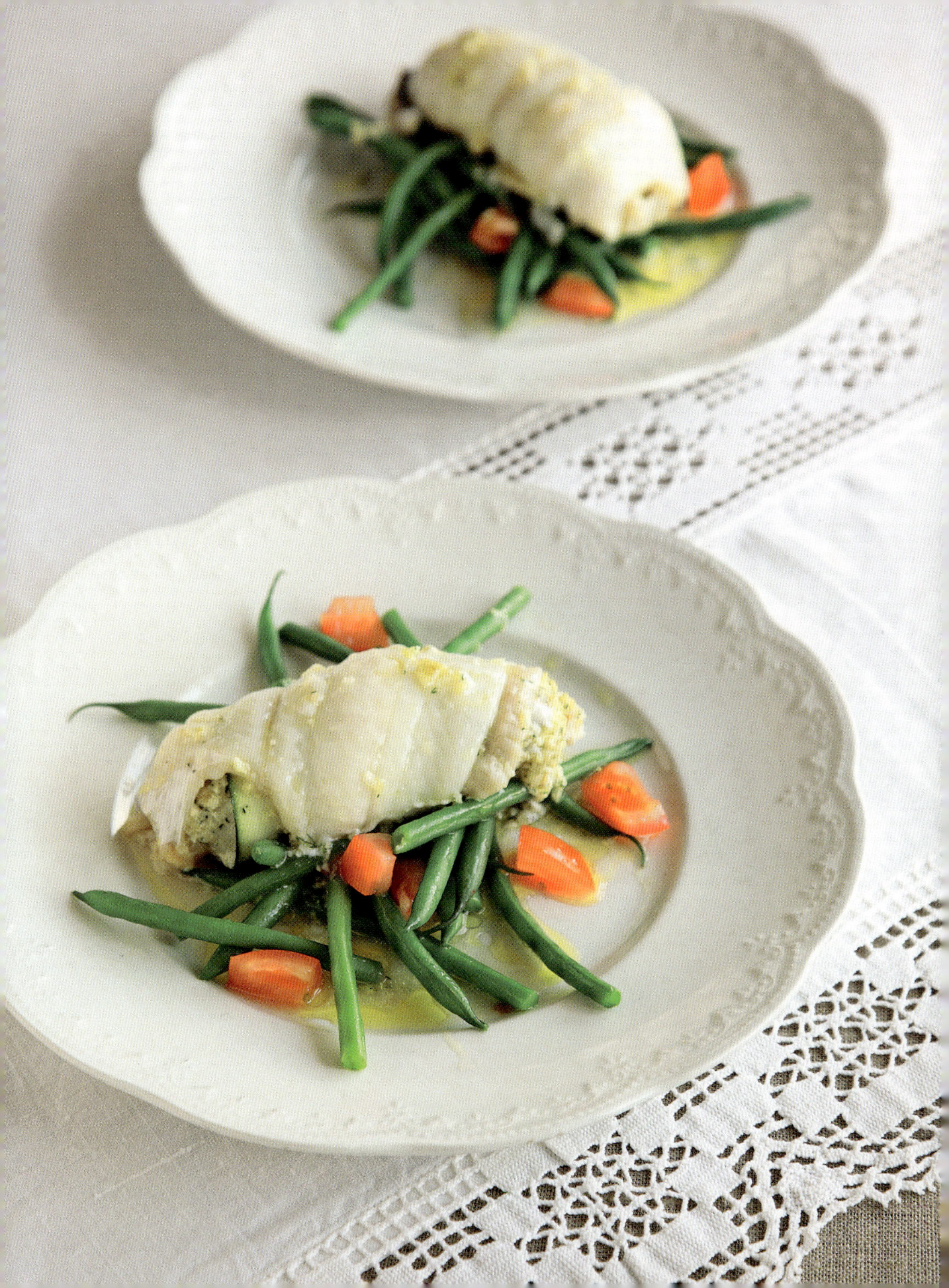

20 Shrimp and Spinach Curry

Serves 4

4 tomatoes
2 tablespoons peanut oil
2 red onions, chopped
1-inch piece of fresh ginger root, peeled and grated
4 garlic cloves, sliced
¼ teaspoon chili powder
½ teaspoon turmeric
1 teaspoon ground coriander
1¾ cups coconut milk
1 (5 oz) package fresh spinach, chopped
1 lb raw peeled jumbo shrimp
1 tablespoon toasted slivered almonds
cooked long-grain rice, to serve

- Place the tomatoes in a heatproof bowl and pour over boiling water to cover. Let stand for 1–2 minutes, then drain, cut a cross at the stem end of each tomato, and peel off the skins and chop.

- Heat the oil in a wok or large skillet, add the onions, ginger, and garlic, and stir-fry for 2–3 minutes. Add the spices and cook for another 2–3 minutes, then add the tomatoes.

- Pour in the coconut milk and bring to a simmer. Gradually add the spinach, stirring until wilted. Cook for 4–5 minutes.

- Stir in the shrimp and cook for another 2 minutes or until the shrimp turn pink.

- Sprinkle with the almonds and serve with cooked rice.

---

10 Shrimp Skewers with Spinach Salad

Thread 24 cooked, peeled jumbo shrimp onto 8 metal skewers. Mix together ¼ cup each of soy sauce and ketchup with 2 crushed garlic cloves in a bowl, then brush over the shrimp. Cook under a preheated hot broiler for 2–3 minutes on each side. Meanwhile, whisk together 3 tablespoons olive oil, the juice of ½ lemon, ½ teaspoon French mustard, and ½ teaspoon honey in a large bowl. Add 2 handfuls of spinach, ½ sliced red onion, and 2 peeled and sliced avocados and toss well. Serve with the skewers.

30 Shrimp and Spinach Soufflés

Heat 1 tablespoon olive oil in a saucepan, add 1 (7 oz) package baby spinach leaves, and cook for 2–3 minutes, until wilted. Meanwhile, melt 3 tablespoons butter in a small saucepan, then stir in ⅓ cup all-purpose flour to make a roux. Gradually whisk in 1½ cups milk and cook, stirring continuously, for 2–3 minutes, until the sauce is thick and smooth. Stir in ½ cup grated Parmesan cheese, season, and pour into a large bowl. Stir in the spinach and let cool for 3–4 minutes. Put 3 cooked, peeled jumbo shrimp in each of 4 greased ramekins, then place on a baking sheet. Whisk 4 egg yolks into the spinach sauce. Whisk 4 egg whites in a clean bowl until stiff, then gently fold into the spinach mixture. Spoon into the ramekins, running a finger around the rim to help even rising. Sprinkle with 2 tablespoons grated Parmesan and bake in a preheated oven, at 400°F, for 20 minutes, until risen and golden.

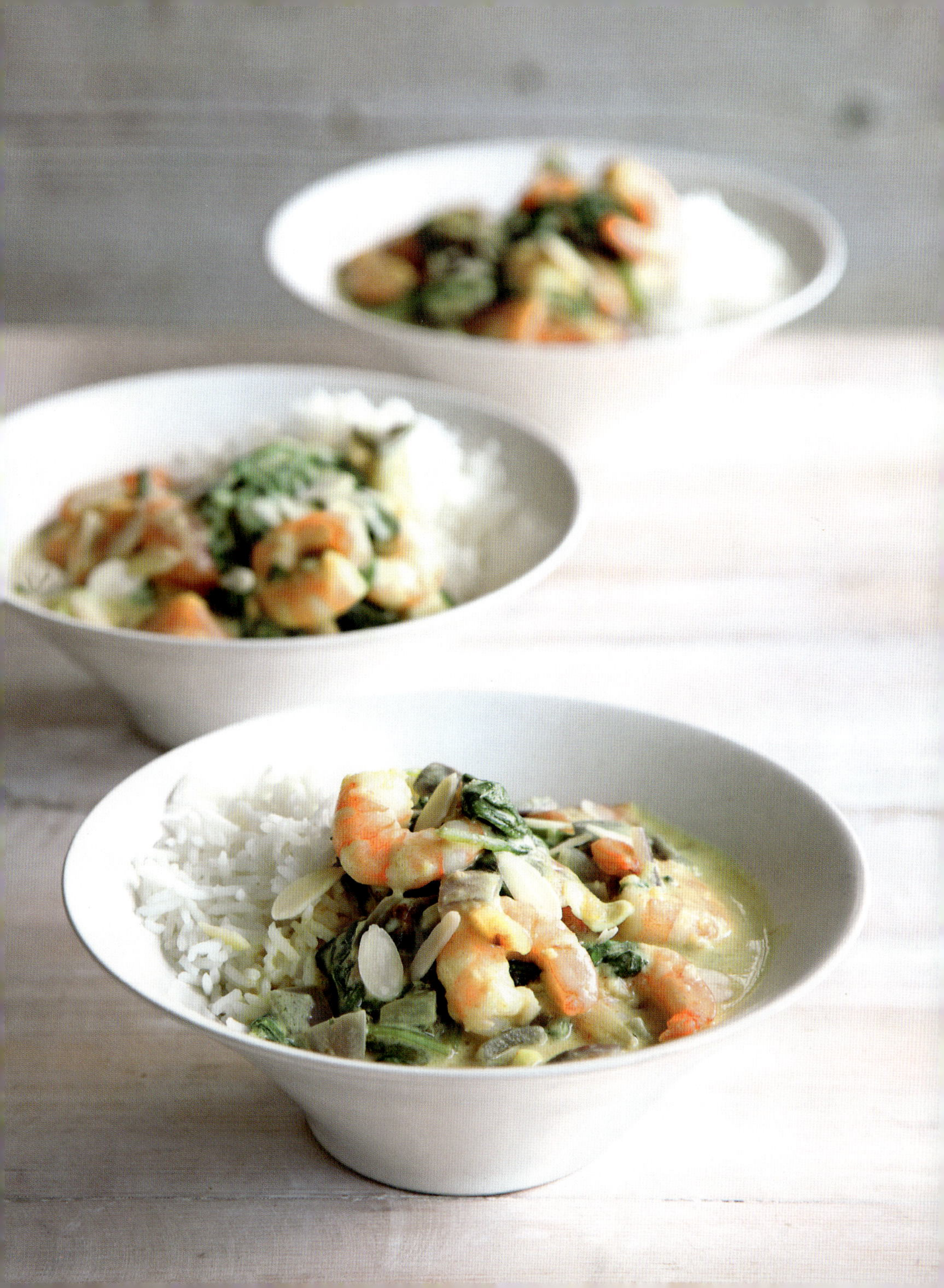

1 Broiled Lemon and Mustard Sardines

Serves 4

small handful of parsley leaves, chopped
1 tablespoon whole-grain mustard
juice of 1 lemon
8 sardines, boned, cleaned, and gutted
2 tablespoons olive oil
lemon halves, to serve

- Mix together the parsley, mustard, and lemon juice in a bowl, then spoon into the sardine cavities. Brush the fish with the oil.

- Cook under a preheated hot broiler for 4 minutes on each side or until cooked through. Serve with lemon halves.

2 Sardine and Lemon Spaghetti

Cook 1 lb spaghetti in a saucepan of boiling water according to the package directions, until "al dente." Meanwhile, heat 1 tablespoon olive oil in a skillet, add ½ teaspoon mustard seeds and 3 sliced garlic cloves, and cook for 1 minute. Stir in a pinch of dried red pepper flakes, the grated rind of 1 lemon, ¾ cup canned diced tomatoes, and 2 (3¾ oz) cans sardines in tomato sauce. Break up the sardines, then stir in ¾ cup pitted ripe black olives, 1 tablespoon capers, rinsed and drained, and 2 tablespoons chopped parsley and heat through. Drain the pasta, toss in the sardine sauce, and serve.

3 Lemony Sardine Fish Cakes

Cook 5 peeled and chopped russet potatoes in a saucepan of boiling water for 12–15 minutes, until tender. Place 1 (7 oz) package spinach leaves in a saucepan with a small amount of water, then cover and cook until wilted. Drain, squeeze dry, and coarsely chop. Drain the potatoes, return to the pan, and mash until smooth. Place in a bowl with the spinach and 2 (3¾ oz) cans sardines, drained, and gently mix together. Stir in 1 tablespoon chopped parsley, ½ tablespoon all-purpose flour, the juice of ½ lemon, and the grated rind of 1 lemon. Using wet hands, shape into patties. Heat 2 tablespoons peanut oil in a skillet, add the fish cakes, and cook for 4–5 minutes on each side until golden. Meanwhile, mix together 3 tablespoons Greek yogurt, the juice of ½ lemon, 1 tablespoon chopped parsley, and 3 tablespoons mayonnaise in a bowl. Serve the fish cakes with the yogurt dressing.

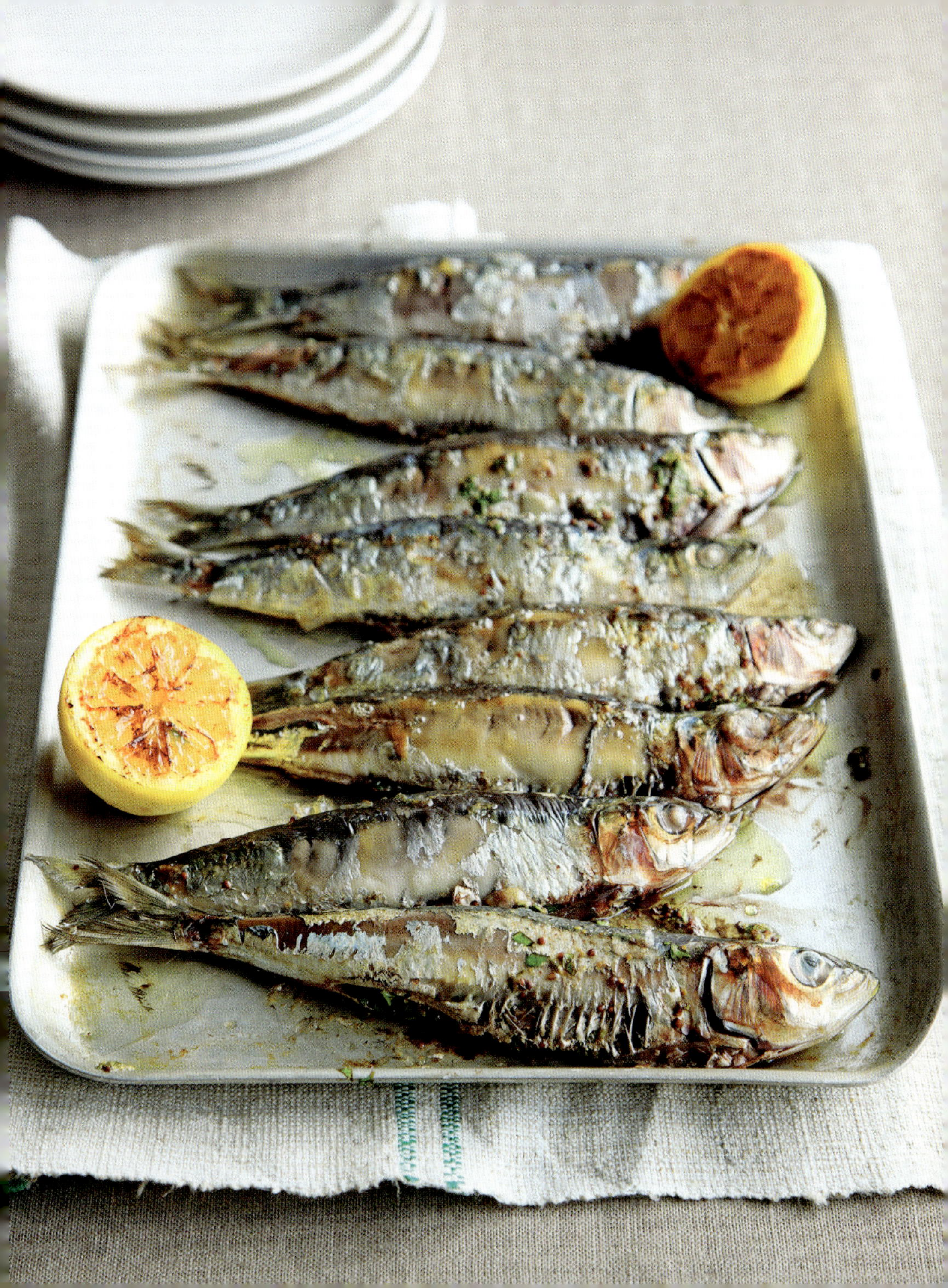

30 Smoked Haddock Omelets

Serves 4
5 oz smoked haddock
  or smoked salmon
½ cup milk
12 eggs
4 tablespoons butter
1 (7 oz) package spinach leaves
salt and black pepper

- Place the haddock or salmon and milk in a saucepan and poach the fish for 3–4 minutes or until cooked. Remove with a slotted spoon, then remove the skin and any bones. Flake the fish into a bowl.

- Beat the eggs in a separate large bowl and season.

- Heat 1 tablespoon of the butter in a skillet until foaming, then pour in one-quarter of the beaten egg. Stir a little with a fork, tipping the skillet so the egg covers the bottom, then cook for 3–4 minutes, until set.

- Place one-quarter of the spinach on the omelet, then top with one-quarter of the fish. Fold the omelet over and cook for another minute. Serve on a warm plate.

- Repeat with the remaining ingredients.

10 Smoked Haddock with Poached Eggs

Place 4 (5 oz) smoked haddock or smoked salmon fillets, 1 bay leaf, and 1¾ cups milk in a large skillet and gently poach for 8–10 minutes or until cooked. Meanwhile, bring a saucepan of water to a gentle simmer and stir with a large spoon to create a swirl. Break 2 eggs into the water and cook for 3 minutes. Remove with a slotted spoon and keep warm. Repeat with another 2 eggs. Serve the fish topped with a poached egg and 1 tablespoon warmed store-bought hollandaise or mustard sauce.

20 Smoked Haddock with Soft-Boiled Eggs

Cook 8 peeled and chopped russet potatoes (about 2 pounds) in a saucepan of boiling water for 12–15 minutes or until tender. Meanwhile, poach 4 (5 oz) smoked haddock or smoked salmon fillets and 8 sliced scallions with 1¾ cups milk (see left). Cook 4 eggs in a saucepan of boiling water for 4–5 minutes, until softly boiled, then drain and cool slightly. Drain the potatoes, then mash in the pan with 1 tablespoon creamed horseradish and 2 teaspoons whole-grain mustard. Peel and halve the eggs. Serve the fish on the mustard mashed potatoes, topped with the eggs and sprinkled with 1 tablespoon chopped chives.

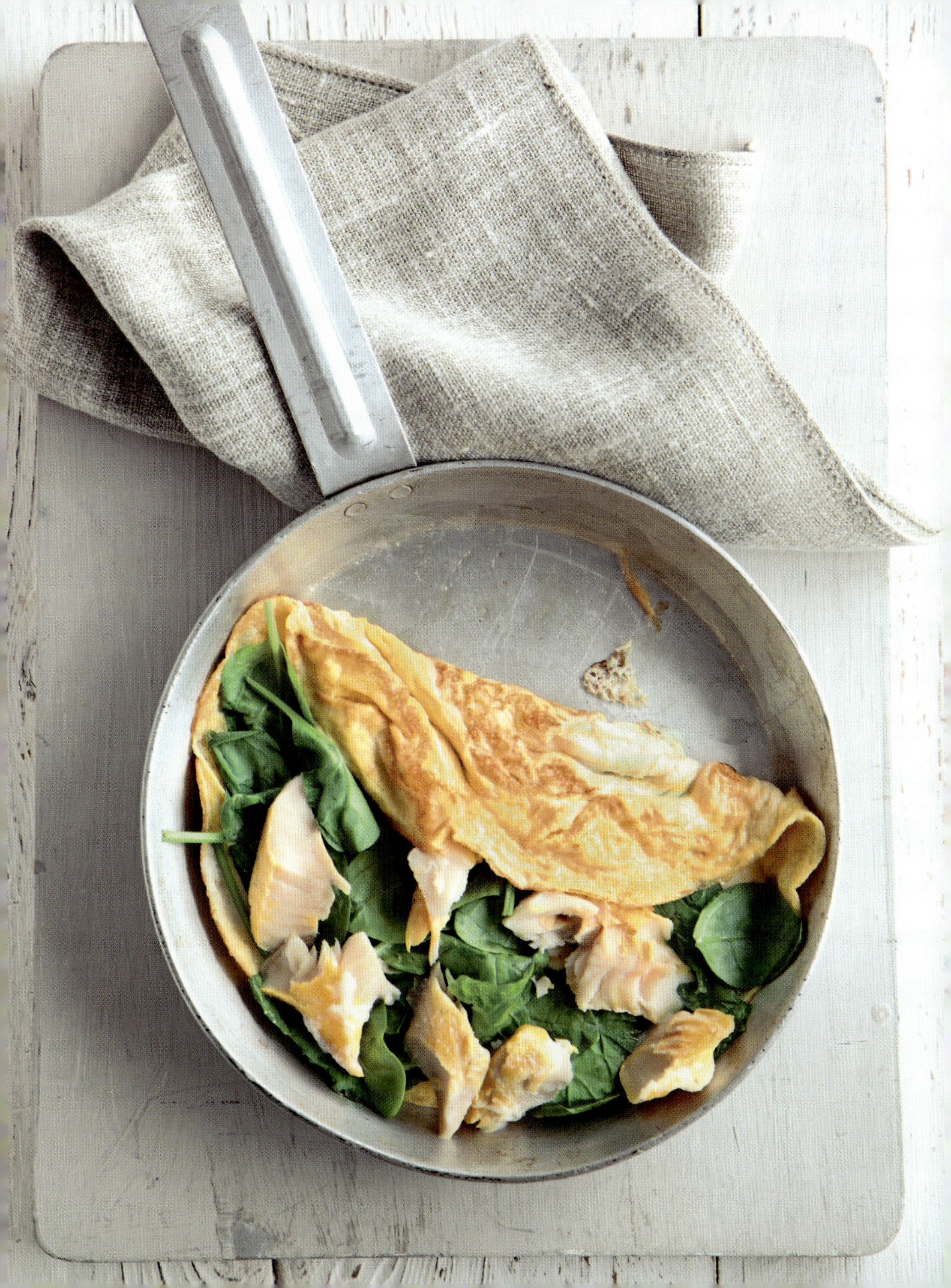

Red Snapper with Warm Potato and Watercress Salad

Serves 4

1 lb new potatoes, halved
2 tablespoons mayonnaise
1 tablespoon plain yogurt
2–3 teaspoons creamed horseradish
1 tablespoon chopped parsley
2 tablespoons olive oil
4 red snapper fillets
½ bunch of watercress or 1 cup arugula
salt and black pepper

- Cook the potatoes in a saucepan of boiling water for 12–15 minutes, until just tender.

- Meanwhile, mix together the mayonnaise, yogurt, horseradish, and parsley in a large bowl, then season well.

- Heat the oil in a skillet, add the red snapper, and cook for 2–3 minutes on each side or until cooked through.

- Drain the potatoes, add to the mayonnaise mixture, and mix well. Stir in the watercress or arugula.

- Divide the potato salad among 4 plates, then top with the fish, pouring the oil from the pan around the plates.

Red Snapper with Mango Salsa and Watercress

Mix together 1 peeled, pitted, and diced mango, ½ diced red onion, 2 diced tomatoes, ½ seeded and diced red chile, 1 tablespoon olive oil, ½ tablespoon balsamic vinegar, and 1 tablespoon chopped cilantro in a bowl. Heat 1 tablespoon olive oil in a skillet, add 4 red snapper fillets, and cook for 2–3 minutes on each side or until cooked through. Serve with the salsa and watercress or arugula.

Spicy Red Snapper with Lentil and Watercress Salad

Heat 2 tablespoons coconut oil in a skillet, add 1 diced red onion, and cook for 2–3 minutes. Add 1 seeded and diced green chile, 1 cored, seeded, and diced yellow bell pepper, and 1 cored and diced apple and cook for another 2–3 minutes. Stir in 1 (15 oz) can lentils, rinsed and drained, 2 diced tomatoes, 1 tablespoon toasted pine nuts, the juice of ½ lime, and 2 tablespoons mint leaves and cook gently for 3–4 minutes. Transfer to a bowl and keep warm. Mix together 2 tablespoons all-purpose flour and 1 teaspoon curry powder in a bowl, then dust 4 red snapper fillets with the spiced flour. Heat 1 tablespoon coconut oil in a skillet, add the fish, and cook for 2–3 minutes on each side or until cooked through. Remove from the skillet and keep warm. Add 1 tablespoon raisins and a pinch each of turmeric and ground cumin to the skillet and cook for 1–2 minutes, then pour in 1 cup coconut milk. Bring to a simmer and cook for 3–4 minutes. Remove from the heat and stir in the grated rind of ½ lemon. Stir ½ bunch chopped watercress or 1 cup arugula into the lentil salad, then serve with the fish and the sauce spooned over the top.

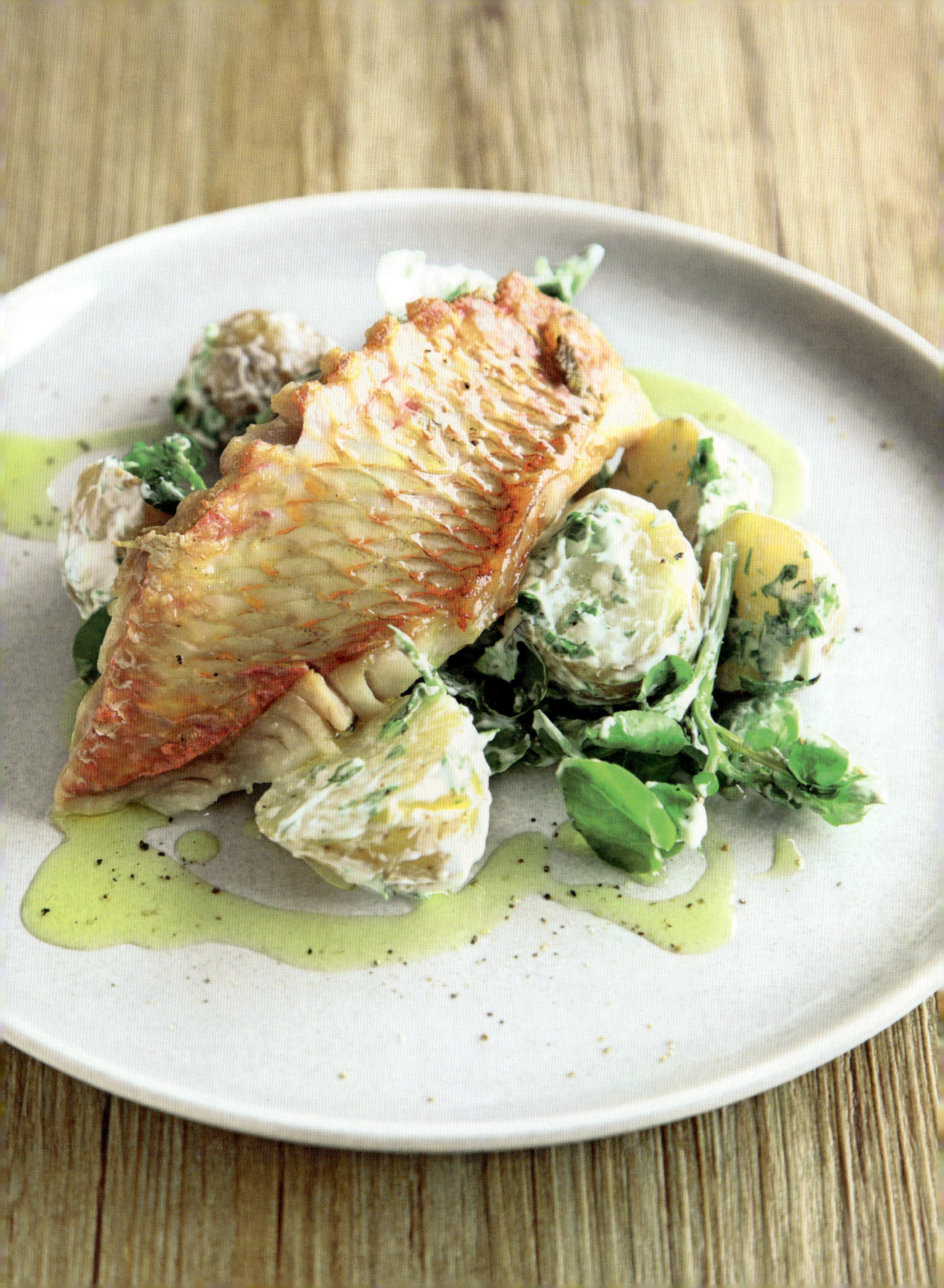

Salmon and Grapefruit Salad

Serves 4

2 tablespoons pumpkin seeds
4 grapefruits
1 red bell pepper, cored, seeded, and sliced
4 scallions, sliced
1 (15 oz) can great Northern beans, rinsed and drained
2 avocados, peeled and sliced
2 handfuls of baby spinach leaves
12 oz smoked salmon fillets, broken into large flakes
2 tablespoons olive oil
1 teaspoon honey
½ teaspoon Dijon mustard

- Heat a nonstick skillet over medium-low heat and dry-fry the pumpkin seeds for 2–3 minutes, stirring frequently, until golden and toasted. Set aside.

- Segment the grapefruits over a bowl to catch the juice. Place the segments in a separate bowl and add the red bell pepper, scallions, great Northern beans, avocados, spinach, and salmon.

- Add the oil, honey, and mustard to the grapefruit juice and whisk together. Pour the dressing over the salad ingredients and toss together gently.

- Serve sprinkled with the toasted pumpkin seeds.

Breaded Salmon with Grapefruit

Heat 1 tablespoon olive oil in a skillet, add 4 (5 oz) skinless salmon fillets, and cook for 30 seconds on each side. Transfer the fish to a baking sheet and place in a preheated oven, at 425°F, for 3–4 minutes. Meanwhile, heat 1 tablespoon olive oil and 2 tablespoons butter in a skillet, add 3 cups fresh whole-wheat bread crumbs, ¼ cup mustard powder, and ¼ cup chopped hazelnuts and cook for 2–3 minutes. Remove the fish from the oven and sprinkle with the bread crumb mixture, then cook under a preheated hot broiler for 2–3 minutes, until crisp and cooked through. Heat a little olive oil in a saucepan, add 1 lb fresh spinach leaves, and cook until wilted, then divide among 4 plates. Top with the fish and the segments of 1 pink grapefruit.

Salmon with Grapefruit Dressing and Roasted Veg

Core, seed, and quarter 1 yellow and 2 red bell peppers, then place in a roasting pan with 1 sliced eggplant and 1 sliced zucchini. Drizzle with olive oil and cook in a preheated oven, at 400°F, for 16–18 minutes. Meanwhile, heat 1 tablespoon oil in a saucepan, add 4 (5 oz) skinless salmon fillets, and cook for 4–5 minutes on each side. Segment 1 pink grapefruit over a bowl to catch the juice, then chop the segments and add to the bowl. Stir in 1 cup plain yogurt and 2 tablespoons chopped mint. Serve the vegetables topped with the fish and with the dressing.

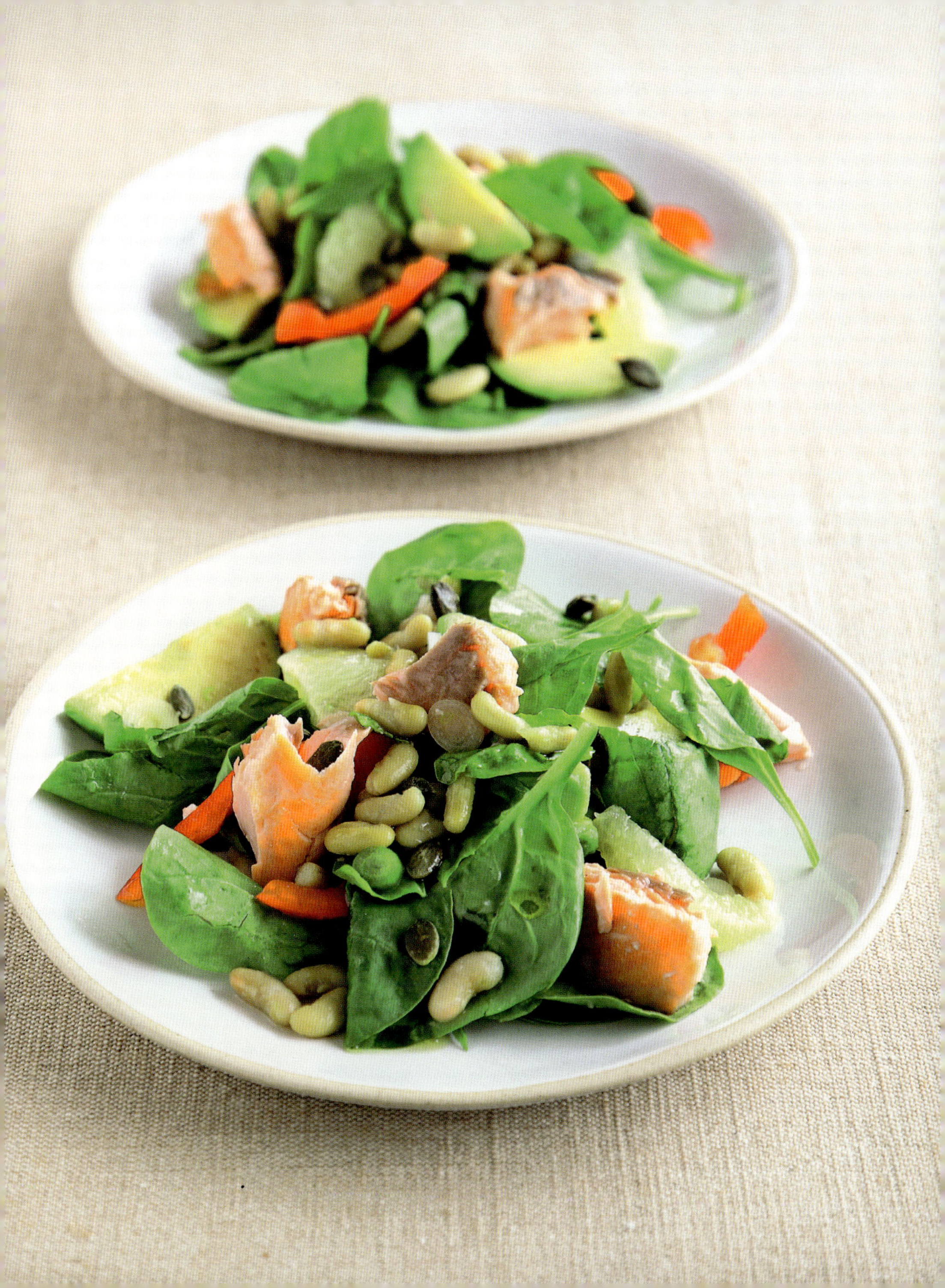

Keralan Fish Curry

Serves 4

1 red chile, seeded and chopped
1 teaspoon canola oil
1 teaspoon ground coriander
½ teaspoon ground cumin
½ teaspoon turmeric
4 garlic cloves
1-inch piece of fresh ginger root, peeled and chopped
1 tablespoon coconut oil
¼ teaspoon fenugreek seeds
2 onions, finely sliced
½ cup coconut milk
1¼ cups water
1 lb fresh mackerel fillets, skinned and cut into 2-inch pieces
salt and black pepper

- Place the chile, canola oil, ground coriander, cumin, turmeric, garlic, and ginger in a mini food processor or small blender and blend to form a paste.
- Heat the coconut oil in a wok or large skillet, add the paste and fenugreek seeds, and cook for 2–3 minutes. Add the onions, coconut milk, and measured water, season, and bring to a boil, then cook for about 5 minutes, until reduced.
- Add the mackerel and simmer gently for 5–8 minutes or until cooked through.

Curried Fish Kebabs Mix together 3 tablespoons plain yogurt, 1 teaspoon each of chopped garlic and ginger puree, the juice of ½ lime, 2 tablespoons curry paste, and ½ teaspoon honey in a nonmetallic bowl. Toss in 1 lb chopped, skinless salmon fillet and let marinate for 2–3 minutes. Thread the fish onto metal skewers, then cook on a barbecue grill or under a preheated hot broiler for 2–3 minutes on each side or until cooked through. Serve with a crisp green salad.

Indian-Spiced Fish Cakes Cook 8 peeled and chopped russet potatoes (about 2 lb) in a saucepan of boiling water for 15–17 minutes, until tender. Meanwhile, dry-fry 1 teaspoon cumin seeds in a nonstick skillet for 2–3 minutes, stirring frequently, until toasted. Drain the potatoes, then mash in the pan with the toasted cumin seeds, 2 finely chopped scallions, 1 seeded and diced red chile, 3 tablespoons chopped cilantro, and salt and black pepper. Beat in 1 beaten egg, then carefully stir in 8 oz flaked, smoked salmon fillets. Using wet hands, shape into 8 fish cakes, then coat in ¼ cup all-purpose flour. Heat 2 tablespoons butter and 1 tablespooon sunflower oil in a skillet, add the fish cakes, and cook for about 2 minutes on each side until golden. Serve with yogurt raita and a arugula salad.

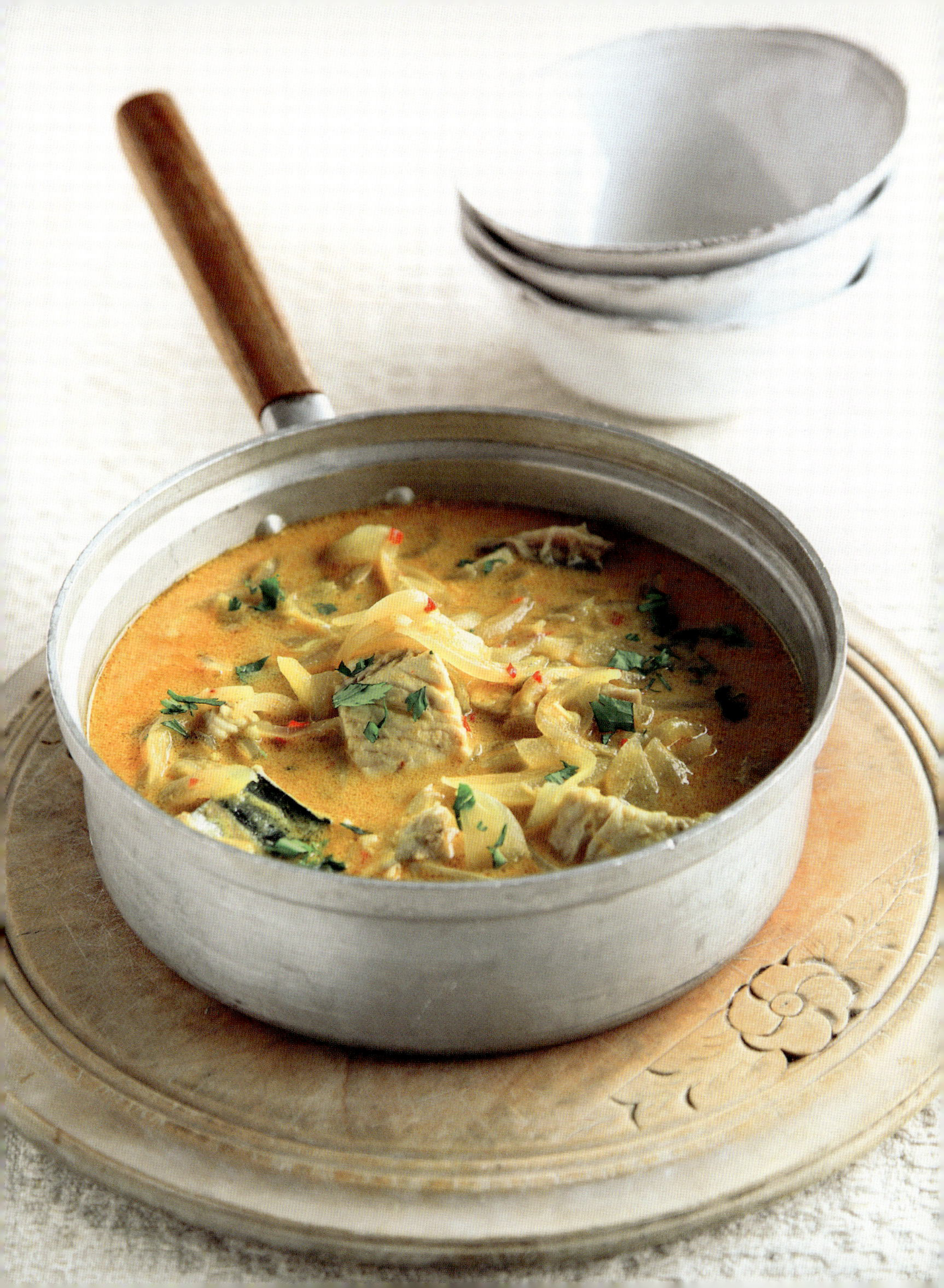

20 Smoked Haddock with a Cider and Cheese Sauce

Serves 4

1 cup apple cider or apple juice
4 tablespoons butter
⅓ cup all-purpose flour
2 cups shredded sharp cheddar cheese
1½ teaspoons English mustard
1 tablespoon Worcestershire sauce
4 (5 oz) skinless smoked haddock or smoked salmon fillets
salt and black pepper

To serve

1 bunch of watercress or 2 cups arugula
4 tomatoes, sliced

- Heat the cider or apple juice in a small saucepan until warm.
- Melt the butter in a separate small saucepan, then stir in the flour to make a roux. Cook for 1–2 minutes, then gradually whisk in the cider and cook, stirring continuously, until the sauce is thick and smooth. Add the cheese, mustard, and Worcestershire sauce and stir until the cheese has melted. Season to taste.
- Cook the haddock or salmon under a preheated hot broiler for 3 minutes on each side or until just cooked through.
- Spoon the cheese mixture onto the fish and broil for another 2–3 minutes, until bubbling and golden. Serve on a bed of watercress or arugula and sliced tomato.

10 Smoked Haddock and Tangy Cheese on Toast

Place 8 oz skinless smoked haddock or smoked salmon and 1¼ cups milk in a skillet and gently poach for 2–3 minutes or until just cooked through, then remove any bones and break into large flakes. Meanwhile, toast 4 slices of whole-wheat bread under a preheated hot broiler for 2–3 minutes on each side. Spread one side of each slice with ½ tablespoon mango chutney, then top with the flaked fish. Sprinkle with ¼–⅓ cup shredded sharp cheddar cheese. Broil for 2–3 minutes, until bubbling and golden.

30 Smoked Mackerel and Cheese Toasts

Place 4 sliced ripe tomatoes on a serving plate, then sprinkle with ½ thinly sliced red onion. Drizzle with 1 tablespoon vinaigrette and let stand. Skin and flake 2 smoked mackerel fillets into a bowl, then mix together with ¼ cup plain yogurt, ½ cup grated Parmesan cheese, 1 teaspoon creamed horseradish, and 1 tablespoon chopped chives. Bring a saucepan of water to a gentle simmer and stir with a large spoon to create a swirl. Break 2 eggs into the water and cook for 3 minutes. Remove with a slotted spoon and keep warm. Repeat with another 2 eggs. Toast 4 thick slices of whole-grain bread under a preheated hot broiler for 2–3 minutes on each side. Spoon the fish mixture over the toast and sprinkle with ½ cup grated Parmesan. Broil for 3–4 minutes, until bubbling, then top with the poached eggs and serve with the tomato salad.

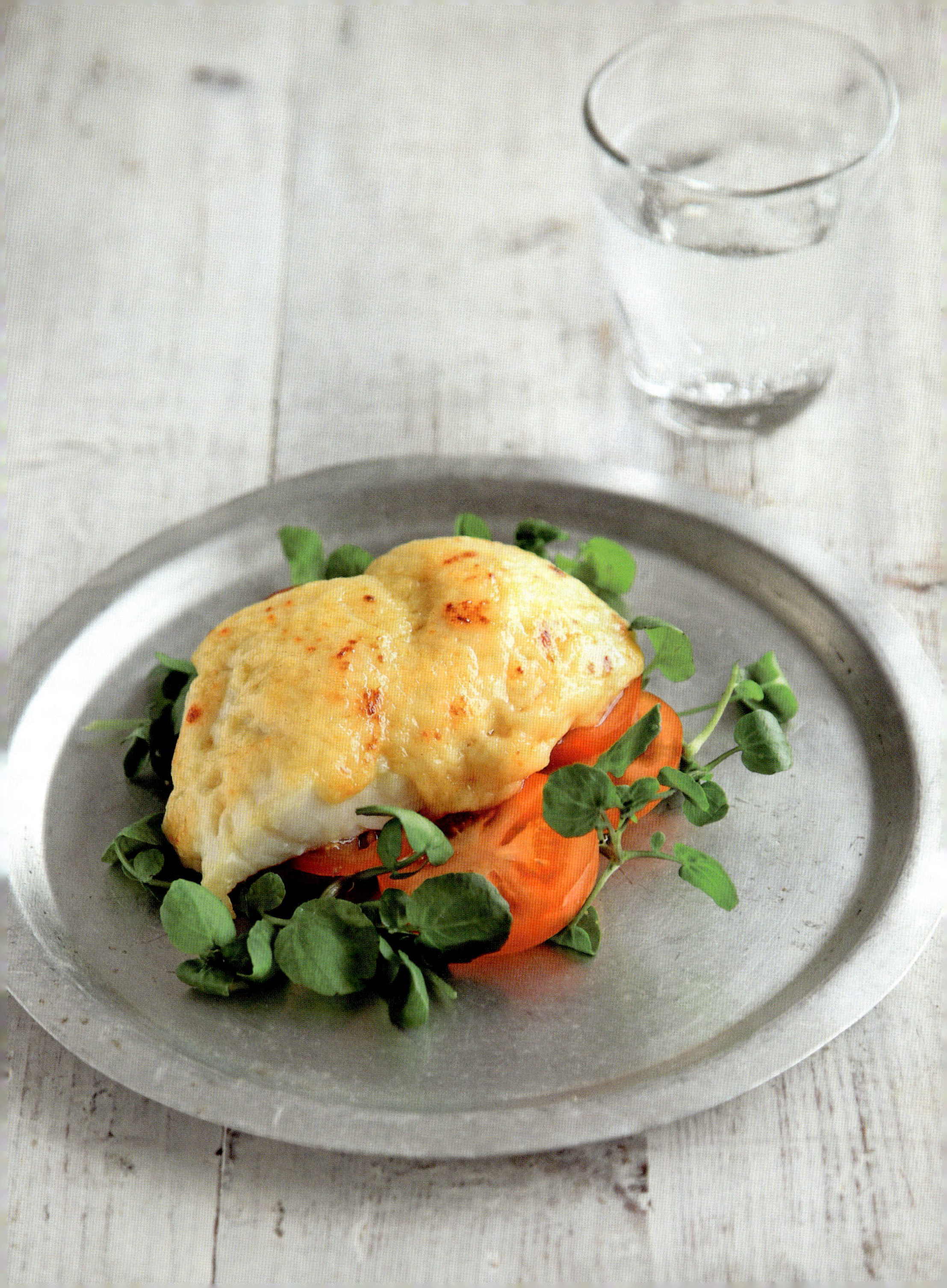

10 Jumbo Shrimp Caesar Salad

Serves 4

1 tablespoon olive oil
2 slices of white bread, crusts removed, cut into small squares
2 garlic cloves
4 anchovy fillets in oil, drained
2 teaspoons lemon juice
1 teaspoon Dijon mustard
½ teaspoon Worcestershire sauce
1 cup plain yogurt
1 large romaine lettuce, torn
8 oz cooked peeled jumbo shrimp
3 tablespoons grated Parmesan cheese

- To make the croutons, heat the oil in a skillet until hot, then toss the bread in the skillet for 3–4 minutes, until golden. Remove with a slotted spoon and drain on paper towels.

- Place the garlic, anchovies, lemon juice, mustard, Worcestershire sauce, and yogurt in a mini food processor or small blender and blend until smooth.

- Place the lettuce and shrimp in a salad bowl with the croutons, then add the yogurt mixture and cheese. Toss lightly to coat the salad with the dressing.

---

20 Spicy Jumbo Shrimp Noodles

Heat 1 tablespoon coconut oil in a wok or skillet, add 12 oz raw peeled, jumbo shrimp, and stir-fry for 1–2 minutes or until they turn pink and are cooked through. Remove with a slotted spoon. Add 1 seeded and chopped red chile and 1 cored, seeded, and diced red bell pepper to the wok and stir-fry for 2 minutes, then add 2 cups sugar snap peas and 4 sliced scallions and stir-fry for another 2 minutes. Stir in 2 tablespoons sweet chili sauce, 1 tablespoon soy sauce, and a pinch of sugar, then add 12 oz straight-to-wok noodles and ½ cup water and simmer for 2–3 minutes, until the sauce is syrupy. Return the shrimp to the wok and cook for 1 minute or until heated through. Serve sprinkled with 2 tablespoons chopped cilantro.

30 Jumbo Shrimp and Coconut Curry

Heat 1 tablespoon coconut oil in a wok or skillet, add 2 grated onions, and cook for 2–3 minutes, then add 1 teaspoon turmeric, 6 crushed cardamom pods, 1 teaspoon chili powder, 3 crushed garlic cloves, and 2 tablespoons peeled and grated ginger root and stir-fry for another 1–2 minutes. Blend a small handful of cilantro leaves and 1¼ cups coconut milk in a small blender, then stir into the onion mixture and bring to a boil. Reduce the heat and simmer for 15 minutes. Add 1¾ lb raw, peeled jumbo shrimp and cook for 3–4 minutes, until they turn pink. Serve with cooked rice.

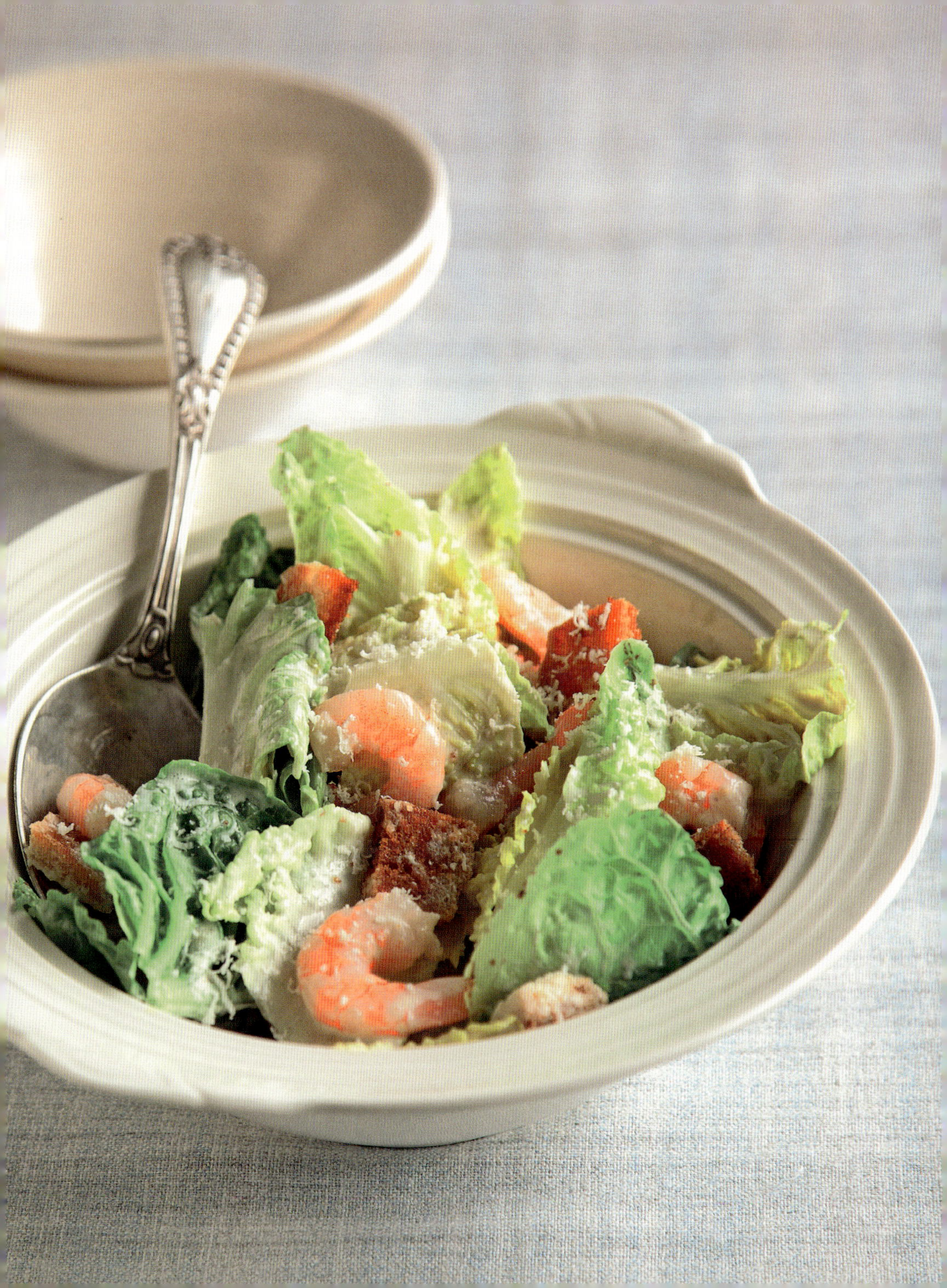

Smoked Mackerel and Spring Vegetable Tabbouleh

Serves 4

1 cup couscous
1½ cups halved green beans
⅔ cup fresh or frozen peas
5 oz asparagus tips
4 scallions, sliced
2 garlic cloves, finely diced
¼ cup chopped mint
¼ cup chopped parsley
3 peppered smoked mackerel fillets, skinned and flaked
3 tablespoons olive oil
juice of 1 lime
1 romaine lettuce, roughly torn
12 cherry tomatoes, halved
2 tablespoons toasted pine nuts
salt and black pepper

- Place the couscous in a large heatproof bowl and just cover with boiling water. Let stand for 15 minutes.

- Meanwhile, steam or boil the green beans, peas, and asparagus tips for 4–5 minutes, until just tender. Refresh under cold running water and drain.

- Fluff up the couscous with a fork, then stir in the scallions, garlic, herbs, mackerel, oil, and lime juice. Season to taste.

- Arrange the lettuce and tomatoes on a serving plate, spoon the couscous over the vegetables, and sprinkle with the pine nuts.

Smoked Mackerel and Spring Vegetable Salad Lightly steam 1½ cups broccoli florets, ⅔ cup peas, and 4 oz halved asparagus tips for 2–3 minutes, then refresh under cold running water and drain. Place in a large bowl with 2 chopped celery sticks, 4 sliced scallions, ½ cup halved green grapes, 3 skinned and flaked smoked mackerel fillets, and 8 cherry tomatoes. Toss with salad dressing and serve sprinkled with 2 tablespoons toasted slivered almonds.

Smoked Mackerel and Spring Vegetable Paella Heat 1 tablespoon olive oil in a large skillet or paella pan, add 1 chopped onion and 2 crushed garlic cloves, and cook for 1–2 minutes. Add 2 chopped zucchini and 2 peeled and diced carrots and cook for another 1–2 minutes. Stir in 1⅓ cups paella or risotto rice and 1 cup canned diced tomatoes. Stir in a pinch of paprika and a pinch of saffron threads, then pour in 3¾ cups hot vegetable stock. Bring to a boil, then reduce the heat and simmer for 18–20 minutes, until the rice is tender, adding ⅔ cup peas, 4 oz asparagus tips, and 2 skinned and thinly sliced smoked mackerel fillets 2 minutes before the end of the cooking time. Stir in 2 tablespoons chopped parsley and season to taste.

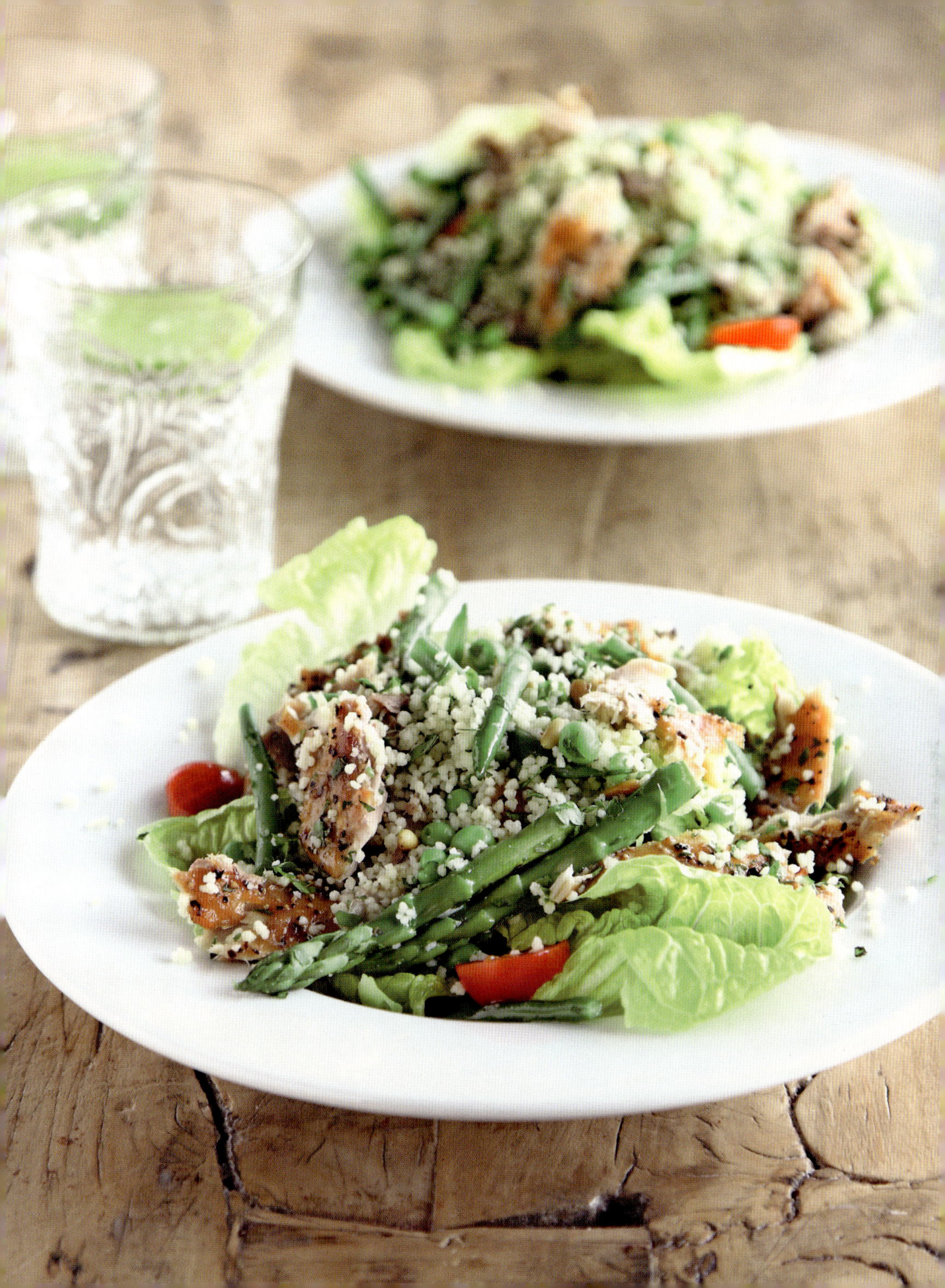

20 Pan-Fried Sea Bass with Warm Leek and Lentil Salad

Serves 4

3 tablespoons olive oil
1 lb leeks, trimmed and sliced
1 (15 oz) can lentils, rinsed and drained, or 2 cups cooked lentils
3 teaspoons creamed horseradish
2 tablespoons crème fraîche or sour cream
4 sea bass fillets
black pepper

- Heat 1 tablespoon of the oil in a skillet, add the leeks, and season with black pepper, then cook over medium heat for 8–10 minutes, until soft. Add the lentils and cook for another 2–3 minutes. Stir in the horseradish and crème fraîche or sour cream and continue to cook for 2–3 minutes.

- Meanwhile, heat 1 tablespoon of the oil in a skillet, add the sea bass, and cook for 3–4 minutes on each side or until cooked through.

- Serve the sea bass with the lentils, drizzled with the remaining oil.

10 Sea Bass, Leek, and Lentil Soup

Heat 1 tablespoon coconut oil in a skillet, add 1 chopped onion, 2 chopped garlic cloves, and 3 trimmed and chopped leeks, and cook for 3–4 minutes, until softened. Stir in 1 (15 oz) can lentils, rinsed and drained, or 2 cups cooked lentils, and 5 cups hot vegetable stock and bring to a boil, then reduce the heat and simmer for 6 minutes, adding 8 oz sea bass fillets, skinned and cut into bite-size pieces, 2 minutes before the end of the cooking time. Season, stir in 2 tablespoons chopped parsley, and serve.

30 Sea Bass with Spicy Leek and Lentil Casserole

Heat 1 tablespoon olive oil in a skillet, add 2 chopped onions and 1 crushed garlic clove, and cook for 3–4 minutes, until softened. Stir in 1 teaspoon peeled and grated fresh ginger root, 1 teaspoon garam masala, and ½ teaspoon turmeric and cook for another 1–2 minutes. Pour in ½ cup rinsed and drained canned lentils or cooked lentils and 1½ cups hot vegetable stock and simmer for 2–3 minutes, until all the liquid has been absorbed. Meanwhile, steam 4 trimmed leeks, cut into 1-inch lengths, for 4–5 minutes, then place in an ovenproof dish. Mash the lentils until smooth, then pour over the leeks and top with 2 tablespoons chopped walnuts. Bake in a preheated oven, at 400°F, for 18–20 minutes or until browned. Meanwhile, heat 1 tablespoon of olive oil in a skillet, add 4 (5 oz) sea bass fillets, and cook for 3–4 minutes on each side or until cooked through, then serve with the lentil casserole.

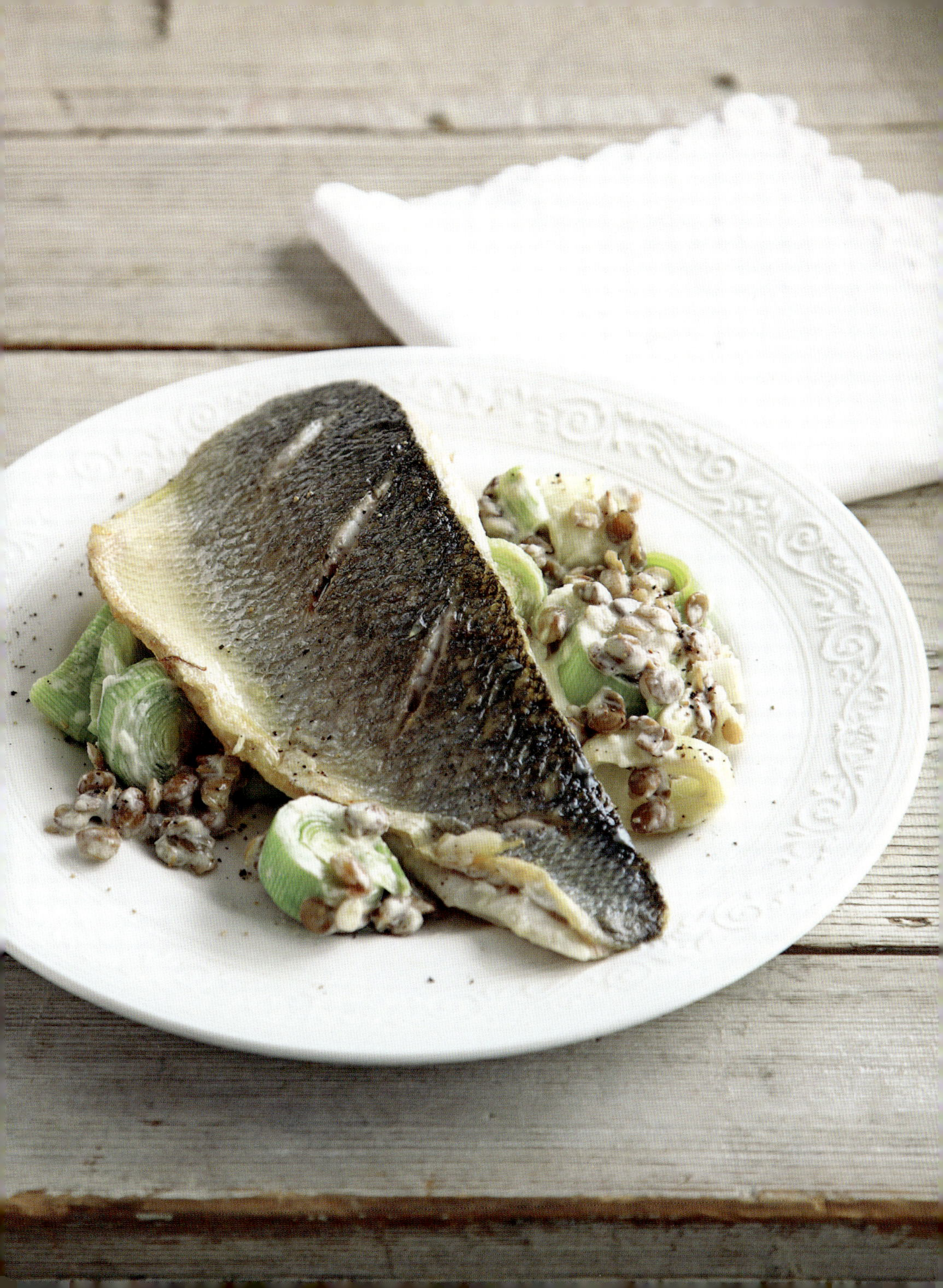

20 Broiled Salmon with Avocado Salsa

Serves 4

2 avocados, peeled, pitted, and diced
juice of ½ lime
½ cup diced baby plum tomatoes
1 tablespoon chopped cilantro
1 tablespoon olive oil
4 (5 oz) salmon fillets

- Mix together the avocados and lime juice in a bowl to prevent discoloration. Add the tomatoes, cilantro, and oil and mix well. Let stand.

- Meanwhile, cook the salmon under a preheated medium broiler, skin side up, for about 6–8 minutes, until the skin starts to turn golden. Turn the fish over and cook for another 4–5 minutes or until cooked through.

- Serve the salmon with a spoonful of salsa.

10 Salmon and Avocado Salad

Whisk together 3 tablespoons extra virgin olive oil, the grated rind and juice of 1 lemon, 1 teaspoon honey, ½ teaspoon Dijon mustard, 2 tablespoons shredded basil leaves, and salt and black pepper in a bowl. Using a vegetable peeler, slice 1 large zucchini into long, thin strips and divide among 4 plates. Tear 1 lb mozzarella cheese into chunks and divide among the plates, then top with 5 oz smoked salmon, cut into strips, 1 cup sun-dried tomatoes, and 2 peeled, pitted, and sliced avocados. Drizzle with the dressing and sprinkle with 2 tablespoons toasted pine nuts.

30 Salmon Packages with Avocado Sauce

Place 2 avocados, 1 garlic clove, 1 teaspoon sherry vinegar, and ½ teaspoon freshly ground black pepper in a food processor and blend until smooth. Place in a bowl and stir in 1 cup crème fraîche. Cover and chill until required. Mix together 1 sliced red onion, 2 sliced garlic cloves, 2 chopped tomatoes, 1 teaspoon chopped dill, and ½ cup white wine. Place 4 (5 oz) skinless salmon fillets in a nonmetallic bowl and pour the marinade over the fish. Let stand for 5 minutes. Place the salmon and marinade in the center of 4 large sheets of wax paper, then fold up to make sealed packages. Place on a baking sheet and bake in a preheated oven, at 400°F, for 6–8 minutes or until cooked through. Serve with watercress or arugula and the avocado sauce.

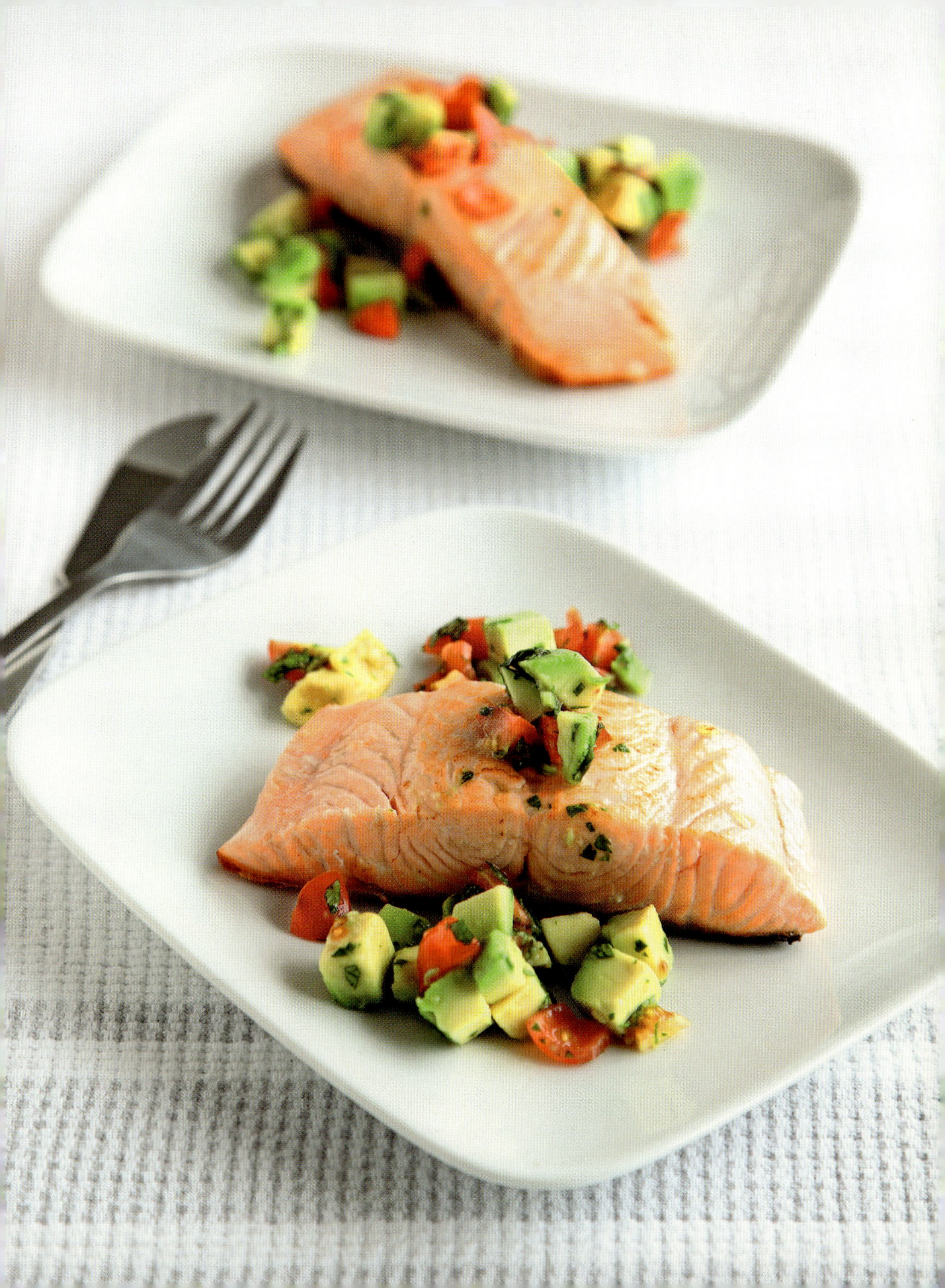

30 Fish Casserole

Serves 4

3 large sweet potatoes, peeled and chopped
1½ cups milk
4 oz skinless salmon fillet, cut into bite-size pieces
12 oz skinless cod fillet, cut into bite-size pieces
2 eggs
2 tablespoons butter
1 tablespoon all-purpose flour
½ teaspoon mustard
3 cups baby spinach leaves
8 oz cooked, peeled jumbo shrimp
¾ cup shredded cheddar cheese
black pepper

- Cook the sweet potatoes in a saucepan of boiling water for 12 minutes or until tender.

- Meanwhile, pour the milk into a skillet. Add the salmon and cod. Bring to a simmer and gently cook for 5–6 minutes or until the fish is just cooked through. Drain the fish, reserving the milk.

- Cook the eggs in a saucepan of boiling water for 4–5 minutes, until softly boiled. Refresh under cold running water.

- Melt the butter in a small saucepan, then stir in the flour to make a roux. Cook for 1–2 minutes, then stir in the mustard. Gradually whisk in the reserved milk and cook, stirring continuously, until the sauce is thick and smooth.

- Lay the spinach in an ovenproof dish and add the fish. Peel the eggs and cut into quarters, then place on the fish. Sprinkle in the shrimp. Pour the white sauce over the top.

- Drain the sweet potatoes, then mash in the pan with plenty of black pepper. Spoon the sweet potatoes over the fish and spread with a fork, then sprinkle with the cheese. Bake in a preheated oven, at 400°F, for 12–15 minutes, until bubbling.

1 Fish Pâté

Chop 5 oz smoked salmon into small pieces. Place 1 cup cream cheese, 1 tablespoon plain yogurt, the juice of ½ lemon, and salt and black pepper in a food processor and process until smooth. Add the salmon and pulse to form a chunky pâté. Stir in a small bunch of chopped dill or chives. Serve with warm toast or breadsticks.

2 Fish Soup

Heat 2 tablespoons olive oil in a large saucepan, add 1 chopped onion, 1 chopped fennel bulb, 2 crushed garlic cloves, and ½ teaspoon fennel seeds and cook for 2–3 minutes. Stir in a 1 (14½ oz) can diced tomatoes and cook for another 6–8 minutes. Pour in 8 cups hot fish stock and a pinch of saffron threads and bring to a boil. Add 8 oz cooked, peeled shrimp, 8 oz live clams, cleaned, and 12 oz skinless salmon fillet, cut into bite-size pieces, and simmer for 5–6 minutes or until the fish is cooked through and the clams have opened. Discard any shells that remain shut. Add 2 tablespoons chopped parsley and serve with crusty bread.

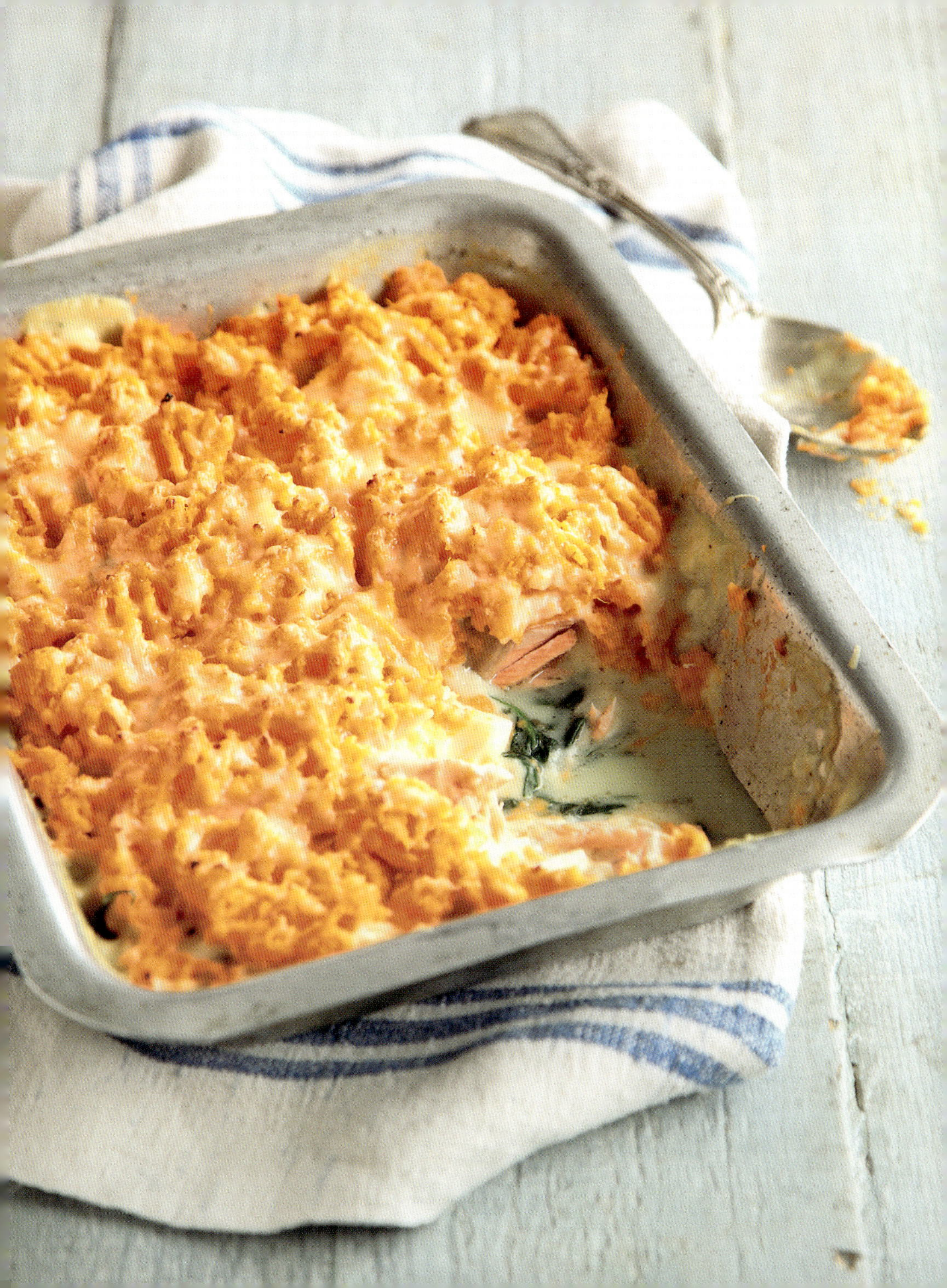

Shrimp and Goat Cheese Salad

Serves 4

2 tablespoons walnut pieces
juice of 1 lime
1 tablespoon olive oil
1 fennel bulb, halved and sliced
1 red bell pepper, cored, seeded, and sliced
2 pears, cored and sliced
8 oz cooked, peeled jumbo shrimp
2 heads of endives, leaves separated
7 oz firm goat cheese, cut into 4 slices

- Heat a nonstick skillet over medium-low heat and dry-fry the walnuts for 3–4 minutes, stirring frequently, until slightly golden. Set aside.
- Meanwhile, whisk together the lime juice and oil in a bowl.
- Toss together the fennel, red bell pepper, pears, shrimp, and endive and place on a serving plate.
- Cook the goat cheese under a preheated hot broiler for 3–4 minutes, until golden. Serve on the salad, drizzled with the dressing and sprinkled with the toasted walnuts.

Shrimp and Cheese Soufflés

Melt 2 tablespoons butter in a small saucepan, then stir in 2 tablespoons all-purpose flour. Cook for 1–2 minutes, then gradually whisk in ¼ cup milk and cook, stirring, until thick and smooth. Add a pinch of cayenne pepper and season. Stir in ¾ cup shredded cheddar cheese and 3 egg yolks. Whisk 3 egg whites in a clean bowl until stiff. Stir 1 tablespoon of the egg white into the cheese sauce, then fold in the remainder. Place 4 oz cooked, peeled shrimp in 4 greased ramekins. Spoon the egg mixture into the ramekins and place on a baking sheet. Bake in a preheated oven, at 350°F, for 12–14 minutes. Serve immediately with a salad.

Shrimp and Cheese Gratin

Toss 12 oz raw, peeled jumbo shrimp with the juice of 1 lime and a few drops of Tabasco sauce in a nonmetallic bowl. Cover and let marinate in the refrigerator for 15 minutes. Meanwhile, heat 1 tablespoon olive oil in a skillet, add 2 finely sliced red onions, and cook for 2–3 minutes. Add 2 crushed garlic cloves and 2 seeded and diced chiles and cook for another 3–4 minutes. Divide the onion mixture among 4 gratin dishes. Drain the shrimp and add to the onions. Pour over ⅔ cup heavy cream and ⅔ cup plain yogurt, then sprinkle with ¾ cup shredded cheddar cheese. Cook under a preheated hot broiler for 6–7 minutes, until bubbling and the shrimp turn pink. Serve with a crisp green salad.

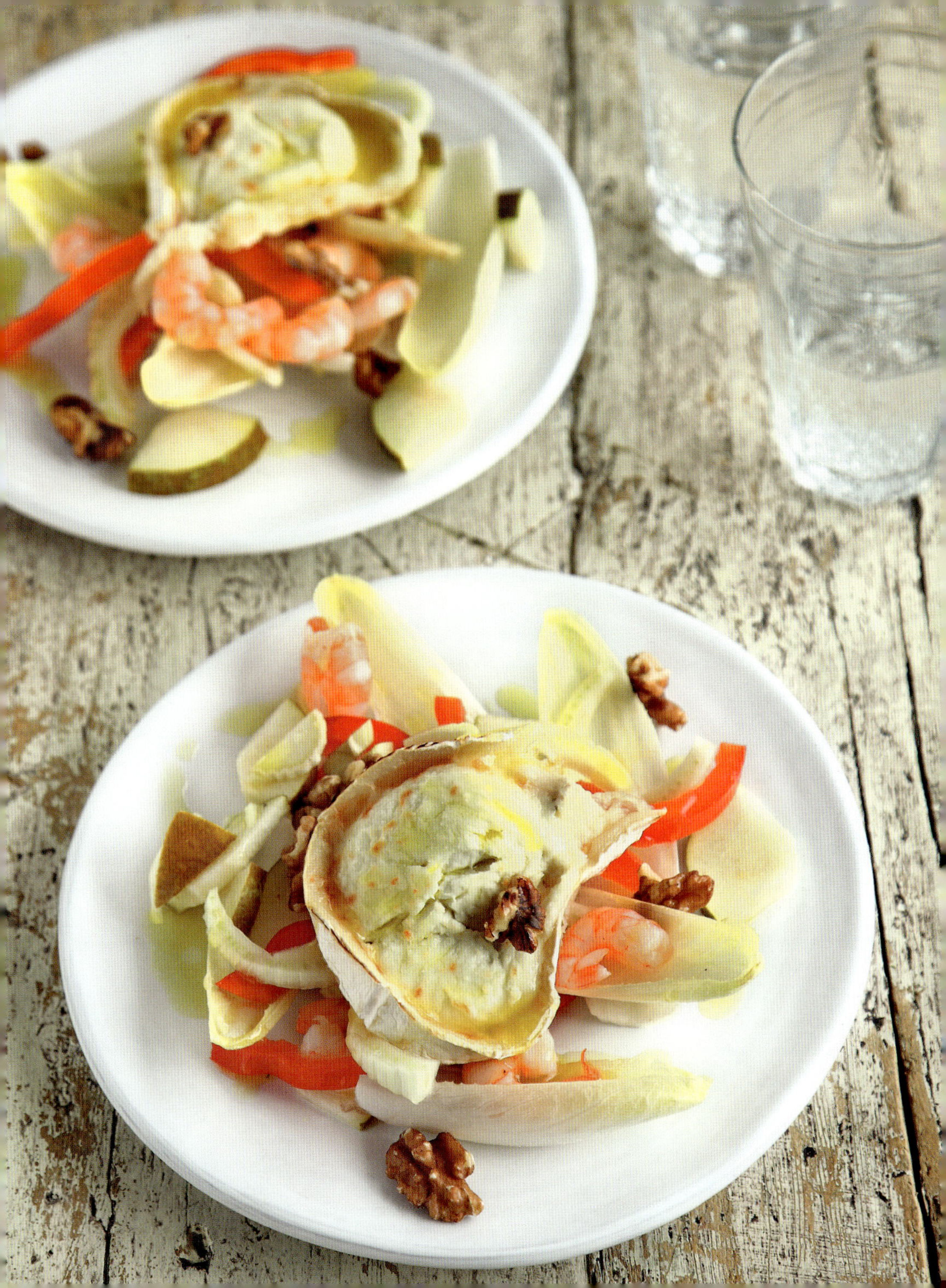

Chunky Cod, Red Snapper, and Shrimp Stew

Serves 4

1 tablespoon olive oil
1 fennel bulb, quartered and thinly sliced
2 garlic cloves, thinly sliced
1 (14½ oz) can diced tomatoes
pinch of saffron threads
4 cups hot fish stock
8 oz cod fillet, cut into bite-size pieces
8 oz cooked, peeled jumbo shrimp
2 red snapper fillets, halved lengthwise
2 cups spinach leaves
crusty whole-wheat bread, to serve

- Heat the oil in a large skillet, add the fennel and garlic, and cook for 4–5 minutes, until softened. Stir in the tomatoes and saffron, then pour in the stock and bring to a simmer.
- Add the cod, shrimp, and red snapper and simmer for 6–8 minutes or until the fish is cooked through.
- Stir in the spinach until wilted, then serve immediately with crusty whole-wheat bread.

Quick Cod, Red Snapper, and Shrimp Curry Heat 1 tablespoon oil in a large skillet or wok, add 1 chopped onion and 2 chopped garlic cloves, and sauté for 1 minute. Stir in 2 tablespoons curry paste and 1¾ cups coconut milk and bring to a simmer. Add 8 oz cod and 2 red snapper fillets, cut into bite-size pieces, and 8 oz cooked, peeled jumbo shrimp. Simmer for 6–8 minutes, until the fish is cooked through. Stir in 4 cups spinach leaves and 2 tablespoons coarsely chopped cilantro. Season and serve with rice.

Cod, Red Snapper, and Shrimp Casserole Cook 6 peeled and chopped russet potatoes in a saucepan of boiling water for 10–12 minutes, until tender. Meanwhile, place 12 oz red snapper and 8 oz cod fillet in a skillet with enough milk to cover and gently simmer for 5 minutes or until just cooked through. Drain, then skin and flake the fish. Return the fish to the pan with ⅔ cup peas, 4 oz cooked, peeled shrimp, 1 cup crème fraîche or sour cream, and 2 tablespoons chopped chives and cook for 2–3 minutes. Drain the potatoes, then mash in the pan with 2 tablespoons butter and 2 tablespoons milk. Season well. Spoon the fish mixture into an ovenproof dish and top with the mashed potatoes. Bake in a preheated oven, at 400°F, for 10 minutes, until golden. Serve with steamed green vegetables.

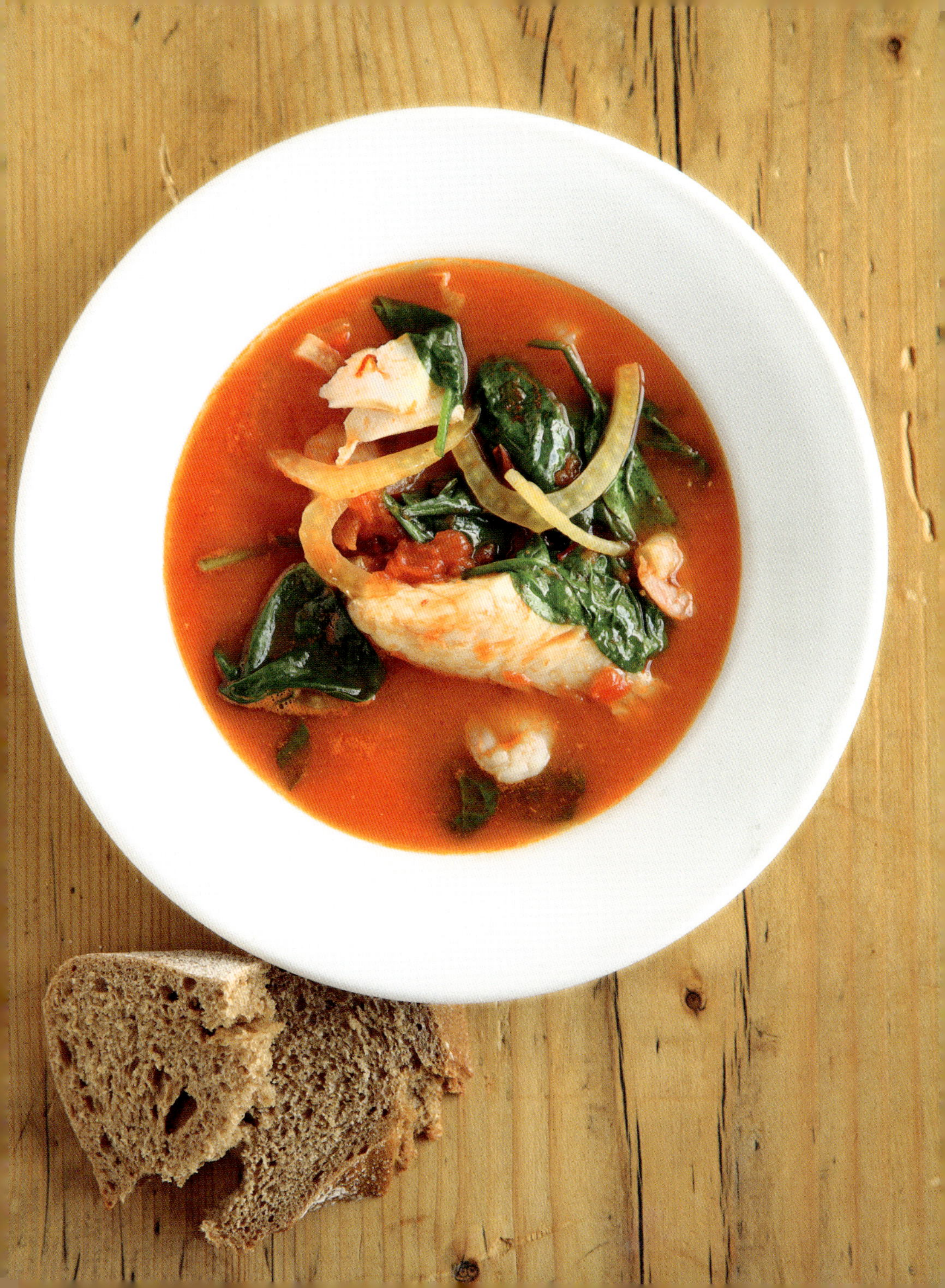

QuickCook
Vegetarian Dishes

Recipes listed by cooking time

30

Spinach and Mozzarella Roulade	184
Red Pepper and Coconut Curry	186
Butternut and Broccoli Soup with Mushroom Bruschetta	188
Moroccan Vegetable Stew	190
Fava Bean and Feta Mashed Potatoes	192
Macaroni and Cheese with Cauliflower	194
Roasted Bell Peppers	196
Lima Bean and Mushroom Tagine	198
Cheesy Pesto Grits	200
Asparagus and Pea Tart	202
Falafels with Greek Salsa	204
Cumin-Roasted Fennel and Veg	206
Mushroom, Tomato, and Herb Pancakes	208
Pea and Mint Soufflés	210
Spaghetti with Roasted Tomato and Chickpea Sauce	212

Cheese and Spinach Muffins	214
Lentil, Chickpea, Chicken, and Mustard Curry	216
Carrot and Cashew Nut Rice	218
Spicy Broccoli and Red Pepper Noodles	220
Simple Baked Leeks and Sweet Potatoes	222
Mushroom and Tofu Thai Curry	224
Spinach, Mushroom, and Feta-Stuffed Peppers	226
Falafel Cheese Burgers	228
Pesto and Broccoli Potato Cakes	230

20

Spinach and Mozzarella Tagliatelle	184
Roasted Red Peppers and Veg with Coconut Rice	186
Butternut, Broccoli, and Mushroom Gratin	188
Moroccan Roasted Vegetables	190
Fava Bean and Feta Salad	192
Cauliflower Cheese Soup	194
Italian Fried Bell Peppers	196
Lima Bean and Mushroom Soup	198
Polenta with Pesto Roasted Veg	200
Asparagus and Pea Quinoa Risotto	202
Greek Pita Pockets	204
Fennel, Cumin, and Butternut Soup	206
Tomato and Herb-Stuffed Mushrooms	208
Pea and Mint Pancakes	210
Linguine with Chickpea and Tomato Sauce	212

Cheese and Spinach Quesadillas		214
Lentil, Mustard, and Chickpea Soup		216
Carrot and Cashew Nut Curry		218
Spicy Broccoli Pasta with Poached Eggs		220
Leek and Sweet Potato Soup		222
Mushroom and Tofu Stew		224
Cheesy Spinach-Stuffed Mushrooms		226
Falafel and Tabbouleh Salad		228
Crunchy Pesto Broccoli with Poached Eggs		230

Quick Spinach and Mozzarella Pizzas		184
Coconut-Crusted Tofu		186
Cheesy Mashed Butternut Squash with Broccoli and Poached Eggs		188
Moroccan Vegetable Soup		190
Fava Bean and Feta Tagliatelle		192
Cauliflower Cheese Gratin		194
Bell Pepper and Zucchini Salad		196
Warm Lima Bean and Mushroom Salad		198
Polenta Salad with Pesto Dressing		200
Warm Asparagus and Pea Rice Salad		202
Greek Salad		204
Fennel and Cumin Waldorf Salad		206
Mushroom, Tomato, and Herb Toasts		208
Pea and Mint Dip		210
Chickpea, Tomato, and Pasta Salad		212

Cheese and Spinach Pancakes		214
Lentil and Chickpea Salad with Warm Mustard Dressing		216
Carrot and Cashew Nut Slaw		218
Spicy Broccoli and Cheese		220
Roasted Baby Leeks and Sweet Potatoes		222
Mushroom and Tofu Stir-Fry		224
Spinach, Mushrooms, and Cheese on Toast		226
Falafels with Spicy Sauce		228
Broccoli Pesto Pasta		230

10 Quick Spinach and Mozzarella Pizzas

Serves 4

4 flour tortillas
1 tablespoon olive oil
3 (6 oz) packages baby spinach leaves
2/3 cup tomato puree or tomato sauce
½ cup thinly sliced roasted red pepper from a jar
6 scallions, sliced
4 eggs
1 teaspoon dried oregano
2 cups shredded mozzarella cheese

- Place the tortillas on 2 large baking sheets and warm through in a preheated oven, at 475°F, for 2 minutes.

- Meanwhile, heat the oil in a large skillet, add the spinach, and cook briefly until wilted.

- Spread each tortilla with tomato puree or sauce, then divide the spinach, roasted red pepper, and scallions among them. Break an egg in the middle of each pizza, then sprinkle with the oregano and cheese.

- Return to the oven for another 3–5 minutes, until the edges are lightly browned and the cheese is melted.

---

20 Spinach and Mozzarella Tagliatelle

Cook 1 lb tagliatelle in a large saucepan of boiling water according to the package directions, until "al dente." Meanwhile, heat 1 tablespoon olive oil in a large skillet, add 1 (12 oz) package baby spinach leaves and 2 crushed garlic cloves, and cook until the spinach is wilted. Remove from the heat and stir in ½ cup thinly sliced roasted red pepper from a jar. Drain the pasta and toss with the spinach mixture and 8 oz mozzarella cheese, chopped. Serve sprinkled with chopped basil leaves and 2 tablespoons toasted pine nuts.

30 Spinach and Mozzarella Roulade

Whisk 3 egg whites and 1 teaspoon lemon juice in a clean bowl until stiff. In a separate bowl, mix together 1 teaspoon cornstarch, 1 cup milk, 1 teaspoon Dijon mustard, and 3 egg yolks and season with salt and black pepper, then fold into the egg whites. Pour into a jelly roll pan lined with wax paper, spreading it out to the corners. Bake in a preheated oven, at 350°F, for 5–8 minutes, until it springs back when pressed. Lift the roulade from the pan, then using the paper, roll it into a log and let cool for 5 minutes. Meanwhile, heat 1 tablespoon olive oil in a skillet, add 1 (6 oz) package baby spinach leaves, and cook briefly until wilted, then stir in 2 chopped tomatoes and 4 oz sliced mozzarella cheese. Unroll the roulade, spread over the spinach filling, then reroll. Serve with store-bought tomato sauce and a crisp green salad.

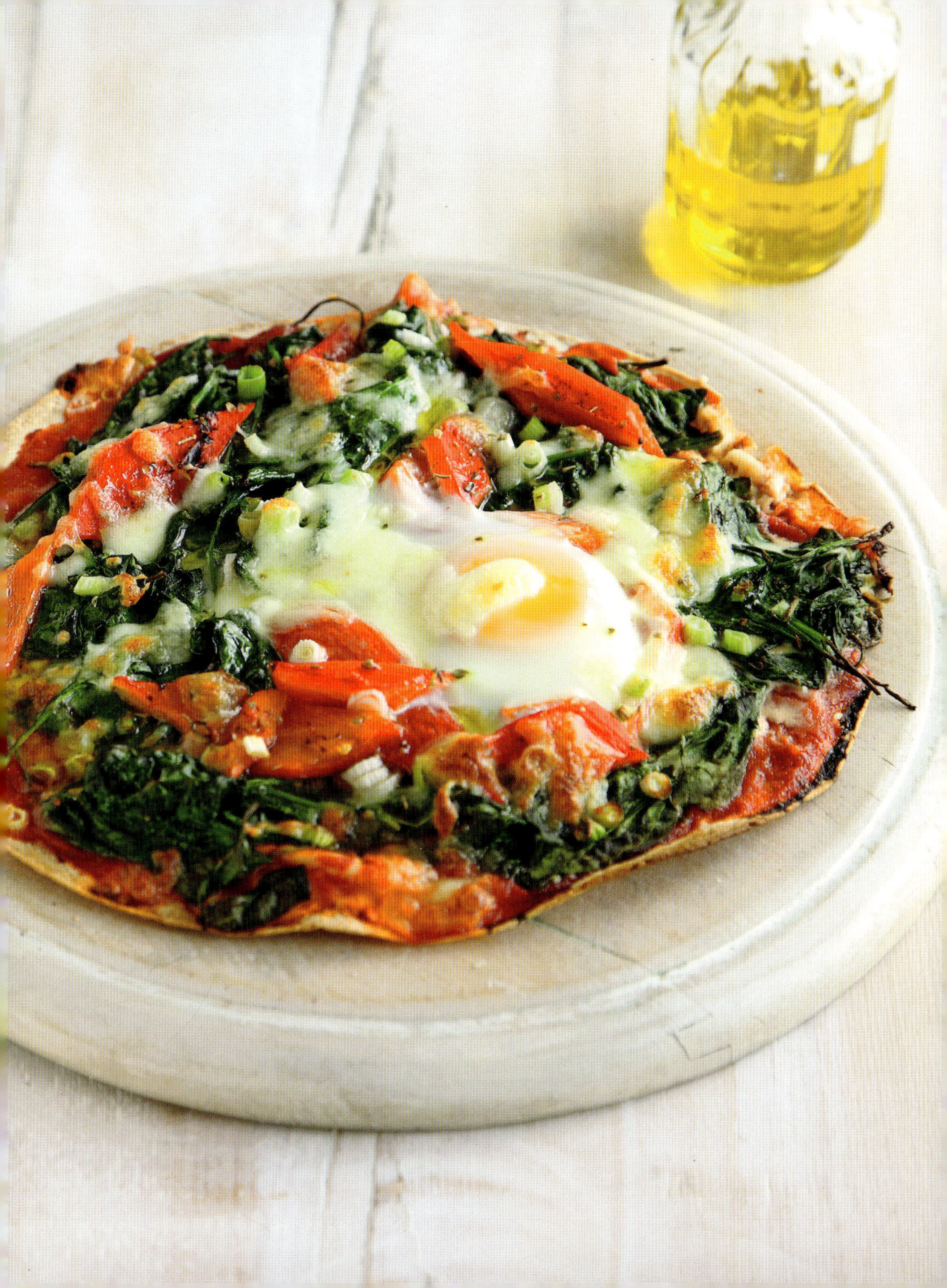

30 Red Pepper and Coconut Curry

Serves 4

1 teaspoon tamarind paste
1 teaspoon turmeric
½ teaspoon chili powder
1 tablespoon mango juice
½ tablespoon coconut oil
1 teaspoon mustard seeds
2 teaspoons cumin seeds
2 garlic cloves, crushed
1 onion, sliced
1 teaspoon prepared minced ginger
3⅓ cups coconut milk
1¼ cups peeled, seeded, and chopped butternut squash
1 potato, peeled and chopped
1 red bell pepper, cored, seeded, and chopped
1 parsnip, peeled and chopped
1 cup cauliflower florets

To serve

2 tablespoons chopped cilantro
2 tablespoons slivered almonds

- To make a spice paste, place the tamarind paste, powdered spices, and mango juice in a mini food processor or small blender and blend together. Set aside.

- Heat the oil in a saucepan, add the mustard seeds and cumin seeds, and cook until the mustard seeds begin to pop. Add the garlic, onion, and ginger and cook for another 3–4 minutes, until softened.

- Add the spice paste and cook, stirring, for 1 minute, then pour in the coconut milk and bring to a boil. Add the vegetables and simmer for 20–22 minutes.

- Serve sprinkled with chopped cilantro and slivered almonds.

---

10 Coconut-Crusted Tofu
Mix together 1½ cups shredded dried coconut, 1 tablespoon all-purpose flour, and 2 teaspoons cornstarch on a plate. Cut 1 (14 oz) package tofu into thick slices and dip in a little milk and the dried coconut mixture. Heat 1 tablespoon olive oil in a skillet, add the tofu, and cook for 1–2 minutes on each side until slightly golden. Serve the salsa with the tofu and arugula salad.

20 Roasted Red Peppers and Veg with Coconut Rice
Place 1½ cups peeled, seeded, and chopped butternut squash, 1 chopped red onion, cut into wedges, 2 cored, seeded, and chopped red bell peppers, and 1 large sliced zucchini in a roasting pan and toss with 1 tablespoon olive oil. Place in a preheated oven, at 400°F, for 18–19 minutes, until tender. Meanwhile, place 1 cup long-grain rice, 1½ cups coconut milk, and ⅔ cup water in a saucepan and season. Bring to a simmer, then cover and cook gently until all the liquid has been absorbed, adding a handful of defrosted frozen peas 3 minutes before the end of the cooking time. Stir in 4 chopped scallions and 2 tablespoons chopped cilantro. Serve with the roasted vegetables spooned over the top.

186 VEGETARIAN DISHES

HEA-VEGE-RUY

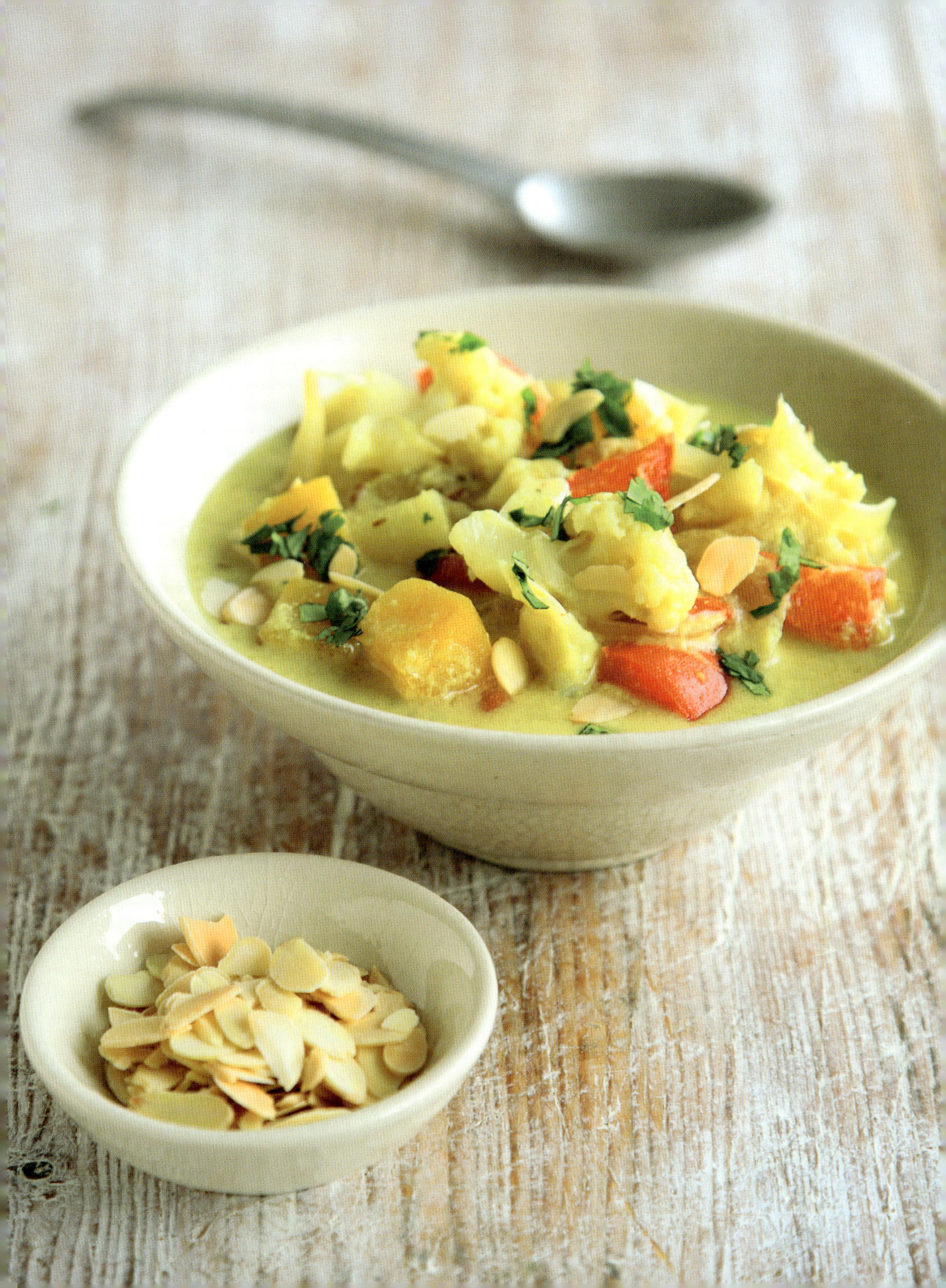

20 Butternut, Broccoli, and Mushroom Gratin

Serves 4

8 oz baby broccoli, trimmed
2 cups peeled, seeded, and chopped butternut squash
3 cups halved mushrooms
4 tablespoons butter
2 tablespoons all-purpose flour
1¾ cups milk
2 teaspoons whole-grain mustard
1 cup shredded cheddar cheese

- Steam the vegetables in a steamer for 8–10 minutes, until tender. Transfer the vegetables to an ovenproof dish.

- Meanwhile, melt the butter in a small saucepan, then stir in the flour to make a roux. Cook for 1–2 minutes, then gradually whisk in the milk, and cook, stirring continuously, until the sauce is thick and smooth. Stir in the mustard and half the shredded cheese.

- Pour the sauce over the vegetables and sprinkle with the remaining cheese. Cook under a preheated hot broiler for 5–6 minutes, until bubbling and golden.

1 Cheesy Mashed Butternut Squash with Broccoli and Poached Eggs

Cook 3 cups peeled, seeded, and diced butternut squash and 1 cup peeled and diced russet potatoes in a saucepan of boiling water for 8 minutes, until tender. Meanwhile, bring a saucepan of water to a gentle simmer and stir with a large spoon to create a swirl. Break 2 eggs into the water and cook for 3 minutes. Remove with a slotted spoon and keep warm. Repeat with another 2 eggs. In a separate saucepan, steam 5½ cups broccoli florets until tender. Drain the squash and potatoes, then mash in the pan with ¾ cup shredded cheddar cheese. Serve topped with the broccoli and poached eggs, sprinkled with 2 tablespoons grated Parmesan cheese.

3 Butternut and Broccoli Soup with Mushroom Bruschetta

Place 1 (2 lb) peeled, seeded, and chopped butternut squash and 1 head of broccoli, broken into large florets, in a roasting pan and sprinkle with 2 tablespoons olive oil. Place in a preheated oven, at 425°F, for 25 minutes, until tender. Meanwhile, heat 1 tablespoon olive oil in a skillet, add 2 cups sliced cremini mushrooms, and sauté for 7–8 minutes, then stir in 2 tablespoons chopped parsley. Toast 8 slices of baguette under a preheated hot broiler for 2–3 minutes on each side. Rub one side of each slice with a garlic clove. Spoon the mushroom mix over the toasts and sprinkle with 2 tablespoons grated Parmesan cheese. Five minutes before the squash is cooked, heat 1 tablespoon olive oil in a saucepan, add 1 chopped onion and 1 teaspoon cumin seeds, and cook until softened. Add the roasted vegetables and 6 cups hot vegetable stock and bring to a boil. Remove from the heat and, using a handheld blender, blend the soup until smooth. Serve with the mushroom bruschetta.

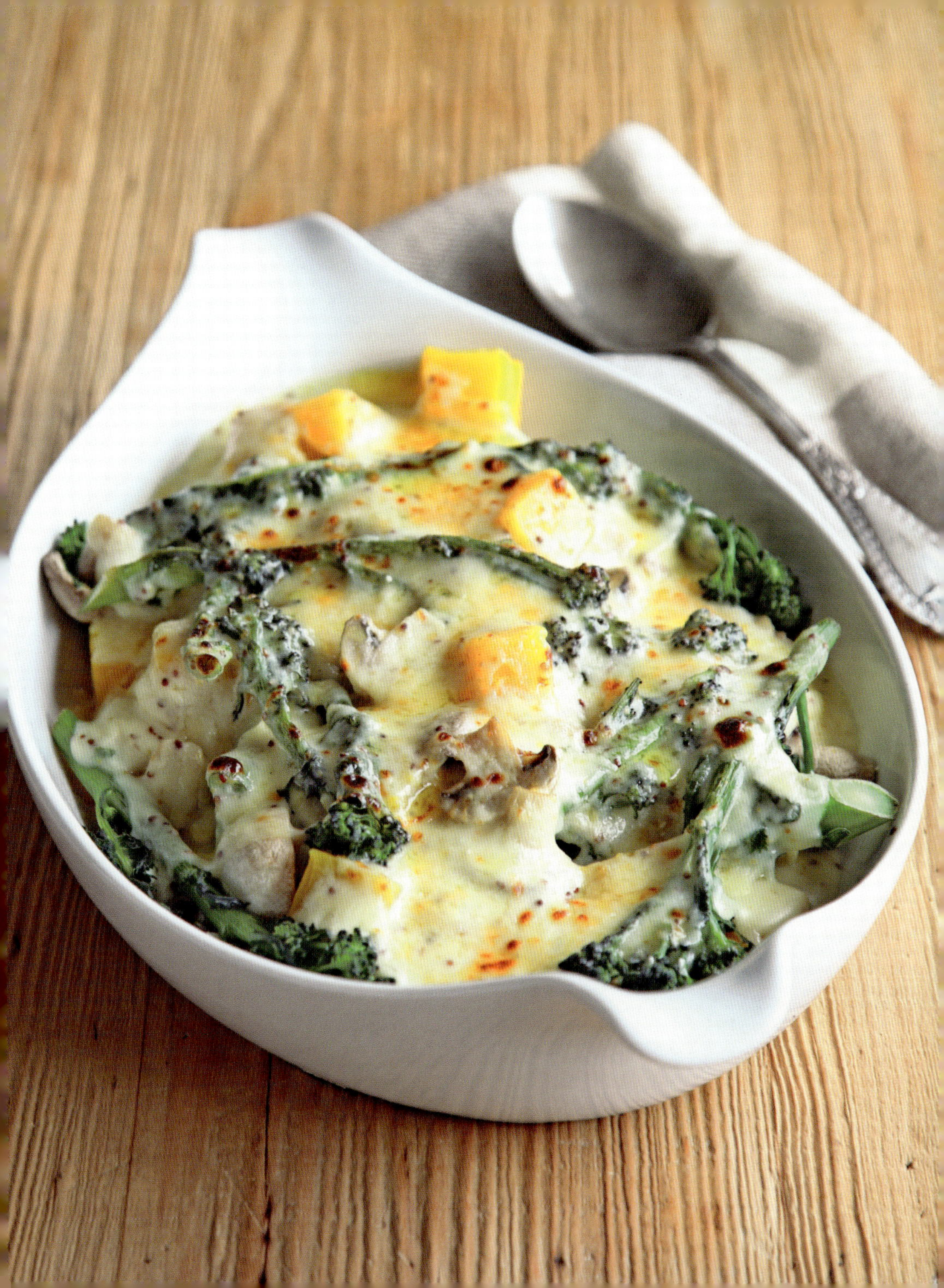

30 Moroccan Vegetable Stew

Serves 4

1 tablespoon olive oil
1 onion, chopped
2 garlic cloves, chopped
2 sweet potatoes, peeled and chopped
2 small parsnips, chopped
1 small rutabaga, chopped
2 large carrots, chopped
12 Brussels sprouts
½ teaspoon ground cumin
1 teaspoon ground coriander
½ teaspoon turmeric
¼ teaspoon cayenne pepper
½ teaspoon ground cinnamon
1 (14½ oz) can tomatoes
1¾ cups vegetable stock
cooked couscous, to serve

- Heat the oil in a large, heavy saucepan, add the onion and garlic, and sauté for 2–3 minutes. Add all the vegetables, reduce the heat to low, and cook, stirring occasionally, for 2–3 minutes without browning.

- Add the spices and mix well to coat all the vegetables, then pour in the tomatoes and vegetable stock. Bring to a boil, then reduce the heat and simmer, breaking up the tomatoes with a wooden spoon, for 20–22 minutes or until the vegetables are tender.

- Serve with couscous to soak up the juices.

1 Moroccan Vegetable Soup

Heat 1 tablespoon oil in a saucepan, add 1 sliced red onion and 2 minced garlic cloves, and cook for 1 minute. Stir in ½ teaspoon each of turmeric and ground cumin, ¼ teaspoon cayenne pepper, and a pinch of ground cinnamon. Add 1 peeled, diced sweet potato, 2 cored, seeded, and sliced red bell peppers, and ½ savoy cabbage, shredded. Pour in 5 cups vegetable stock and bring to a boil. Reduce the heat and simmer for 8 minutes. Process the soup briefly with a handheld blender, then serve sprinkled with toasted slivered almonds.

2 Moroccan Roasted Vegetables

Chop 1 large peeled carrot, 2 peeled sweet potatoes, 1 cored and seeded red bell pepper, 1 cored and seeded yellow bell pepper, and 1 large peeled parsnip, then place in 2 roasting pans and sprinkle with 2 tablespoons cumin seeds and ½ teaspoon each of coriander seeds and turmeric. Pour 2–3 tablespoons olive oil over the vegetables and toss together. Place in a preheated oven, at 400°F, for 15–17 minutes, until all the vegetables are cooked and starting to char a little at the edges. Meanwhile, place 1 cup couscous in a heatproof bowl and just cover with boiling water. Let stand for 12–15 minutes. Dry-fry 2 tablespoons cashew nuts in a nonstick skillet for 3–4 minutes, stirring frequently, until golden. Fluff up the couscous with a fork. Stir in 2 tablespoons each of chopped cilantro, chopped mint, and chopped parsley, the juice of ½ lemon, and 2 tablespoons extra virgin olive oil. Serve the vegetables over the couscous, topped with the toasted cashews.

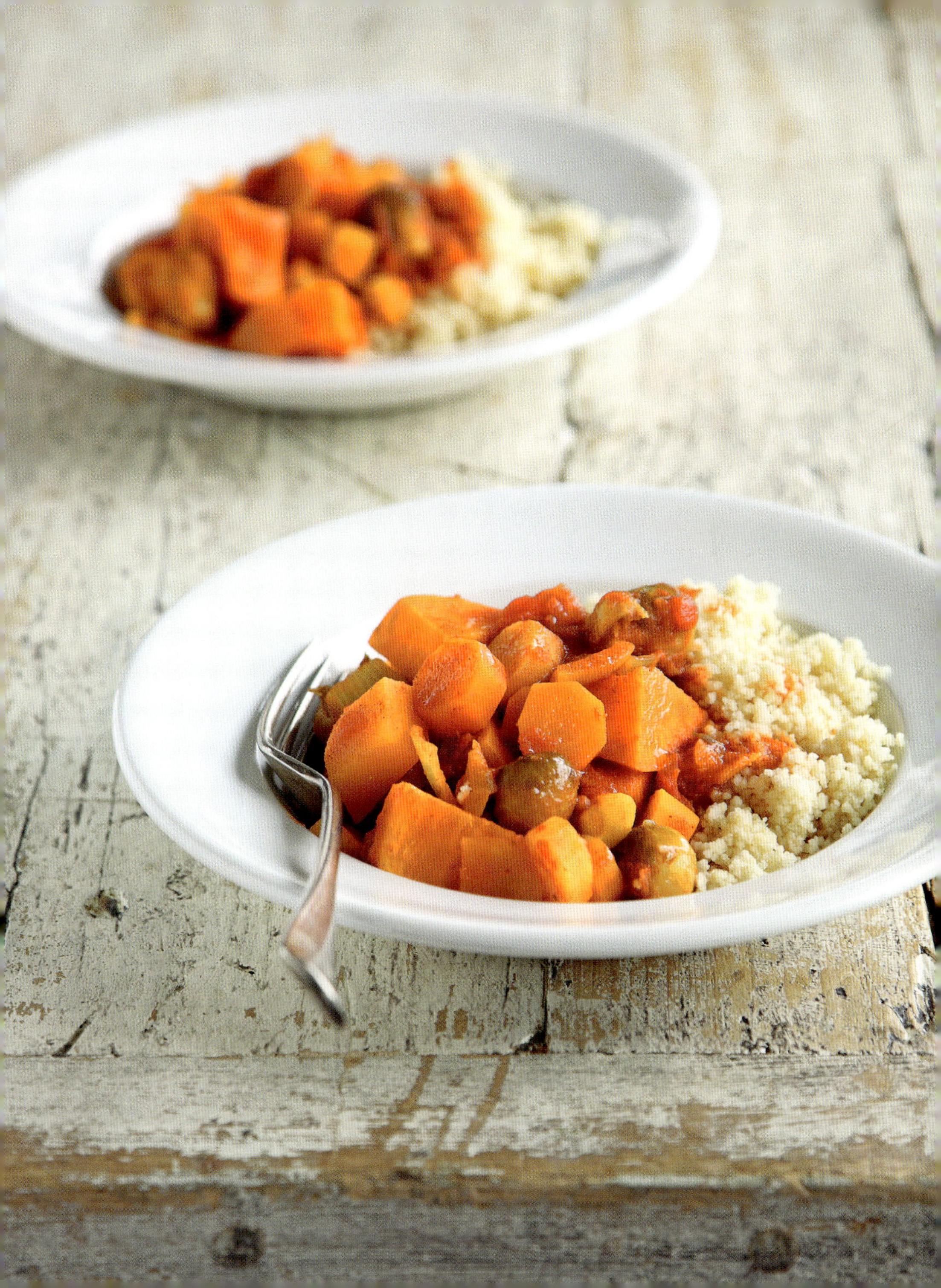

Fava Bean and Feta Tagliatelle

Serves 4

12 oz tagliatelle
2 cups fresh or frozen fava beans
2 tablespoons olive oil
6 scallions, sliced
½ teaspoon dried red pepper flakes
1½ bunches of watercress or 3 cups arugula, coarsely chopped
grated rind of 1 lemon
1⅓ cups crumbled feta cheese
2 tablespoons toasted pine nuts

- Cook the pasta in a large saucepan of boiling water according to the package directions, until "al dente." Add the fava beans 3 minutes before the end of the cooking time.

- Meanwhile, heat the oil in a large skillet, add the scallions and red pepper flakes, and cook for 2–3 minutes. Stir in the watercress or arugula and lemon rind.

- Drain the pasta and beans and add to the watercress mixture with the feta. Mix well.

- Serve sprinkled with the toasted pine nuts.

Fava Bean and Feta Salad

Place 1½ cups couscous in a large heatproof bowl and just cover with boiling water. Let stand for 10–12 minutes. Meanwhile, cook 2 cups frozen fava beans in a saucepan of boiling water for 4–5 minutes, until tender, then drain. Heat 1 tablespoon olive oil in a skillet, add 1 (4 oz) package baby spinach leaves, and cook briefly until wilted. Fluff up the couscous with a fork, then stir in the fava beans, spinach, 2 tablespoons chopped mint, ¾ cup sliced, pitted ripe black olives, and 1⅓ cups crumbled feta cheese. Whisk together the juice of ½ lemon and 2 tablespoons olive oil in a small bowl, then drizzle over the salad and serve.

Fava Bean and Feta Mashed Potatoes

Cook 6 peeled and chopped russet potatoes in a saucepan of boiling water for 12–15 minutes, until tender. Add 1 cup defrosted and skinned fava beans and cook for another minute, then drain. Meanwhile, heat a ridged grill pan until hot, add 12 trimmed asparagus spears, and cook for 4–5 minutes, turning occasionally, until chargrilled. Keep warm. Bring a saucepan of water to a gentle simmer and stir with a large spoon to create a swirl. Break 2 eggs into the water and cook for 3 minutes. Remove with a slotted spoon and keep warm. Repeat with another 2 eggs. Drain the potatoes and beans, then mash in the pan with ⅔ cup crumbled feta cheese, 1 tablespoon plain yogurt or sour cream, and salt and black pepper until almost smooth. Serve topped with the asparagus and poached eggs.

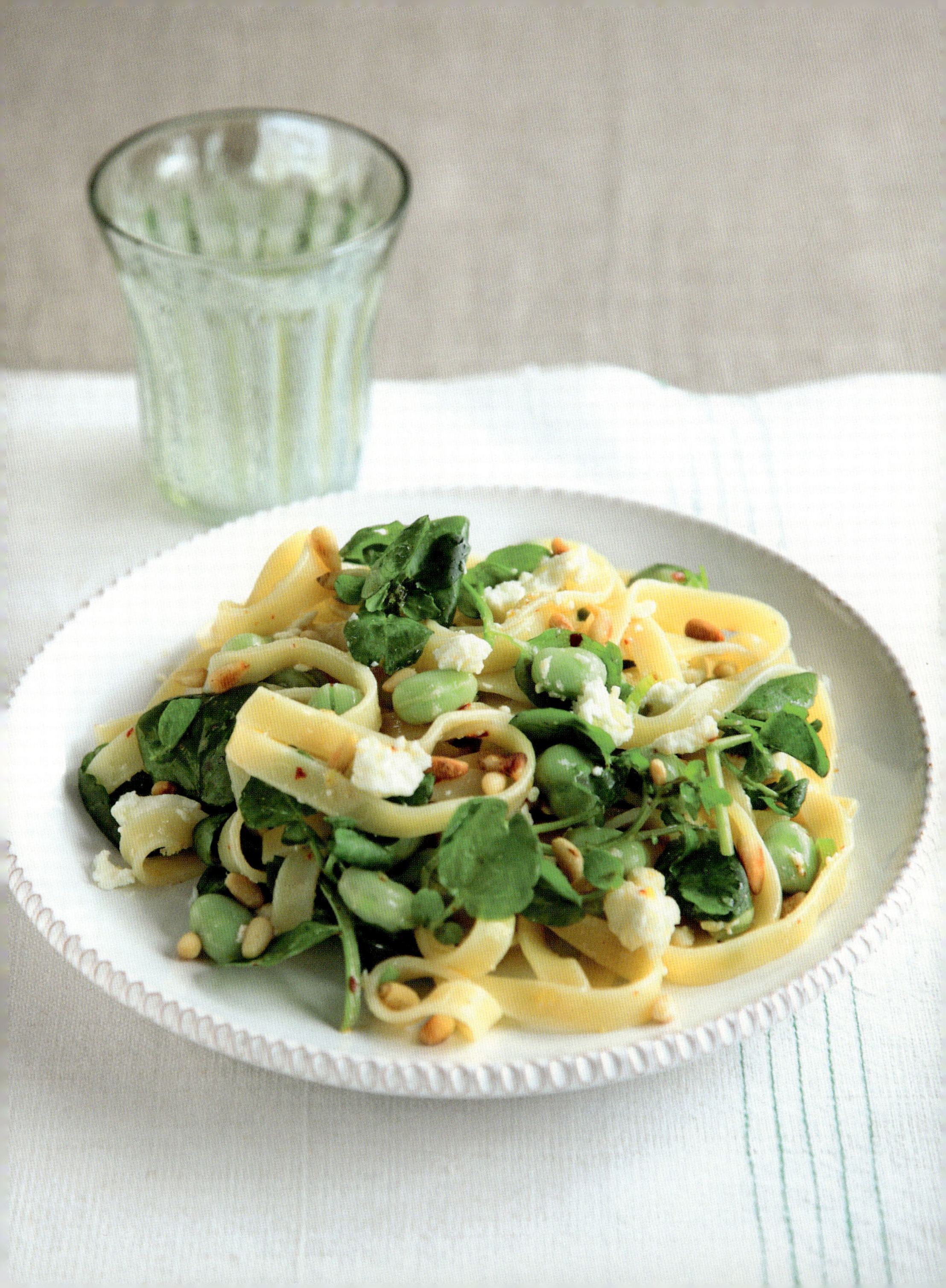

10 Cauliflower Cheese Gratin

Serves 4

1 large cauliflower, broken into pieces
4 tablespoons butter
¼ cup all-purpose flour
½ teaspoon English mustard powder
2 cups milk
1 cup shredded sharp cheddar cheese
2 tablespoons pumpkin seeds

- Cook the cauliflower in a large saucepan of boiling water for 5–6 minutes, until tender.

- Meanwhile, melt the butter in a small saucepan, then stir in the flour and mustard powder to make a roux. Cook for 1–2 minutes, then gradually whisk in the milk and cook, stirring continuously, until the sauce is thick and smooth. Simmer for 1 minute, then stir in half the cheese.

- Drain the cauliflower and place in an ovenproof dish. Pour the cheese sauce over the cauliflower, then sprinkle with the pumpkin seeds and remaining cheese. Cook under a preheated hot broiler for 2–3 minutes, until bubbling and golden.

20 Cauliflower Cheese Soup

Melt 2 tablespoons butter in a saucepan, add 1 finely chopped onion, and cook for 2–3 minutes. Add the florets of 1 large head of cauliflower, 1 peeled and chopped potato, 2½ cups hot vegetable stock, and 1¾ cups milk, season with salt and black pepper, and bring to the boil. Reduce the heat and simmer for 15–16 minutes, until the vegetables are soft. Using a handheld blender, blend the soup until smooth, adding a little more milk, if needed. Sprinkle with 2 tablespoons shredded sharp cheddar cheese.

30 Macaroni and Cheese with Cauliflower

Cook 8 oz macaroni in a saucepan of boiling water according to the package directions, adding the florets of 1 large cauliflower 5 minutes before the end of the cooking time. Meanwhile, dry-fry ½ cup walnut pieces in a nonstick skillet for 3–4 minutes, stirring frequently, until slightly golden, then set aside. Melt 2 tablespoons butter in small saucepan, then stir in 2 tablespoons all-purpose flour and 1 teaspoon English mustard powder to make a roux. Cook for 1–2 minutes, then gradually whisk in 2 cups milk and cook, stirring continuously, until the sauce is thick and smooth. Stir in ½ cup shredded sharp cheddar cheese and season. Drain the macaroni and cauliflower, then return to the pan and stir in 4 chopped tomatoes and the toasted walnuts. Stir in the sauce, then transfer to an ovenproof dish and sprinkle with ½ cup shredded sharp cheddar and 2 tablespoons grated Parmesan cheese. Place in a preheated oven, at 400°F, for 10 minutes. Serve with a crisp green salad.

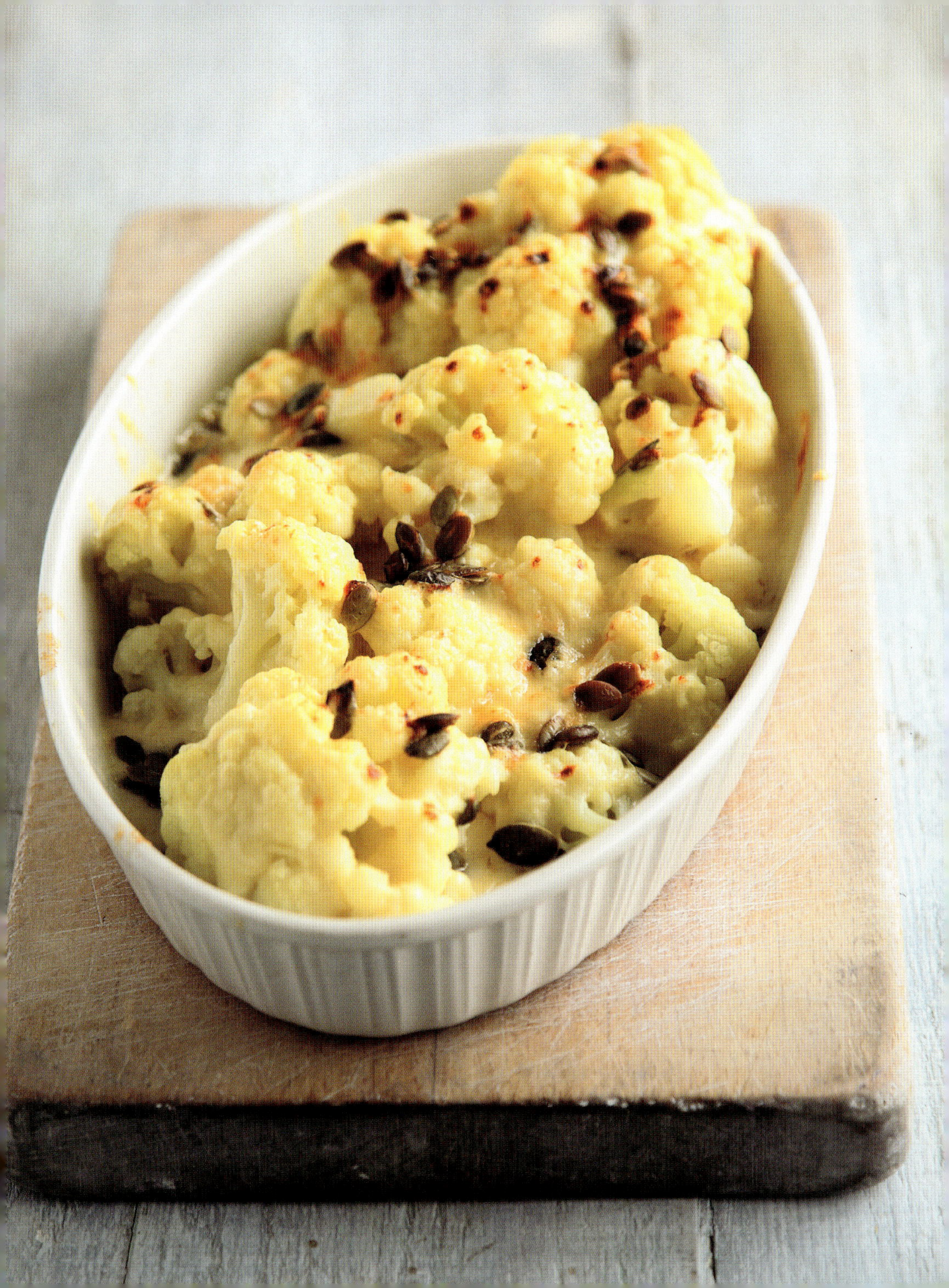

30 Roasted Bell Peppers

Serves 4

2 red bell peppers, halved, cored, and seeded
2 yellow bell peppers, halved, cored, and seeded
1 small red onion, cut into 8 wedges
1 cup trimmed and halved green beans
1 zucchini, sliced
3 garlic cloves, sliced
2 tablespoons extra virgin olive oil
1 teaspoon cumin seeds
salt and black pepper
4 oz feta or goat cheese, to serve (optional)

- Place the bell pepper halves, cut side up, in a roasting pan and divide the vegetables and garlic among them.
- Sprinkle with the oil and cumin seeds and season with salt and black pepper. Place in a preheated oven, at 375°F, for 25 minutes, until tender. Sprinkle with feta or goat cheese, to serve, if liked.

---

1 Bell Pepper and Zucchini Salad

Dry-fry 2 tablespoons pumpkin seeds in a nonstick skillet for 2–3 minutes, stirring frequently, until golden brown. Set aside. Meanwhile, core, seed, and slice 2 red bell peppers and 1 yellow bell pepper. Place in a bowl with 6 halved cherry tomatoes, 1 bunch of watercress or 2 cups arugula, and 2 shredded zucchini. Toss with salad dressing and serve sprinkled with the toasted pumpkin seeds.

2 Italian Fried Bell Peppers

Heat 2 tablespoons olive oil in a skillet, add 1 sliced large onion, and cook for 2–3 minutes, until softened. Meanwhile, core, seed, and slice 2 red bell peppers, 2 yellow bell peppers, and 2 orange bell peppers. Add 3 thinly sliced garlic cloves, the sliced bell peppers, and 2 teaspoons dried oregano to the skillet and cook for 3–4 minutes, then add 4 chopped tomatoes and 2 tablespoons torn basil leaves and cook for another 12 minutes, until the bell peppers are tender. Season with black pepper and a squeeze of lemon juice.

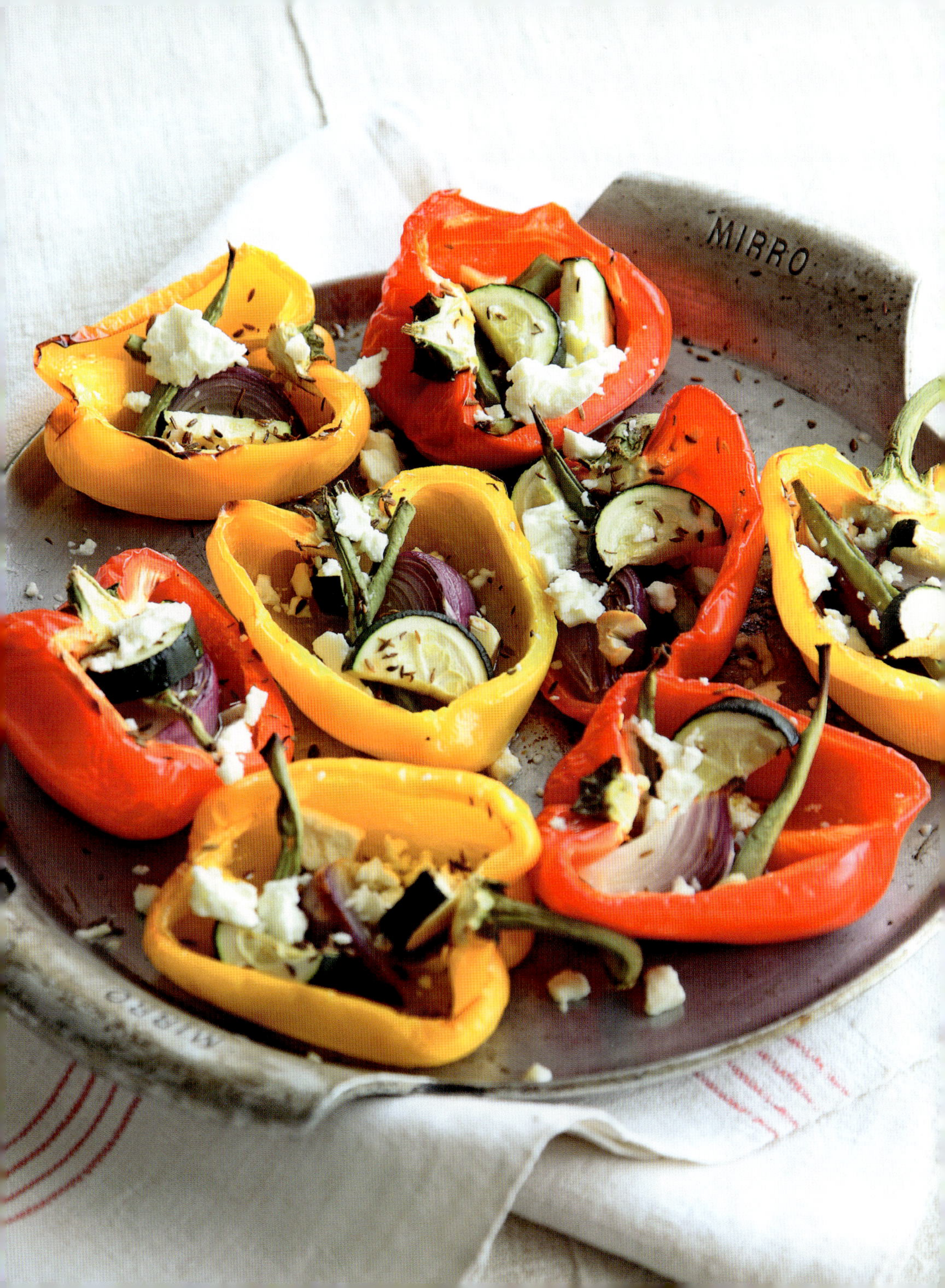
MIRRO

Lima Bean and Mushroom Tagine

Serves 4

1 tablespoon olive oil
1 red onion, sliced
2 carrots, peeled and sliced
½ teaspoon mustard seeds
½ teaspoon cumin seeds
¼ teaspoon turmeric
3⅓ cups hot vegetable stock
1 tablespoon tomato paste
4 cups chopped mushrooms
1 (15 oz) can lima beans, rinsed and drained
2 tablespoons chopped dill
salt and black pepper
cooked rice, to serve

- Heat the oil in a saucepan, add the onion, and sauté for 5–6 minutes, until softened. Add the carrot and spices and cook for another 2 minutes.

- Pour in the stock and stir in the tomato paste, then add the mushrooms and lima beans. Season with salt and black pepper and add the dill, then simmer for 12–15 minutes.

- Serve with cooked rice.

---

1 Warm Lima Bean and Mushroom Salad Heat 2 tablespoons olive oil in a large skillet, add 3 cups sliced cremini mushrooms, and cook for 5–6 minutes, until softened. Stir in 1 (15 oz) can lima beans, rinsed and drained, 1 tablespoon balsamic vinegar, ½ teaspoon multigrain mustard, and 1 teaspoon honey and stir well. Divide 1 (6 oz) package baby spinach leaves among 4 plates and spoon the lima bean mixture over the leaves. Serve sprinkled with 2 tablespoons chopped chives.

2 Lima Bean and Mushroom Soup Soak ½ oz dried porcini in a small heatproof bowl of boiling water for 5 minutes. Meanwhile, heat 1 tablespoon olive oil in a skillet, add 1 sliced onion and 2 crushed garlic cloves, and cook for 4–5 minutes, until softened. Add 1 (15 oz) can lima beans, rinsed and drained, and stir to coat with the oil. Drain and chop the porcini, then add to the skillet with the soaking water, 3 cups sliced cremini mushrooms, and 4 cups hot vegetable stock. Bring to a simmer and cook for 12–14 minutes. Meanwhile, dry-fry 2 tablespoons pumpkin seeds in a nonstick skillet for 2–3 minutes, stirring frequently, until lightly toasted. Using a handheld blender, blend the soup until smooth, then stir in 3 tablespoons plain yogurt. Serve sprinkled with the toasted pumpkins seeds and a swirl of olive oil.

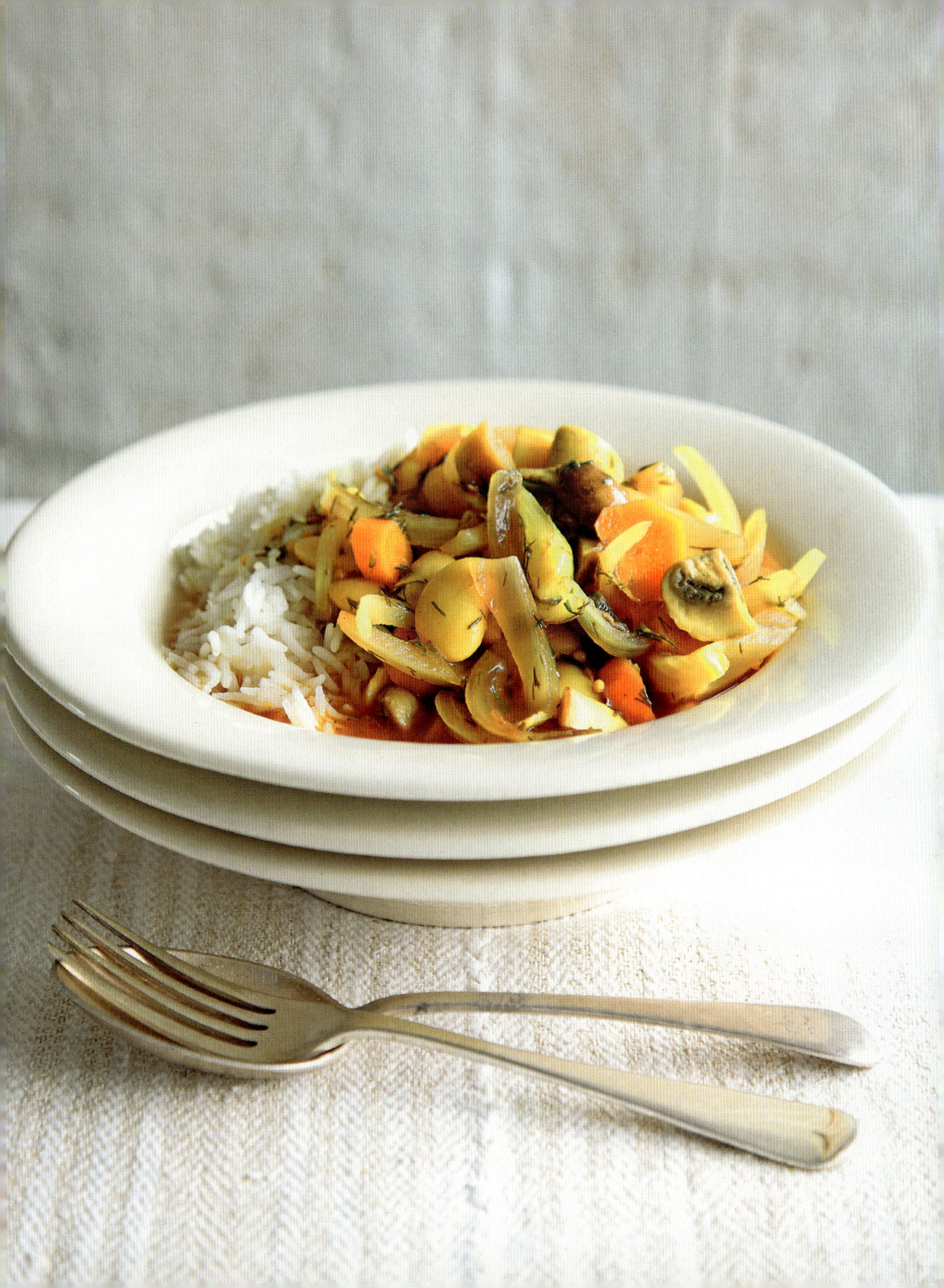

30 Cheesy Pesto Grits

Serves 4

½ (2 lb) butternut squash, peeled, seeded, and diced
3 tablespoons olive oil
1 large onion, chopped
½ teaspoon dried sage
3 cups water
1 cup cornmeal or instant polenta
½ cup toasted pine nuts
3 tablespoons butter
2 tablespoons store-bought pesto
½ cup grated Parmesan cheese
salt and black pepper
steamed baby broccoli, to serve

- Place the squash in a roasting pan and sprinkle with 1 tablespoon of the oil. Place in a preheated oven, at 400°F, for 20–22 minutes, until tender.

- Meanwhile, heat the remaining oil in a skillet, add the onion and sage, and season with salt and black pepper, then cook over low heat for 16–18 minutes, stirring occasionally, until soft and golden.

- In a separate saucepan, bring the water to a boil, then add the cornmeal or polenta in a steady stream, whisking continuously. Simmer over low heat for 10–12 minutes, until bubbling and cooked.

- Remove the squash from the oven, add the pine nuts, and coarsely mash with a fork. Stir the butter, pesto, cheese, onions, and squash into the grits, then serve with broccoli.

---

10 Polenta Salad with Pesto Dressing

Heat 1 tablespoon oil in a saucepan, add 1 seeded and diced chile, 2 sliced garlic cloves, and 12 oz sliced store-bought polenta log, and cook for 3–4 minutes on each side. Meanwhile, toss together 1 chopped romaine lettuce, 1 sliced red onion, 2 seeded and sliced red bell peppers, 2 tablespoons olives, 3 sliced tomatoes, and 2 sliced avocados in a bowl. In a separate bowl, whisk together 2 teaspoons pesto, 3 tablespoons olive oil, and 1 tablespoon white wine vinegar; pour it over the salad. Sprinkle the polenta with 3 tablespoons grated Parmesan and serve with the salad.

20 Polenta with Pesto Roasted Veg

Chop 1 cored and seeded red bell pepper, 1 cored and seeded bell yellow pepper, 2 zucchini, 2 red onions, 2 peeled carrots, and 1 small peeled sweet potato, then place in 2 roasting pans and sprinkle each with 1 tablespoon olive oil and season with salt and black pepper. Place in a preheated oven, at 400°F, for 16–18 minutes, until roasted. Meanwhile, heat 1 tablespoon peanut oil in a skillet, add 2 tablespoons cumin seeds, and cook for 1 minute, then add 12 oz sliced store-bought polenta log and cook for 3–4 minutes on each side, until golden. Remove the vegetables from the oven and stir in 2 tablespoons store-bought pesto. Serve the vegetables spooned over the polenta.

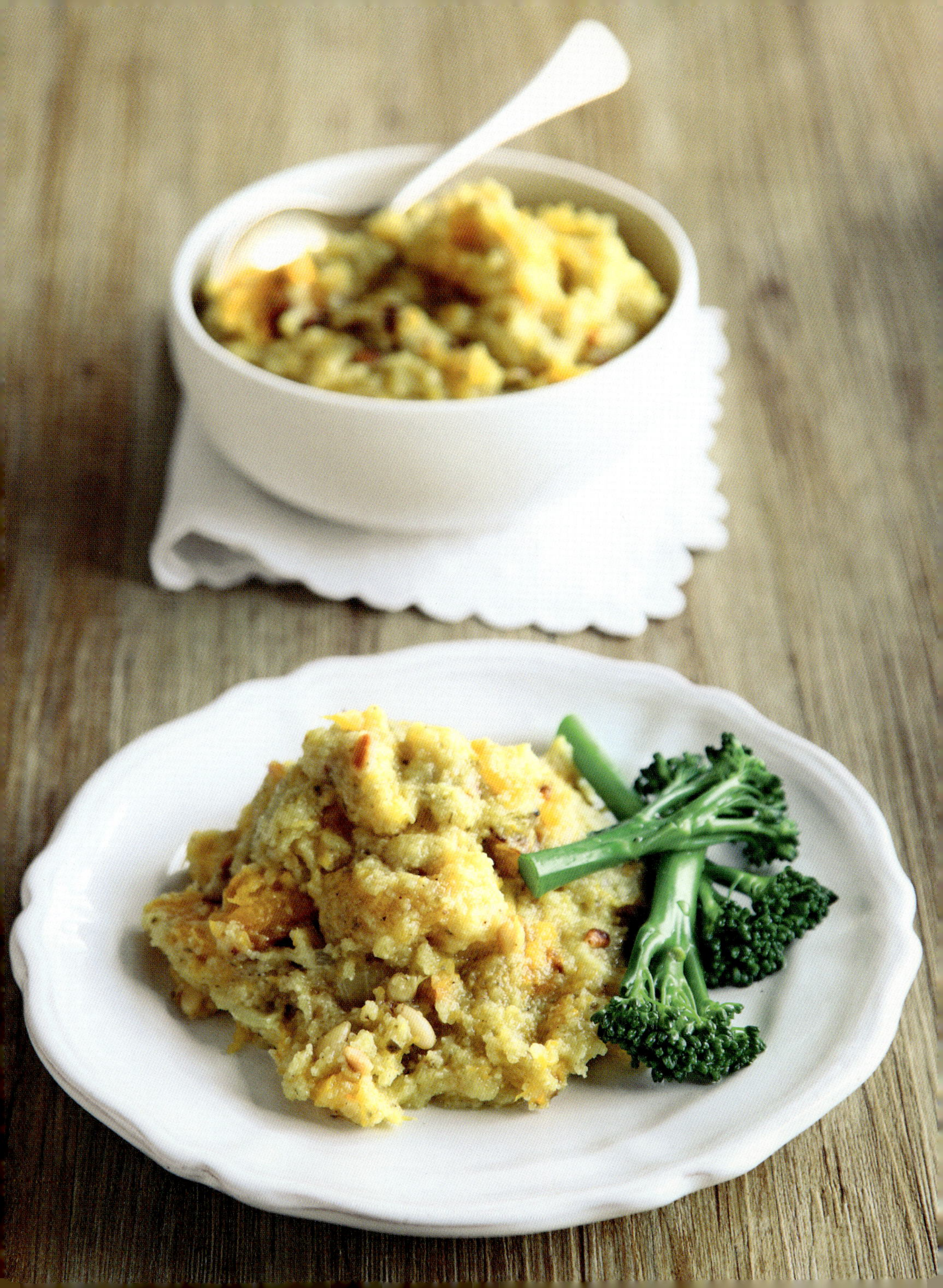

20 Asparagus and Pea Quinoa Risotto

Serves 4

1 1/3 cups quinoa, rinsed
2 1/2 cupshot vegetable stock
8 oz asparagus, chopped
1 1/3 cups frozen peas
1 tablespoon chopped mint
3 tablespoons grated Parmesan cheese
black pepper

- Place the quinoa and stock in a saucepan and bring to a boil, then reduce the heat and simmer for 12–15 minutes, until the quinoa is cooked, adding the asparagus and peas about 2 minutes before the end of the cooking time.

- Drain the quinoa and vegetables, then return to the pan with the mint and 2 tablespoons of the cheese and season with black pepper. Mix well.

- Serve sprinkled with the remaining Parmesan.

10 Warm Asparagus and Pea Rice Salad

Toss together 8 oz asparagus tips and 1 tablespoon olive oil in a bowl, then cook in a preheated hot ridged grill pan for 2–3 minutes. Meanwhile, prepare 1 (7 oz) container heat-and-eat rice according to the package directions. Place the asparagus and rice in a large bowl. Cook 1 1/3 cups frozen peas in a saucepan of boiling water for 1–2 minutes, until tender, then drain and add to the rice with 2 tablespoons chopped mint, 1 tablespoon toasted pine nuts, 3 sliced scallions, 1 tablespoon diced dried apricots, and salad dressing. Toss together and serve.

30 Asparagus and Pea Tart

Unroll a sheet of ready-to-bake puff pastry and place on a baking sheet. Mix together 1 cup cream cheese and 1 tablespoon Dijon mustard in a bowl, then spread over the pastry, leaving a 3/4 inch border around the edge. Top with 10 oz trimmed asparagus and 2/3 cup defrosted peas. Drizzle with 2 tablespoons olive oil, then season with black pepper and sprinkle with 1/2 cup grated Parmesan cheese. Place in a preheated oven, at 400°F, for 20–22 minutes. Serve with a crisp green salad.

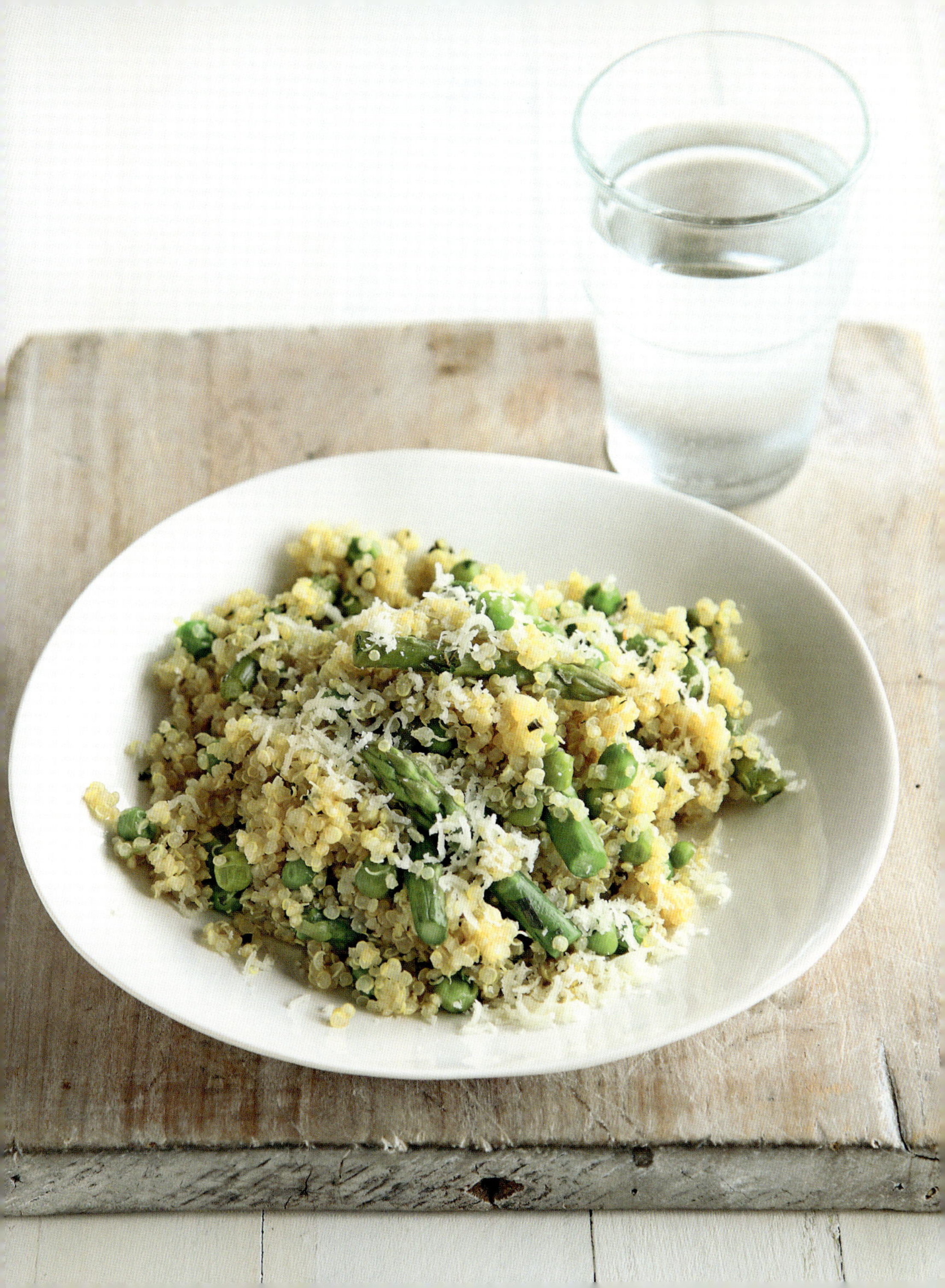

20 Greek Pita Pockets

Serves 4

8 store-bought cooked falafels
4 whole-wheat pita breads
¼ iceburg lettuce, shredded
½ cucumber, diced
12 cherry tomatoes, halved
10–12 mint leaves, torn
¾ cup store-bought hummus
¼ cup crumbled feta cheese

- Place the falafels on a baking sheet and bake in a preheated oven, at 375°F, for 10–12 minutes, or according to the package directions, turning once.
- Meanwhile, cook the pita breads under a preheated medium broiler for 4–5 minutes on each side, until toasted, then halve each down a long side to make a pocket.
- Toss together the lettuce, cucumber, tomatoes, and mint in a bowl. Spoon the hummus into the pita breads, then add the salad. Halve the falafels and place on the salad. Spoon the feta over the falafels to serve.

10 Greek Salad

Mix together 4 chopped tomatoes, 1 sliced red onion, 1⅓ cups crumbled feta cheese, ½ chopped cucumber, 20 pitted ripe black olives, 1 tablespoon chopped parsley, 1 tablespoon chopped mint, ¼ cup olive oil, and the juice of 1 lemon in a serving bowl. Serve with pita breads.

30 Falafels with Greek Salsa

Put 1 (15 oz) can chickpeas, rinsed and drained, 2 tablespoons tahini paste, 1 egg, 1 tablespoon grated lemon rind, the juice of ½ lemon, 1 teaspoon each of ground cumin and ground coriander, and ½ teaspoon chili powder in a food processor and pulse until almost smooth but still chunky. Transfer to a bowl and stir in 1 small chopped onion, 1 tablespoon chopped parsley, ½ tablespoon all-purpose flour, and ½ teaspoon baking powder. Using wet hands, shape into 1-inch patties, then cover and chill for 15 minutes. Meanwhile, mix together 4 chopped tomatoes, 1 tablespoon chopped parsley, 1 diced small red onion, 2 tablespoons chopped, pitted ripe black olives, and 1 tablespoon chopped mint in a bowl. Season and stir in 2 tablespoons olive oil. Heat ¼ inch olive oil in a skillet and cook the falafels for 3 minutes on each side until golden brown. Drain on paper towels, then serve with the salsa.

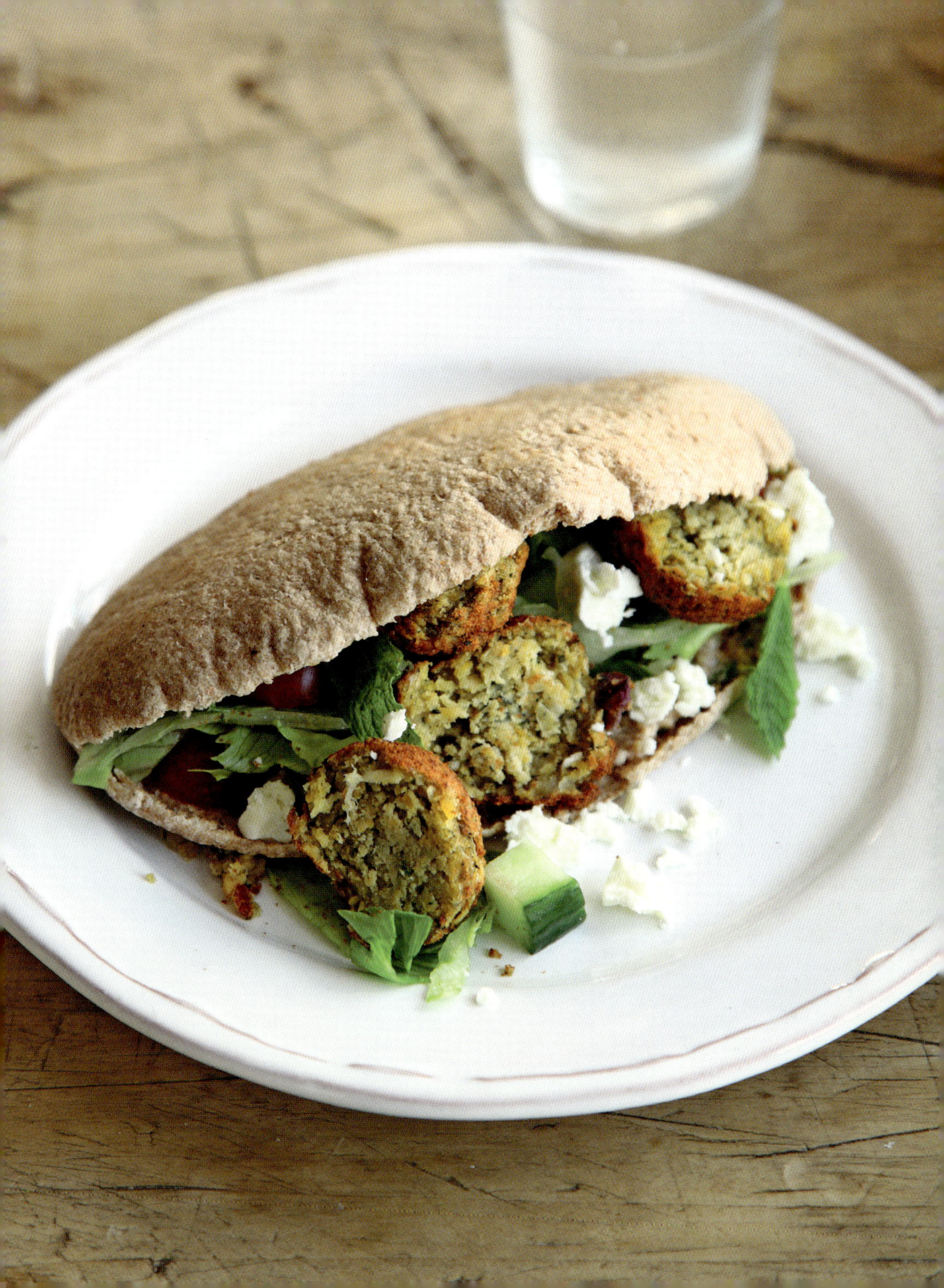

10 Fennel and Cumin Waldorf Salad

Serves 4

½ cup walnut pieces
1 teaspoon ground cumin
1¼ cups plain yogurt
⅔ cup halved green grapes
1 small fennel bulb, thinly sliced
6 celery sticks, sliced diagonally
1 green apple, cored, quartered, and thinly sliced
½ cup golden raisins

- Heat a nonstick skillet over medium-low heat and dry-fry the walnuts for 3–4 minutes, stirring frequently, until slightly golden. Let cool slightly.

- Mix together the cumin and yogurt in a large bowl. Add the remaining ingredients and the toasted walnuts and toss in the dressing until well coated.

- Serve immediately or cover and chill until required.

---

20 Fennel, Cumin, and Butternut Soup

Heat 1 tablespoon olive oil in a saucepan, add 1 chopped onion and 1 teaspoon cumin seeds, and cook for 1–2 minutes. Stir in 1 sliced fennel bulb, 2 peeled and diced carrots, 2 sliced celery sticks, and ½ (2 lb) peeled, seeded, and chopped butternut squash and cook for another 3–4 minutes. Pour in 3 cups hot vegetable stock and bring to a boil, then reduce the heat and simmer for 12–14 minutes, until the vegetables are tender. Using a handheld blender, blend the soup until smooth. Season to taste. Serve with swirls of plain yogurt and crusty bread.

30 Cumin-Roasted Fennel and Veg

Toss together 2 fennel bulbs, cut into wedges, 2 large sweet potatoes, peeled and coarsely chopped, 1 red onion, cut into wedges, 2 peeled and chopped carrots, 2 cored, seeded, and chopped red bell peppers, 2 sliced zucchini, 2 tablespoons olive oil, and 2 teaspoons cumin seeds in a roasting pan and season to taste. Place in a preheated oven, at 400°F, for 20–24 minutes, until tender. Serve with baby spinach leaves, drizzled with balsamic glaze.

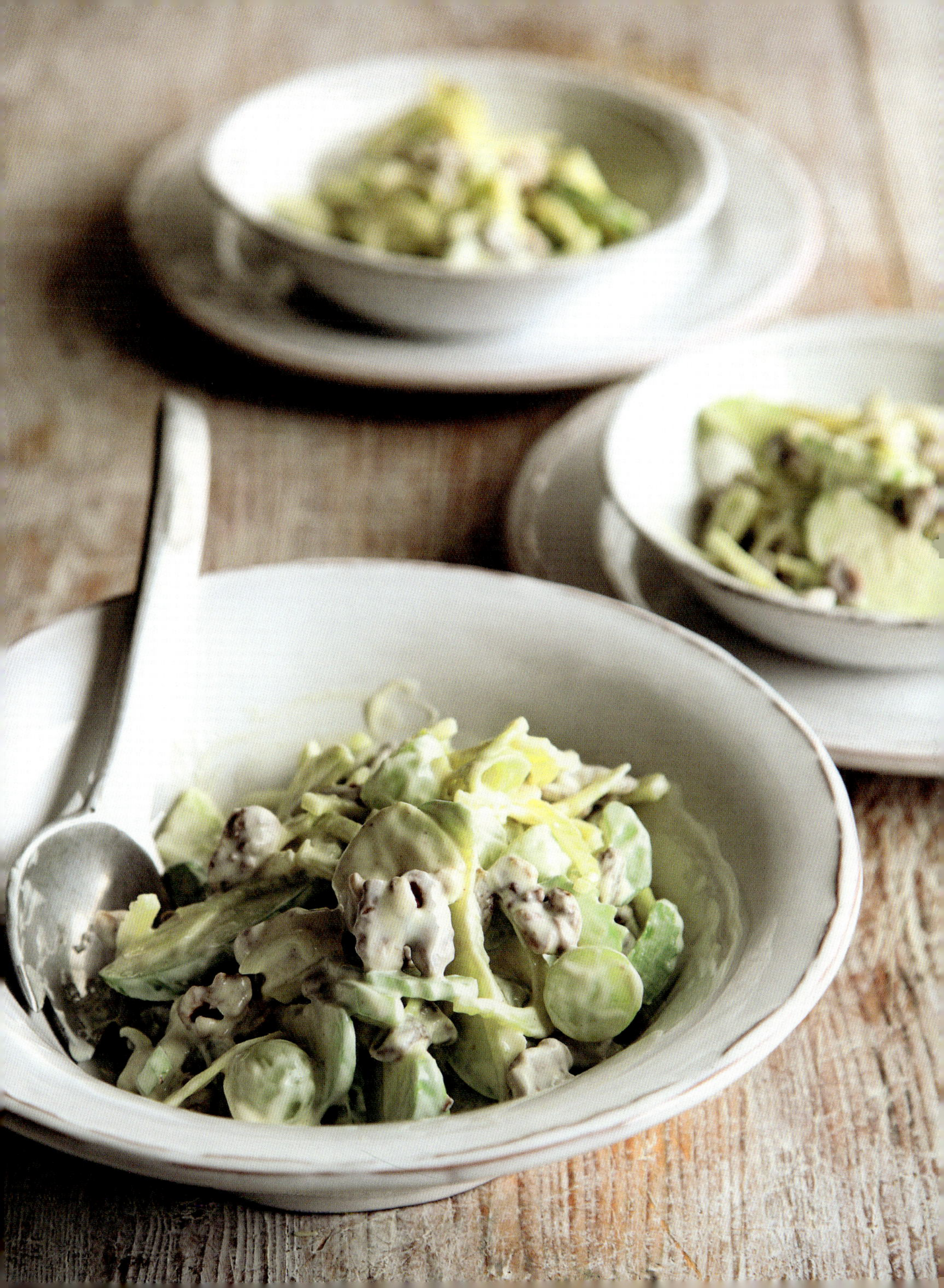

30 Mushroom, Tomato, and Herb Pancakes

Serves 4

- ⅓ cup plus 1 tablespoon buckwheat flour
- ⅓ cup plus 1 tablespoon all-purpose flour
- 1 egg
- 1 egg white
- 1¼ cups milk
- 2 tomatoes
- 1 stick unsalted butter
- 1 cup sliced cremini mushrooms
- 1 tablespoon chopped parsley
- 1 tablespoon chopped basil
- 2 tablespoons shredded cheddar cheese, to serve

- Sift the flours into a large bowl, then make a well in the center. Gradually whisk in the egg, egg white, and milk until smooth. Let rest for 8 minutes.

- Meanwhile, place the tomatoes in a heatproof bowl and pour over boiling water to cover. Let stand for 1–2 minutes, then drain, cut a cross at the stem end of each tomato, and peel off the skins. Seed and chop the flesh.

- Heat half the butter in a skillet, add the tomatoes, mushrooms, and herbs, and cook for 5 minutes. Keep warm.

- Melt the remaining butter in 2 skillets until foaming, then pour in enough of the batter to just cover the bottoms. Cook each pancake for about 3 minutes, then turn over and cook for another 2 minutes. Remove from the skillets and keep warm. Repeat with the remaining batter to make 8 pancakes.

- Divide the vegetable mixture among the pancakes and serve sprinkled with the cheese.

---

1 Mushroom, Tomato, and Herb Toasts

Heat 1 tablespoon olive oil and 2 tablespoons butter in a skillet, add 2 cups sliced cremini mushrooms, and 1 crushed garlic clove and cook for 5–6 minutes, until softened. Stir in 1 tablespoon chopped parsley and 12 quartered cherry tomatoes. Meanwhile, toast 4 slices of whole-grain bread under a preheated hot broiler for 2–3 minutes on each side. Spoon the mushrooms over the toasts and serve sprinkled with 1 tablespoon grated Parmesan cheese.

2 Tomato and Herb-Stuffed Mushrooms

Heat 1 tablespoon olive oil in a skillet, add 1 chopped onion and 2 crushed garlic cloves, and sauté for 1–2 minutes, then remove from the skillet with a slotted spoon. Trim the stems from 4 portobello mushrooms, then add the cups to the skillet, gill side up, and cook for 3–4 minutes. Mix together the onion mixture, 5 chopped tomatoes, ½ cup shredded cheddar cheese, 1 tablespoon chopped parsley, and 1 teaspoon thyme leaves in a bowl. Season well. Transfer the mushrooms to a baking sheet, spoon in the tomato mixture, and sprinkle with 2 tablespoons grated Parmesan cheese. Place in a preheated oven, at 350°F, for 10–12 minutes. Serve with a herb salad tossed with a little olive oil and a squeeze of lemon juice.

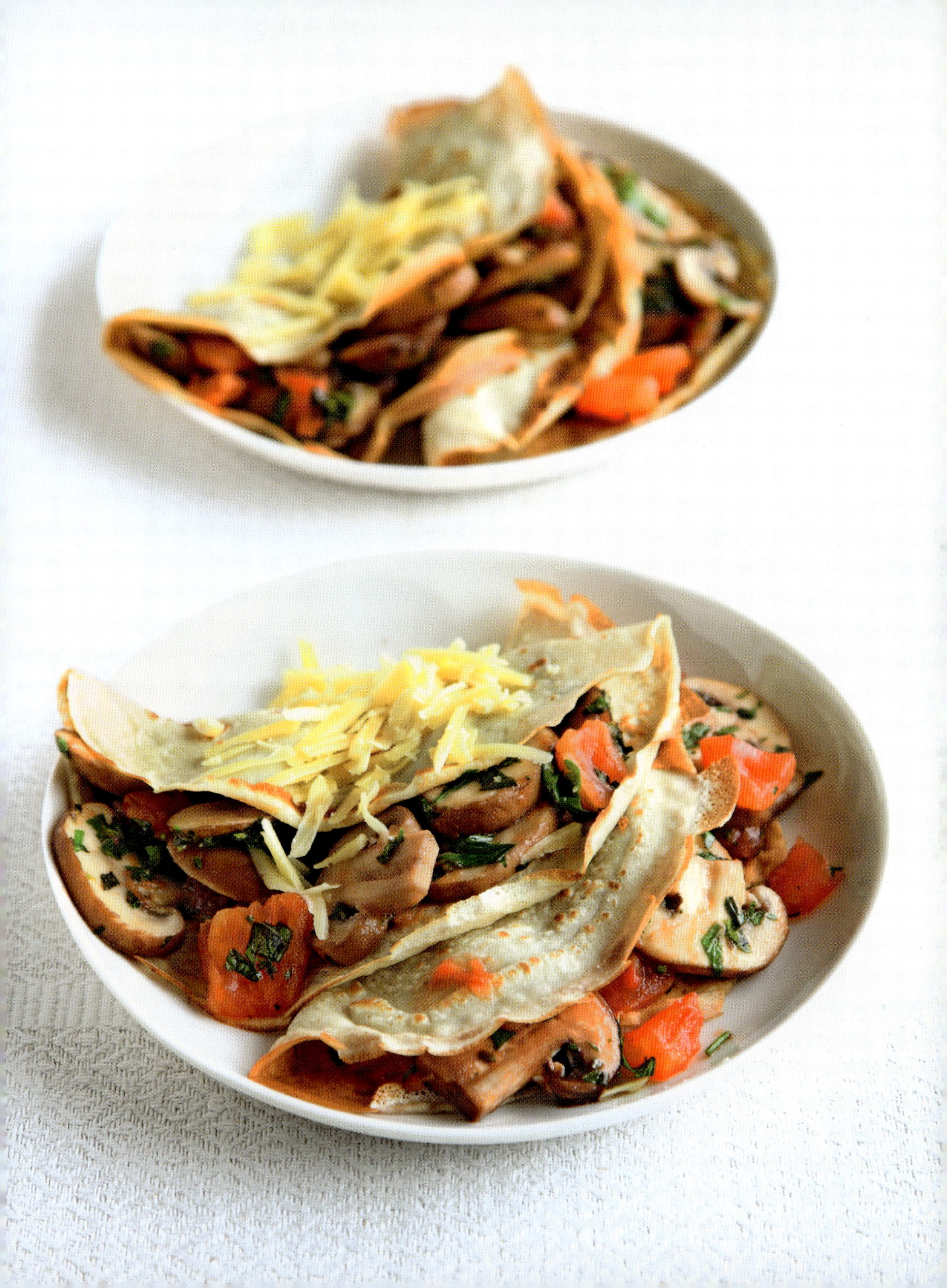

Pea and Mint Pancakes

Serves 4

2½ cups fresh or frozen peas
1 large handful of mint leaves, chopped
4 tablespoons butter, melted
¼ cup all-purpose flour
¼ cup plain yogurt
2 tablespoons grated Parmesan cheese
1 extra-large egg
2 tablespoons peanut oil
12 oz baby broccoli, steamed
salt and black pepper
4 extra-large eggs, poached, to serve

- Cook the peas in a saucepan of boiling water for 2 minutes. Drain, then refresh under cold running water and drain again. Place in a food processor with the mint and process to form a rough texture. Add the butter, flour, yogurt, cheese, and egg and season with salt and black pepper. Process again to form a stiff paste.

- Heat the oil in a large skillet, then drop 2 tablespoons of the pea mixture into the skillet for each pancake. Smooth the tops and cook over medium heat for 3–4 minutes. Turn the pancakes over and cook for another 2 minutes. Remove from the skillet and keep warm. Repeat with the remaining mixture to make about 12 pancakes.

- Heat a ridged grill pan until hot, add the broccoli, and cook for 5–6 minutes, turning frequently, until slightly charred Top the pancakes with the poached eggs and serve with the charred broccoli.

Pea and Mint Dip

Cook 3⅓ cups frozen peas in a saucepan of boiling water for 2 minutes. Drain, then refresh under cold running water and drain again. Place in a food processor with ½ cup plain yogurt, a small handful of mint leaves, and the juice of ½ lemon. Season well and process until nearly smooth. Serve with vegetable crudités and toasted pita breads.

Pea and Mint Soufflés

Place 4 oz asparagus tips, 1⅓ cups frozen peas, 20 mint leaves, and ⅔ cup hot vegetable stock in a small saucepan and cook for 3–4 minutes, until the vegetables are tender. Meanwhile, brush 4 ramekins with melted butter, then dust with 1 tablespoon grated Parmesan cheese. Transfer the vegetable mixture to a food processor or blender and process to a puree. Melt 2 tablespoons butter in a small saucepan, then stir in 1–2 tablespoons all-purpose flour to make a roux. Cook for 2–3 minutes, then gradually whisk in 1 cup milk and cook, stirring continuously, until the sauce is thick and smooth. Let cool, then put in a large bowl. Fold 4 egg yolks into the white sauce with the pea puree. Whisk 4 egg whites in a clean bowl until stiff, then gently fold into the pea mixture. Spoon into the ramekins, gently tap the dishes on the work surface, and run a finger around the rims to make sure they will rise evenly. Place on a baking sheet and bake in a preheated oven, at 400°F, for 15 minutes, until risen and golden.

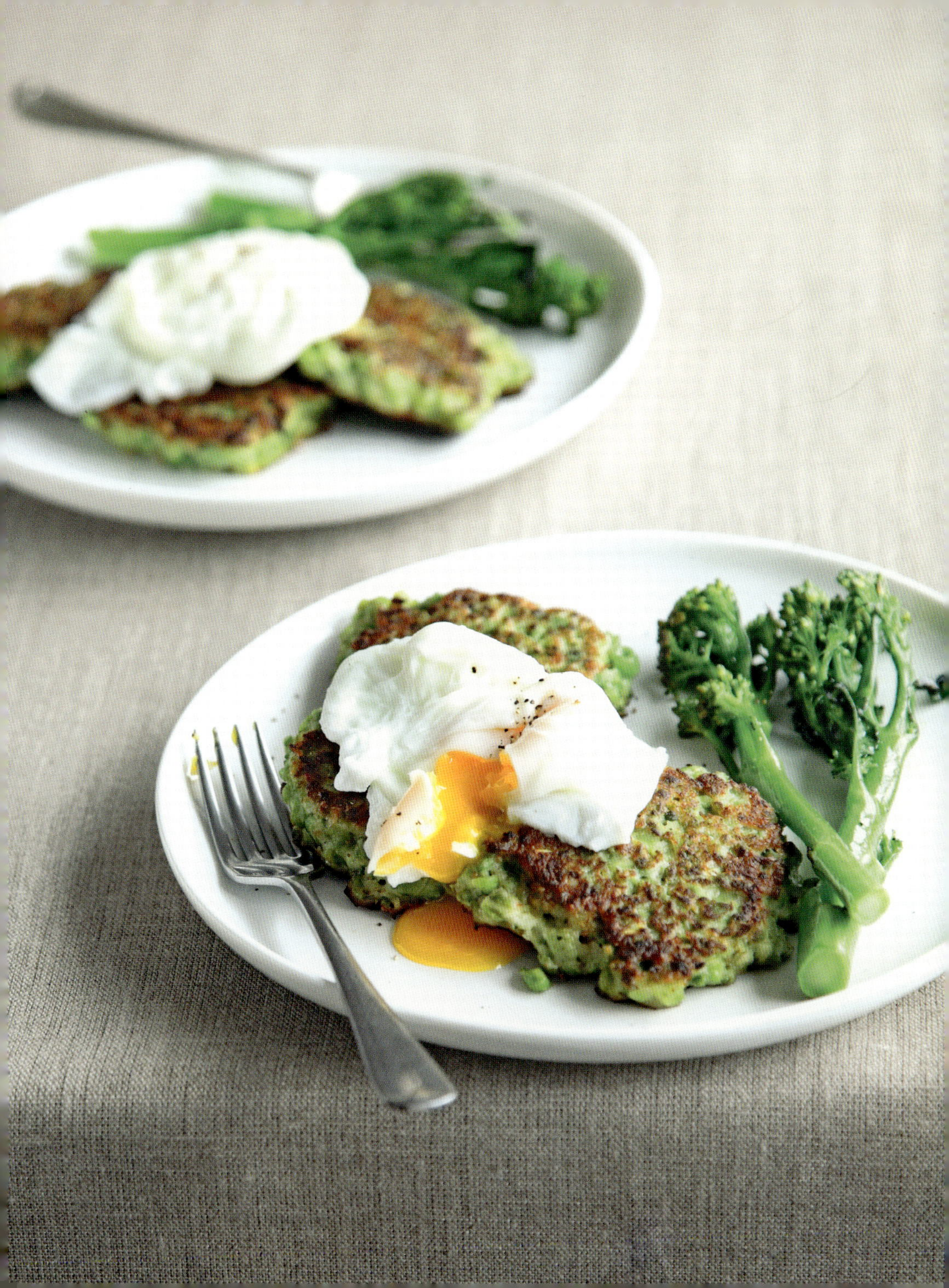

Linguine with Chickpea and Tomato Sauce

Serves 4

2 tablespoons olive oil
1 onion, chopped
2 garlic cloves, crushed
1 celery stick, sliced
1 (15 oz) can diced tomatoes
1 (6 oz) package baby spinach leaves
1 (15 oz) can chickpeas, rinsed and drained
12 oz linguine
10 basil leaves, torn
½ cup grated Parmesan cheese, to serve

- Heat the oil in a large saucepan, add the onion, garlic, and celery, and cook for 3–4 minutes, until softened. Add the tomatoes and bring to a boil, then reduce the heat and simmer for 10 minutes. Stir in the spinach and chickpeas and cook until the spinach is wilted.

- Meanwhile, cook the pasta in a saucepan of boiling water according to the package directions, until "al dente." Drain, then add to the tomato sauce with the basil and toss together.

- Serve sprinkled with the Parmesan.

Chickpea, Tomato, and Pasta Salad

Cook 12 oz farfalle in a saucepan of boiling water according to the package directions, until "al dente." Drain, then refresh under cold running water and drain again. Place in a serving bowl and toss together with 1 (15 oz) can chickpeas, rinsed and drained, 1 diced red onion, 4 chopped tomatoes, 6 torn basil leaves, 2 cups arugula leaves, 2 tablespoons Parmesan cheese shavings, 2 tablespoons olive oil, and 1 tablespoon balsamic vinegar. Season to taste and serve.

Spaghetti with Roasted Tomato and Chickpea Sauce

Place 4 halved tomatoes in a roasting pan, cut side up. Press 3 chopped garlic cloves into the tomatoes, then sprinkle with black pepper and 2 tablespoons olive oil. Place in a preheated oven, at 400°F, for 25 minutes, until very soft, adding 1 cup rinsed and drained, canned chickpeas 2–3 minutes before the end of the cooking time. Meanwhile, cook 12 oz spaghetti in a saucepan of boiling water according to the package directions, until "al dente." Drain, then toss together with the tomatoes and chickpeas and 8 torn basil leaves. Serve sprinkled with 3 tablespoons toasted pine nuts.

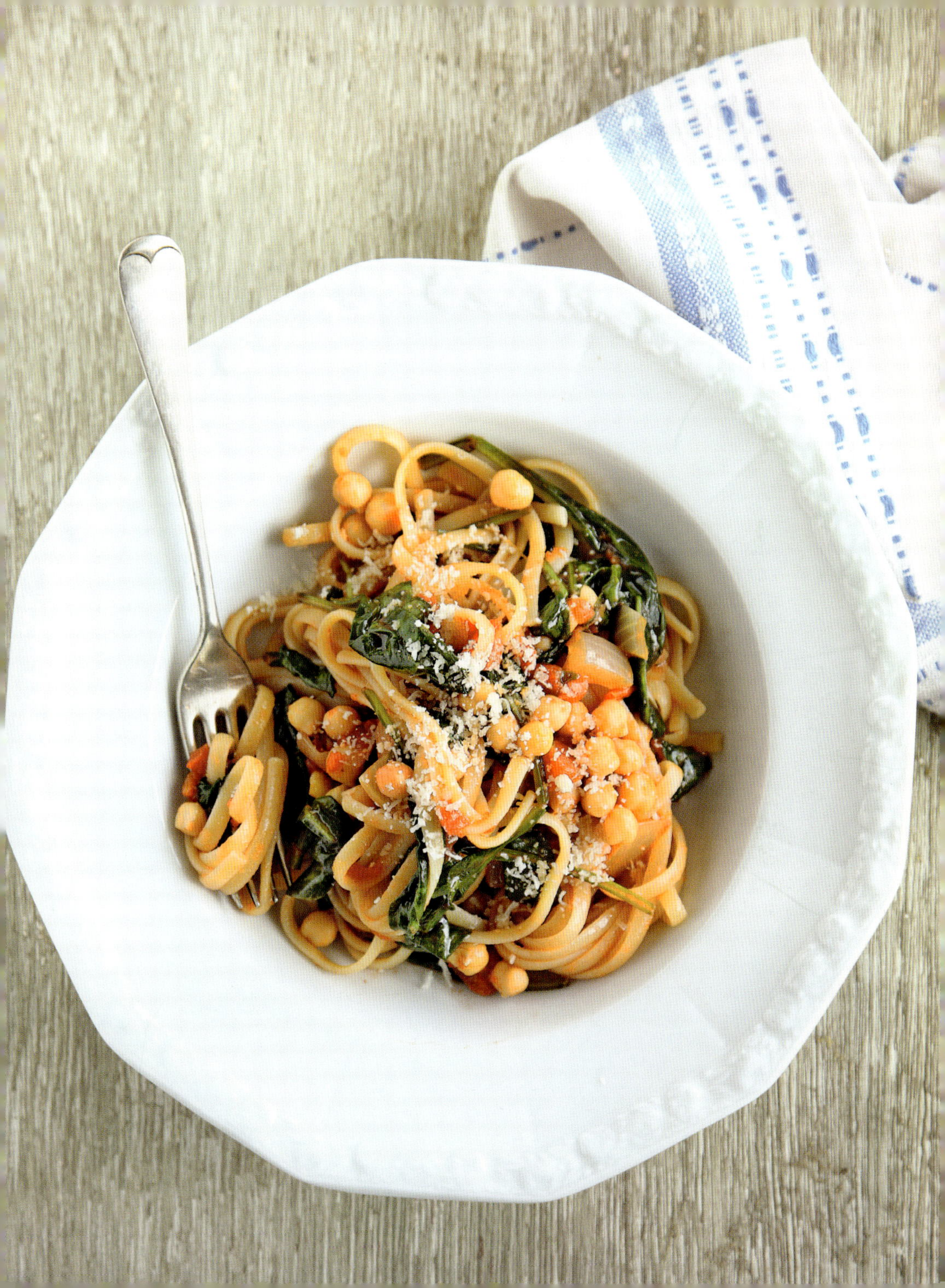

20 Cheese and Spinach Quesadillas

Serves 4

1½ (6 oz) packages baby spinach leaves
8 flour tortillas
8 oz goat cheese
2 tablespoons chopped sun-dried tomatoes
2 avocados, peeled, pitted, and diced
1 red onion, thinly sliced
juice of 1 lime
2 tablespoons chopped cilantro
salt and black pepper

- Place the spinach in a saucepan with a small amount of water, then cover and cook until wilted. Drain and squeeze dry.

- Heat 2 nonstick skillets, add 1 tortilla to each, and crumble in one-quarter of the goat cheese over each tortilla, then add one-quarter of the spinach and sun-dried tomatoes. Season well.

- Place 1 tortilla on top of each and cook over medium heat for 3–4 minutes, until golden underneath. Gently turn the quesadillas over and cook for another 3–4 minutes. Remove from the skillets and keep warm. Repeat with the remaining 4 tortillas.

- Meanwhile, mix together the avocados, onion, lime juice, and cilantro in a bowl.

- Serve the quesadillas in wedges with the avocado salsa.

10 Cheese and Spinach Pancakes

Heat through 8 store-bought pancakes according to the package directions. Meanwhile, heat 2 tablespoons olive oil in a skillet, add 2 cups sliced cremini mushrooms, and cook for 3–4 minutes. Add 1 crushed garlic clove and 1 (6 oz) package baby spinach leaves and cook until wilted. Stir in 2 tablespoons shredded cheddar cheese. Divide the mixture among the pancakes, then roll them up and serve sprinkled with ½ cup shredded cheddar and 1 tablespoon snipped chives.

30 Cheese and Spinach Muffins

Heat 2 tablespoons butter in a skillet, add ½ diced onion, and cook for 2–3 minutes, until soft. Meanwhile, mix together 2¾ cups all-purpose flour, 2½ teaspoons baking powder, 1 teaspoon paprika, and 2¼ cups shredded cheddar cheese in a large bowl. Beat together 1 cup milk and 1 egg in a small bowl, then pour into the dry ingredients and mix together until just combined—do not overmix. Gently stir in the cooked onion and butter and 3 cups coarsely chopped baby spinach leaves. Spoon into 12 paper muffin liners arranged in a muffin pan and cook in a preheated oven, at 350°F, for 25–26 minutes, until golden.

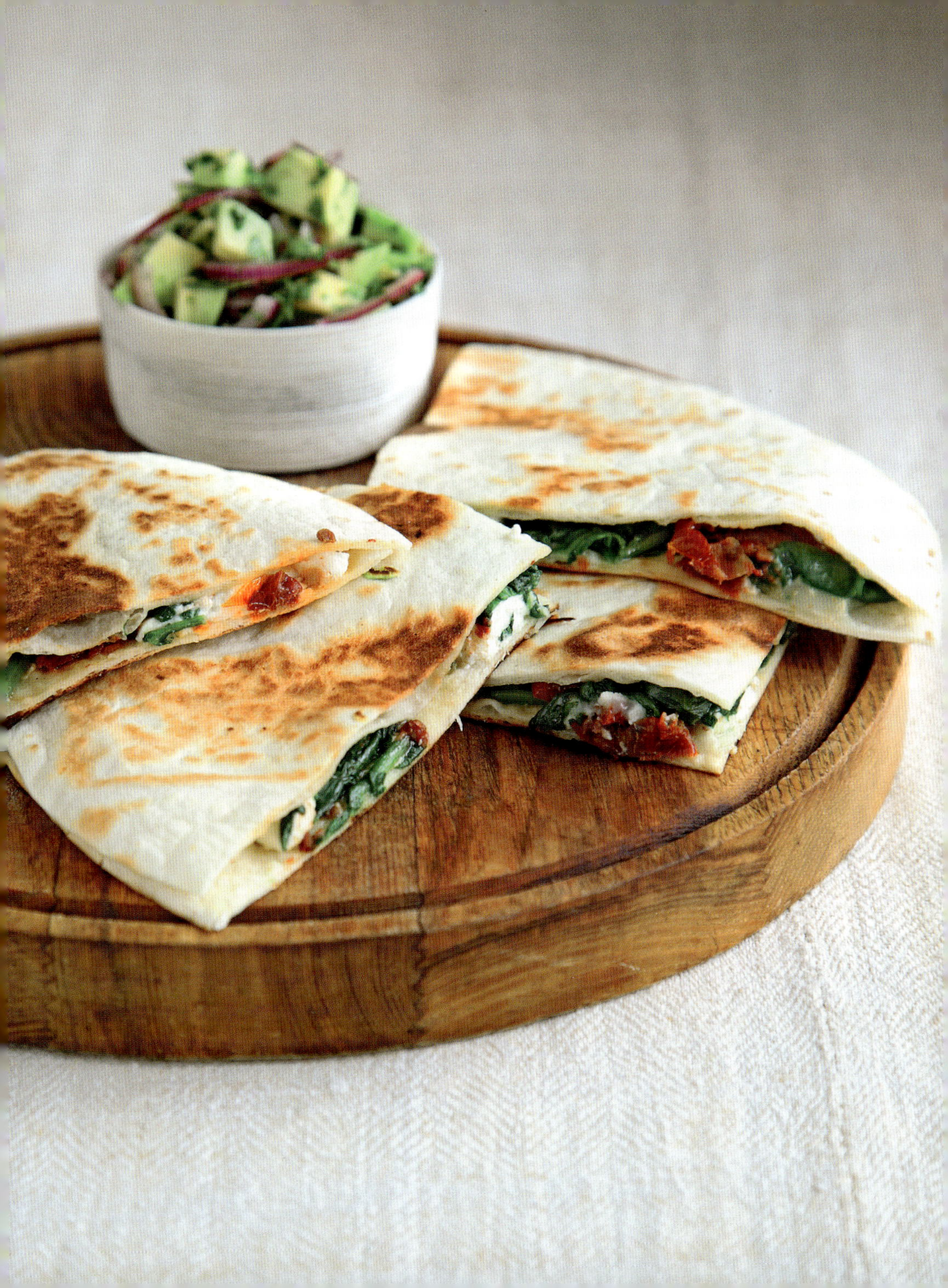

Lentil, Mustard, and Chickpea Soup

Serves 4

½ teaspoon coconut oil or olive oil
¼ teaspoon mustard seeds
½ teaspoon ground cumin
½ teaspoon turmeric
1 small onion, diced
¾-inch piece of fresh ginger root, finely chopped
1 garlic clove, finely chopped
½ cup red lentils
1 cup rinsed and drained, canned chickpeas
4 cups hot vegetable stock
2 cups baby spinach leaves
salt and black pepper

- Heat the oil in a saucepan and add the dry spices. When the mustard seeds start to pop, add the onion, ginger, and garlic and cook until the onion softens.

- Add the lentils and chickpeas and stir well to coat. Pour in the stock and bring to a boil, then reduce the heat and simmer for 14–16 minutes, until the lentils are cooked.

- Stir in the spinach until wilted, then season to taste. Ladle the soup into bowls and serve.

Lentil and Chickpea Salad with Warm Mustard Dressing

Heat 3 tablespoons olive oil in a large skillet, add 1 seeded and chopped red chile, ½ teaspoon mustard seeds, 2 sliced garlic cloves, and 1-inch piece of ginger root, peeled and grated, and sauté for 2 minutes. Remove from the heat and stir in 1 small sliced red onion, 1 (15 oz) can lentils, rinsed and drained, or 2 cups cooked lentils, 1 (15 oz) can chickpeas, rinsed and drained, the juice of ½ lemon, and 2 tablespoons chopped sun-dried tomatoes. Stir together, pour into a serving bowl, and toss with 2 cups arugula leaves and 1 cup crumbled feta cheese.

Lentil, Chickpea, Chicken, and Mustard Curry

Heat 1 tablespoon olive oil in a saucepan, add 1 lb chopped skinless, boneless chicken breasts, and cook until browned. Remove from the pan with a slotted spoon and set aside. Sauté 1 finely chopped onion, 1 teaspoon mustard seeds, 2 crushed garlic cloves, and 1 diced red chile in the pan for 2–3 minutes. Stir in ½ teaspoon turmeric, ½ teaspoon paprika, 1 teaspoon ground cumin, ½ teaspoon garam masala, and 1 teaspoon ground coriander and cook for 1 minute. Stir in 1 (14½ oz) can diced tomatoes and 1 cup hot vegetable stock, then return the chicken to the pan. Simmer for 12–15 minutes. Stir in 1 (15 oz) can lentils, rinsed and drained, or 2 cups cooked lentils, and 1 (15 oz) can chickpeas, rinsed and drained, and simmer for 5 minutes, until cooked through and piping hot. Stir in 2 tablespoons chopped cilantro and serve with cooked long-grain rice.

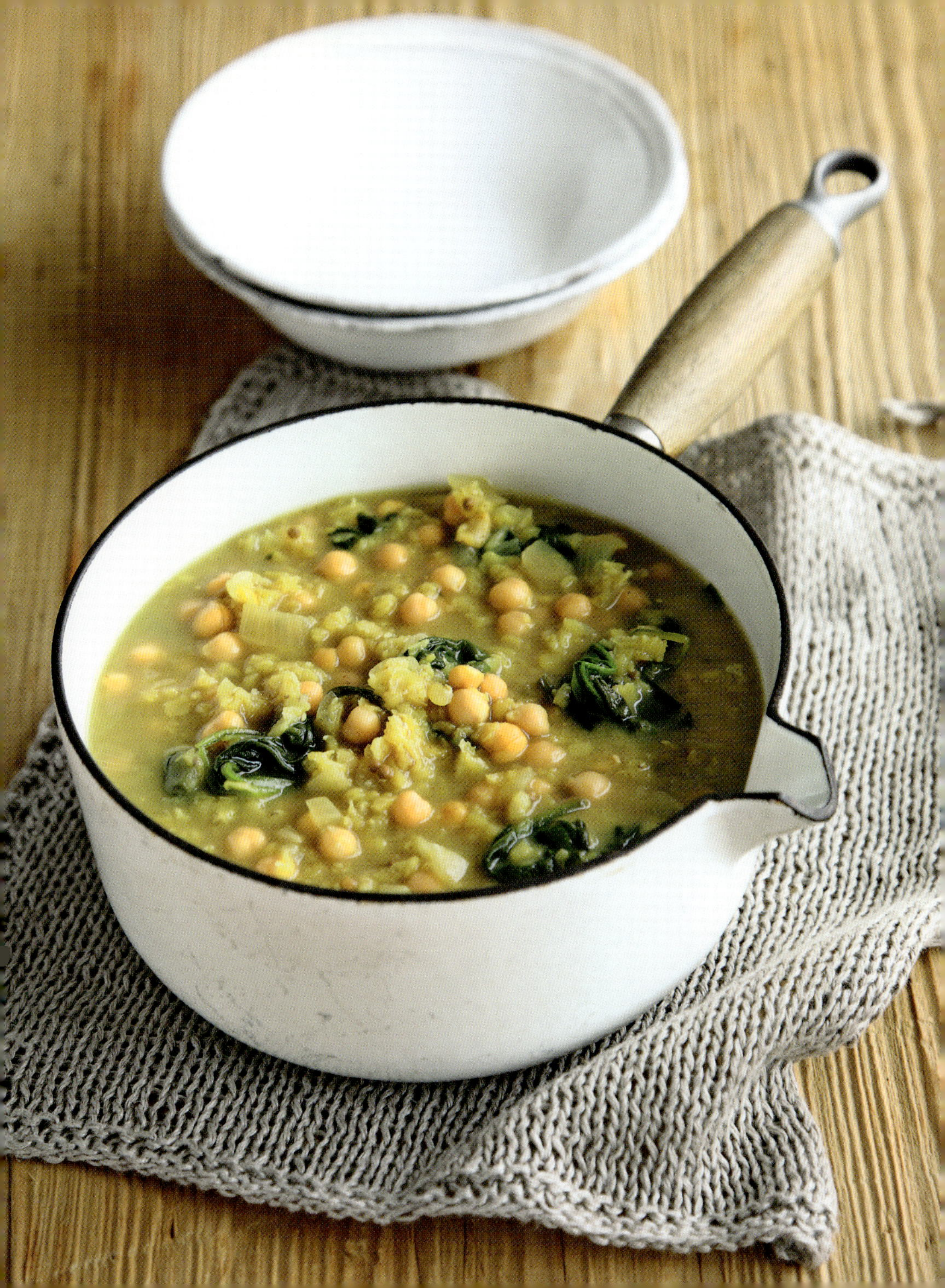

30 Carrot and Cashew Nut Rice

Serves 4

1 tablespoon olive oil
1 red onion, chopped
2 garlic cloves, sliced
2 teaspoons mustard seeds
1 teaspoon cumin seeds
1 teaspoon coriander seeds
1 teaspoon ground coriander
1 teaspoon turmeric
2¼ cups peeled, shredded carrots
1⅓ cups long-grain rice
2 cups hot vegetable stock
½ cup cashew nuts
2 tablespoons chopped cilantro
salt and black pepper

- Heat the oil in a saucepan, add the onion and garlic, and cook for 2–3 minutes. Stir in the spices and cook for 1 minute, then stir in the carrots and rice.

- Pour in the stock and season with salt and black pepper. Bring to a boil, then cover tightly and cook over medium heat for 15 minutes. Remove from the heat and let stand for 10 minutes.

- Meanwhile, heat a nonstick skillet over medium-low heat and dry-fry the cashew nuts for 3–4 minutes, stirring frequently, until golden and toasted.

- Fluff up the rice with a fork, then stir in the toasted cashew nuts and cilantro.

10 Carrot and Cashew Nut Slaw

Dry-fry 1¼ cups cashew nuts as above. Mix together 5 peeled and shredded carrots, 1 shredded small green cabbage, and 1 thinly sliced small red onion in a serving bowl, then toss in the cashew nuts. Heat 1 tablespoon olive oil in a skillet, add 2 teaspoons mustard seeds and 1 tablespoon cumin seeds, and cook until the mustard seeds start to pop. Stir in 2 tablespoons white wine vinegar and season. Pour the dressing over the vegetables and toss together with 2 tablespoons cilantro leaves.

20 Carrot and Cashew Nut Curry

Heat 1 tablespoon coconut oil in a wok or large skillet, add 1 chopped onion, and stir-fry for 1 minute. Stir in 2 tablespoons peeled and grated fresh ginger root, 2 crushed garlic cloves, 2 teaspoons garam masala, ½ teaspoon chili powder, and 1 teaspoon turmeric. Add 1½ lb carrots, cut into sticks, 1⅔ cups cashew nuts, 1 cup canned diced tomatoes, and ¼ cup hot vegetable stock. Bring to a simmer, then cook, covered, for 15–16 minutes, until the carrots are soft. Serve with cooked long-grain rice.

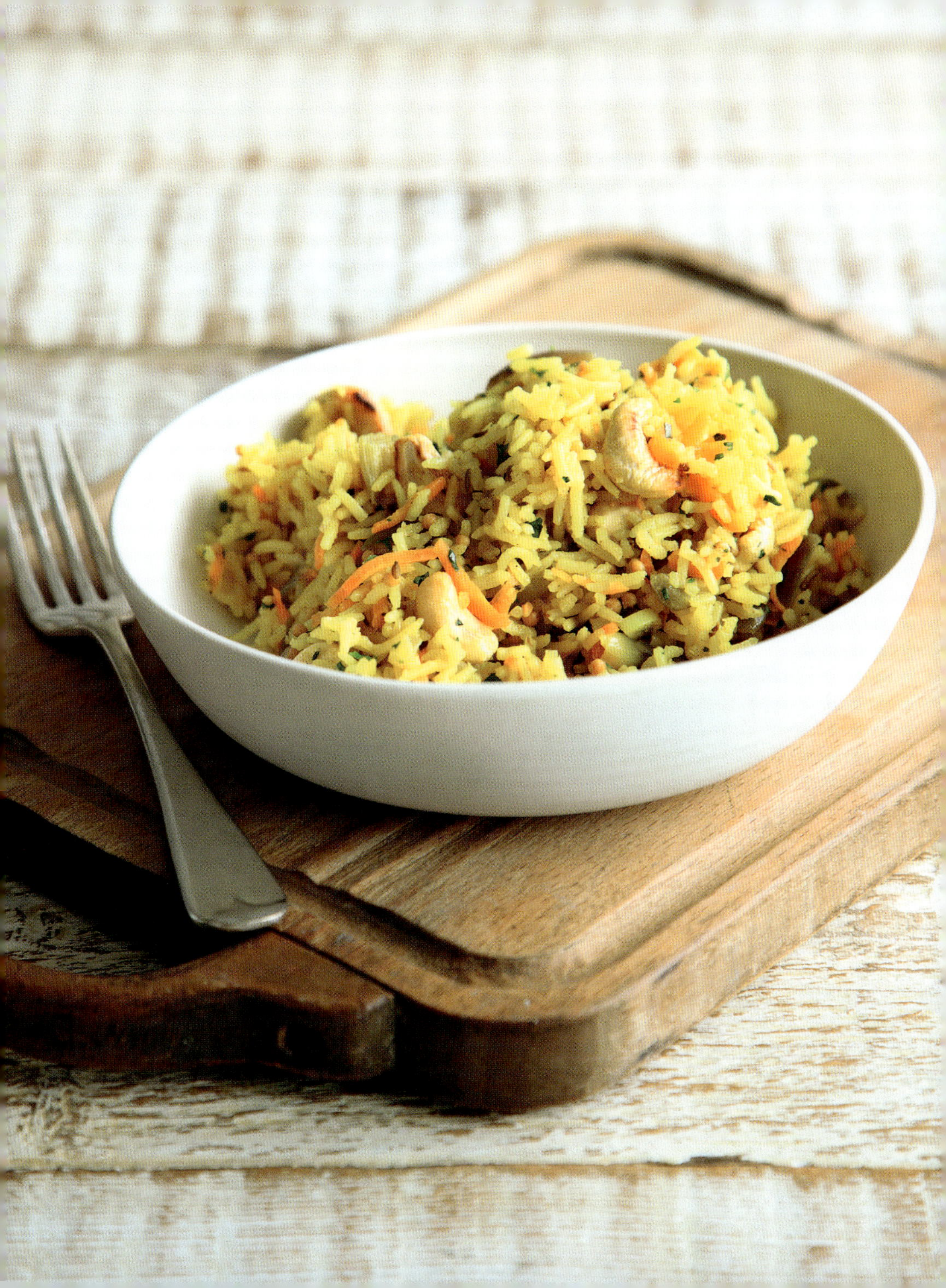

20 Spicy Broccoli Pasta with Poached Eggs

Serves 4

12 oz linguine
8 oz baby broccoli
4 eggs
2 tablespoons olive oil
6 scallions, sliced
1 teaspoon dried red pepper flakes
12 cherry tomatoes, halved

- Cook the pasta in a large saucepan of boiling water according to the package directions, until "al dente," adding the broccoli for the last 4–5 minutes of the cooking time, until tender.

- Meanwhile, bring a saucepan of water to a gentle simmer and stir with a large spoon to create a swirl. Break 2 of the eggs into the water and cook for 3 minutes. Remove with a slotted spoon and keep warm. Repeat with the remaining eggs.

- Drain the pasta and broccoli and keep warm. Heat the oil in the pasta pan, add the scallions, red pepper flakes, and tomatoes, and sauté, stirring, for 2–3 minutes. Return the pasta and broccoli to the pan and toss well to coat with the chili oil.

- Serve the pasta topped with the poached eggs.

---

10 Spicy Broccoli and Cheese

Cook 1¼ lb baby broccoli in boiling water for 3 minutes. Drain, then toss with 1 tablespoon olive oil, ½ teaspoon dried red pepper flakes, and ½ tablespoon black pepper. Cook in a preheated hot ridged grill pan for 2 minutes on each side. Meanwhile, heat 8 oz sliced Muenster cheese in a nonstick skillet for 2 minutes on each side. Whisk together the juice of ½ lemon, 2 tablespoons olive oil, 2 tablespoons tahini, and 1 tablespoon white wine vinegar in a small bowl. Place the broccoli and cheese on a large serving plate, sprinkle with 3 tablespoons toasted chopped walnuts, and drizzle with the dressing.

30 Spicy Broccoli and Red Pepper Noodles

Halve, core, and seed 3 red bell peppers and cook under a preheated hot broiler, skin side up, for 10–12 minutes, until blackened. Place in a bowl, cover with plastic wrap, and let cool for 5 minutes. Meanwhile, cook 12 oz baby broccoli in a saucepan of boiling water for 5–6 minutes, until tender, then drain, refresh under cold running water, and drain again. Cut in half lengthwise. Cook 4 oz ramen noodles according to the package directions, adding ⅔ cup soybeans 2 minutes before the end of the cooking time. Drain and place in a large bowl with the broccoli. Mix together 1 tablespoon soy sauce, 1 teaspoon dried red pepper flakes, 2 teaspoons sesame oil, ½ teaspoon peeled and grated fresh ginger root, 2 sliced scallions, and 2 tablespoons olive oil in a bowl. Peel the skin from the red bell peppers, then cut into strips. Add to the broccoli and toss with the dressing and 1 cup crumbled feta cheese.

220 VEGETARIAN DISHES

HEA-VEGE-TOT

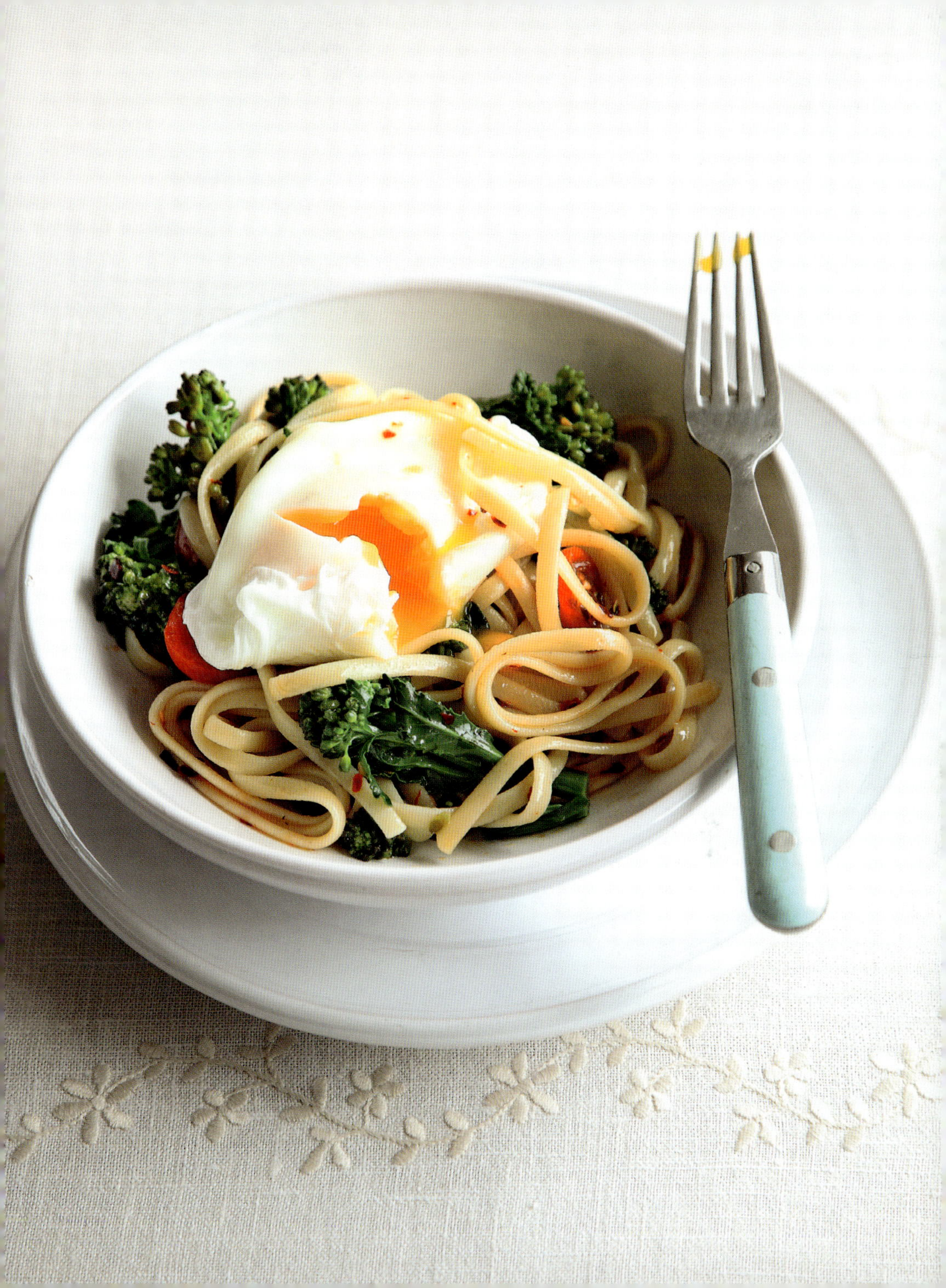

30 Simple Baked Leeks and Sweet Potatoes

Serves 4

4 small sweet potatoes
4 teaspoons sea salt
4 leeks, trimmed, halved and sliced
$\frac{2}{3}$ cup white wine
2 tablespoons extra virgin olive oil
1 cup grated Parmesan cheese
2 garlic cloves, crushed
$\frac{1}{3}$ cup pine nuts
black pepper

- Prick the sweet potatoes with a knife or fork, then wash and rub with the salt. Bake in a preheated oven, at 400°F, for 25 minutes, until tender.

- Meanwhile, place the leeks in a shallow ovenproof dish and sprinkle with the wine and oil. Season with black pepper. Mix together the cheese, garlic, and pine nuts in a bowl, then sprinkle with the leeks.

- Cover with aluminum foil and place in the oven for 15 minutes, then remove the foil and cook for another 12–13 minutes.

- Halve the sweet potatoes and serve with the leeks.

1 Roasted Baby Leeks and Sweet Potatoes

Blanch 16 trimmed baby leeks and 2 small peeled and finely diced sweet potatoes in a saucepan of boiling water for 2 minutes, then drain and place in a roasting pan. Toss together with 2 tablespoons olive oil and bake in a preheated oven, at 400°F, for 8 minutes, until tender. Meanwhile, mix together 4 chopped tomatoes, 2 tablespoons olive oil, 2 tablespoons chopped sun-dried tomatoes, 1 tablespoon red wine vinegar, 4 sliced scallions, and 1 tablespoon chopped parsley in a bowl. Spoon over the leeks and sweet potatoes, then sprinkle with 2 tablespoons Parmesan cheese shavings.

2 Leek and Sweet Potato Soup

Heat 2 tablespoons olive oil in a large saucepan, add 1 chopped onion and 2 trimmed and chopped leeks, and sauté for 2–3 minutes. Add $1\frac{2}{3}$ cups peeled and chopped sweet potatoes and 5 cups hot vegetable stock and bring to a boil. Season, then reduce the heat and simmer for 15–16 minutes until the vegetables are tender. Using a handheld blender, blend the soup until smooth, then stir in 2–3 tablespoons plain yogurt. Serve with a sprinkling of chopped parsley.

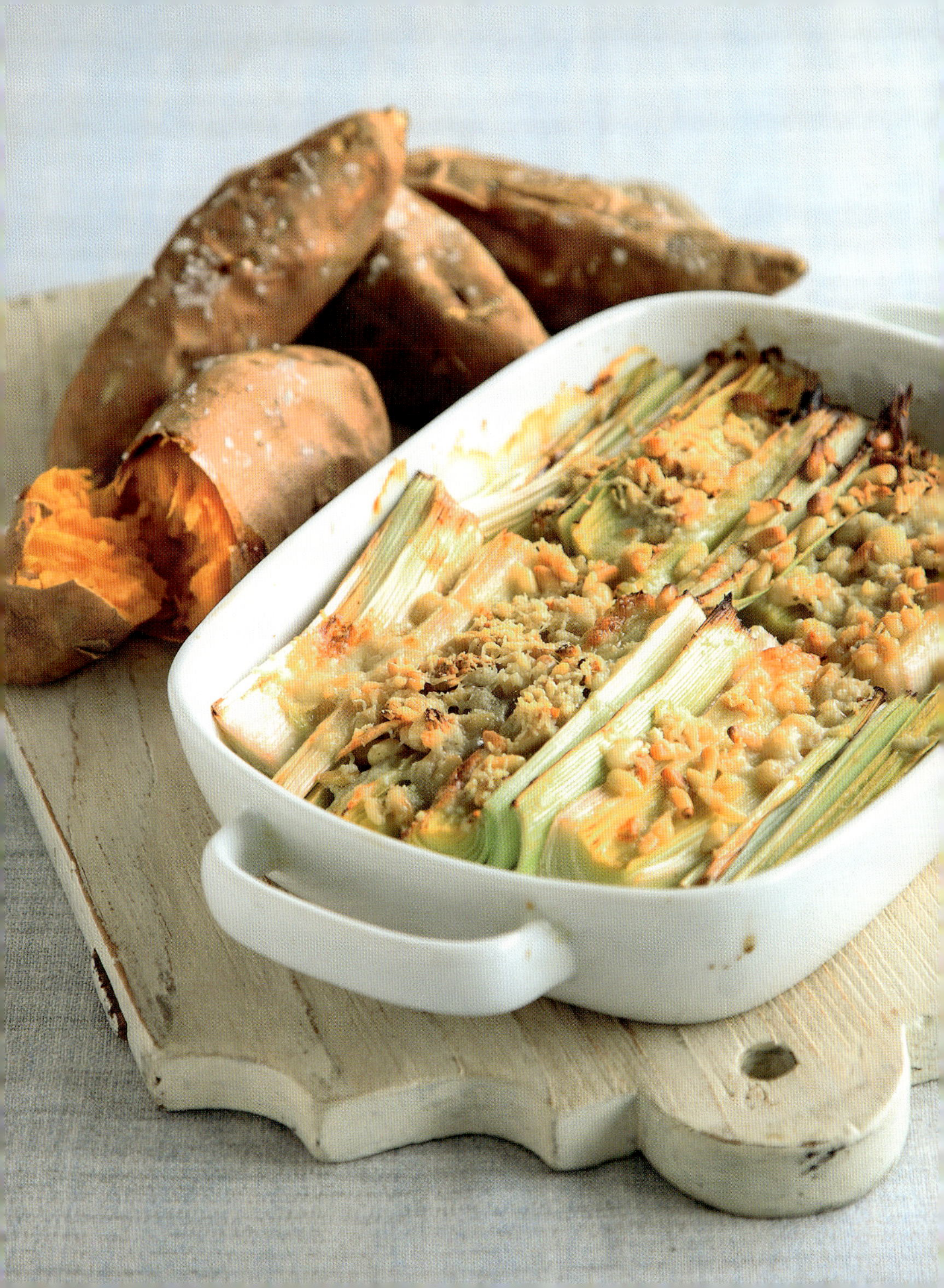

Mushroom and Tofu Stew

Serves 4

1 tablespoon olive oil
1 onion, sliced
1 lb cremini mushrooms, quartered
2 sweet potatoes, peeled and chopped
½ tablespoon pomegranate molasses or balsamic syrup
1 tablespoon whole-wheat flour
2 cups hot vegetable stock
1 tablespoon dark brown sugar
dash of Worcestershire sauce
8 oz tofu, cubed
steamed baby broccoli, to serve

- Heat the oil in a large saucepan or flameproof casserole dish, add the onion, and cook for 1–2 minutes, until it starts to soften. Add the mushrooms and cook for another 1–2 minutes, stirring occasionally.

- Add the sweet potatoes, molasses or syrup, and flour and stir well. Slowly pour in the stock, stirring continuously. Add the sugar and Worcestershire sauce and stir again until well mixed.

- Bring to a simmer, cover, and cook for 15 minutes, until the sweet potatoes are tender. Add the tofu 5 minutes before the end of the cooking time.

- Serve with steamed broccoli.

Mushroom and Tofu Stir-Fry

Heat 1 tablespoon coconut oil in a wok or large skillet, add 2 sliced red onions, 1 tablespoon mustard seeds, and 2 chopped garlic cloves, and stir-fry for 1–2 minutes. Add 1 lb sliced cremini mushrooms and stir-fry for 2–3 minutes, then add 1 cored, seeded, and sliced red bell pepper, ½ shredded napa cabbage, and 5 oz cubed tofu and stir-fry for another 4–5 minutes. Stir in 2 teaspoons soy sauce. Serve sprinkled with 2 tablespoons toasted sesame seeds.

Mushroom and Tofu Thai Curry

Heat 1 tablespoon coconut oil in a wok or large skillet, add 1 red onion, 2 kaffir lime leaves, 1 tablespoon mustard seeds, and 2 chopped garlic cloves, and stir-fry for 1–2 minutes. Stir in 2 teaspoons Thai red chili paste. Pour in 1¾ cups can coconut milk and simmer for 3–4 minutes, stirring occasionally, then add 2 cored, seeded, and chopped red bell peppers, 1 cup peeled and chopped sweet potatoes, 1 lb sliced cremini mushrooms, and 2 chopped tomatoes and cook for 18–20 minutes, until the sweet potatoes are tender. Stir in 2 tablespoons cilantro leaves and serve with cooked long-grain rice.

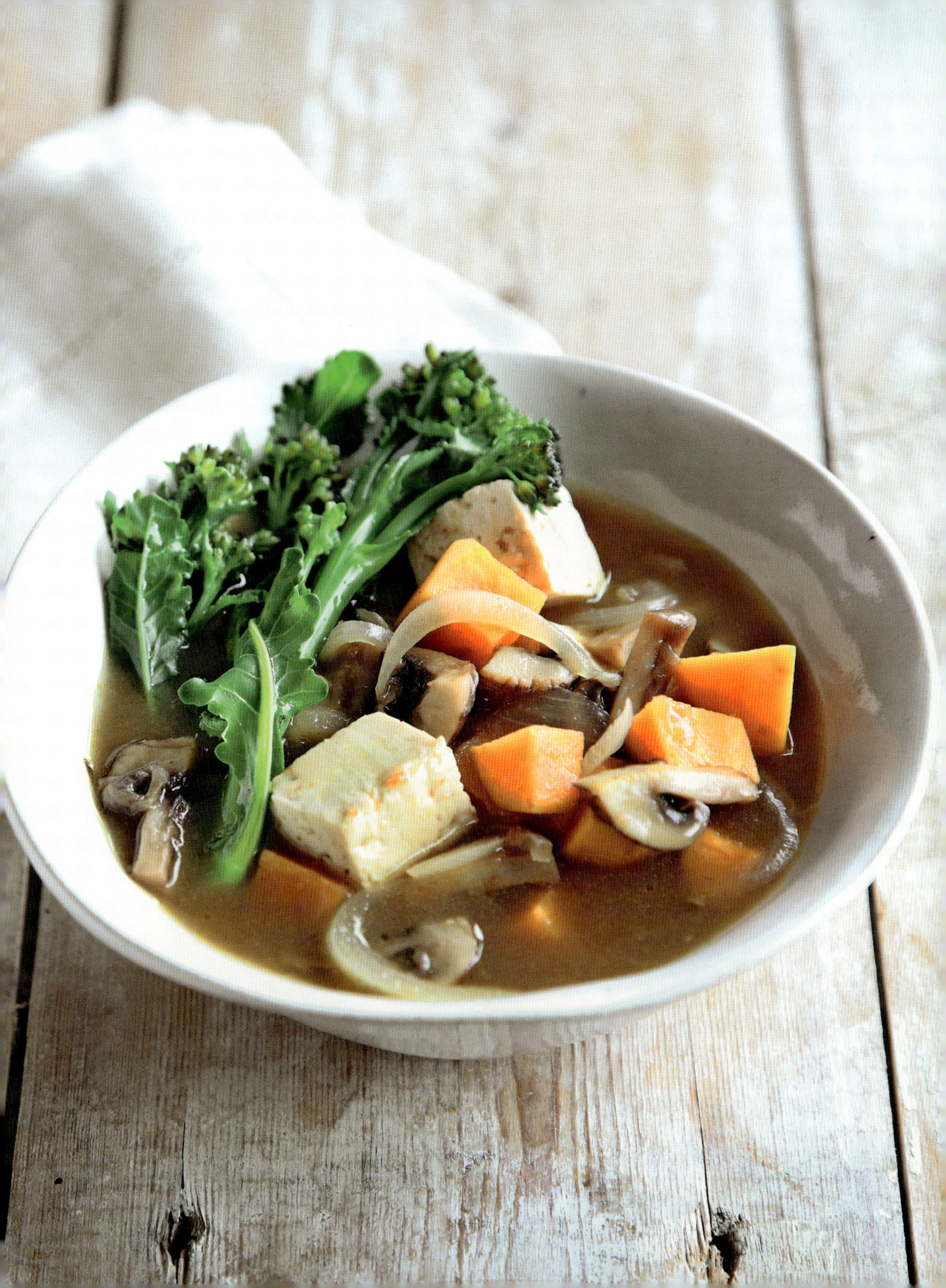

Cheesy Spinach-Stuffed Mushrooms

Serves 4

8 portobello mushrooms, stalks removed
¼ cup olive oil
6 scallions, sliced
2 (6 oz) packages baby spinach leaves
1 (7 oz) container heat-and-eat rice
1 cup grated Manchego cheese or pecorino Romano cheese
salt and black pepper

- Place the mushrooms, gill side up, in a large roasting pan, drizzle with 1 tablespoon of the oil, and cook in a preheated oven, at 400°F, for 6–8 minutes.

- Meanwhile, heat the remaining oil in a large skillet, add the scallions, and sauté for 3–4 minutes. Gradually add the spinach, stirring until wilted. Add the rice and half the cheese and season to taste, then mix well.

- Remove the mushrooms from the oven and divide the spinach mixture among the caps. Sprinkle with the remaining cheese and cook for another 8–10 minutes.

Spinach, Mushrooms, and Cheese on Toast

Heat 1 tablespoon olive oil in a skillet, add 4 scallions, and sauté for 1 minute, then add 3 cups sliced cremini mushrooms and cook for 5–6 minutes. Add 3½ cups baby spinach leaves, stirring until wilted. Meanwhile, toast 4 slices of whole-grain bread under a preheated hot broiler for 2–3 minutes on each side. Stir 1 cup crumbled blue cheese into the mushroom mixture and spoon over the toasts to serve.

Spinach, Mushroom, and Feta-Stuffed Peppers

Place 4 halved, cored, and seeded bell peppers in a roasting pan, cut side up. Heat 1 tablespoon olive oil in a skillet, add 1 large chopped red onion and 1 teaspoon cumin seeds, and cook for 2–3 minutes. Add 6 sliced cremini mushrooms and cook for another 2 minutes, then add 1 (12 oz) package baby spinach leaves, cover, and cook for 2–3 minutes, until the spinach is wilted. Remove from the heat and add ¼ cup chopped walnuts, 2 tablespoons pumpkin seeds, and 1⅓ cups crumbled feta cheese. Season well, then spoon the mixture into the bell peppers. Place in a preheated oven, at 400°F, for 20–22 minutes until the bell peppers are tender. Meanwhile, cook ½ (2 lb) peeled, seeded, and chopped butternut squash and 1⅓ cups peeled and chopped russet potatoes in a saucepan of boiling water for 12–15 minutes, until tender. Drain, then mash in the pan with 1 tablespoon plain yogurt and 1 teaspoon chopped thyme leaves. Serve the stuffed peppers with the mashed potatoes.

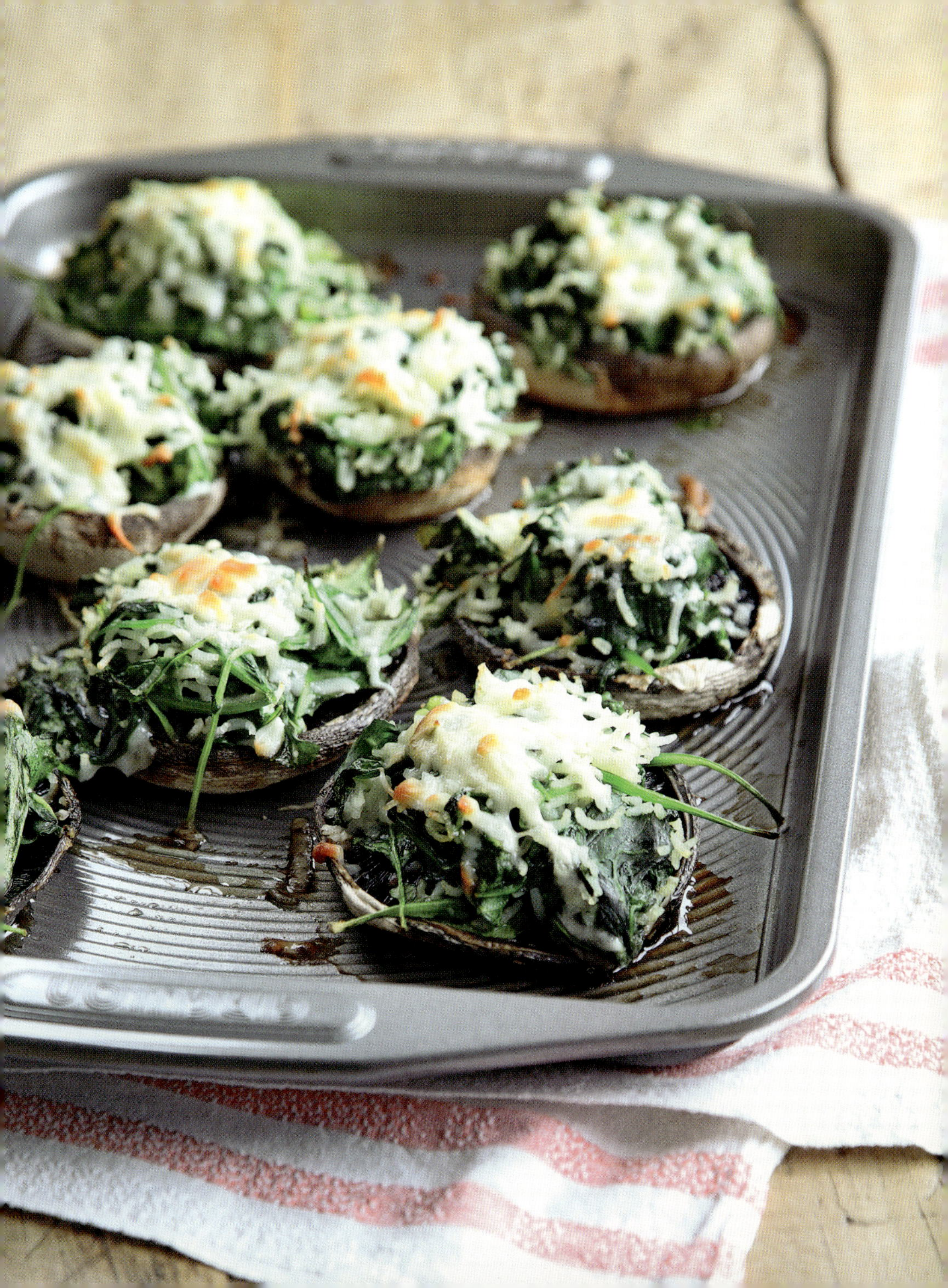

Falafels with Spicy Sauce

Serves 4

1 (15 oz) can chickpeas, rinsed and drained
1 onion, finely diced
2 garlic cloves, chopped
3 tablespoons chopped parsley
1 teaspoon ground coriander
1 teaspoon ground cumin
2 tablespoons all-purpose flour
2–3 tablespoons vegetable oil
salt and black pepper
½ iceburg lettuce, shredded, to serve

For the spicy sauce

⅓ cup tomato paste
½–1 teaspoon harissa paste, to taste
2 garlic cloves, crushed
1 teaspoon lemon juice
¼ cup water
1 tablespoon chopped parsley

- To make the sauce, place all the ingredients in a small saucepan and simmer for 10 minutes.
- Meanwhile, place all the falafel ingredients except the oil in a large bowl and mash together with a fork. Alternatively, place the ingredients in a food processor and process until smooth. Using wet hands, shape the mixture into small balls and flatten slightly.
- Heat the vegetable oil in a skillet and cook the falafels for 5–7 minutes, until golden.
- Serve on the lettuce with the spicy sauce.

Falafel and Tabbouleh Salad

Make the falafels as above. Meanwhile, place 1½ cups couscous in a heatproof bowl and just cover with boiling water. Let stand for 10 minutes. Fluff up the couscous with a fork, then stir in 2 tablespoons each of chopped mint, chopped parsley, and chopped chives, 3 diced tomatoes, and ½ diced cucumber. Serve with the falafels and dollops of store-bought hummus.

Falafel Cheese Burgers

Place 3 cups rinsed and drained canned chickpeas, 2 teaspoons ground cumin, 1 teaspoon ground coriander, 2 seeded and diced green chiles, 2 chopped garlic cloves, 6 chopped scallions, ½ teaspoon salt, and 2 tablespoons all-purpose flour in a food processor and process until coarsely blended. Transfer to a bowl and stir in 8 oz diced Muenster cheese. Using wet hands, shape into 4 patties, then cover and chill for 15 minutes. Heat 1 tablespoon olive oil in a skillet, add the patties, and cook for 3–4 minutes on each side until golden. Meanwhile, toast 4 burger buns under a preheated medium broiler for 3–4 minutes on each side. Top the bottoms with 2 tablespoons shredded iceburg lettuce. Place a burger on top, then 3 sliced tomatoes. Top with the lids and serve immediately.

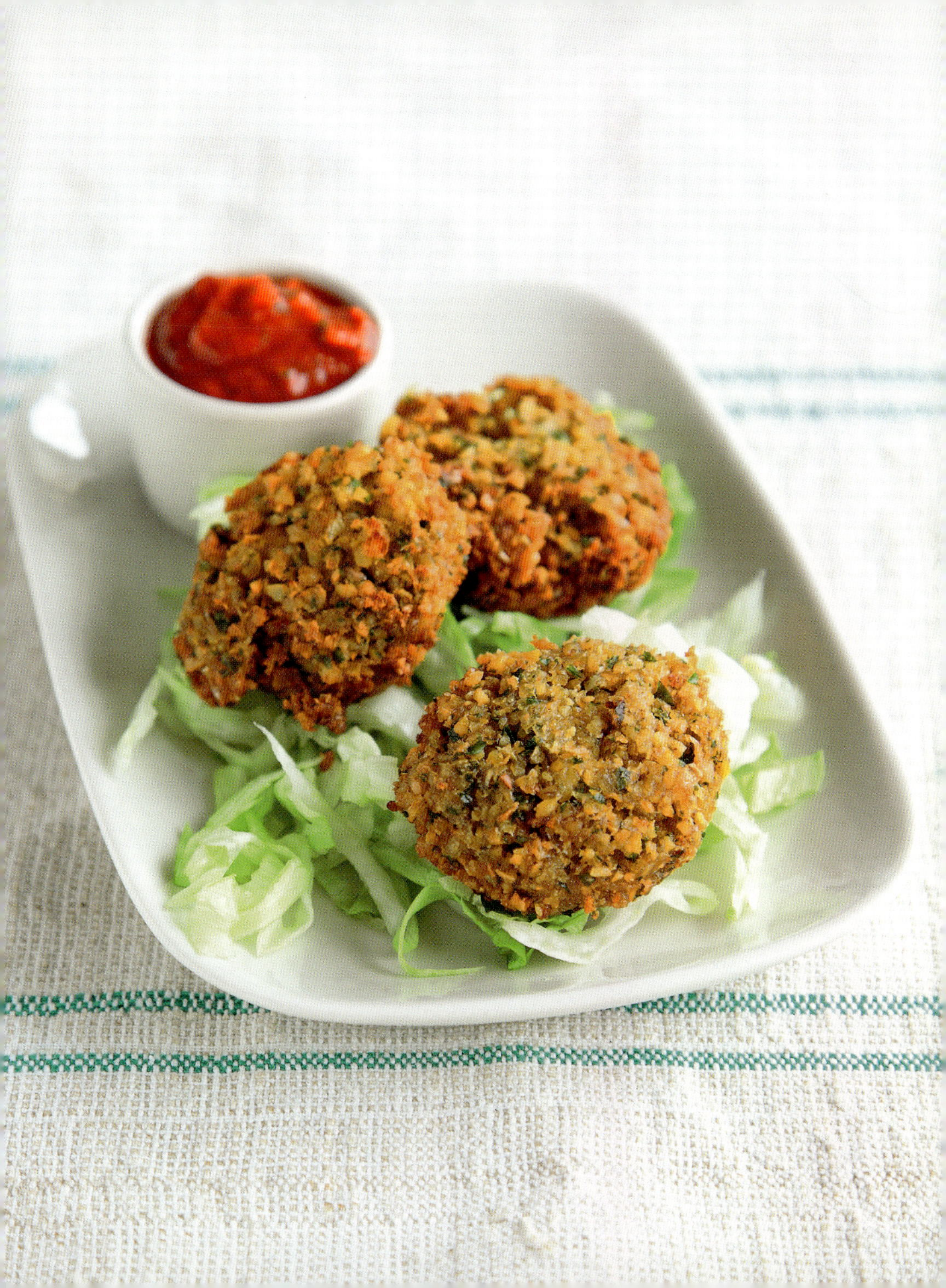

Crunchy Pesto Broccoli with Poached Eggs

Serves 4

9 cups broccoli florets
5 cups sugar snap peas
4 eggs
1½ cups chopped sun-dried tomatoes
black pepper
Parmesan cheese shavings, to serve

For the pesto
⅓ cup basil leaves
½ tablespoon toasted pine nuts
1 tablespoon grated Parmesan cheese
1 small garlic clove, crushed
3–4 teaspoons olive oil

- To make the pesto, place the basil and pine nuts in a food processor and process until broken down. Add the cheese and garlic and process briefly. With the motor still running, slowly pour in the oil through the feed tube until combined.

- Cook the broccoli and sugar snap peas in a large saucepan of boiling water for 7–8 minutes, until "al dente."

- Meanwhile, bring a saucepan of water to a gentle simmer and stir with a large spoon to create a swirl. Break 2 of the eggs into the water and cook for 3 minutes. Remove with a slotted spoon and keep warm. Repeat with the remaining eggs.

- Drain the vegetables, then return to the pan and add 1½ tablespoons of the pesto (store any remaining pesto in an airtight container in the refrigerator) and the sun-dried tomatoes. Gently toss together until well coated.

- Serve topped with the poached eggs and Parmesan shavings and sprinkled with black pepper.

Broccoli Pesto Pasta Cook 1 lb green tagliatelle in a saucepan of boiling water according to the package directions, until "al dente," adding 2 cups broccoli florets 3 minutes before the end of the cooking time. Drain, then return to the pan with ¼ cup store-bought pesto, 4 chopped scallions, and 4 oz chopped goat cheese. Toss together and serve immediately.

Pesto and Broccoli Potato Cakes Cook 8 peeled and chopped russet potatoes (about 2 lb) in a saucepan of boiling water for 12–15 minutes, until tender, adding 1½ cups broccoli florets 2 minutes before the end of the cooking time. Drain, then mash in the pan with 2 tablespoons crème fraîche or sour cream. Stir in 1 tablespoon store-bought pesto and 4 sliced scallions and season well. Using wet hands, shape into 4 patties. Heat 2 tablespoons olive oil in a skillet, add the potato cakes, and cook for 2–3 minutes on each side until golden. Meanwhile, poach 4 eggs as above. Serve the potato cakes topped with the poached eggs.

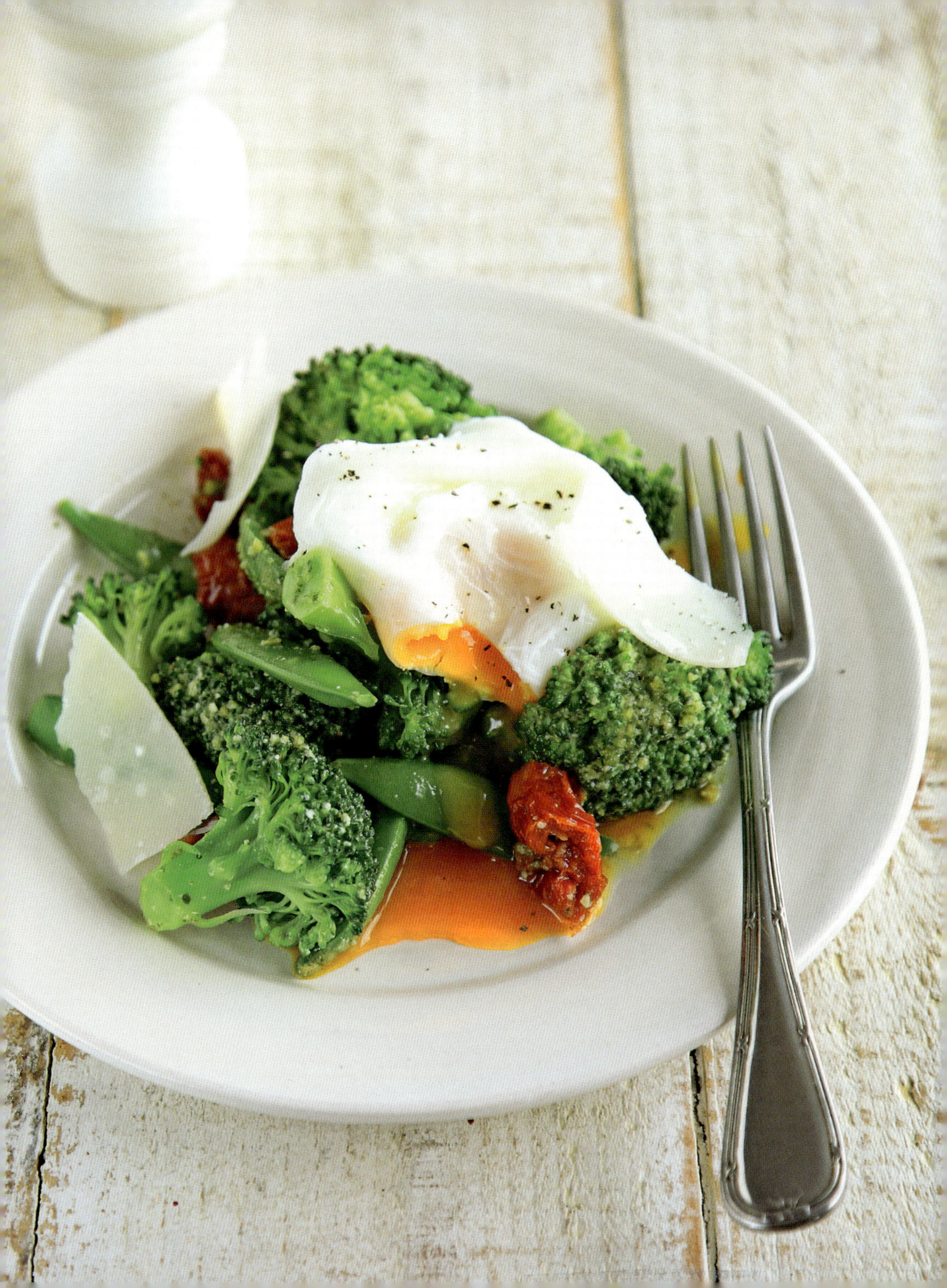

QuickCook
Cakes and Desserts

Recipes listed by cooking time

30

Lemon and Raisin Scones	236
Ginger Poached Pears	238
Berry Muffins	240
Cocoa, Orange, and Pecan Oat Bars	242
Apricot Tarts with Cardamom Yogurt	244
Blackberry Pancakes	246
Oat, Banana, and Ginger Muffins	248
Roasted Honey Peaches	250
Sesame Cookies	252
Minted Mixed Berry Desserts	254
Spicy Fruit Bread Puddings	256
Strawberry and Almond Muffins	258
Tropical Fruit Crisp	260
Whole-Wheat Raspberry Coconut Muffins	262
Winter Fruit Cobbler with Cinnamon Ricotta	264
Lemon and Golden Raisin Rice Pudding	266
Gingered Sesame Fruit Compote	268
Whole-Wheat Blueberry Pancakes with Lemon Yogurt	270
Spiced Banana Muffins	272
Fall Fruits in Mulled Wine	274
Rhubarb, Coconut, and Honey Tarts	276
Raspberry Oat Crisp	278

20

Lemon and Cardamom Cookies	236
Oat-Topped Pear and Ginger Dessert	238
Berry and Rhubarb Whips	240
Cocoa, Orange, and Pecan Scones	242
Sweet Semolina with Cardamom Poached Apricots	244
Blackberry Mousse	246
Oat, Banana, and Ginger Cookies	248
Broiled Peaches with Honey Syrup	250
Mango Whips with Sesame Brittle	252
Berry and Mint Compote	254
Spicy Fruit-Topped French Toast	256
Roasted Strawberries with Almond Yogurt	258
Tropical Fruit Salsa	260
Raspberry and Coconut French Toast	262

10

Winter Fruits with Orange Ricotta		264
Whole-Wheat Lemon and Golden Raisin Scones		266
Gingered Sesame Fruit Kebabs		268
Blueberry and Lemon Cheesecake Desserts		270
Baked Spiced Bananas		272
Caramelized Fall Fruits		274
Honey-Roasted Rhubarb with Coconut Rice		276
Raspberry Whips with Crunchy Oats		278
Lemon Mousse		236
Caramelized Pears with Ginger Yogurt		238
Berry and Meringue Desserts		240
Cocoa, Orange, and Pecan Muesli		242
Cardamom Rice Pudding with Apricots		244
Blackberry Brûlées		246
Banana and Ginger Oatmeal		248
Honeyed Peach Bruschetta		250
Sesame French Toast		252
Berry and Mint Smoothies		254
Spicy Fruit-Topped Sweet Bruschetta		256
Strawberry and Almond Desserts		258
Tropical Fruit Brûlées		260
Raspberry Coconut Whips		262
Winter Fruit Salad with Lemon Ricotta		264
Quick Lemon and Golden Raisin Rice		266
Gingered Sesame Fruit Salad		268
Blueberry Lemon Yogurt		270
Bananas with Spiced Chocolate Sauce		272
Fall Fruit Compote		274
Rhubarb with Toasted Coconut and Honeyed Ice Cream		276
Oaty Raspberry Dessert		278

30 Lemon and Raisin Scones

Makes 12

¼ cup raisins
juice of ½ lemon
grated rind of 2 lemons
2¾ cups all-purpose flour, sifted
1 tablespoon baking powder
6 tablespoons chilled butter, diced
3 tablespoons sugar
1¼ cups milk

To serve

2 tablespoons Greek yogurt
2 tablespoons lemon curd (available in well-stocked grocery stores and gourmet food stores)

- Place the raisins in a small bowl and pour the lemon juice over them. Let stand for 10 minutes.

- Meanwhile, place the lemon rind and flour in a large bowl, add the butter, and rub in with the fingertips until the mixture resembles fine bread crumbs. Drain the raisins, then stir in with the sugar. Using a spatula, gradually mix in the milk to form a dough—do not overmix or knead.

- Turn the dough out onto a floured surface and press out lightly to about ¾ inch thick, then cut out 12 circles, using a 1½–2-inch plain cookie cutter, using the leftover dough as necessary.

- Place on a baking sheet and bake in a preheated oven, at 400°F, for 12–15 minutes, until risen and slightly brown. Transfer to a wire rack to cool.

- Serve with Greek yogurt and lemon curd.

---

10 Lemon Mousse

Whisk together 1¼ cups heavy cream, the grated rind of 1 lemon, and ⅓ cup superfine or granulated sugar in a bowl until the mixture starts to thicken. Add the juice of 1 lemon and whisk again until thickened. Whisk 2 egg whites in a clean bowl until they form soft peaks, then gently fold into the cream mixture. Spoon into 4 glasses and chill for a few minutes before serving.

20 Lemon and Cardamom Cookies

Beat together 1¾ sticks softened unsalted butter, ¾ cup granulated sugar, and the grated rind of 1 lemon until light and fluffy. Beat in 2 cups all-purpose flour, 1 cup ground almonds (almond meal), and 2 teaspoons ground cardamom to form a stiff dough. Roll the dough into 24 balls and place, well spaced apart, on a baking sheet lined with parchment paper. Press each ball to flatten slightly, then bake in a preheated oven, at 375°F, for 12–14 minutes, until golden. Let cool on the baking sheet for 2 minutes, then transfer to a wire rack to cool completely.

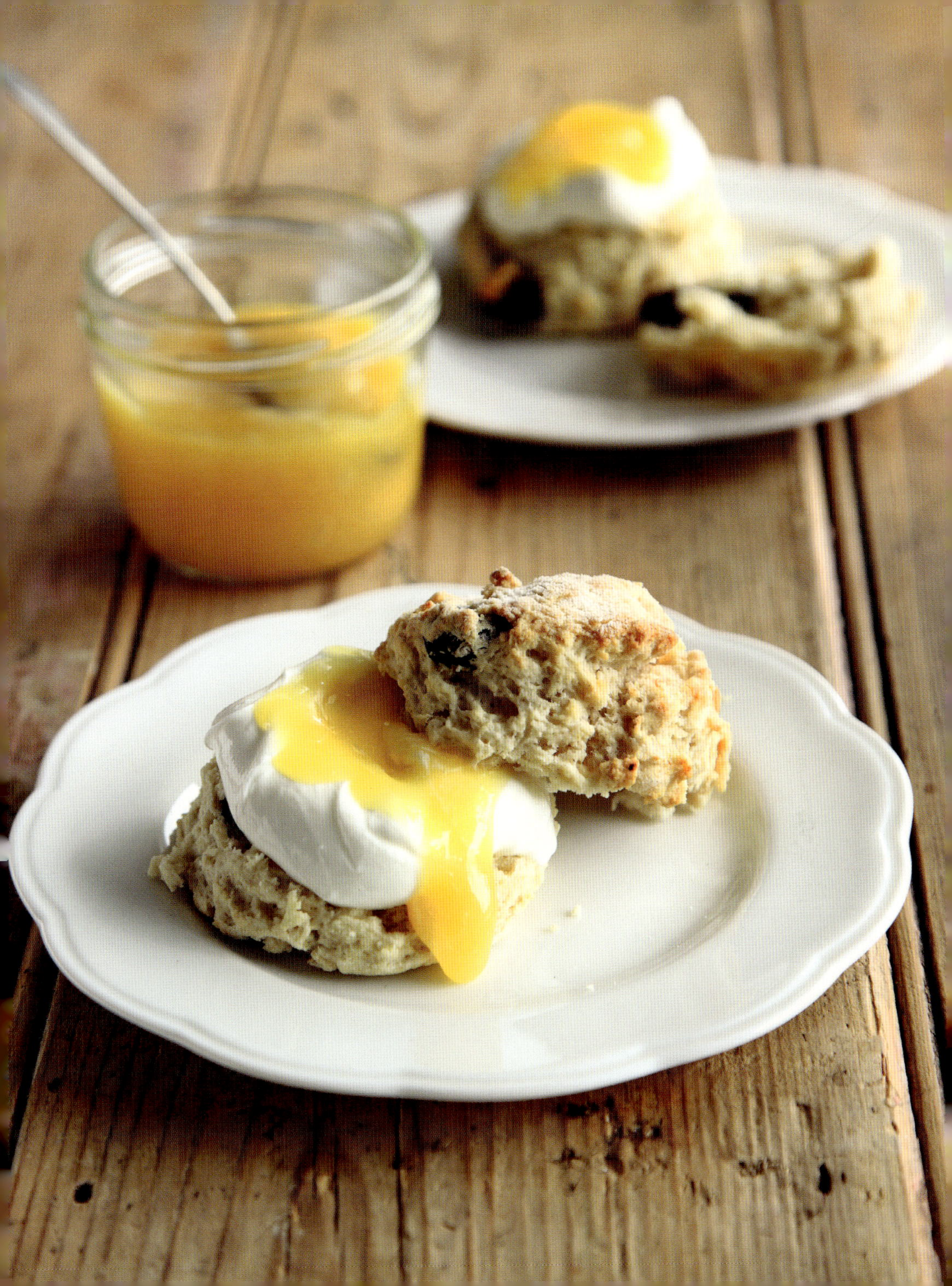

20 Oat-Topped Pear and Ginger Dessert

Serves 4–6

8 ripe pears, peeled, cored, and chopped
4–5 knobs of preserved ginger, diced
3 tablespoons preserved ginger syrup
¼ cup coconut oil
2 tablespoons molasses
2 tablespoons light brown sugar
1⅓ cups rolled oats
2 tablespoons pumpkin seeds
1 tablespoon sesame seeds

- Place the pears in a shallow ovenproof dish, then sprinkle with the preserved ginger. Pour the preserved ginger syrup over the pears.
- Heat the oil, molasses, and sugar in a saucepan over gentle heat, stirring until the sugar is dissolved. Add the remaining ingredients and mix well. Spoon the mixture over the pears.
- Bake in a preheated oven, at 375°F, for 15–17 minutes, until golden.

10 Caramelized Pears with Ginger Yogurt

Heat 2 tablespoons butter in a skillet, add 4 peeled, cored, and sliced pears, and cook for 3–4 minutes on each side. Meanwhile, stir 4 diced knobs of preserved ginger and 2 tablespoons preserved ginger syrup into 1 cup thick plain yogurt. Serve the pears topped with spoonfuls of the ginger yogurt and a sprinkling of slivered almonds.

30 Ginger Poached Pears

Place 3¾ cups granulated sugar, 1 cinnamon stick, 2 strips of lemon rind, 1 star anise, 1 vanilla bean, 5 cloves, and a 1-inch piece of fresh ginger root, peeled and sliced, in a large saucepan. Fill the pan halfway with water, then bring to a boil. Add 4 peeled ripe pears, cover, and gently poach for about 20 minutes, until tender. Turn off the heat and let cool slightly. Serve the pears with a little of the syrup, sprinkled with 1 chopped knob of preserved ginger and scoops of vanilla ice cream, if liked.

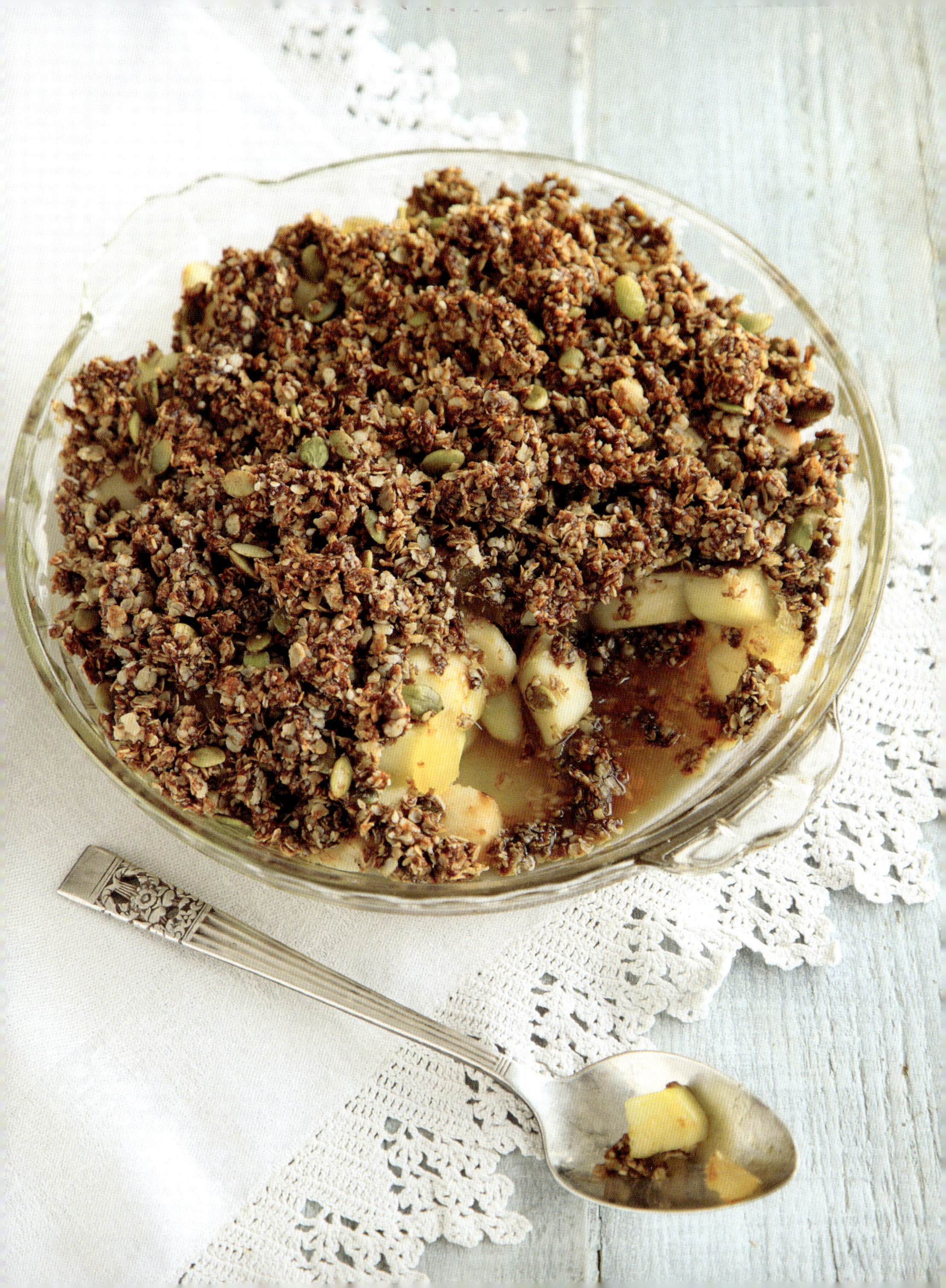

10 Berry and Meringue Desserts

Serves 4

- 2 oz meringue cookies or nests, broken into chunks
- 3 cups mixed berries, such as strawberries, raspberries, blueberries, and blackberries, defrosted if frozen
- 1⅓ cups plain yogurt
- 2 knobs of preserved ginger, diced

- Place the meringues in a large bowl and add the berries and yogurt. Mix very gently so the meringue pieces do not break up too much.
- Divide among 4 glasses or bowls and sprinkle with the preserved ginger.

20 Berry and Rhubarb Whips

Place 1 lb trimmed and chopped rhubarb, 1⅓ cups hulled and halved strawberries, the juice of 1 orange, and 2 tablespoons sugar in a saucepan and bring to a simmer, then cook gently for 8–10 minutes. Transfer to a bowl and chill for 6 minutes. Meanwhile, finely chop a small handful of mint leaves and stir into 1¾ cups Greek or plain yogurt. Layer the fruit and yogurt in 4 glasses and serve each with a light sweet cookie, if desired.

30 Berry Muffins

Sift 1⅔ cups all-purpose flour and 1½ teaspoons baking powder into a large bowl and stir in 1 cup granulated sugar. Beat together the grated rind of 1 orange, 1 cup Greek or plain yogurt, 4 tablespoons melted butter, and 1 beaten egg in a small bowl, then pour into the dry ingredients and mix together—do not overmix. Gently stir in 1 cup mixed berries and the segments from 1 orange until just combined. Spoon into 12 paper muffin liners arranged in a muffin pan and bake in a preheated oven, at 375°F, for 20–25 minutes, until golden and firm to the touch. Transfer to a wire rack to cool or serve warm.

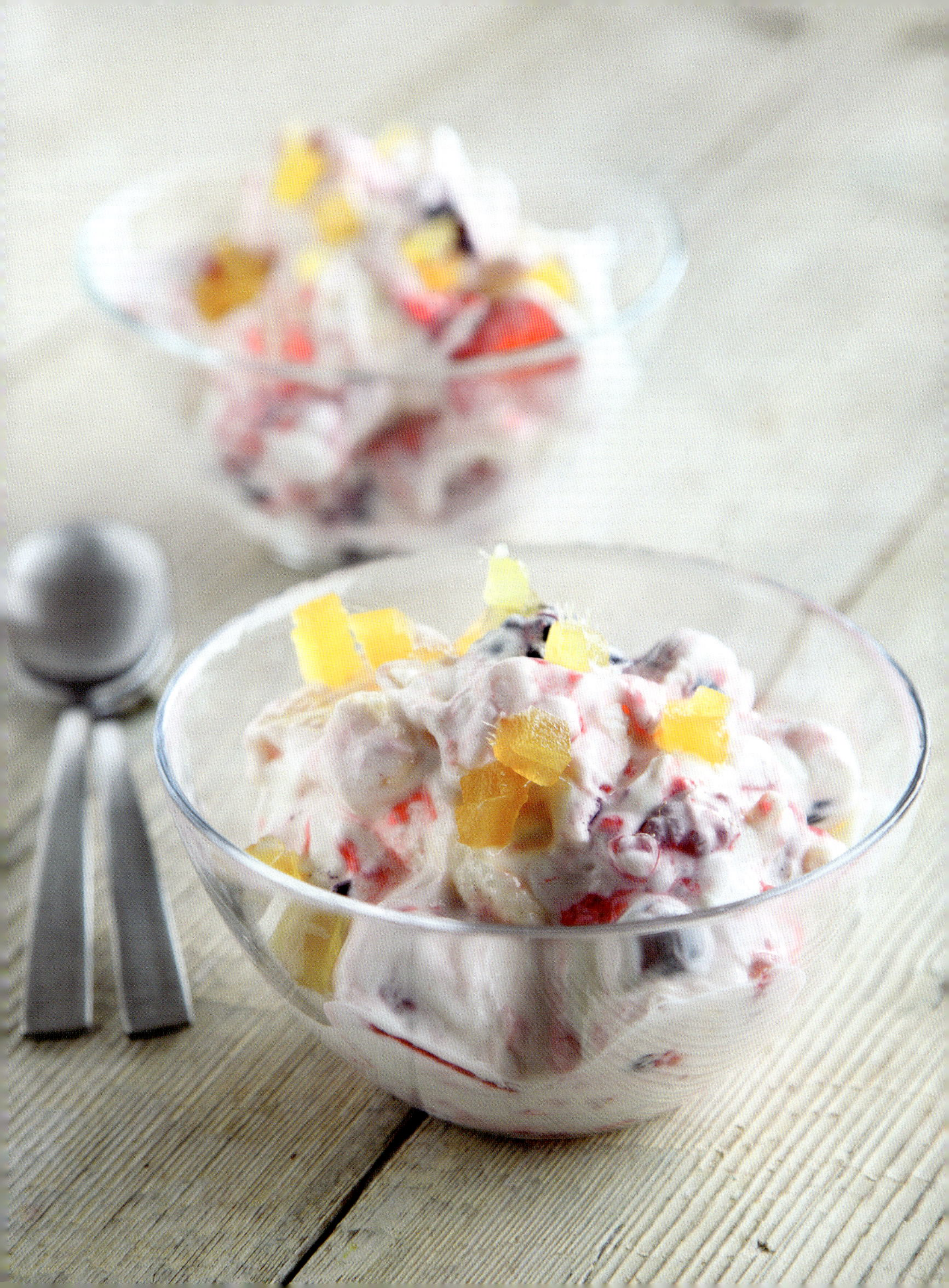

30 Cocoa, Orange, and Pecan Oat Bars

Makes 9–12

½ cup coconut oil, plus extra for greasing
¼ cup molasses
2 tablespoons dark brown sugar
1 tablespoon agave syrup
2¾ cups rolled oats
½ cup coarsely chopped pecans
½ cup cocoa nibs or semisweet chocolate chips
grated rind of 1 orange

- Heat the oil, molasses, sugar, and agave syrup in a large saucepan over gentle heat, stirring until the sugar is dissolved. Add the remaining ingredients and mix well.
- Pour into a greased 7 inch-square baking pan and level the surface. Bake in a preheated oven, at 350°F, for 18–20 minutes.
- Cool in the pan for 2 minutes, then cut into squares. Let cool completely in the pan.

1 Cocoa, Orange, and Pecan Muesli

Dry-fry ½ cup pecans in a nonstick skillet for 3–4 minutes, stirring frequently, until toasted. Let cool, then mix together with 2¾ cups rolled oats, ½ cup cocoa nibs or semisweet chocolate chips, ⅓ cup diced dried apricots, and the grated rind of 2 oranges. Soak for a few minutes in the juice of 2 oranges, then serve with fresh fruit and plain yogurt.

2 Cocoa, Orange, and Pecan Scones

Toast ¼ cup pecans (see left), then chop. Set aside. Sift together 1¾ cups all-purpose flour, 2 teaspoons baking powder, and a pinch of salt in a large bowl. Add 6 tablespoons diced, chilled unsalted butter and rub in with the fingertips until the mixture resembles fine bread crumbs. Stir in the pecans, 3 tablespoons granulated sugar, the grated rind of 1 orange, and ¼ cup cocoa nibs or semisweet chocolate chips. Beat together 1 egg and 2 tablespoons buttermilk in a small bowl, then add to the dry ingredients and mix with a spatula to a soft dough. Roll or press out on a floured surface to 1-inch thick, then cut out circles using a 2 inch plain cookie cutter or glass. Place on a baking sheet and bake in a preheated oven, at 425°F, for 10–12 minutes, until risen. Transfer to a wire rack to cool.

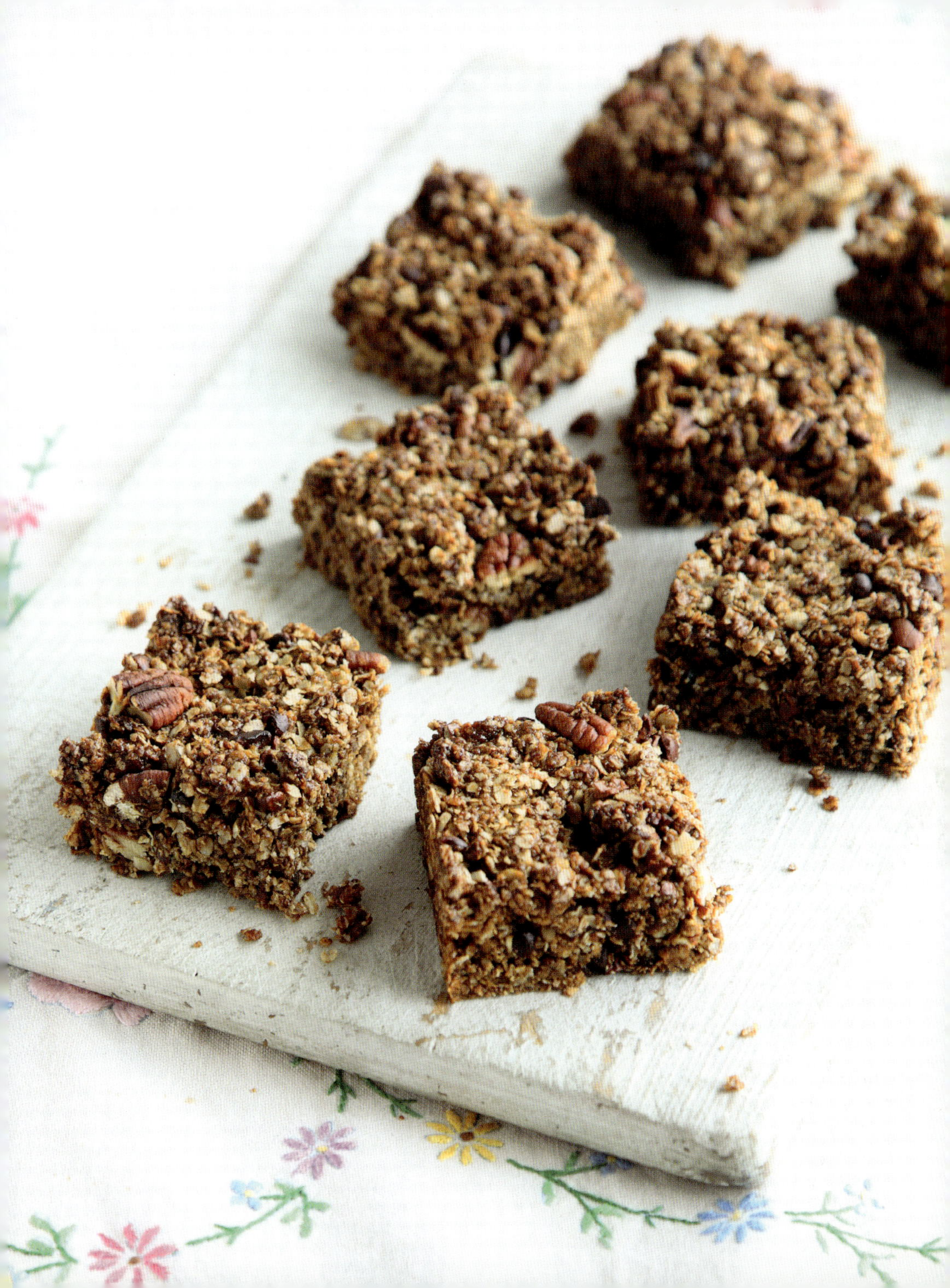

Sweet Semolina with Cardamom Poached Apricots

Serves 4

½ vanilla bean, split lengthwise
2 tablespoons honey
6 cardamom pods, lightly crushed
1 cup water
4 apricots, halved and pitted
2½ cups milk
¼ cup semolina
2 tablespoons granulated sugar
pinch of nutmeg
1 tablespoon pistachio nuts, chopped

- Scrape the seeds from the vanilla bean and add the seeds and bean to a saucepan with the honey, cardamom pods, and measured water. Bring to a boil, stirring occasionally, until the honey dissolves.

- Add the apricots and simmer for 2–5 minutes, until just tender. Remove the apricots with a slotted spoon.

- Boil the remaining syrup over high heat for 6–8 minutes, until reduced by about half, then strain.

- Meanwhile, bring the milk to a boil in a separate saucepan, then slowly pour in the semolina and sugar, stirring continuously. Simmer and stir for 8–10 minutes, until thickened and cooked. Add the nutmeg.

- Spoon the semolina into 4 small bowls and add the apricots. Pour the syrup over the dessert and serve sprinkled with the pistachios.

Cardamom Rice Pudding with Apricots
Place ¾ cup flaked rice, 3 cups low-fat milk, and 4 lightly crushed cardamom pods in a saucepan and bring to a boil, stirring occasionally. Reduce the heat and simmer, stirring occasionally, for 7 minutes. Stir in 4–5 teaspoons granulated sugar. Serve the rice pudding topped with 1 (15 oz) can apricots in syrup.

Apricot Tarts with Cardamom Yogurt
Unroll a sheet of ready-to-bake puff pastry and cut into 4 rectangles. Place on a baking sheet and top each one with 1 tablespoon ground almonds (almond meal). Lay 2–3 halved and pitted apricots on top and dust with 2 tablespoons confectioners' sugar. Bake in a preheated oven, at 425°F, for 20–25 minutes, until golden. Meanwhile, remove the seeds from 3–4 cardamom pods and crush using a mortar and pestle, then mix together with 1 cup Greek yogurt in a bowl. Serve the apricots tarts with the yogurt, sprinkled with a few chopped pistachio nuts and a drizzle of honey.

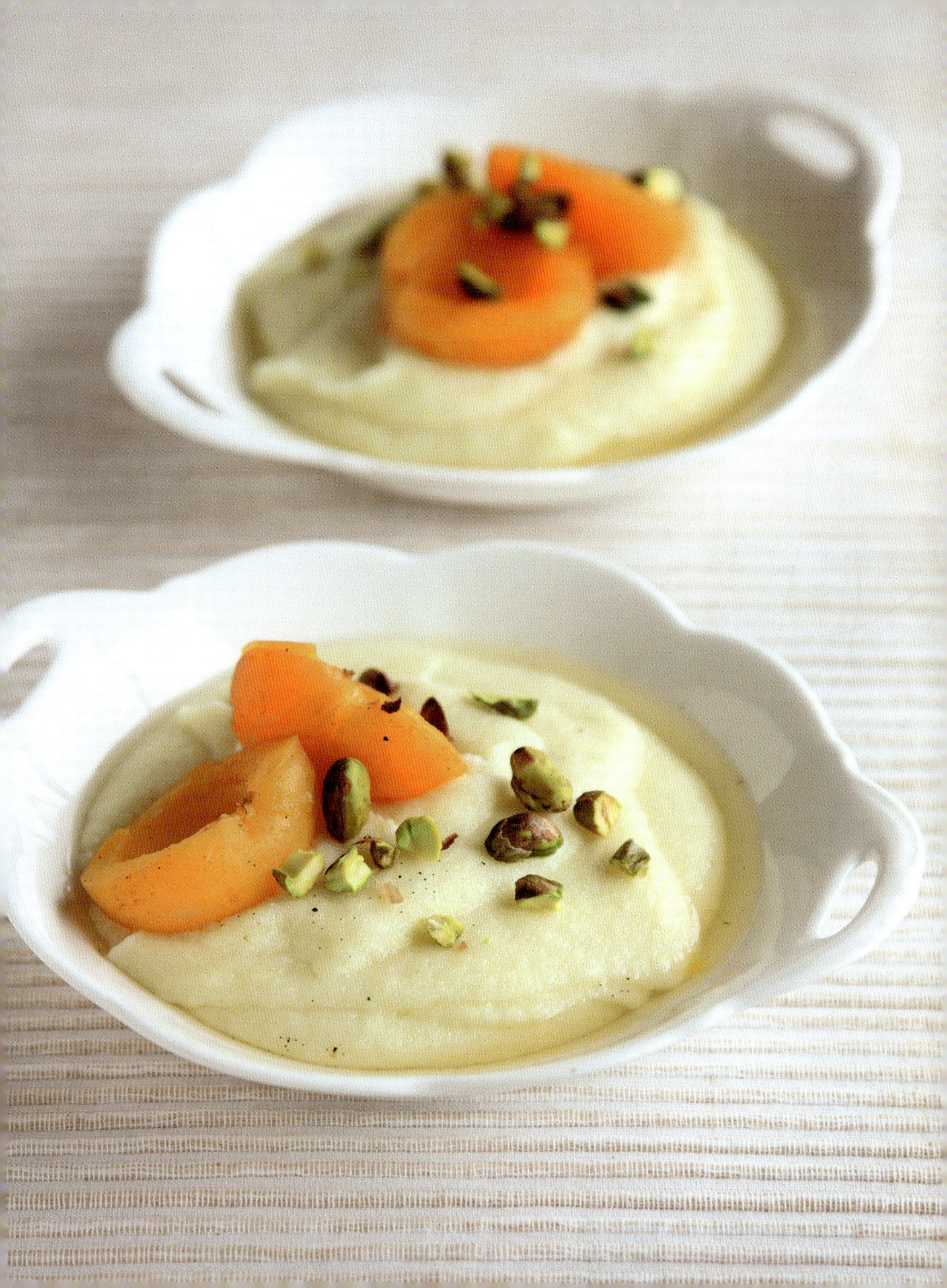

10 Blackberry Brûlées

Serves 4

1½ cups blackberries
2 tablespoons apple juice
2–3 teaspoons superfine or granulated sugar, to taste
½ cup Greek yogurt
2 tablespoons firmly packed dark brown sugar

- Place the blackberries, apple juice, and sugar in a saucepan and simmer for 2–3 minutes. Spoon into 4 ramekins and let cool for 2–3 minutes.
- Spoon the yogurt over the blackberries, then sprinkle with the brown sugar.
- Cover and chill until required.

20 Blackberry Mousse

Place 2 cups blackberries, ⅔ cup confectioners' sugar, and the juice of ½ lemon in a food processor or blender and process to a puree, then pass through a strainer into a large bowl. Stir in ⅔ cup heavy cream and ⅔ cup Greek or plain yogurt and whisk until thick. Divide among 4 dishes or glasses, then cover and chill for 10–12 minutes. Serve with spoonfuls of plain yogurt and a few blackberries.

30 Blackberry Pancakes

Sift 1⅔ cups all-purpose flour and 1 tablespoon baking powder into a large bowl, then make a well in the center. Beat together 1¼ cups milk and 1 egg in a small bowl, then whisk into the dry ingredients until thick and smooth. Beat in 2 tablespoons melted butter, then gently stir in ½ cup blackberries. Heat 1 teaspoon sunflower oil in a nonstick skillet, then drop 3–4 tablespoonfuls of the batter into the skillet to form small pancakes. Cook for about 3 minutes, until bubbles appear on the surface, then turn the pancakes over and cook for another 2–3 minutes, until golden. Remove from the skillet and keep warm. Repeat with the remaining batter. Serve drizzled with honey and ½ cup blackberries.

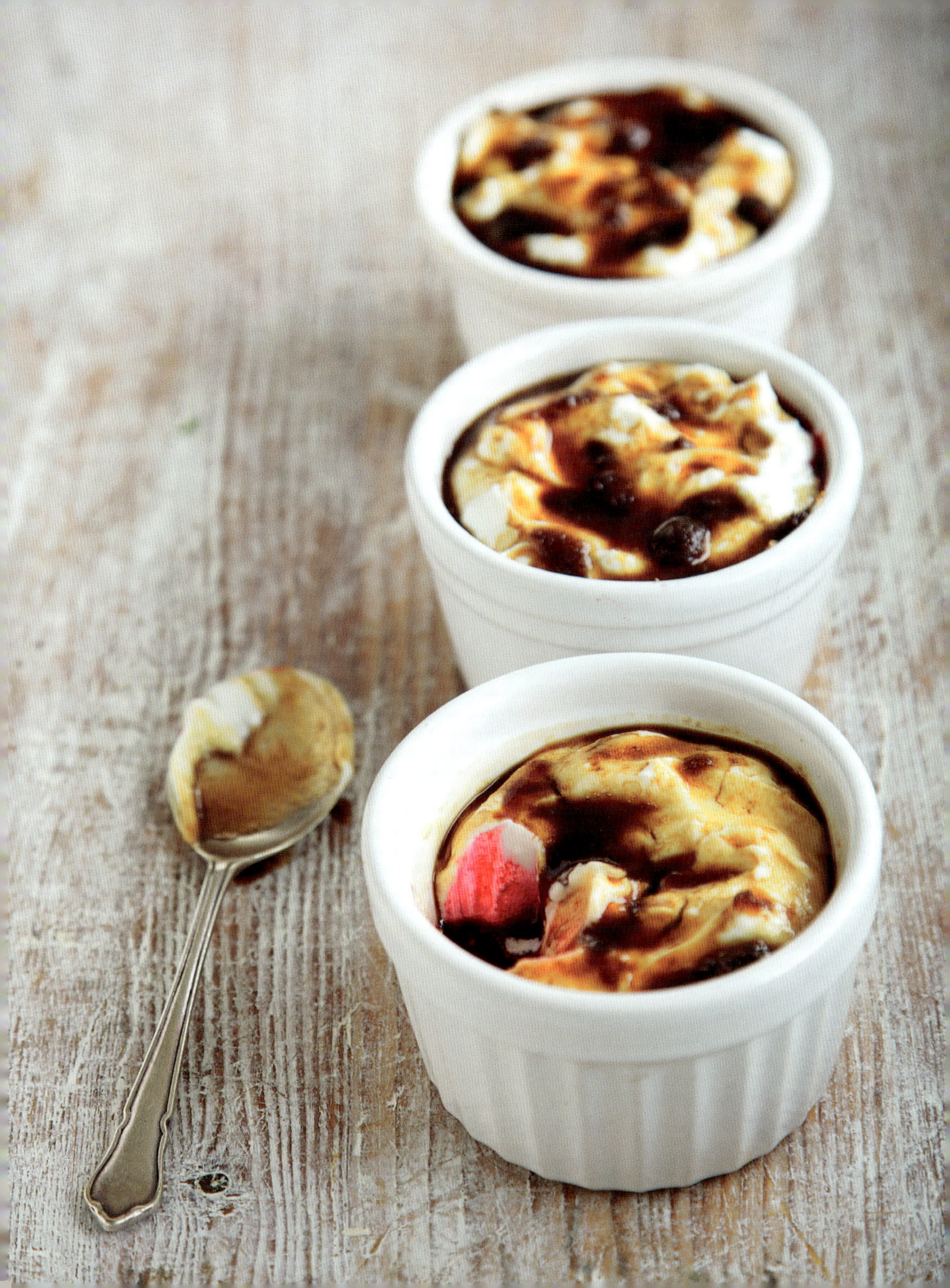

30 Oat, Banana, and Ginger Muffins

Makes 12

1¼ cups all-purpose flour
1⅔ cups whole-wheat flour
1 teaspoon baking powder
½ cup rolled oats
½ cup coconut oil, melted and cooled
2 eggs, beaten
1 cup milk
⅓ cup firmly packed light brown sugar
2 bananas, chopped
4 knobs of preserved ginger, diced
2 tablespoons preserved ginger syrup

- Line a 12-cup muffin pan with paper muffin liners.
- Sift the flours and baking powder into a large bowl, then stir in the oats. In a separate bowl, beat together the oil, eggs, milk, and sugar, then pour into the dry ingredients and mix together until just combined—do not overmix.
- Gently stir in the bananas and preserved ginger, then spoon the batter into the paper liners. Bake in a preheated oven, at 400°F, for 20 minutes.
- Remove the muffins from the pan, then pour the ginger syrup over them and let cool on a wire rack.

1 Banana and Ginger Oatmeal

Place 2 cups rolled oats, 3 cups water, and 3 cups soy milk in a saucepan and bring to a boil, then reduce the heat and simmer for 4–5 minutes, stirring occasionally, until thickened. Pour into bowls and top each one with 2 tablespoons Greek or plain yogurt, ½ chopped banana, and 1 chopped knob of preserved ginger. Stir a little to mix and then drizzle with a little preserved ginger syrup to serve.

2 Oat, Banana, and Ginger Cookies

Beat together 1¼ sticks softened unsalted butter and 1 cup firmly packed light brown sugar in a bowl until creamy. Beat in 1 egg and ½ cup mashed banana. Mix together 1 cup all-purpose flour, ½ teaspoon baking soda, 1 teaspoon ground cinnamon, ¼ teaspoon ground cloves, and 2 diced knobs of preserved ginger in a separate bowl, then stir into the banana mixture. Mix in 2½ cups rolled oats. Drop 36 heaping spoons of the batter, well spaced apart, onto baking sheets. Bake in a preheated oven, at 350°F, for 8–10 minutes, until golden. Let cool on the baking sheets for 5 minutes, then transfer to a wire rack to cool completely.

248 CAKES AND DESSERTS

HEA-CAKE-DEO

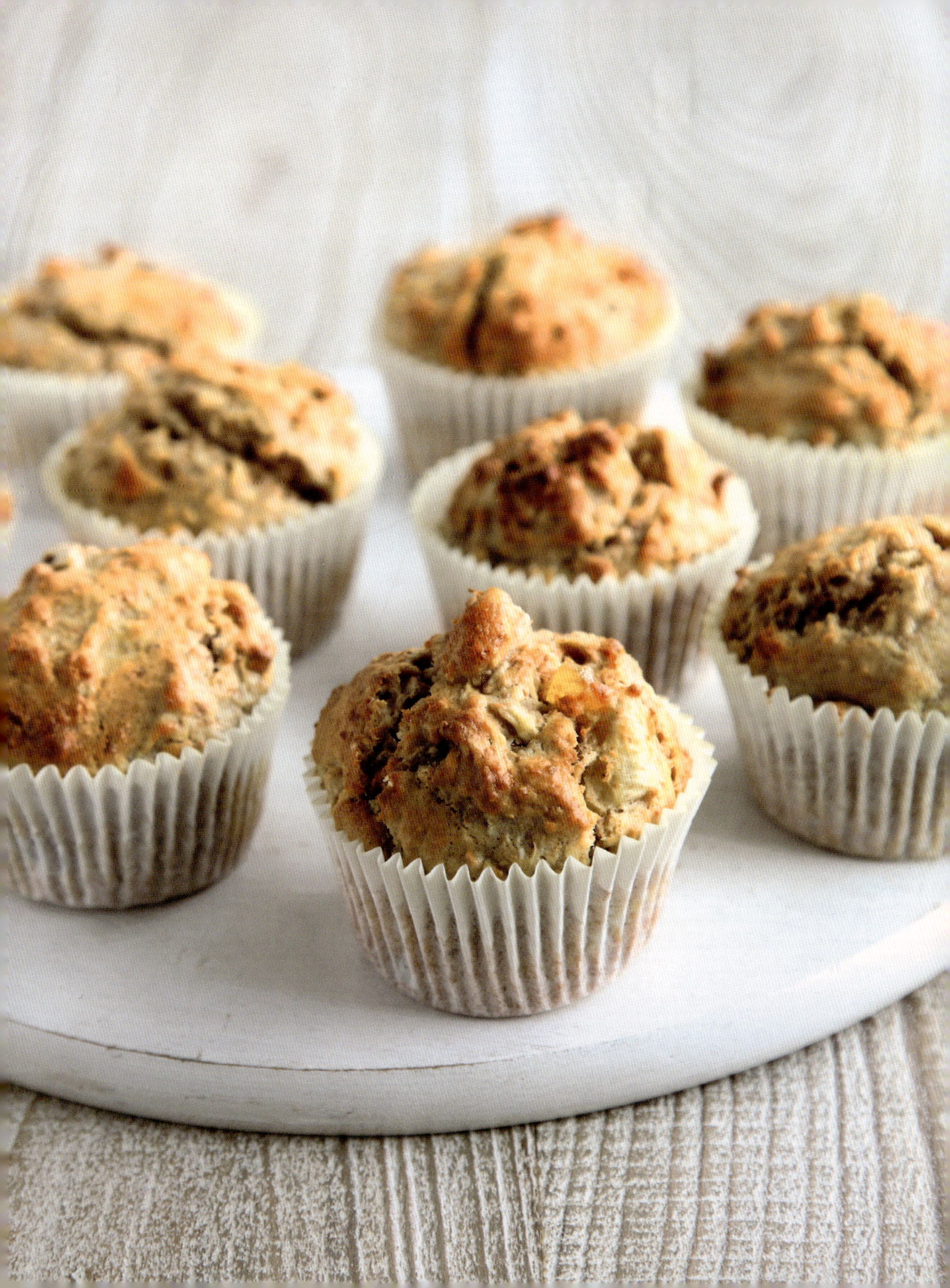

30 Roasted Honey Peaches

Serves 4

2 tablespoons orange blossom honey
1 vanilla bean, split lengthwise
2–3 teaspoons sesame seeds
4 peaches, halved and pitted
vanilla ice cream or crème fraîche, to serve (optional)

- Pour the honey into a small saucepan. Scrape the seeds from the vanilla bean and add the seeds and bean to the pan. Heat gently, stirring occasionally. Stir in the sesame seeds.

- Place the peaches in a roasting pan and pour the honey mixture over them. Bake in a preheated oven, at 350°F, for 20–25 minutes, until the peaches are soft. Baste a couple of times with the juices.

- Serve warm with vanilla ice cream or crème fraîche, if liked.

10 Honeyed Peach Bruschetta

Toast 8 slices of baguette under a preheated hot broiler for 2–3 minutes on each side, until golden. Spread each slice with ½ tablespoon cream cheese. Halve, pit, and slice 3 peaches and place the slices on the toasts. Drizzle each with ½ teaspoon honey and sprinkle with ½ teaspoon sesame seeds. Cook under the broiler for another 1–2 minutes.

20 Broiled Peaches with Honey Syrup

Halve and pit 4 small peaches, then place on a baking sheet. Dot with 2 tablespoons butter and cook under a preheated hot broiler for 6–7 minutes, until softened and golden. Place 2 tablespoons honey and the seeds scraped from 1 vanilla bean in a small saucepan and heat gently. Place the peaches in a bowl with 8 hulled and halved strawberries, then pour the syrup over them. Let stand for 5 minutes, then sprinkle with 1 tablespoon chopped mint and 4 crushed amaretti cookies.

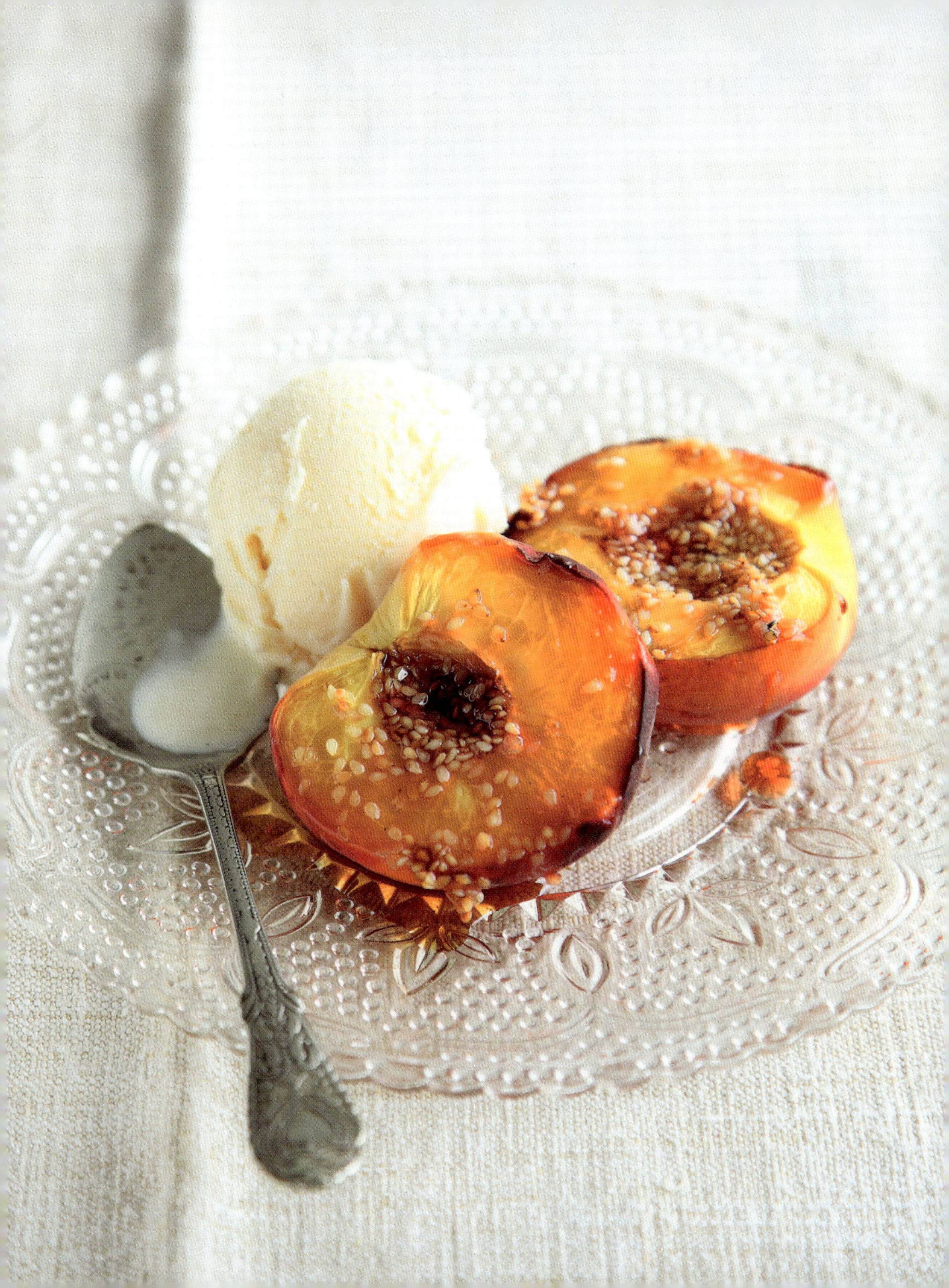

30 Sesame Cookies

Makes about 20

6 tablespoons butter, softened
½ cup granulated sugar
½ teaspoon sesame oil
1 egg, beaten
1¼ cups all-purpose flour
½ cup ground almonds (almond meal)
⅓ cup sesame seeds

- Beat together the butter, sugar, and oil in a bowl. Beat in the egg, then fold in the flour and ground almonds. Bring the mixture together using your hands to form a dough.
- Place the sesame seeds on a plate. Roll walnut-size pieces of the dough into balls, then roll them in the seeds. Place, spaced a little apart, on a baking sheet.
- Bake in a preheated oven, at 325°F, for 20 minutes, until light golden. Transfer to a wire rack to cool.

---

10 Sesame French Toast Beat together 4 eggs, ⅔ cup milk, 2 tablespoons granulated sugar, 1 teaspoon ground cardamom, and a pinch of ground cinnamon in a bowl. Heat 2 tablespoons butter in a large skillet. Dip 4 slices of whole-wheat bread into the egg mixture, then sprinkle each one with 1–2 teaspoons sesame seeds on each side. Add to the skillet and cook for 2–3 minutes on each side until golden. Serve topped with fruit and spoonfuls of Greek or plain yogurt.

20 Mango Whips with Sesame Brittle Dry-fry ⅓ cup sesame seeds in a nonstick skillet for 2–3 minutes, stirring frequently, until golden. Heat ½ cup granulated sugar, 2 tablespoons corn syrup, and 1 tablespoon water in a small saucepan over low heat, without stirring, until a dark brown caramel forms. Stir in the sesame seeds and transfer onto a piece of nonstick parchment paper. Let cool, then break into shards. Meanwhile place, 3 peeled, pitted, and coarsely chopped mangoes in a food processor or blender and process to a puree, then mix together with 1 cup Greek yogurt in a bowl. Spoon into 4 glasses and serve with shards of the sesame brittle.

252 CAKES AND DESSERTS

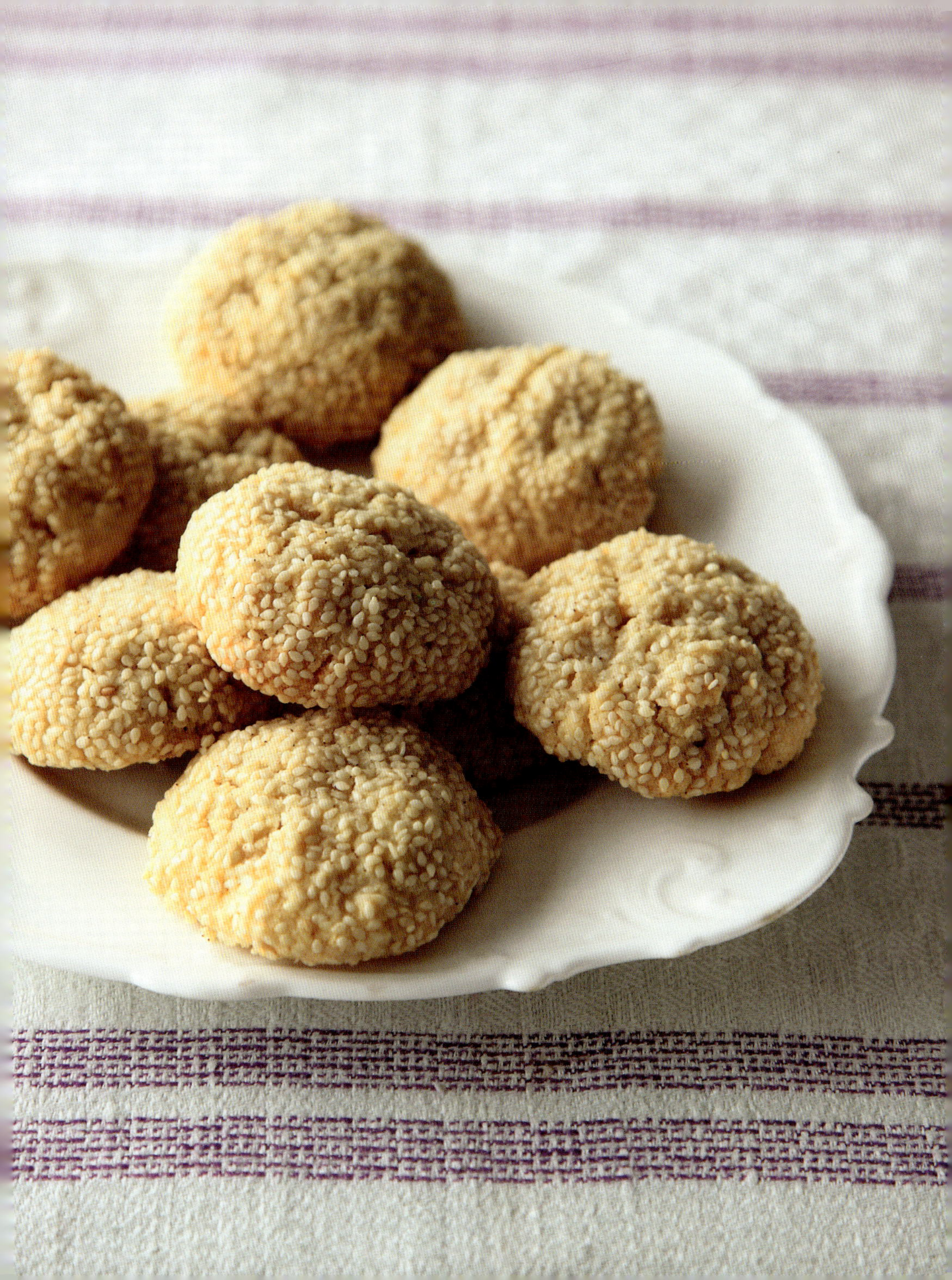

20 Berry and Mint Compote

Serves 4
1 lb mixed fruit, such as strawberries, blackberries, raspberries, and halved and pitted plums
1 cinnamon stick
grated rind and juice of 1 orange
8 mint leaves, shredded
Greek or plain yogurt, to serve (optional)

- Place the fruit, cinnamon stick, and orange rind and juice in a small saucepan and simmer gently for 12–15 minutes.
- Remove the cinnamon stick and let the compote cool for 3–4 minutes, then stir in the mint.
- Serve with spoonfuls of yogurt, if desired.

10 Berry and Mint Smoothies

Place 1⅓ cups plain yogurt, 1¾ cups soy milk, 5–6 ice cubes, 2½ cups mixed raspberries, blueberries, and hulled strawberries, and 5–6 mint leaves in a food processor or blender and blend until smooth. Pour into 4 glasses and serve topped with mint sprigs.

30 Minted Mixed Berry Desserts

Place 1¼ cups raspberries and 2 teaspoons sugar in a food processor or blender and process to a puree, then pass through a strainer into a small bowl and set aside. Place 1¼ cups mixed berries in a large bowl and toss together with 2 tablespoons sugar and 10 torn mint leaves. Lightly oil 4 small dessert molds, then line with plastic wrap. Dip 12 thin slices of bread, crusts removed, into the raspberry puree, then use to line the molds. Fill each lined mold with the fruit mixture and press down well. Top each mold with a final slice of bread to enclose the filling, then cover and chill for 5–6 minutes. To serve, carefully invert the desserts onto plates and drizzle the remaining raspberry puree over them. Decorate with basil sprigs and serve with crème fraîche or Greek yogurt, if desired.

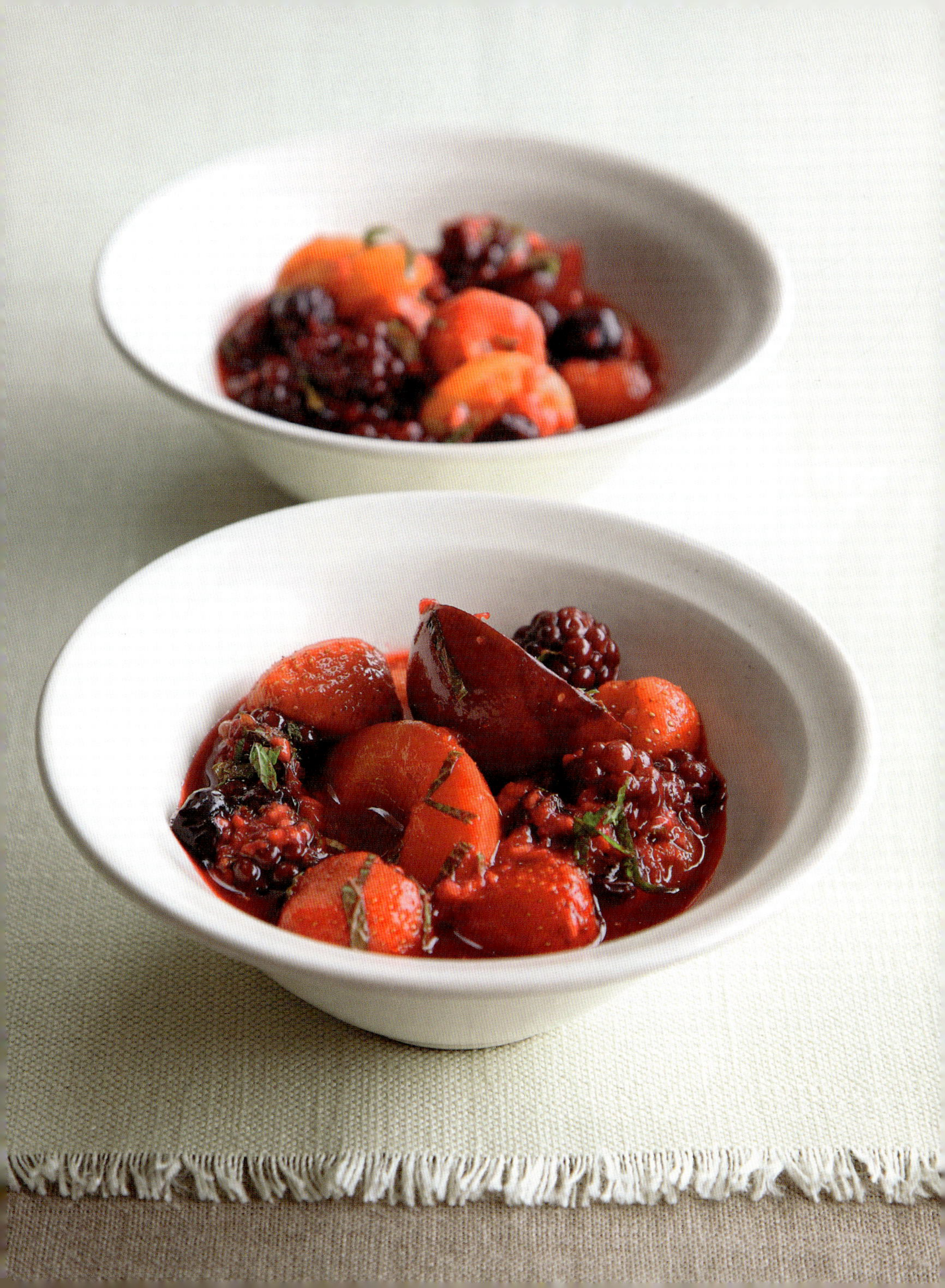

30 Spicy Fruit Bread Puddings

Serves 4

2 tablespoons chilled butter, grated, plus extra for greasing
5 slices whole-wheat bread
2/3 cup milk
1/4 cup golden raisins
1/3 cup diced dried apricots
1/3 cup blueberries
1/4 cup firmly packed dark brown sugar
1/2 teaspoon allspice
1 teaspoon sunflower seeds
1 teaspoon pumpkin seeds
1 egg, beaten
Greek yogurt or crème fraîche, to serve (optional)

- Lightly grease 4 ramekins. Break the bread into small chunks and place in a large bowl. Pour the milk over the bread and let soak for 10–12 minutes.

- Add the remaining ingredients and mix well. Spoon into the prepared ramekins and bake in a preheated oven, at 350°F, for 12–15 minutes, until just golden.

- Serve immediately with Greek yogurt or crème fraîche, if desired.

---

10 Spicy Fruit-Topped Sweet Bruschetta

Place 1/3 cup blueberries and 1/3 cup hulled strawberries in a small saucepan. Add the grated rind of 1 orange, then segment the orange over the pan to catch the juice and add the segments. Heat gently for 3–4 minutes, until slightly softened. Meanwhile, toast 8 slices of baguette under a preheated hot broiler for 2–3 minutes on each side, until golden. Mix together 2/3 cup cream cheese, 1/2 teaspoon allspice, and 2 diced knobs of preserved ginger in a bowl, then spread over the toasts. Top with the fruit and serve dusted with confectioners' sugar.

20 Spicy Fruit-Topped French Toast

Whisk together 2 extra-large eggs, 1/2 teaspoon allspice, 1/4 cup milk, and 1 teaspoon granulated sugar in a shallow bowl until the sugar dissolves. Dip 4 slices of whole-wheat bread into the egg mixture and let soak for 1 minute, then turn the bread over and soak for another minute. Heat 1 tablespoon olive oil in a skillet, add the bread, and cook for 3–4 minutes on each side until golden. Meanwhile, segment 2 oranges over a small saucepan to catch the juice. Add the orange segments, 2 cups hulled and halved strawberries, 1 cup blueberries, and 2 tablespoons honey to the pan and simmer for 3–4 minutes, until heated through. Serve the toasts topped with the warm fruit and sprinkled with 1 tablespoon sesame seeds.

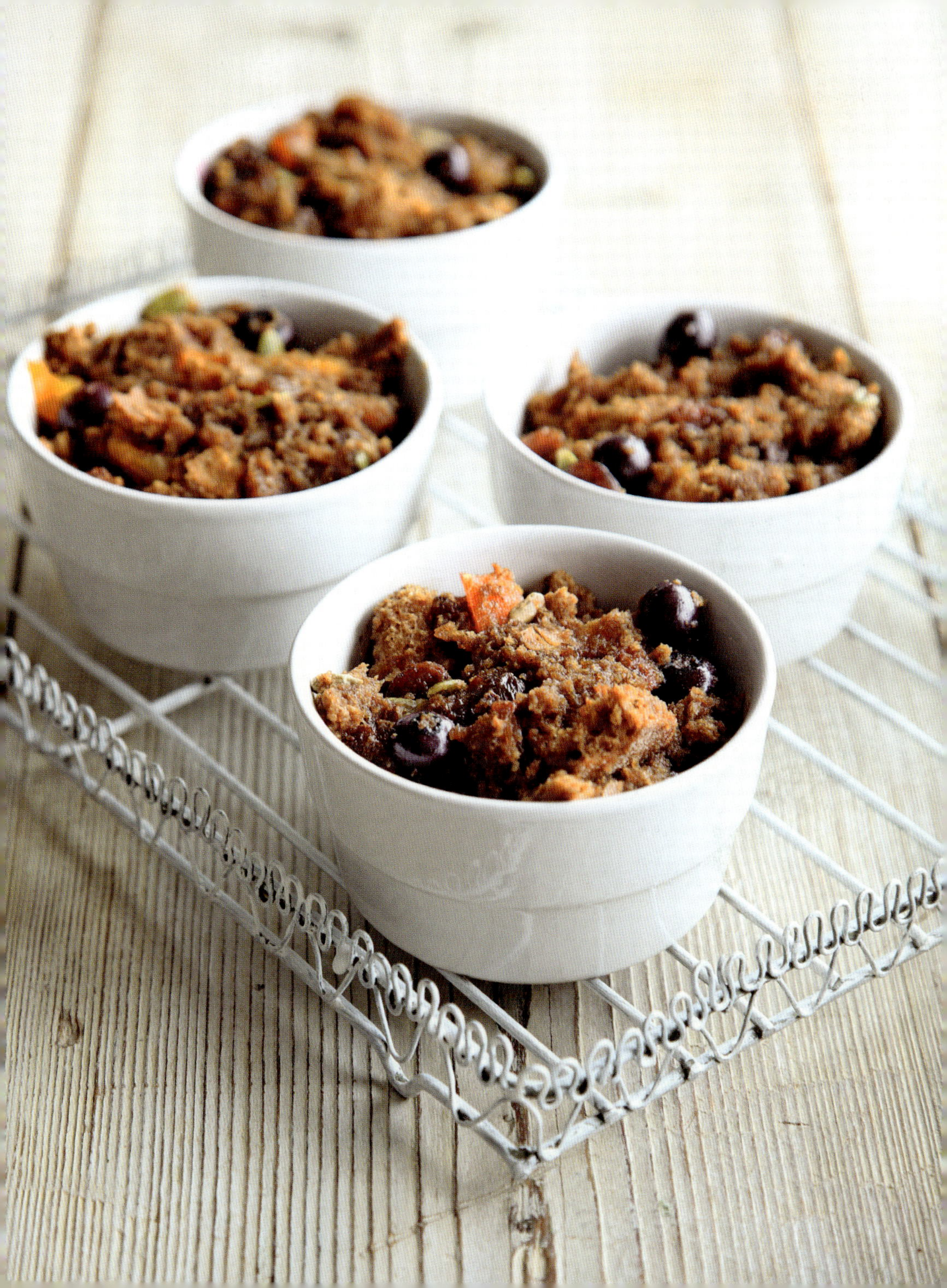

10 Strawberry and Almond Desserts

Serves 4
¼ cup slivered almonds
¼ cup flaked dried coconut
2 cups hulled and sliced strawberries
1 cup Greek or plain yogurt
4 teaspoons honey

- Place the slivered almonds and coconut on a baking sheet and cook under a preheated medium-hot broiler for 3–4 minutes, until golden, turning at least once. Let cool.
- Spoon half of the almond and coconut mixture into 4 glasses. Layer with half the sliced strawberries, then the yogurt.
- Top with the remaining strawberries, almonds, and coconut. Spoon the honey over the top and serve.

20 Roasted Strawberries with Almond Yogurt
Place 3 cups hulled and halved strawberries in a roasting pan and sprinkle with 2 tablespoons dark brown sugar. Place in a preheated oven, at 350°F, for 10–12 minutes. Remove from the oven and gently stir in 2 tablespoons shredded mint leaves. Divide among 4 small bowls or glasses, then top each with 1 scoop of vanilla yogurt and sprinkle with 2 tablespoons toasted slivered almonds.

30 Strawberry and Almond Muffins
Mix together 2⅓ cups all-purpose flour, 2 teaspoons baking powder, and ⅓ cup firmly packed dark brown sugar in a bowl. Beat together 6 tablespoons melted butter, ½ cup milk, and 1 beaten egg in a small bowl, then pour into the dry ingredients and mix together until just combined. Mash 2 bananas with the juice of 1 lemon in a separate bowl, then gently stir into the batter with ⅔ cup hulled and chopped strawberries and 1 tablespoon slivered almonds—do not overmix. Spoon into 8 paper muffin liners arranged in a muffin pan and bake in a preheated oven, at 375°F, for 20–25 minutes.

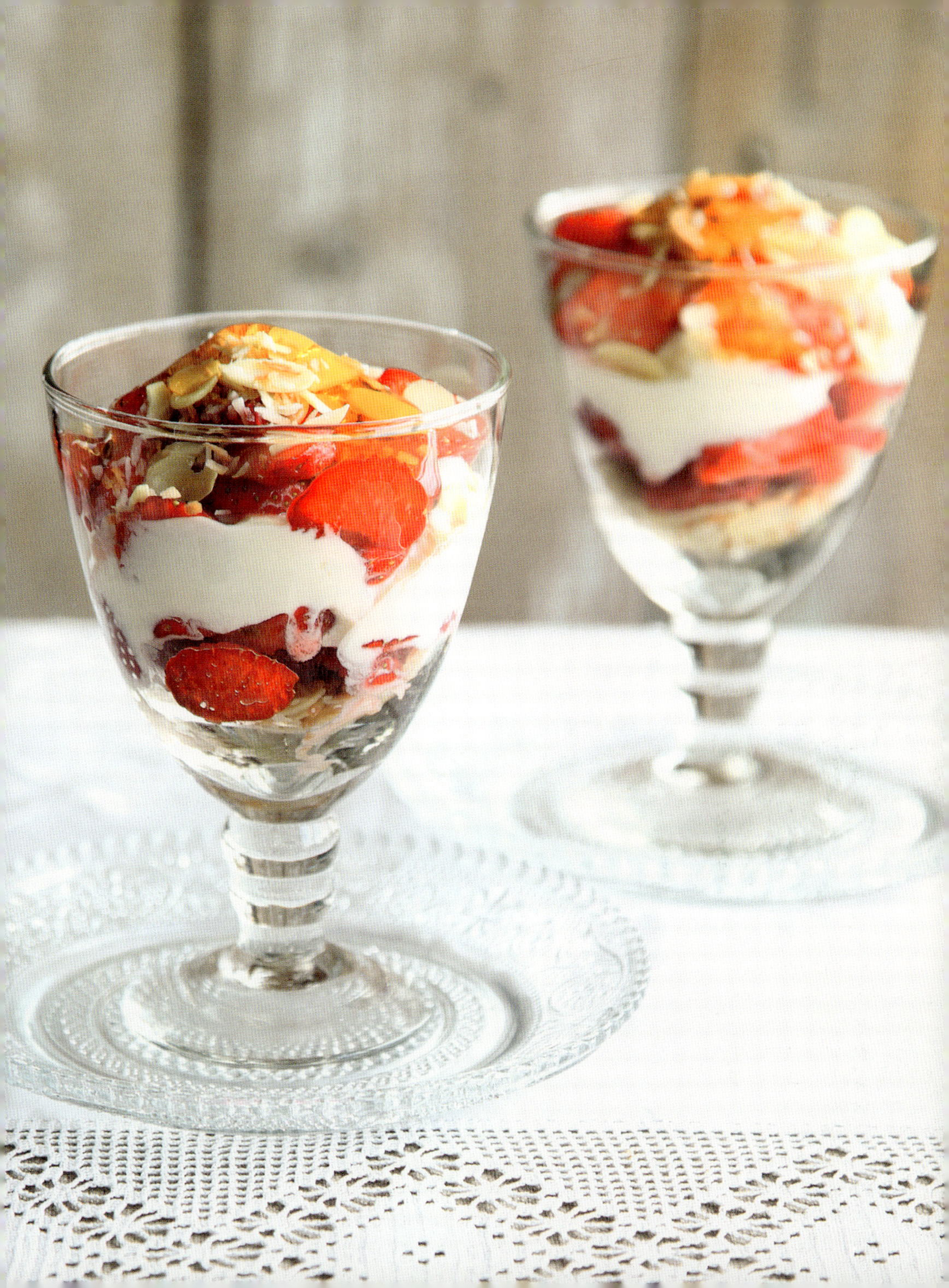

20 Tropical Fruit Salsa

Serves 4

1 passionfruit
1 ripe mango, peeled, pitted, and finely diced
⅔ cup finely diced pineapple
1 knob of preserved ginger, finely diced
1 teaspoon preserved ginger syrup
1 teaspoon finely shredded mint
½ teaspoon finely shredded cilantro
ice cream, to serve (optional)

- Halve the passionfruit, spoon out the flesh, and place in a strainer over a bowl. Using the back of a spoon, press the seeds to squeeze out all the juice. Discard the seeds.
- Add the fruit and preserved ginger, then stir in the preserved ginger juice. Stir in the herbs, then let stand at room temperature for 10 minutes to let the flavors steep.
- Spoon into bowls and serve with ice cream, if desired.

10 Tropical Fruit Brûlées

Halve 1 passionfruit, spoon out the flesh, and place in a strainer over a bowl. Press the seeds to squeeze out all the juice. Discard the seeds. Divide the mixture among 4 ramekins. Stir together ½ peeled, pitted, and chopped mango and 1¾ cups Greek yogurt in a bowl, then spoon it over the passion fruit. Sprinkle each one with 1 tablespoon dark brown sugar. Cover and chill for 1–2 minutes before serving.

30 Tropical Fruit Crisp

Place 2 peeled, pitted and chopped mangoes, ⅔ cup chopped pineapple, 2 chopped bananas, and the juice of 2 passionfruits (prepared as above) in an ovenproof dish. Sprinkle with 2 tablespoons preserved ginger syrup and 2 chopped knobs of preserved ginger. Place the grated rind of 1 orange, ¾ cup rolled oats, ¼ cup slivered almonds, ¼ cup walnuts, and 3 tablespoons rye flour in a food processor and process until it forms large crumbs. Add ⅓ cup coconut oil and ⅓ cup packed dark brown sugar and process again to form a crisp mixture. Spoon over the fruit and bake in a preheated oven, at 375°F, for 25–26 minutes, until golden. Serve with Greek or plain yogurt.

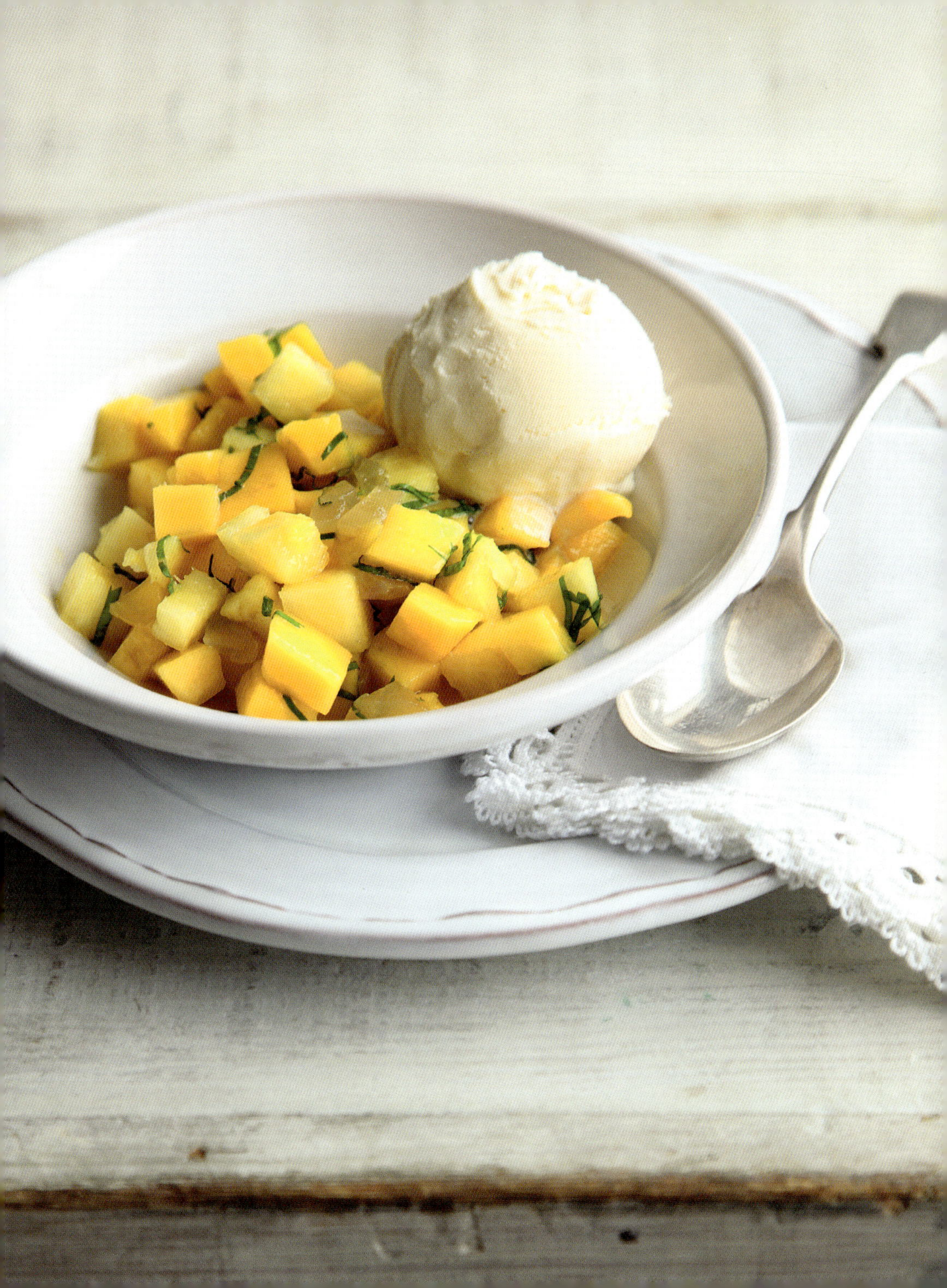

30 Whole-Wheat Raspberry Coconut Muffins

Makes 12

- 1¼ cups all-purpose white flour
- 1¼ cups whole-wheat flour
- 1 teaspoon baking powder
- ½ cup coconut oil, melted and cooled
- 2 eggs, beaten
- ½ cup milk
- ⅓ cup firmly packed light brown sugar
- 2 cups raspberries
- 2 tablespoons dried coconut

- Line a 12-cup muffin pan with paper muffin liners.
- Sift the flours and baking powder into a large bowl. In a separate bowl, whisk together the oil, eggs, milk, and sugar, then pour into the dry ingredients and mix together until just combined—do not overmix.
- Gently stir in the raspberries, then spoon the batter into the paper cases and sprinkle with the dried coconut.
- Bake in a preheated oven, at 400°F, for 20 minutes. Transfer to a wire rack to cool.

10 Raspberry Coconut Whips

Place 2 tablespoons dried coconut on a baking sheet and cook under a preheated medium-hot broiler for 3–4 minutes, until golden, turning at least once. Let cool slightly. Meanwhile, heat 3 cups raspberries and 1 tablespoon honey in a small saucepan over low heat for 2 minutes, pressing the fruit gently with the back of a spoon to burst a few. Let cool slightly. Stir together 1 cup crème fraîche, 1 cup Greek yogurt, and the toasted coconut in a bowl, then gently stir in the raspberries, reserving 1 tablespoon. Divide the whips among 4 small bowls or glasses, then spoon the reserved raspberries over them and serve drizzled with honey.

20 Raspberry and Coconut French Toast

Heat 2½ cups raspberries, ½ tablespoon honey, and the grated rind of 1 orange in a saucepan over low heat for 2–3 minutes. Mix together 4 eggs, ⅔ cup milk, 2 tablespoons granulated sugar, 1 tablespoon dried coconut, and a pinch of ground cinnamon in a shallow bowl. Dip 4 slices of sliced brioche loaf into the egg mixture and let soak for 1 minute, then turn over and soak for another minute. Heat 2 tablespoons butter in a large skillet, add the brioche, and cook for 3–4 minutes on each side until golden. Serve topped with the raspberries and spoonfuls of Greek or plain yogurt.

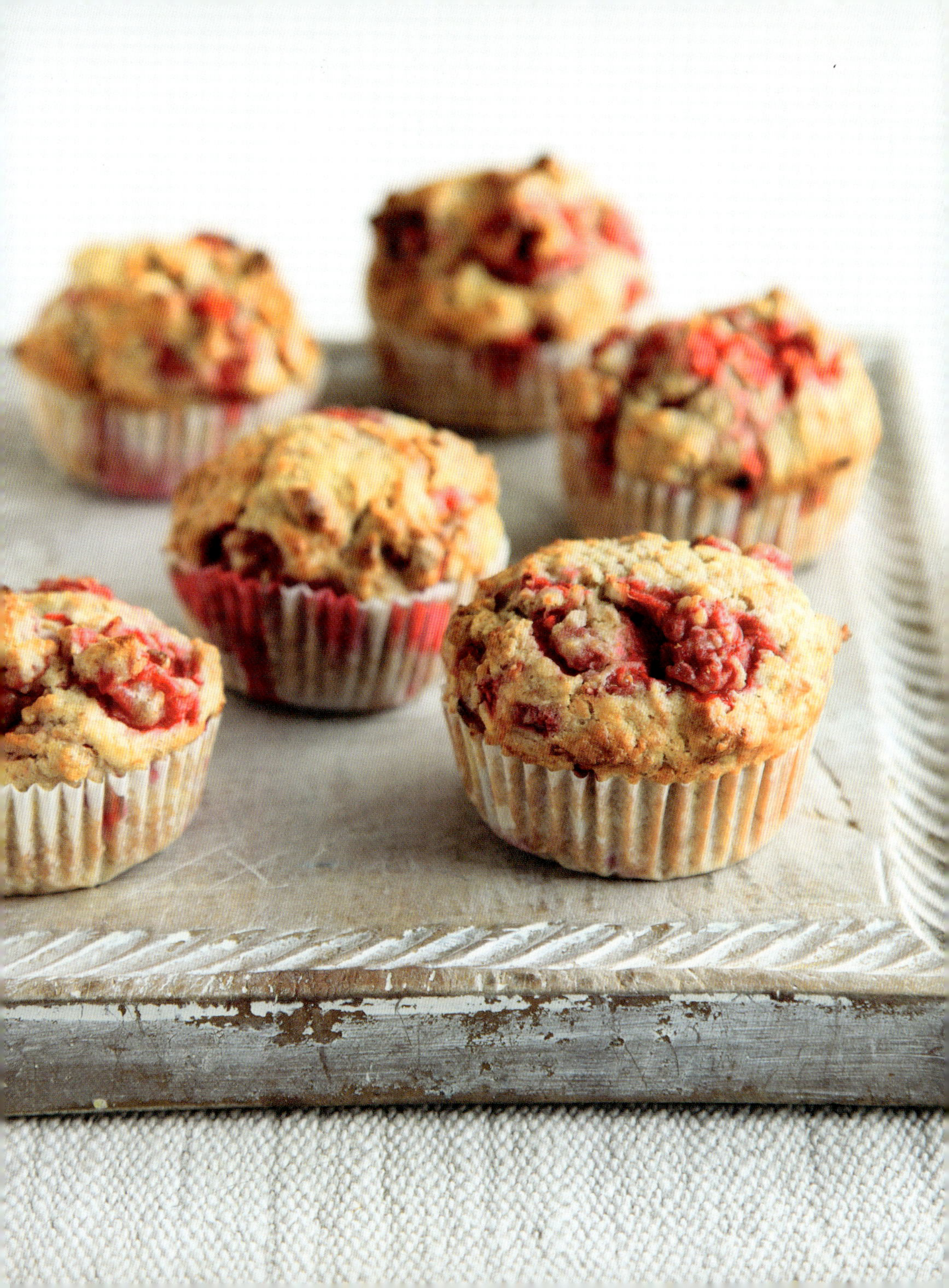

Winter Fruits with Orange Ricotta

Serves 4

¾ cup coarsely chopped dried apricots
½ cup chopped dried figs
10 prunes (dried plums), pitted
2 tablespoons raisins
2 tablespoons dried cherries
2 plums, halved and pitted
1 pear, peeled cut into wedges
3 tablespoons orange juice
grated rind of 2 oranges
3 tablespoons honey
½ cup boiling water
1 cup ricotta cheese
½ cup Greek or plain yogurt

- Stir together all the fruit, 2 tablespoons of the orange juice, the grated rind of 1 orange, and 2 tablespoons of the honey in a saucepan. Pour in the measured water and bring to a gentle simmer, then cook for 6–7 minutes, stirring occasionally. Let stand for 8–10 minutes.

- Meanwhile, beat together the remaining orange juice, orange rind, and honey with the ricotta and yogurt in a large bowl.

- Spoon the winter fruits into 4 bowls and serve with the orange ricotta.

Winter Fruit Salad with Lemon Ricotta

Heat the juice of 1 lime with 1 tablespoon sugar in a saucepan, stirring, until the sugar dissolves. Pour into a bowl and let cool slightly, then stir in 1 tablespoon chopped mint. In a large bowl, mix together 2 peeled, cored, and sliced pears, 2 apples, cored and cut into wedges, 3 plums, halved, pitted, and quartered, and the seeds from 1 pomegranate. Segment 1 orange over a bowl to catch the juice. Add the segments to the fruits, and the juice to the lime syrup. Pour the syrup over the fruits. Mix together the grated rind of 2 lemons, 1 tablespoon sugar and 1 cup ricotta cheese in a bowl and serve with the fruit.

Winter Fruit Cobbler with Cinnamon Ricotta

Place 4 peeled, cored, and chopped ripe pears, the juice of 1 lemon, ¼ cup granulated sugar, and 1 tablespoon water in a saucepan and bring to a boil, then cover and cook for 3 minutes. Stir in 6 halved and pitted plums and cook for another 2 minutes. Meanwhile, place ¾ cup all-purpose flour, ¾ teaspoon baking powder, and 1 teaspoon ground cinnamon in a bowl, add 4 tablespoons diced chilled butter, and rub in with the fingertips until the mixture resembles fine bread crumbs. Stir in ¼ cup granulated sugar, then mix in 1 beaten egg and ¼ cup milk to form a soft batter. Turn the fruit into a greased ovenproof dish, then drop spoonfuls of the batter over the fruit, leaving gaps between. Sprinkle with 2 tablespoons chopped pecans and bake in a preheated oven, at 350°F, for 5 minutes, until crisp and golden. Meanwhile, whisk together ½ cup ricotta cheese, ½ cup mascarpone cheese, ¼ teaspoon ground cinnamon, and a pinch of nutmeg in a bowl. Serve the with the cinnamon ricotta.

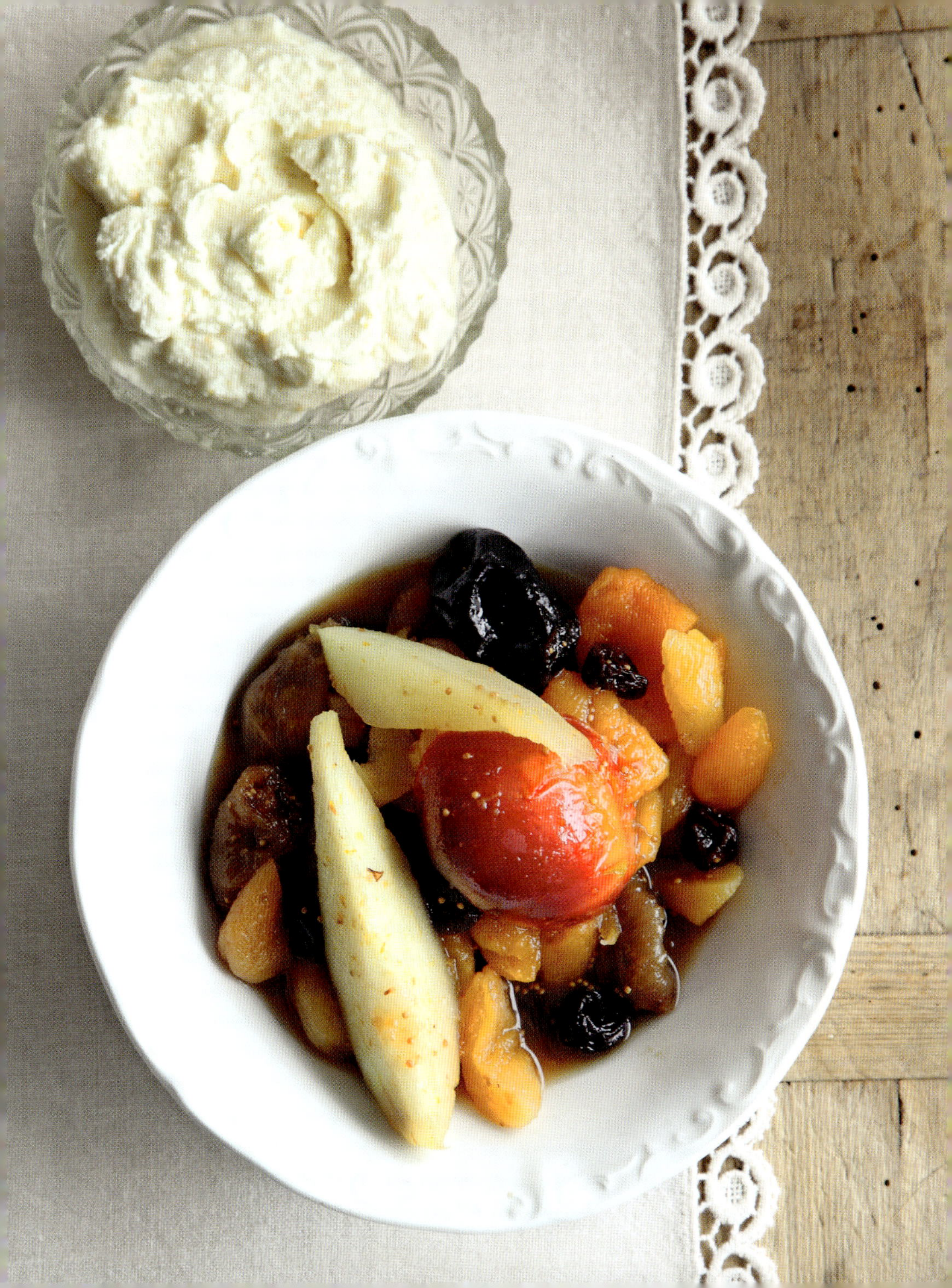

Lemon and Golden Raisin Rice Pudding

Serves 4

1 vanilla bean, split lengthwise
1 cup short grain rice
3 cups milk
2 tablespoons golden raisins
grated rind of 2 lemons
2 teaspoons granulated sugar, or to taste
2/3 cup Greek or plain yogurt
ground nutmeg, to serve

- Scrape the seeds from the vanilla bean and add the seeds and bean to a saucepan with the rice, milk, golden raisins, and lemon rind.

- Bring to a boil, then reduce the heat and simmer for 15–18 minutes, until the rice is swollen and soft.

- Add the sugar to taste and let cool for 10 minutes.

- Remove the vanilla bean from the rice, then stir in the yogurt. Serve sprinkled with a little ground nutmeg.

Quick Lemon and Golden Raisin Rice

Mix together 2/3 cup golden raisins, the grated rind of 2 lemons, and the juice of 1 lemon in a small saucepan. Sprinkle in 1 teaspoon sugar and simmer for 4–5 minutes. Mix together 4 (4 oz) containers rice puddings, 1 tablespoon lemon curd, and 2 tablespoons Greek or plain yogurt in a bowl, then stir in the golden raisin mixture.

Whole-Wheat Lemon and Golden Raisin Scones

Sift 1 cup all-purpose flour, ¾ cup whole-wheat flour, and 1 teaspoon baking powder into a bowl and add the grated rind of 2 lemons in a bowl. Add 3 tablespoons diced chilled butter and rub in with the fingertips until the mixture resembles fine bread crumbs. Stir in 2/3 cup golden raisins, then add 2/3 cup milk and mix with a spatula to a soft dough. Press out on a floured surface to about ¾ inch thick, then cut out circles using a 1¼–1½-inch plain cookie cutter or glass. Place on a baking sheet and bake in a preheated oven, at 425°F, for 12–15 minutes, until risen and golden. Transfer to a wire rack to cool, then serve with butter and lemon curd.

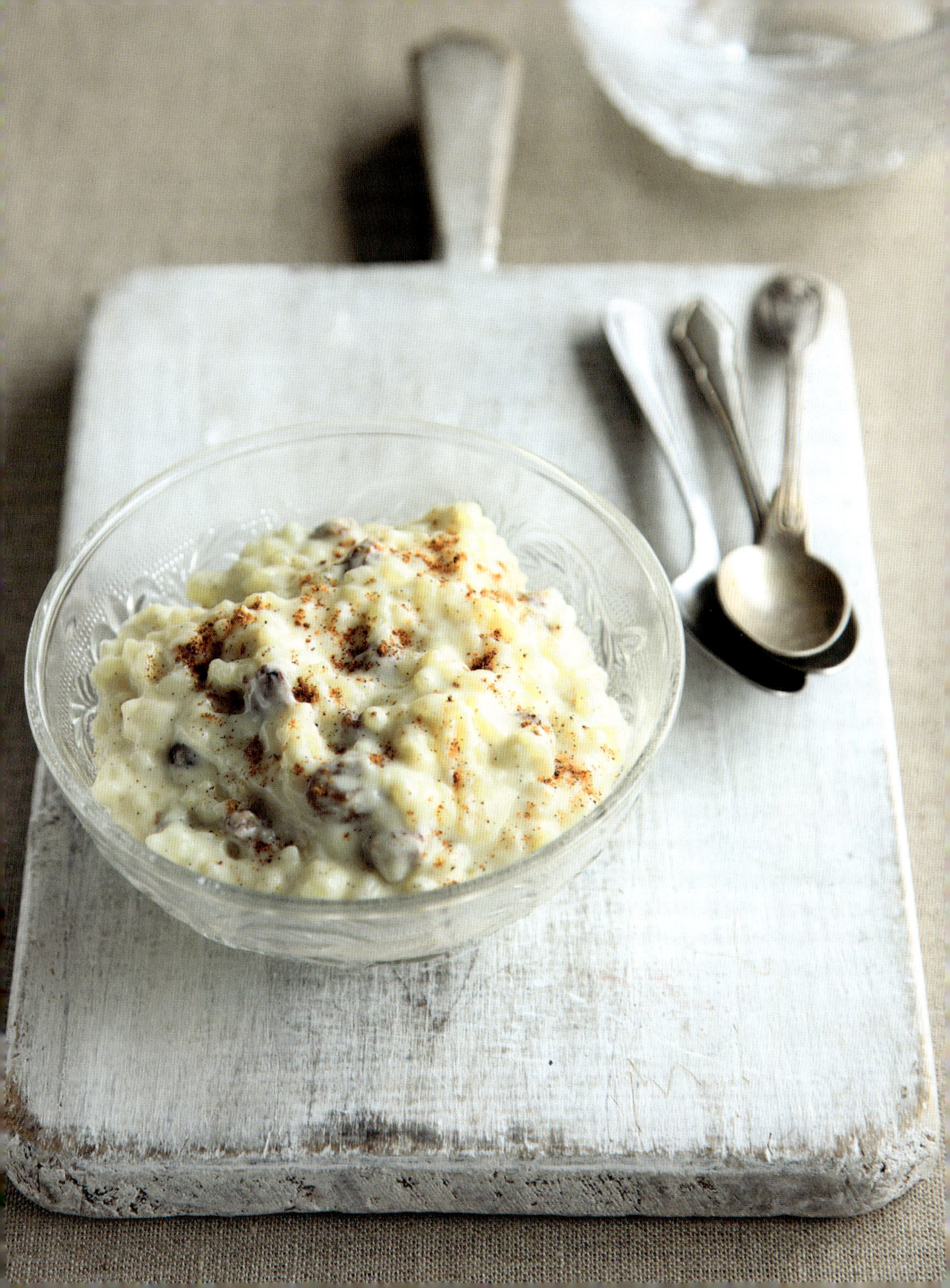

Gingered Sesame Fruit Kebabs

Serves 4

1 tablespoon rapeseed oil
⅓ cup firmly packed light brown sugar
juice of 1 lime
pinch of nutmeg
2 tablespoons chopped mint
3 knobs of preserved ginger, diced
1 mango, peeled, pitted, and cut into chunks
2 kiwis, peeled and cut into chunks
10–12 strawberries, hulled
2 tablespoons sesame seeds
2 tablespoons preserved ginger syrup
1 cup Greek yogurt

- Soak 8 wooden skewers in water for 10 minutes.
- Meanwhile, mix together the oil, sugar, lime juice, nutmeg, mint, and ginger in a bowl and stir until the sugar has dissolved.
- Thread the fruit onto the skewers and brush with the syrup. Sprinkle with the sesame seeds.
- Place on a baking sheet and cook under a preheated medium-hot broiler for 6–8 minutes, turning once, until turning golden.
- Mix together the ginger syrup and yogurt in a bowl and serve with the kebabs.

Gingered Sesame Fruit Salad

Dry-fry 1 tablespoon sesame seeds in a nonstick skillet for 2 minutes, stirring frequently, until golden. Set aside. Mix together 12 hulled and halved strawberries, 2 peeled and chopped kiwifruits, 1 peeled, pitted, and chopped mango, and 1 chopped banana in a large bowl. Mix together the juice of 1 orange, 2 tablespoons preserved ginger syrup, 2 diced knobs of preserved ginger, and 1 tablespoon shredded mint in a small bowl, then gently stir into the fruit. Sprinkle with the toasted sesame seeds and serve with Greek or plain yogurt.

Gingered Sesame Fruit Compote

Place 2 tablespoons each of dried apricots, figs, prunes, and raisins in a saucepan, then pour in 1¼ cups ginger beer and bring to a boil. Reduce the heat and simmer for 20 minutes, until the liquid is reduced and syrupy. Stir in 1 peeled, pitted, and chopped mango, 2 peeled, and chopped kiwifruits, and 10 hulled and halved strawberries. Let stand for 6–8 minutes. Meanwhile, dry-fry 1 tablespoon sesame seeds in a nonstick skillet for 2 minutes, stirring frequently, until golden. Sprinkle with the compote and serve with thick Greek or plain yogurt.

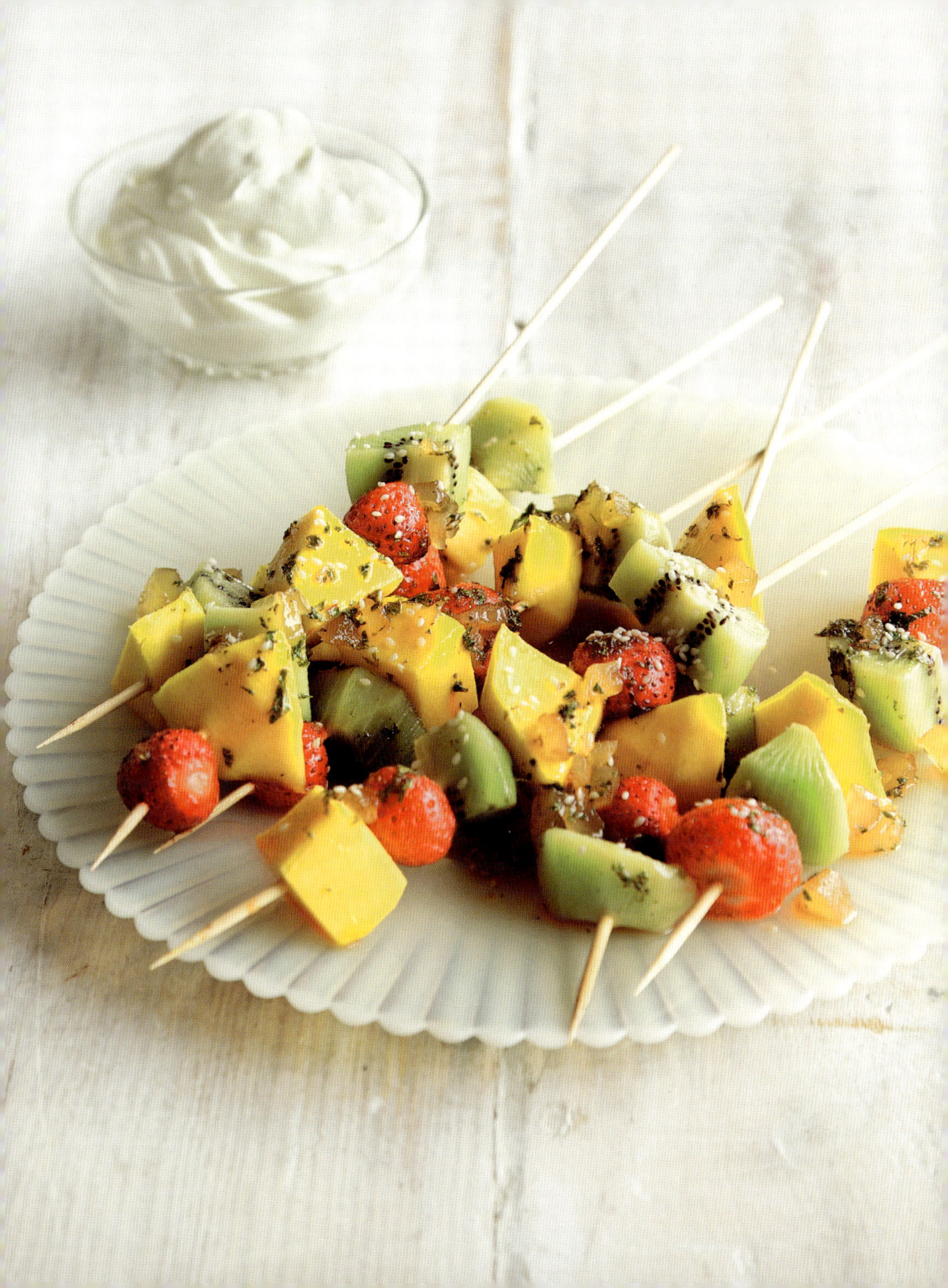

30 Whole-Wheat Blueberry Pancakes with Lemon Yogurt

Serves 4

1¼ cups whole-wheat flour
⅓ cup all-purpose flour
1 teaspoon baking powder
1¼ cups milk
1 egg, beaten
2 tablespoons honey
1¼ cups blueberries
2 tablespoons coconut oil
½ cup lemon curd or lemon-flavored yogurt
2 tablespoons honey

- Sift the flours and baking powder into a large bowl, then make a well in the center. Mix together the milk, egg, and honey in a small bowl, then pour into the dry ingredients and whisk until mixed. Stir in 1 cup of the blueberries.

- Heat the oil in a large skillet, then drop 2 tablespoons of the batter into the skillet for each pancake to form 4 and cook for 4–5 minutes, until golden, then turn over and cook for another 2–3 minutes. Remove from the skillet and keep warm. Repeat with the remaining mixture to make about 12.

- Serve the pancakes with spoonfuls of the lemon yogurt, sprinkled with the remaining blueberries and drizzled with honey.

1 Blueberry Lemon Yogurt

Place a few saffron threads in a bowl with 2 tablespoons warmed milk and let steep for 3–4 minutes. Put 1 peeled, pitted, and chopped mango in a food processor or blender and blend until smooth, then transfer to a bowl and mix together with 2 cups Greek or plain yogurt, 1 cup blueberries, the grated rind of ½ lemon, and the saffron milk. Spoon into glasses and serve with a drizzle of honey.

2 Blueberry and Lemon Cheesecake Pots

Place 1 cup blueberries and 2 tablespoons honey in a small saucepan and heat gently for about 3–4 minutes, until the colour starts to run. Let cool slightly. Put 5 graham crackers in a food processor and process to form crumbs, then stir in 2 tablespoons melted butter and 1 teaspoon lemon juice. Spoon the cookie mixture into 4 small glasses or ramekins. Mix together 1 cup mascarpone cheese, ⅔ cup Greek or plain yogurt, the grated rind of 1 lemon, and 1 tablespoon confectioners' sugar in a bowl, then spoon over the cookie bottoms. Top with the blueberries and serve.

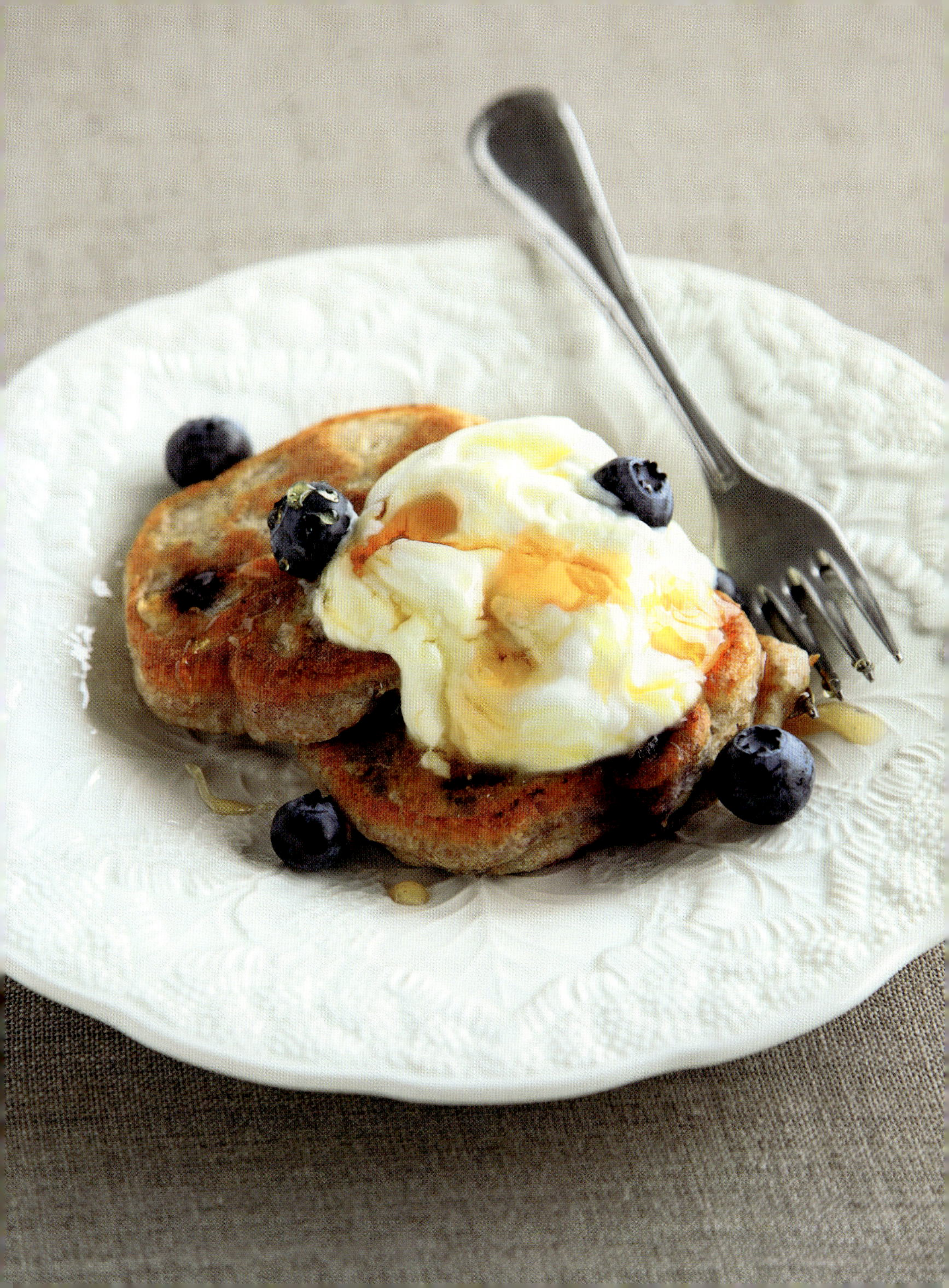

Baked Spiced Bananas

Serves 4

4 ripe bananas, sliced lengthwise
butter, for greasing
1 teaspoon ground allspice
½ teaspoon ground nutmeg
juice of 1 lemon
½ cup slivered almonds
3 knobs of preserved ginger, diced
1 cup Greek or plain yogurt

- Place the bananas in a lightly greased ovenproof dish. Sprinkle with the spices, lemon juice, and almonds.
- Bake in a preheated oven, at 350°F, for 12–15 minutes.
- Meanwhile, mix together the preserved ginger and yogurt in a bowl.
- Serve the bananas with spoonfuls of the yogurt.

Bananas with Spiced Chocolate Sauce

Melt 8 g oz semisweet chocolate, broken into pieces, 2 tablespoons unsalted butter, 1 tablespoon light corn syrup, 1 diced knob of preserved ginger, and 1 teaspoon ground cinnamon in a heatproof bowl set over a saucepan of simmering water. Slice 4 bananas and divide among 4 glass bowls. Pour over the chocolate sauce and serve sprinkled with 2 tablespoons toasted slivered almonds.

Spiced Banana Muffins

Sift 2 cups all-purpose flour, 1 tablespoon baking powder, and ½ teaspoon each of baking soda, ground cinnamon, and ground nutmeg into a large bowl. Stir in ⅔ cup granulated sugar. Beat together 2 eggs, ½ cup milk, 6 tablespoons melted unsalted butter, and 2 large mashed bananas in a separate bowl, then stir into the dry ingredients and mix together until just combined—do not overmix. Spoon into 10 paper muffin liners arranged in a muffin pan and bake in a preheated oven, at 400°F, for 20–22 minutes.

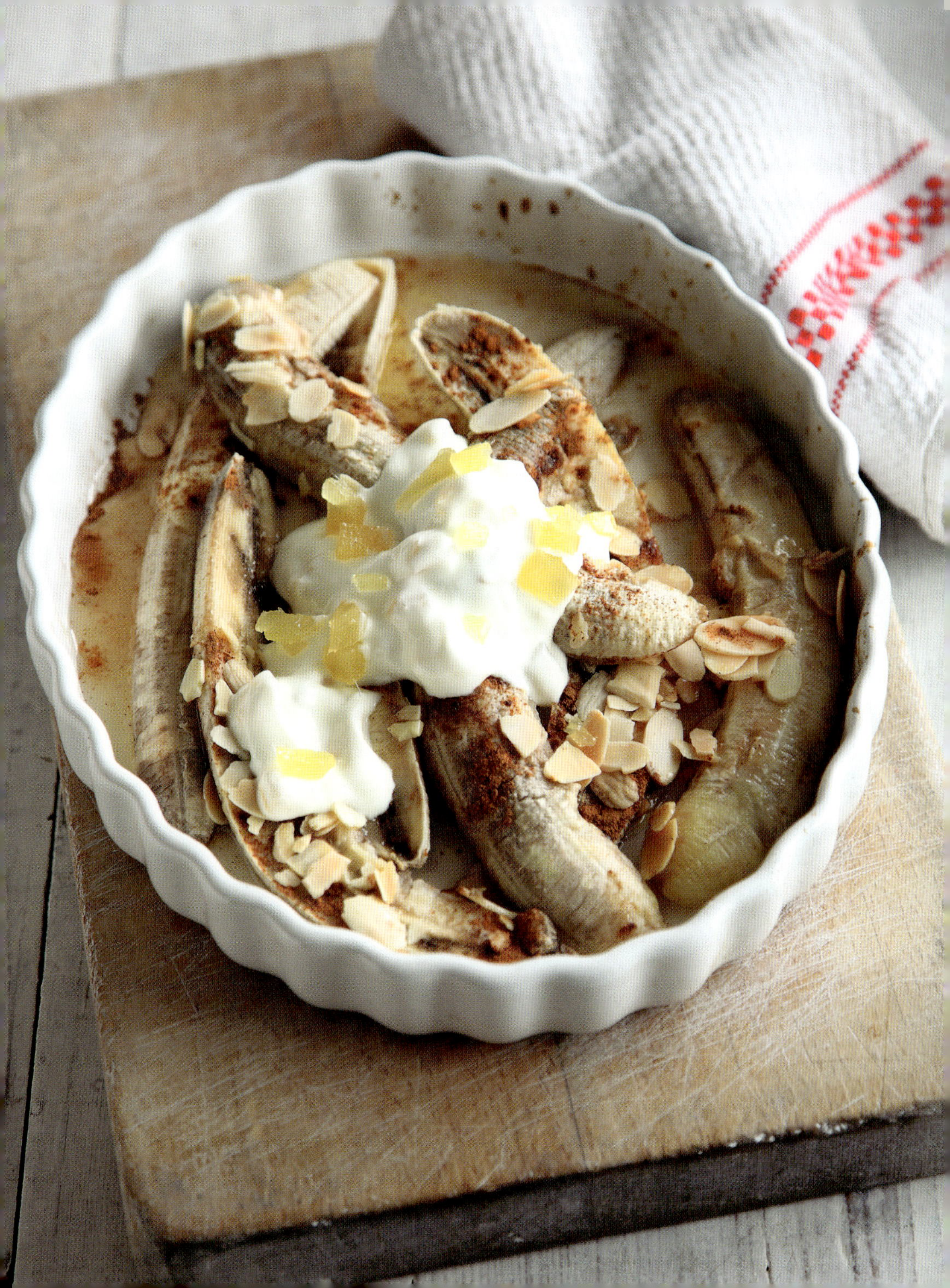

Caramelized Fall Fruits

Serves 4

4 tablespoons butter
¼ cup granulated sugar
juice of 1 orange
3 Pippin apples, peeled, cored, and quartered
3 pears, peeled, cored, and quartered
4 plums, halved and pitted

- Heat the butter in a large skillet, add the sugar and orange juice, and cook, stirring, until the sugar dissolves. Increase the heat and cook for 6–8 minutes, until the mixture turns golden.
- Add the apples and pears and stir into the caramel. Cook for 4–5 minutes, until they start to soften.
- Stir in the plums and cook for another 4–5 minutes, until all the fruit is soft and coated in caramel. Serve warm.

Fall Fruit Compote

Place 2 cored and sliced apples, 2 cored and sliced pears, 4 halved and pitted plums, 6 dried apricots, and 6 pitted prunes, the juice of 2 oranges, 2 tablespoons honey, 3 cloves, and a cinnamon stick in a large saucepan and bring to a boil, then reduce the heat and simmer for 8–9 minutes. Serve with spoonfuls of Greek or plain yogurt, sprinkled with ground nutmeg.

Fall Fruits in Mulled Wine

Place 1 cup red wine, 1 cinnamon stick, 4 cloves, 1 bay leaf, 1 cup firmly packed light brown sugar, and the peel of 1 orange in a saucepan and bring to a boil, then reduce the heat and simmer for 5 minutes. Let cool. Meanwhile, peel, halve, and core 2 ripe pears and 2 Pippin apples, then cut into 6 wedges, and halve and pit 4 plums. Place the prepared fruit in a bowl with 1 cup blackberries and pour the mulled wine over them. Cover and let stand for 20 minutes. Serve with Greek or plain yogurt.

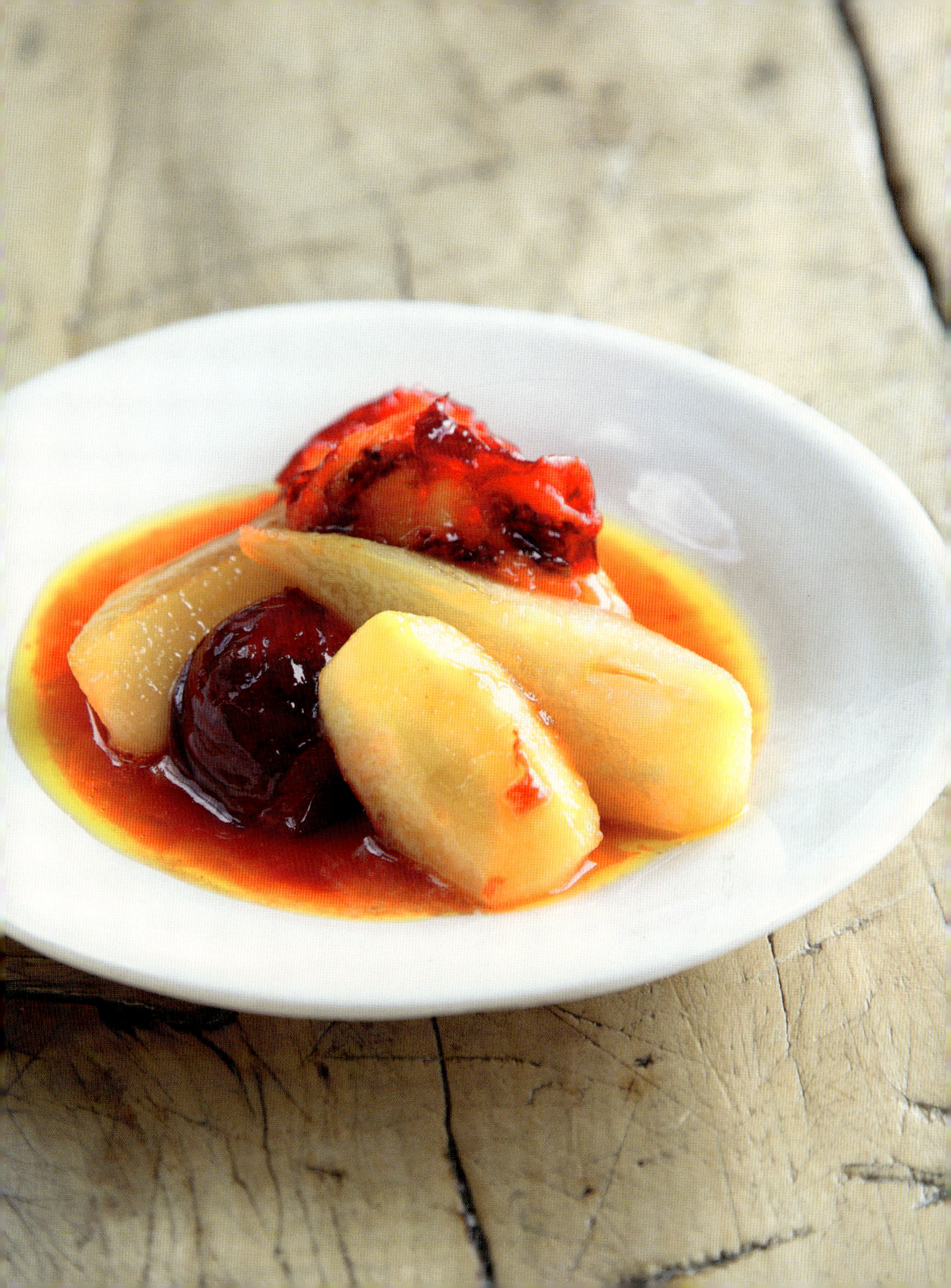

Honey-Roasted Rhubarb with Coconut Rice

20

Serves 4
- 1½ tablespoons honey
- 1 lb rhubarb, trimmed and chopped
- ½ cup long-grain basmati rice
- 1¾ cups coconut milk
- ½ cup water
- 1 tablespoon toasted slivered almonds

- Heat 1 tablespoon of the honey in a small saucepan. Put the rhubarb in a roasting pan and pour the honey over it. Place in a preheated oven, at 400°F, for 10 minutes.

- Meanwhile, place the rice, coconut milk, measured water, and remaining honey in a saucepan and bring to a simmer, then cook, stirring occasionally, for 12–15 minutes, until the rice is tender.

- Serve the rice pudding topped with the roasted rhubarb, sprinkled with a few slivered almonds.

---

10 Rhubarb with Toasted Coconut and Honeyed Ice Cream Put 1 lb trimmed rhubarb, cut into chunks, in a roasting pan and drizzle with 2 tablespoons preserved ginger syrup and 2 knobs of diced preserved ginger. Place in a preheated oven, at 400°F, for 10 minutes until tender. Meanwhile, place 2 tablespoons dried coconut on a baking sheet and cook under a preheated medium-hot grill for 3–4 minutes, until golden, turning at least once, until toasted. Sprinkle the toasted coconut over the rhubarb, then serve with scoops of vanilla ice cream drizzled with honey.

30 Rhubarb, Coconut, and Honey Tarts Toss together 1 lb trimmed and chopped rhubarb, 1 teaspoon ground cinnamon, 1 tablespoon all-purpose flour, and 2 tablespoons dark brown sugar in a bowl. In a separate bowl, rub together 2 tablespoons all-purpose flour, 3 tablespoons diced chilled butter, 2 tablespoons flaked dried coconut, ½ cup rolled oats, and 3 tablespoons dark brown sugar with the fingertips to form a rough crisp mixture. Unroll a sheet of ready-to-bake puff pastry and cut into 4 rectangles, then place on a baking sheet lined with parchment paper. Divide the rhubarb between the pastry, leaving a ½-inch border around the edge. Sprinkle with the crisp mixture and drizzle with 2 tablespoons honey. Bake in a preheated oven, at 400°F, for 20–25 minutes, until golden. Serve with Greek or plain yogurt.

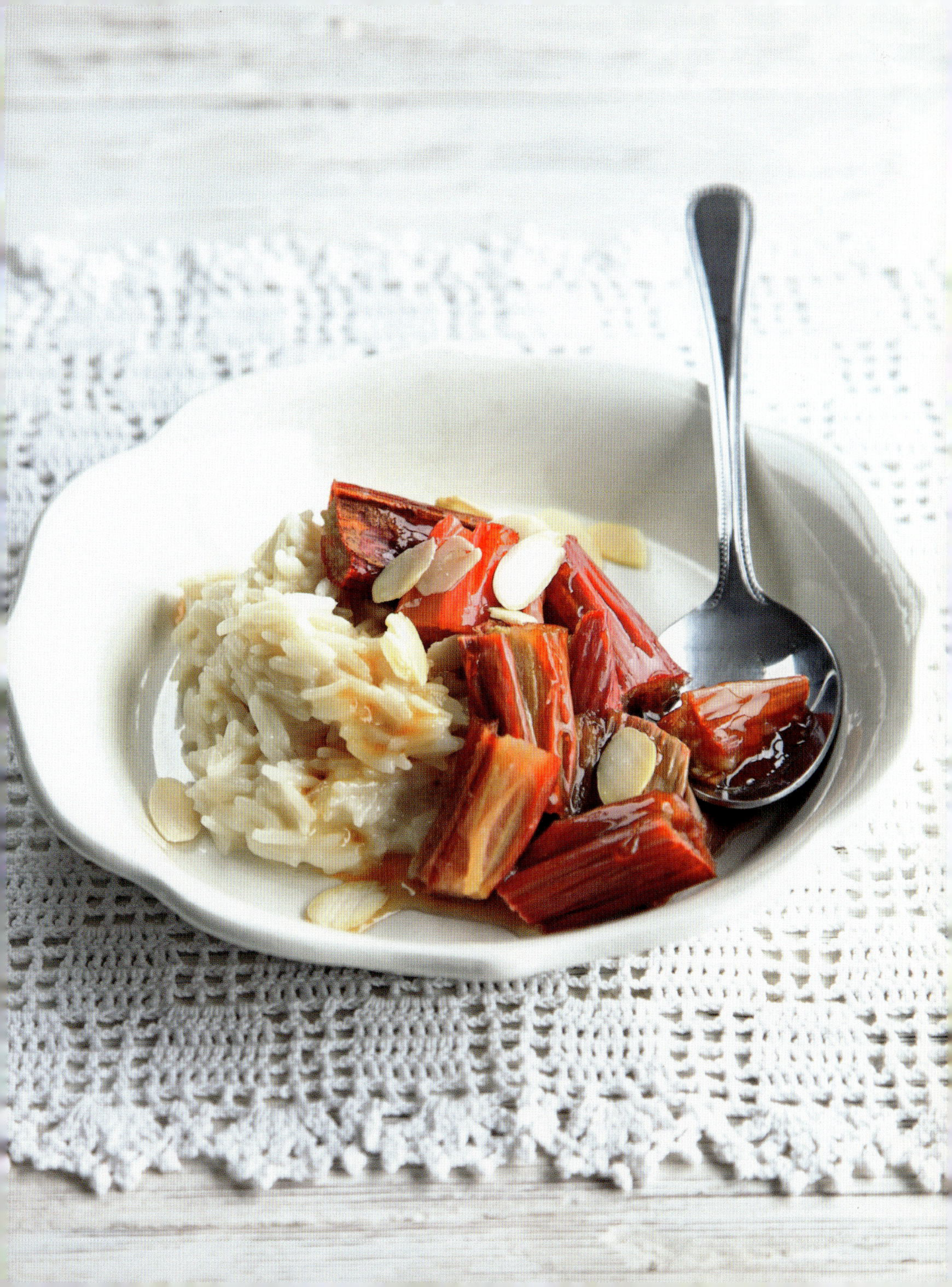

10 Oaty Raspberry Dessert

Serves 4

1 cup rolled oats
¼ cup heather honey, plus extra to serve
1¼ cups Greek yogurt
1 tablespoon whiskey (optional)
2 cups raspberries

- Place the oats on a baking sheet, drizzle with the honey, and stir around a little. Toast under a preheated medium grill for about 6–8 minutes, turning occasionally, until golden, watching carefully to make sure they do not burn. Transfer to a plate to cool slightly.

- Gently mix together the toasted oats, yogurt, whiskey, if using, and raspberries in a bowl until just combined—do not overmix.

- Divide among 4 small bowls or glasses and serve drizzled with extra honey.

20 Raspberry Whips with Crunchy Oats

Place ¼ cup rolled oats on a baking sheet and drizzle with 1 tablespoon honey. Toast under a preheated medium broiler for 2–3 minutes, until golden, then let cool. Place 2½ cups raspberries in a food processor and process to a puree, then pass through a strainer into a bowl. Mix together 1 cup crème fraîche and ½ cup Greek yogurt in a separate bowl, then stir in the raspberry puree. Spoon into 4 glasses and chill for 10 minutes. Serve sprinkled with the toasted oats and decorated with a few raspberries.

30 Raspberry Oat Crisp

Place 3 peeled, cored, and sliced Pippin apples and 2 peeled, cored, and sliced pears in a large bowl. Whisk together the juice of 1 orange and 1 tablespoon agave syrup in a small bowl, then pour into the fruit and toss to coat. Gently stir in 1 cup raspberries, then spoon into an ovenproof dish. Place the grated rind of 1 orange, ¾ cup rolled oats, ¼ cup slivered almonds, ¼ cup walnuts, and 3 tablespoons rye flour in a food processor and process until it forms large crumbs. Add ⅓ cup coconut oil and ⅓ cup firmly packed dark brown sugar and process again to form a crisp mixture. Spoon it over the fruit and bake in a preheated oven, at 375°F, for 25–26 minutes, until golden. Serve with Greek or plain yogurt.

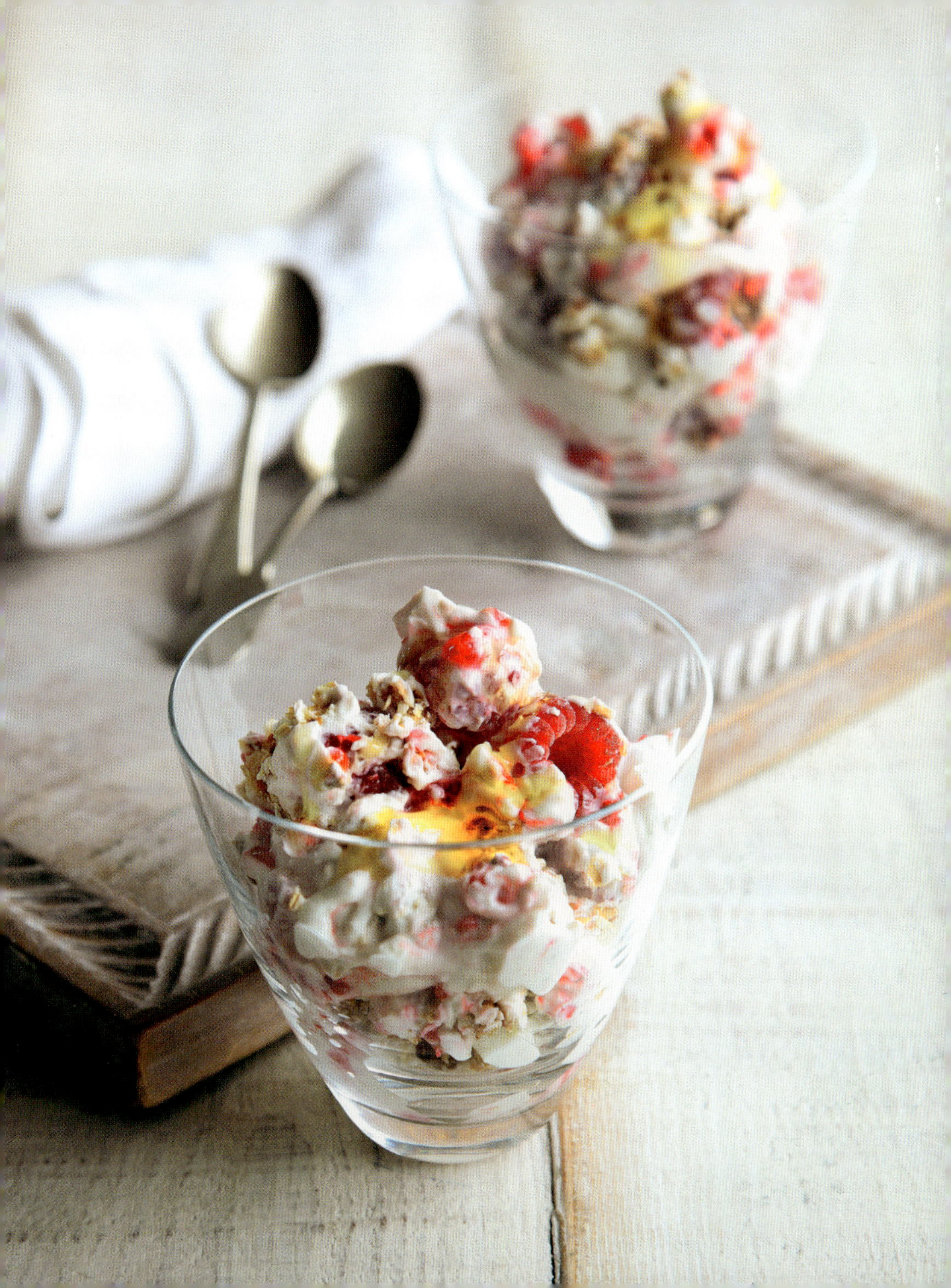

Index

Page references in *italics* indicate photographs

anchovies
    chorizo and olive tapenade toasts *18*, *70*, *71*

apples
    apple and ginger pork 102
    breakfast muesli 26
    broiled pork cutlets with apple and ginger coleslaw 102
    cheese, cumin, and apple salad 66
    cheese, cumin, and apple scones 66, *67*
    cheese, cumin, and apple toasts 66
    fennel and cumin Waldorf salad 206, *207*
    pork, apple and ginger stir-fry *15*, 102, *103*

apricots
    apricot tarts with cardamom yogurt 244
    cardamom rice pudding with apricots 244
    chicken and apricot kebabs 96
    chicken and apricot stew *19*, 96, *97*
    chicken and apricot wraps 96
    sweet semolina with cardamom poached apricots *16*, 244, *245*

asparagus
    asparagus and pea quinoa risotto *13*, 202, *203*
    asparagus and pea tart 202
    pancetta-wrapped asparagus with cannellini bean salad 80
    pan-fried duck breasts with grilled asparagus 54
    smoked duck and asparagus tarts 54
    warm asparagus and pea rice salad 202
    warm smoked duck and asparagus salad *12*, 54, *55*

avocados
    avocado, red pepper, and olive salad *13*, 50, *51*
    broiled salmon with avocado salsa 172, *173*
    chicken kebabs with avocado dip 126
    coconut chicken with avocado salsa 126
    curried chicken with avocado salad *12*, 126
    guacamole *14*, 34, *35*
    Mediterranean pepper salad 44
    Muenster cheese with avocado, red pepper, and olive salsa 50
    peperonata with avocado and olives 50
    red pepper tarts 44
    salmon and avocado salad 172
    salmon packages with avocado sauce 172
    shrimp and avocado salad 34
    smoked mackerel superfood toasts 56
    smoked salmon and avocado terrines 34

bacon
    bacon and leek penne 112
    bacon and leek tortilla *17*, 112, *113*
    leek, butternut, and bacon soup 112

bananas
    baked spiced bananas 272, *273*
    banana and ginger oatmeal 248
    bananas with spiced chocolate sauce 272
    breakfast muffins 26
    breakfast smoothies *14*, 26, *27*
    oat, banana, and ginger cookies 248
    oat, banana, and ginger muffins *13*, 248, *249*
    spiced banana muffins 272

beans
    bean and garlic stew 68
    bean and sardine salad 30
    beef and lentil chili *19*, 98, *99*
    Boston baked beans 76
    broccoli and black-eyed pea curry 38
    broccoli and black-eyed pea salad 38
    broccoli and black-eyed pea soup *13*, 38, *39*
    fava bean and feta mashed potatoes 192
    fava bean and feta salad 192
    fava bean and feta tagliatelle *17*, 192, *193*
    lima bean and mushroom soup 198
    lima bean and mushroom tagine *16*, 198, *199*
    Mediterranean beans *17*, 68, *69*
    mixed bean goulash 68
    pancetta and cannellini bean bruschetta *17*, 80, *81*
    pancetta and cannellini bean spaghetti 80
    pancetta-wrapped asparagus with cannellini bean salad 80
    sardine bean burgers 30
    smashed bean and sardine dip 30, *31*
    spicy barbecue beans on toast *16*, 76, *77*
    spicy bean quesadillas 76
    warm lima bean and mushroom salad 198

beef
    beef and leek phyllo pie 128
    beef and lentil casserole 98
    beef and lentil chili *19*, 98, *99*
    steak and caramelized leek sandwiches 128
    harissa beef fajitas *16*, 108, *109*
    harissa beef salad 108
    harissa hamburgers 108
    horseradish beef with quinoa 116, *117*
    horseradish beef sandwiches 116
    quick spaghetti with lentil meat sauce 98
    steak and chickpea salad with horseradish dressing 116
    stir-fried beef and leeks 128, *129*

beets
    beet and goat cheese salad *13*, *58*, 58
    beet soup with goat cheese 58
    roasted beet and goat cheese salad 58

bell peppers
    avocado, red pepper, and olive salad *13*, 50, *51*
    bell pepper and zucchini salad 196
    Italian fried bell peppers 196
    Mediterranean pepper salad 44
    Muenster cheese with avocado, red pepper, and olive salsa 50
    peperonata with avocado and olives 50
    red pepper and coconut curry *16*, 186
    red pepper tarts 44
    roasted bell peppers *18*, 196, *197*
    roasted red peppers and veg with coconut rice 186
    spicy broccoli and red pepper noodles 220
    spinach, mushroom, and feta-stuffed peppers 226

berries
    berry and meringue desserts *18*, 240, *241*

280 INDEX

berry and mint compote *15*, 254, 255
berry and mint smoothies 254
berry muffins 240
berry and rhubarb whips 240
minted mixed berry desserts 254
spicy fruit bread puddings *19*, 256, *257*
spicy fruit-topped French toast 256
spicy fruit-topped sweet bruschetta 256
blackberries
  blackberry brûlées *19*, 246, *247*
  blackberry mousse 246
  blackberry pancakes 246
blinis, smoked salmon 144
blueberries
  blueberry and lemon cheesecake 270
  blueberry and lemon yogurt 270
  whole-wheat blueberry pancakes with lemon yogurt *13*, 270, *271*
Boston baked beans 76
bread
  butternut and broccoli soup with mushroom bruschetta 188
  cheese, cumin, and apple toasts 66
  cheese and pickle toasts 64
  cheese soda bread 64
  chicken pesto baguettes 94
  chicken and tarragon double-decker sandwiches 100
  chorizo and olive tapenade toasts *18*, 70, *71*
  grilled zucchini bruschetta *14*, 72, *73*
  honeyed peach bruschetta 250
  horseradish beef sandwiches 116
  lentil and tomato flatbreads 46
  mushroom, tomato, and herb toasts 208
  pancetta and cannellini bean bruschetta *17*, 80, *81*
  raspberry and coconut French toast 262
  smoked haddock and tangy cheese on toast 164
  smoked mackerel and cheese toasts 164
  smoked mussel bruschetta 136
  spicy barbecue beans on toast *16*, 76, *77*

spicy fruit bread puddings *19*, 256, *257*
spicy fruit-topped French toast 256
spicy fruit-topped sweet bruschetta 256
spinach, mushrooms, and cheese on toast 226
steak and caramelized leek sandwiches 128
tuna open sandwiches *16*, 74, *75*
broccoli
  broccoli and black-eyed pea curry 38
  broccoli and black-eyed pea salad 38
  broccoli and black-eyed pea soup *13*, 38, *39*
  broccoli pesto pasta 230
  butternut, broccoli, and mushroom gratin *15*, 188, *189*
  butternut and broccoli soup with mushroom bruschetta 188
  cheesy mashed butternut squash with broccoli and poached eggs 188
  crunchy pesto broccoli with poached eggs *15*, 230, *231*
  flounder with mushroom cream and hazelnut broccoli 146
  pesto and broccoli potato cakes 230
  spicy broccoli and cheese 220
  spicy broccoli pasta with poached eggs 220, *221*
  spicy broccoli and red pepper noodles 220
  stir-fried beef and leeks 128, *129*
butternut squash
  butternut and broccoli soup with mushroom bruschetta 188
  butternut, broccoli, and mushroom gratin *15*, 188, *189*
  butternut, sage, and cashew nut dip 42
  cheesy mashed butternut squash with broccoli and poached eggs 188
  fennel, cumin, and butternut soup 206
  leek, butternut, and bacon soup 112
  roasted butternut, sage, and cashew nut soup *19*, 42, *43*

cabbage
  broiled pork chops with cabbage and leek mashed potatoes 120

butternut and sage mashed potatoes 42
pork cutlets with cabbage and leek potato cakes 120
roasted pork loin with creamy cabbage and leeks *14*, 120, *121*
carrots
  carrot and cashew nut curry 218
  carrot and cashew nut rice 218, *219*
  carrot and cashew nut slaw 218
  carrot and Muenster cheese salad with hummus dressing 36
  hummus with carrot and celery sticks *15*, 36, *37*
  hummus and carrot wraps 36
cauliflower
  cauliflower cheese gratin *19*, 194, *195*
  cauliflower cheese soup 194
  macaroni and cheese with cauliflower 194
cheese
  beet and goat cheese salad *13*, *58*, 58
  beet soup with goat cheese 58
  butternut, broccoli, and mushroom gratin 188, *189*
  carrot and Muenster cheese salad with hummus dressing 36
  cauliflower cheese gratin *19*, 194, *195*
  cauliflower cheese soup 194
  cheese, cumin, and apple salad 66
  cheese, cumin, and apple scones 66, *67*
  cheese, cumin, and apple toasts 66
  cheese and pickle toasts 64
  cheese soda bread 64
  cheese and spinach muffins 214
  cheese and spinach pancakes 214
  cheese and spinach quesadillas *13*, 214, *215*
  cheesy mashed butternut squash with broccoli and poached eggs 188
  cheesy pesto grits 200, *201*
  cheesy spinach-stuffed mushrooms *15*, 226, *227*
  falafel cheese burgers 228
  fava bean and feta mashed potatoes 192
  fava bean and feta salad 192
  fava bean and feta tagliatelle *17*, 192, *193*
  fish casserole *19*, 174, *175*

INDEX 281

Greek pita pockets 204, *205*
Greek salad 204
macaroni and cheese with cauliflower 194
Mediterranean beans *17*, 68, *69*
peach, feta, and watercress bruschetta 48
peach, feta, and watercress salad *18*, 48, *49*
quick spinach and mozzarella pizzas 184, *185*
roasted beet and goat cheese salad 58
roasted feta-topped peach and watercress salad 48
shrimp and cheese gratin 176
shrimp and cheese soufflés 176
shrimp and goat cheese salad *12*, 176, *177*
smoked haddock and tangy cheese on toast 164
smoked haddock with a cider and cheese sauce *14*, 164, *165*
smoked mackerel and cheese toasts 164
spicy barbecue beans on toast *16*, 76, *77*
spicy bean quesadillas 76
spicy broccoli and cheese 220
spicy tuna pasta casserole 74
spinach and mozzarella roulade 184
spinach and mozzarella tagliatelle 184
spinach, mushroom, and feta-stuffed peppers 226
spinach, mushrooms, and cheese on toast 226
tomato and herb-stuffed mushrooms 208
warm lentil, tomato, and Muenster cheese salad *18*, 46, *47*
whole-wheat cheese straws 64, *65*
chicken
	chicken and apricot kebabs 96
	chicken and apricot stew *19*, 96, *97*
	chicken and apricot wraps 96
	chicken and nectarine salad 122
	chicken and tarragon double-decker sandwiches 100
	chicken and tarragon risotto *17*, 100, *101*
	chicken and tarragon tagliatelle 100

chicken, cucumber, and radish pita breads 114
chicken dippers with homemade hummus *14*, 90, *91*
chicken kebabs with avocado dip 126
chicken, orange, and olive sandwiches 106
chicken pasta salad with pesto dressing 94, *95*
chicken pesto baguettes 94
chicken satay with nectarine salad 122
chicken with orange and olives *18*, 106, *107*
coconut chicken with avocado salsa 126
curried chicken with avocado salad *12*, 126
ginger chicken soup *16*, 110, *111*
ginger chicken stir-fry 110
ginger chicken wraps 110
grilled chicken, orange, and olive salad 106
lentil, chickpea, chicken, and mustard curry 216
nectarine-glazed chicken kebabs *18*, 122, *123*
roasted chicken breasts with pesto pasta 94
shrimp, chicken, and vegetable spring rolls 84
spicy chicken breasts with hummus 90
spicy chicken with cucumber and radish salad *12*, 114, *115*
spicy chicken with cucumber and radish stir-fry 114
spicy pancetta-wrapped chicken with eggplant dip 90
chickpeas
	broiled salmon with chickpea curry 52
	chicken dippers with homemade hummus *14*, 90, *91*
	chickpea and alfalfa sprout salad 82
	chickpea and bean sprout curry 82
	chickpea and bean sprout patties 82, *83*
	chickpea, tomato and pasta salad 212
	falafels with Greek salsa 204
	falafels with spicy sauce *16*, 228, *229*
	falafel and tabbouleh salad 228

hummus with carrot and celery sticks *15*, 36, *37*
lentil and chickpea salad with warm mustard dressing 216
lentil, chickpea, chicken, and mustard curry 216
lentil, mustard, and chickpea soup *19*, 216, *217*
linguine with chickpea and tomato sauce 212, *213*
salmon and chickpea salad *15*, 52, *53*
salmon en papillote with warm chickpea salad 52
smashed bean and sardine dip 30, *31*
spaghetti with roasted tomato and chickpea sauce 212
spicy chicken breasts with hummus 90
steak and chickpea salad with horseradish dressing 116
chiles
	spicy broccoli and cheese 220
	spicy broccoli and red pepper noodles 220
	spicy broccoli pasta with poached eggs 220, *221*
chocolate
	bananas with spiced chocolate sauce 272
chorizo
	chorizo and olive potatoes 70
	chorizo and olive tapenade toasts *18*, 70, *71*
	chorizo, onion, and olive tart 70
cocoa
	cocoa, orange, and pecan oat bar *12*, 242, *243*
	cocoa, orange, and pecan muesli 242
	cocoa, orange, and pecan scones 242
coconut
	coconut chicken with avocado salsa 126
	coconut-crusted tofu 186
	honey-roasted rhubarb with coconut rice 276, *277*
	jumbo shrimp and coconut curry 166
	raspberry coconut whips 262
	raspberry and coconut French toast 262
	red pepper and coconut curry *16*, 186
	rhubarb, coconut, and honey tarts 276

rhubarb with toasted coconut and honeyed ice cream 276
roasted red peppers and veg with coconut rice 186
whole-wheat raspberry coconut muffins 14, 262, 263

cod
  baked cod, tomatoes, and leeks 148
  chunky cod, red snapper, and shrimp stew 19, 178, 179
  cod with roasted tomato ratatouille 15, 148, 149
  cod, red snapper, and shrimp casserole 178
  fish casserole 19, 174, 175
  pan-fried cod with grilled tomatoes and veg 148
  quick cod, red snapper, and shrimp curry 178

cornmeal
  cheesy pesto grits 200, 201
curried chicken with avocado salad 12, 126

couscous
  chicken and apricot stew 19, 96, 97
  falafel and tabbouleh salad 228
  pancetta-wrapped asparagus with cannellini bean salad 80
  smoked mackerel and spring vegetable tabbouleh 15, 168, 169

cucumber
  chicken, cucumber, and radish pita breads 114
  gazpacho 17, 44, 45
  lamb chops with cucumber and mint salad 92
  salmon and sesame skewers 78, 79
  spicy chicken with cucumber and radish salad 12, 114, 115
  spicy chicken with cucumber and radish stir-fry 114
  tuna open sandwiches 16, 74, 75

duck
  pan-fried duck breasts with grilled asparagus 54
  smoked duck and asparagus tarts 54
  warm smoked duck and asparagus salad 12, 54, 55

eggplants
  spicy pancetta-wrapped chicken with eggplant dip 90
eggs
  bacon and leek tortilla 17, 112, 113
  butternut and sage mashed potatoes 42
  cheesy mashed butternut squash with broccoli and poached eggs 188
  crunchy pesto broccoli with poached eggs 15, 230, 231
  Mediterranean pepper salad 44
  pea and mint pancakes 14, 210, 211
  quick spinach and mozzarella pizzas 184, 185
  smoked haddock omelets 156, 157
  smoked haddock with poached eggs 156
  smoked mackerel and cheese toasts 164
  smoked trout baked eggs 60

fennel
  baked sole with fennel pesto 17, 150, 151
  broiled sole with fennel coleslaw 150
  cumin-roasted fennel and veg 206
  fennel and cumin Waldorf salad 206, 207
  fennel, cumin and butternut soup 206
  sole and fennel soup 150
fish casserole 19, 174, 175
flounder
  baked flounder with mushrooms and hazelnuts 146, 147
  flounder with caper butter, mushroom, and hazelnut green salad 146
  flounder with mushroom cream and hazelnut broccoli 146
fruit
  caramelized fall fruits 15, 274, 275
  fall fruit compote 274
  fall fruits in mulled wine 274
  gingered sesame fruit compote 268
  gingered sesame fruit kebabs 16, 268, 269
  gingered sesame fruit salad 268

tropical fruit brûlées 260
tropical fruit crisp 260
tropical fruit salsa 18, 260, 261

gazpacho 17, 44, 45
ginger
  apple and ginger pork 102
  banana and ginger oatmeal 248
  broiled pork cutlets with apple and ginger coleslaw 102
  caramelized pears with ginger yogurt 238
  ginger chicken soup 16, 110, 111
  ginger chicken stir-fry 110
  ginger chicken wraps 110
  gingered sesame fruit compote 268
  gingered sesame fruit kebabs 16, 268, 269
  gingered sesame fruit salad 268
  ginger poached pears 238
  marinated salmon with ginger rice 140
  oat, banana, and ginger cookies 248
  oat, banana, and ginger muffins 13, 248, 249
  oat-topped pear and ginger dessert 19, 238, 239
  pork, apple, and ginger stir-fry 15, 102, 103
golden raisins
  lemon and golden raisin rice pudding 266, 267
  quick lemon and golden raisin rice 266
  whole-wheat lemon and golden raisin scones 266
grapefruit
  breaded salmon with grapefruit 160
  salmon with grapefruit dressing and roasted veg 160
  salmon and grapefruit salad 12, 160, 161
Greek pita pockets 204, 205
Greek salad 204
guacamole 14, 34, 35

harissa
  harissa beef fajitas 16, 108, 109
  harissa beef salad 108
  harissa hamburgers 108

INDEX 283

hazelnuts
    baked flounder with mushrooms and hazelnuts 146, *147*
    flounder with caper butter, mushroom and hazelnut green salad 146
herbs
    mushroom, tomato, and herb pancakes *14*, 208, *209*
    mushroom, tomato, and herb toasts 208
    tomato and herb-stuffed mushrooms 208

kale
    smoked haddock fish cakes with kale 40
    smoked haddock and kale soup *13*, 40, *41*
    spicy smoked haddock and kale pasta 40
Keralan fish curry *16*, 162, *163*

lamb
    lamb chops with cucumber and mint salad 92
    lamb cutlets with pea and rosemary mashed potatoes *18*, 104, *105*
    lamb koftas with mint yogurt 92, *93*
    lamb racks with rosemary and garlic 104
    mint-crusted rack of lamb 92
    rosemary lamb cutlets with summer salad 104
leeks
    bacon and leek penne 112
    bacon and leek tortilla *17*, 112, *113*
    baked cod, tomatoes, and leeks 148
    beef and leek phyllo pie 128
    broiled pork chops with cabbage and leek mashed potatoes 120
    leek and sweet potato soup 222
    leek, butternut, and bacon soup 112
    pan-fried sea bass with warm leek and lentil salad 170, *171*
    pork cutlets with cabbage and leek potato cakes 120
    roasted baby leeks and sweet potatoes 222
    roasted pork loin with creamy cabbage and leeks *14*, 120, *121*
    sea bass, leek, and lentil soup 170

sea bass with spicy leek and lentil casserole 170
    simple baked leeks and sweet potatoes *15*, 222, *223*
    stir-fried beef and leeks 128, *129*
lemons
    blueberry and lemon cheesecake 270
    blueberry and lemon yogurt 270
    broiled lemon and mustard sardines *12*, 154, *155*
    lemon and cardamom cookies 236
    lemon and golden raisin rice pudding 266, *267*
    lemon and raisin scones *12*, 236, *237*
    lemon mousse 236
    lemony sardine fish cakes 154
    quick lemon and golden raisin rice 266
    sardine and lemon spaghetti 154
    whole-wheat blueberry pancakes with lemon yogurt *13*, 270, *271*
    whole-wheat lemon and golden raisin scones 266
lentils
    beef and lentil casserole 98
    beef and lentil chili *19*, 98, *99*
    chicken and apricot stew *19*, 96, *97*
    lentil and chickpea salad with warm mustard dressing 216
    lentil and tomato flatbreads 46
    lentil and tomato soup 46
    lentil, chickpea, chicken, and mustard curry 216
    lentil, mustard, and chickpea soup *19*, 216, *217*
    pan-fried sea bass with warm leek and lentil salad 170, *171*
    quick spaghetti with lentil meat sauce 98
    sea bass, leek, and lentil soup 170
    sea bass with spicy leek and lentil casserole 170
    spicy red snapper with lentil and watercress salad 158
    warm lentil, tomato, and Muenster cheese salad *18*, 46, *47*
liver
    chicken liver and mustard pâté 130
    calf liver pâté with caramelized onion 124
    chicken liver salad with mustard

dressing *12*, 130, *131*
    calf liver with caramelized onions *13*, 124, *125*
    calf liver with caramelized shallot sauce 124
    chicken livers with mustard mashed potatoes 130

mackerel
    Keralan fish curry *16*, 162, *163*
    pan-fried mackerel with crushed potatoes 142
mangoes
    mango whips with sesame brittle 252
    red snapper with mango salsa and watercress 158
melons
    melon, mint, and strawberry smoothies *18*, 24, *25*
    melon, mint, and strawberry soup 24
    minty melon and strawberry salad 24
mushrooms
    baked flounder with mushrooms and hazelnuts 146, *147*
    butternut, broccoli, and mushroom gratin *15*, 188, *189*
    butternut and broccoli soup with mushroom bruschetta 188
    cheesy spinach-stuffed mushrooms *15*, 226, *227*
    flounder with caper butter, mushroom, and hazelnut green salad 146
    flounder with mushroom cream and hazelnut broccoli 146
    grilled zucchini bruschetta 72, *73*
    lima bean and mushroom soup 198
    lima bean and mushroom tagine *16*, 198, *199*
    mixed bean goulash 68
    mushroom and tofu stew *19*, 224, *225*
    mushroom and tofu stir-fry 224
    mushroom and tofu Thai curry 224
    mushroom, tomato, and herb pancakes *14*, 208, *209*
    mushroom, tomato, and herb toasts 208
    spinach, mushroom, and feta-stuffed peppers 226
    spinach, mushrooms, and cheese on

284 INDEX

toast 226
tomato and herb-stuffed mushrooms 208
warm lima bean and mushroom salad 198
mussels
   moules marinieres *17*, 136, *137*
   mussel and watercress linguine 136
   smoked mussel bruschetta 136

nectarines
   chicken and nectarine salad 122
   chicken satay with nectarine salad 122
   nectarine-glazed chicken kebabs *18*, *122, 123*
noodles
   shrimp and avocado salad 34
   spicy broccoli and red pepper noodles 220
   spicy jumbo shrimp noodles 166
nuts
   breakfast smoothies *14, 26, 27*
   butternut, sage, and cashew nut dip 42
   carrot and cashew nut curry 218
   carrot and cashew nut rice 218, *219*
   carrot and cashew nut slaw 218
   cocoa, orange, and pecan oat bars *12, 242, 243*
   cocoa, orange, and pecan muesli 242
   cocoa, orange, and pecan scones 242
   fennel and cumin Waldorf salad 206, *207*
   homemade nutty muesli 28
   nutty granola *12*, 28, *29*
   nutty muesli muffins 28
   roasted butternut, sage, and cashew nut soup *19, 42, 43*
   roasted strawberries with almond yogurt 258
   strawberry and almond desserts *17, 258, 259*
   strawberry and almond muffins 258

oats
   banana and ginger oatmeal 248
   breakfast muesli 26
   breakfast muffins 26
   breakfast smoothies *14, 26, 27*
   homemade nutty muesli 28
   nutty granola *12*, 28, *29*

oat, banana, and ginger cookies 248
oat, banana, and ginger muffins *13*, 248, *249*
oat-topped pear and ginger dessert *19*, 238, *239*
oaty raspberry dessert *12*, 278, *279*
raspberry whips with crunchy oats 278
raspberry oat crisp 278
rosemary oatcakes 62
olives
   avocado, red pepper, and olive salad *13*, 50, *51*
   chicken, orange, and olive sandwiches 106
   chicken with orange and olives *18*, 106, *107*
   chorizo and olive potatoes 70
   chorizo and olive tapenade toasts *18*, 70, *71*
   chorizo, onion, and olive tart 70
   grilled chicken, orange, and olive salad 106
   Muenster cheese with avocado, red pepper, and olive salsa 50
   peperonata with avocado and olives 50
onions
   calf liver with caramelized onions *13*, 124, *125*
   chorizo, onion and olive tart 70
oranges
   chicken, orange, and olive sandwiches 106
   chicken with orange and olives *18*, 106, *107*
   cocoa, orange, and pecan oat bars *12, 242, 243*
   cocoa, orange, and pecan muesli 242
   cocoa, orange, and pecan scones 242
   grilled chicken, orange, and olive salad 106
oysters
   oysters Kilpatrick 138
   oysters Rockefeller 138, *139*
   oysters with shallot vinaigrette 138

pancetta
   pancetta and cannellini bean bruschetta *17*, 80, *81*
   pancetta and cannellini bean spaghetti 80

pancetta-wrapped asparagus with cannellini bean salad 80
spicy pancetta-wrapped chicken with eggplant dip 90
pasta
   bacon and leek penne 112
   broccoli pesto pasta 230
   chicken and tarragon tagliatelle 100
   chicken pasta salad with pesto dressing 94, *95*
   chickpea, tomato, and pasta salad 212
   fava bean and feta tagliatelle *17*, 192, *193*
   linguine with chickpea and tomato sauce 212, *213*
   macaroni and cheese with cauliflower 194
   mussel and watercress linguine 136
   pancetta and cannellini bean spaghetti 80
   quick spaghetti with lentil meat sauce 98
   quick zucchini pasta 72
   roasted chicken breasts with pesto pasta 94
   sardine and lemon spaghetti 154
   spaghetti with roasted tomato and chickpea sauce 212
   spicy broccoli pasta with poached eggs 220, *221*
   spicy tuna pasta casserole 74
   spinach and mozzarella tagliatelle 184
   zucchini lasagna 72
peaches
   broiled peaches with honey syrup 250
   peach, feta, and watercress bruschetta 48
   peach, feta, and watercress salad *18*, 48, *49*
   roasted feta-topped peach and watercress salad 48
   roasted honey peaches *17*, 250, *251*
pears
   caramelized pears with ginger yogurt 238
   ginger poached pears 238
   oat-topped pear and ginger dessert *19*, 238, *239*

INDEX 285

peas
    asparagus and pea quinoa risotto 13, 202, 203
    asparagus and pea tart 202
    lamb cutlets with pea and rosemary mashed potatoes 18, 104, 105
    pea and mint dip 210
    pea and mint pancakes 14, 210, 211
    pea and mint soufflés 210
    warm asparagus and pea rice salad 202
polenta
    polenta with pesto roasted veg 200
    polenta salad with pesto dressing 200
pork
    apple and ginger pork 102
    broiled pork chops with cabbage and leek mashed potatoes 120
    broiled pork cutlets with apple and ginger coleslaw 102
    pork, apple, and ginger stir-fry 15, 102, 103
    pork cutlets with cabbage and leek potato cakes 120
    roasted pork loin with creamy cabbage and leeks 14, 120, 121
potatoes
    bacon and leek tortilla 17, 112, 113
    beef and lentil casserole 98
    broiled pork chops with cabbage and leek mashed potatoes 120
    calf liver with caramelized onions 13, 124, 125
    chicken livers with mustard mashed potatoes 130
    chorizo and olive potatoes 70
    cod, red snapper, and shrimp casserole 178
    fava bean and feta mashed potatoes 192
    Indian-spiced fish cakes 162
    lamb cutlets with pea and rosemary mashed potatoes 18, 104, 105
    pan-fried mackerel with crushed potatoes 142
    pesto and broccoli potato cakes 230
    pork cutlets with cabbage and leek potato cakes 120

red snapper with warm potato and watercress salad 158, 159
smoked haddock with poached eggs 156
smoked mackerel and new potato salad 142
smoked salmon and potato salad 144

quinoa
    asparagus and pea quinoa risotto 13, 202, 203
    horseradish beef with quinoa 116, 117

radishes
    chicken, cucumber, and radish pita breadss 114
    spicy chicken with cucumber and radish salad 12, 114, 115
    spicy chicken with cucumber and radish stir-fry 114
raspberries
    oaty raspberry dessert 12, 278, 279
    raspberry and coconut French toast 262
    raspberry coconut whips 262
    raspberry oat crisp 278
    raspberry whips with crunchy oats 278
    whole-wheat raspberry coconut muffins 14, 262, 263
red snapper
    chunky cod, red snapper, and shrimp stew 19, 178, 179
    cod, red snapper, and shrimp casserole 178
    quick cod, red snapper, and shrimp curry 178
    red snapper with mango salsa and watercress 158
    red snapper with warm potato and watercress salad 158, 159
    spicy red snapper with lentil and watercress salad 158
rhubarb
    berry and rhubarb whips 240
    honey-roasted rhubarb with coconut rice 276, 277
    rhubarb, coconut, and honey tarts 276
    rhubarb with toasted coconut and

honeyed ice cream 276
rice
    asparagus and pea quinoa risotto 13, 202, 203
    cardamom rice pudding with apricots 244
    carrot and cashew nut rice 218, 219
    chicken and tarragon risotto 17, 100, 101
    honey-roasted rhubarb with coconut rice 276, 277
    lemon and golden raisin rice pudding 266, 267
    marinated salmon with ginger rice 140
    quick lemon and golden raisin rice 266
    roasted red peppers and veg with coconut rice 186
    salmon and rice bhajis 16, 140, 141
    salmon and rice salad 140
    smoked mackerel and spring vegetable paella 168
    warm asparagus and pea rice salad 202
rosemary oatcakes 14, 62, 63
rosemary scones 62

salmon
    breaded salmon with grapefruit 160
    broiled salmon with avocado salsa 13, 172, 173
    broiled salmon with chickpea curry 52
    broiled salmon with sesame salad 78
    curried fish kebabs 162
    fish pâté 174
    fish casserole 19, 174, 175
    fish soup 174
    Indian-spiced fish cakes 162
    marinated salmon with ginger rice 140
    pan-fried sesame-crusted salmon 78
    salmon and avocado salad 172
    salmon and chickpea salad 15, 52, 53
    salmon and rice bhajis 16, 140, 141
    salmon and rice salad 140
    salmon and sesame skewers 78, 79
    salmon ceviche 144, 145
    salmon en papillote with warm chickpea salad 52
    salmon packages with avocado sauce 172

salmon with grapefruit dressing and roasted veg 160
salmon and grapefruit salad *12*, 160, *161*
smoked salmon and avocado terrines 34
smoked salmon and potato salad 144
smoked salmon blinis 144
sardines
    bean and sardine salad 30
    broiled lemon and mustard sardines *12*, 154, *155*
    lemony sardine fish cakes 154
    sardine and lemon spaghetti 154
    sardine bean burgers 30
    smashed bean and sardine dip 30, *31*
sea bass
    pan-fried sea bass with warm leek and lentil salad 170, *171*
    sea bass, leek, and lentil soup 170
    sea bass with spicy leek and lentil casserole 170
sesame cookies *14*, 252, *253*
sesame French toast 252
shallots
    calf liver with caramelized shallot sauce 124
    oysters with shallot vinaigrette 138
shrimp
    chunky cod, red snapper, and shrimp stew *19*, 178, *179*
    cod, red snapper, and shrimp casserole 178
    fish soup 174
    jumbo shrimp Caesar salad *18*, 166, *167*
    jumbo shrimp and coconut curry 166
    quick cod, red snapper, and shrimp curry 178
    shrimp and avocado salad 34
    shrimp and cheese gratin 176
    shrimp and cheese soufflés 176
    shrimp and goat cheese salad *12*, 176, *177*
    shrimp and spinach curry *13*, 152, *153*
    shrimp and spinach soufflés 152
    shrimp and zucchini spring rolls *18*, 84, *85*
    shrimp, chicken, and vegetable spring rolls 84
    shrimp skewers with spinach salad 152
    spicy jumbo shrimp noodles 166
    Vietnamese shrimp spring rolls 84
smoked haddock
    smoked haddock and kale soup *13*, 40, *41*
    smoked haddock and tangy cheese on toast 164
    smoked haddock fish cakes with kale 40
    smoked haddock omelets 156, *157*
    smoked haddock with a cider and cheese sauce *14*, 164, *165*
    smoked haddock with poached eggs 156
    spicy smoked haddock and kale pasta 40
smoked mackerel
    smoked mackerel and cheese toasts 164
    smoked mackerel and horseradish pâté *12*, 32, *33*
    smoked mackerel and new potato salad 142
    smoked mackerel and spring vegetable paella 168
    smoked mackerel and spring vegetable salad 168
    smoked mackerel and spring vegetable tabbouleh *15*, 168, *169*
    smoked mackerel dip 142
    smoked mackerel superfood salad *13*, 56, *57*
    smoked mackerel superfood soup 56
    smoked mackerel superfood toasts 56
smoked mussel bruschetta 136
smoked salmon
    Indian-spiced fish cakes 162
    smoked salmon and avocado terrines 34
    smoked salmon and potato salad 144
    smoked salmon blinis 144
smoked trout
    mini smoked trout quiches *14*, 60, *61*
    smoked trout baked eggs 60
    smoked trout phyllo quiche 60
sole
    baked sole with fennel pesto *17*, 150, *151*
    broiled sole with fennel coleslaw 150
    sole and fennel soup 150
spinach
    cheese and spinach muffins 214
    cheese and spinach pancakes 214
    cheese and spinach quesadillas *13*, 214, *215*
    cheesy spinach-stuffed mushrooms *15*, 226, *227*
    fish casserole *19*, 174, *175*
    oysters Rockefeller 138, *139*
    quick spinach and mozzarella pizzas 184, *185*
    shrimp and spinach curry *13*, 152, *153*
    shrimp and spinach soufflés 152
    shrimp skewers with spinach salad 152
    smoked haddock omelets 156, *157*
    spinach and mozzarella roulade 184
    spinach and mozzarella tagliatelle 184
    spinach, mushroom, and feta-stuffed peppers 226
    spinach, mushrooms, and cheese on toast 226
strawberries
    melon, mint, and strawberry smoothies *18*, 24, *25*
    melon, mint, and strawberry soup 24
    minty melon and strawberry salad 24
    roasted strawberries with almond yogurt 258
    strawberry and almond desserts *17*, 258, *259*
    strawberry and almond muffins 258
sweet potatoes
    leek and sweet potato soup 222
    roasted baby leeks and sweet potatoes 222
    roasted pork loin with creamy cabbage and leeks *14*, 120, *121*
    simple baked leeks and sweet potatoes *15*, 222, *223*

tofu
    coconut-crusted tofu 186
    mushroom and tofu stew *19*, 224, *225*

mushroom and tofu stir-fry 224
mushroom and tofu Thai curry 224
tomatoes
 baked cod, tomatoes, and leeks 148
 chickpea, tomato, and pasta salad 212
 cod with roasted tomato ratatouille *15*, *148*, *149*
 falafels with Greek salsa 204
 Greek salad 204
 grilled zucchini bruschetta 72, *73*
 lentil and tomato flatbreads 46
 lentil and tomato soup 46
 linguine with chickpea and tomato sauce 212, *213*
 Mediterranean beans *17*, *68*, *69*
 mushroom, tomato, and herb pancakes *14*, 208, *209*
 mushroom, tomato, and herb toasts 208
 pan-fried cod with grilled tomatoes and veg 148
 spaghetti with roasted tomato and chickpea sauce 212
 tomato and herb-stuffed mushrooms 208
 warm lentil, tomato, and Muenster cheese salad *18*, *46*, *47*
tuna
 spicy tuna open sandwiches *16*, 74, *75*
 spicy tuna salad Niçoise 74
 spicy tuna pasta casserole 74

vegetables
 cumin-roasted fennel and veg 206
 Moroccan roasted vegetables 190
 Moroccan vegetable soup 190
 Moroccan vegetable stew *16*, 190, *191*
 polenta with pesto roasted veg 200
 roasted red peppers and veg with coconut rice 186
 shrimp, chicken, and vegetable spring rolls 84
 smoked mackerel and spring vegetable paella 168
 smoked mackerel and spring vegetable salad 168
 smoked mackerel and spring vegetable tabbouleh *15*, 168, *169*
 Vietnamese shrimp spring rolls 84

watercress
 mussel and watercress linguine 136
 peach, feta, and watercress bruschetta 48
 peach, feta, and watercress salad *18*, *48*, *49*
 red snapper with mango salsa and watercress 158
 red snapper with warm potato and watercress salad 158, *159*
 roasted feta-topped peach and watercress salad 48
 spicy red snapper with lentil and watercress salad 158

yogurt
 apricot tarts with cardamom yogurt 244
 berry and mint smoothies 254
 blackberry brûlées *19*, *246*, *247*
 blueberry and lemon yogurt 270
 breakfast smoothies *14*, *26*, *27*
 caramelized pears with ginger yogurt 238
 lamb koftas with mint yogurt 92, *93*
 roasted strawberries with almond yogurt 258
 strawberry and almond desserts *17*, *258*, *259*
 whole-wheat blueberry pancakes with lemon yogurt *13*, 270, *271*

zucchini
 baked sole with fennel pesto *17*, 150, *151*
 bell pepper and zucchini salad 196
 cod with roasted tomato ratatouille *15*, *148*, *149*
 grilled zucchini bruschetta *14*, 72, *73*
 pan-fried cod with grilled tomatoes and veg 148
 quick zucchini pasta 72
 shrimp and zucchini spring rolls *18*, *84*, *85*
 smoked mackerel and spring vegetable paella 168
 zucchini lasagna 72

Acknowledgments

Recipes by **Joy Skipper**
Executive Editor **Eleanor Maxfield**
Senior Editor **Leanne Bryan**
Copy Editor **Jo Murray**
Art Direction **Tracy Killick for Tracy Killick Art Direction and Design**
Original Design Concept **www.gradedesign.com**
Designers **Tracy Killick and Sally Bond for Tracy Killick Art Direction and Design**
Photographer **Lis Parsons**
Home Economist **Joy Skipper**
Stylist **Liz Hippisley**
Senior Production Controller **Caroline Alberti**